SOLDADOS RAZOS AT WAR

STEVEN ROSALES

SOLDADOS RAZOS AT WAR

Chicano Politics, Identity, and Masculinity in the U.S. Military from World War II to Vietnam

THE UNIVERSITY OF ARIZONA PRESS
TUCSON

The University of Arizona Press
www.uapress.arizona.edu

First paperback edition 2018

ISBN-13: 978-0-8165-3244-5 (cloth)
ISBN-13: 978-0-8165-3964-2 (paper)

Cover design by Leigh McDonald
Cover photograph: *One of the first gatherings of the American G.I. Forum*, date unknkown. Hector P. Garcia Papers, Special Collections and Archives, Mary and Jeff Bell Library, Texas A&M University–Corpus Christi.

Publication of this book is made possible in part by the proceeds of a permanent endowment created with the assistance of a Challenge Grant from the National Endowment for the Humanities, a federal agency.

Library of Congress Cataloging-in-Publication Data
Names: Rosales, Steven, author.
Title: Soldados razos at war : Chicano politics, identity, and masculinity in the U.S. military from World War II to Vietnam / Steven Rosales.
Other titles: Chicano politics, identity, and masculinity in the U.S. military from World War II to Vietnam
Description: Tucson : The University of Arizona Press, 2017. | Includes bibliographical references and index.
Identifiers: LCCN 2016039135 | ISBN 9780816532445 (cloth : alk. paper)
Subjects: LCSH: Mexican American soldiers—United States—Biography. | Mexican American soldiers—History—20th century. | Mexican American soldiers—Social conditions—20th century. | Citizenship—United States. | Masculinity—United States—History—20th century. | United States—Armed Forces—Mexican Americans—History—20th century. | LCGFT: Biographies.
Classification: LCC UB418.M48 R67 2017 | DDC 355.2/23620896872073—dc23 LC record available at https://lccn.loc.gov/2016039135

Printed in the United States of America
♾ This paper meets the requirements of ANSI/NISO Z39.48-1992 (Permanence of Paper).

For Latinas/os and all other
marginalized communities confronting
social injustice and hate

Sí se puede

CONTENTS

ILLUSTRATIONS

FIGURES

TABLES

ACKNOWLEDGMENTS

AS AN AVID READER of acknowledgements, I am somewhat daunted by the need to produce my own. I shall therefore begin by stating that this manuscript represents the culmination of a long process that first began as an undergraduate when I wrote a senior year honors thesis on this very topic under David Gutíerrez's guidance. He probably doesn't remember me, but I am grateful for the mentoring and kind words he provided as I completed my thesis and prepared for my eventual move to graduate school. I then had the honor and privilege of working under an exceptional dissertation committee that included Vicki L. Ruiz, Gilbert González, and Jon Wiener. An especially heartfelt debt of gratitude is extended to Dr. Ruiz, who served as my advisor and has remained my advocate and friend all these years since my graduation. She may not know it, but she is my role model. Her professionalism, critical pen, and personal integrity have repeatedly challenged me to dig deeper and move beyond the mere obvious, while demonstrating that the historian's craft is best exemplified by a commitment to the human actors that shape historical events. At Grand Valley State University, Paul Murphy, Kathleen Underwood, Gretchen Galbraith, and Jason Crouthamel were indispensable, supportive colleagues during my first academic appointment as I learned the ropes of this profession. At GVSU, the junior faculty reading group—Louis Moore, in particular—provided thoughtful comments and other forms of social interaction. Special mention must also be given to Lynda Coon and Kathryn Sloan, who helped me navigate my transition to the University of Arkansas by offering guidance, support, and much-needed time off to complete this manuscript. In my few years here, Caree Banton, my departmental neighbor, remains a constant source of friendly banter and intellectual engagement. I would also like to thank acquiring editor Kristen Buckles and the anonymous reviewers for the University of Arizona Press. I am eternally grateful to Kristen and her persistent faith in my project since we first met at a conference in Pasadena many years ago. And most importantly, I would like to express my deepest gratitude to all sixty-four narrators that comprise my database. They kindly shared their homes, time, and memories with me across several states. It is my sincere hope that this manuscript is an accurate reflection of their personal biographies and sentiments. Any errors in judgment and interpretation are strictly mine.

On my research trips, I benefitted from the assistance of the staffs at various collections, including the Bancroft Library at the University of California, the Benson Latin American Collection at the University of Texas, and the Special Collections and Archives Division of the Jeff and Mary Bell Library at Texas A&M University, Corpus Christi. At the latter, Grace Charles deserves special thanks for her meticulous support and never-ending photocopying as I negotiated the Hector P. Garcia Papers. I would also like to individually thank Lisa Sharik, deputy director of the Texas Military Forces Museum at Camp Mabry in Austin, Texas, and Leo LeFevre, assistant librarian at the Hoyt Library, Local History and Genealogy Collection, Public Libraries of Saginaw, Michigan.

In conclusion, Yajaira M. Padilla, my wife and colleague, entered my life during my first academic job talk at the University of Kansas, where she had just started her initial appointment as an assistant professor. We talked and flirted throughout the day, and I returned to Southern California where I soon realized that I was not the chosen candidate. About nine months later, through a mutual friend, we began to communicate via e-mail, which then led to phone calls and personal visits. And we fell in love. As the years passed across several states and various institutions, she worked tirelessly to bring us together, which ultimately brought us to the University of Arkansas. And so, while I didn't get that first job, I got the girl—a passionate woman and intellectual who is my partner, confidant, copyeditor, and best friend. She is also an amazing mother to our two beautiful daughters, Sayra and Camila, who entered our lives in 2012 and 2016. They are a consistent bundle of joy and adventure. With all that I am, Yajaira, thank you and I love you.

An earlier version of chapter 2 first appeared as "'This Street is Essentially Mexican': An Oral History of the Mexican American Community of Saginaw, Michigan, 1920–1980," in the *Michigan Historical Review*. Portions of chapters 5 and 6 first appeared as "Macho Nation? Chicano Soldiering, Sexuality, and Manhood During the Vietnam War Era" in *Oral History Review*. Also, segments of chapters 7 and 8 originally appeared as "Fighting the Peace At Home: Mexican American Veterans and the 1944 G.I. Bill of Rights" in the *Pacific Historical Review*. Finally, a survey of Mexican American military service appeared as "The Right to Bear Arms: Enlisting Chicanos into the U.S. Military, 1940–1980" in *The Routledge Handbook of the History of Race and the American Military*.

SOLDADOS RAZOS AT WAR

INTRODUCTION

I AM A TWENTY-EIGHT-YEAR U.S. Navy (USN) veteran. I initially began a four-year tour of active duty in June 1988 upon my graduation from high school that was followed by an immediate affiliation with the U.S. Naval Reserve (USNR), where I have since remained an active drilling reservist. Two of the more notable achievements in my naval career thus far include a nine-month deployment in support of Operation Desert Storm from 1990 to 1991 and, more recently, my commission as a naval officer in 2010. Several factors motivated my decision to enlist. As an only child raised by a single mother in East Los Angeles, I was driven at an early age to find an opportunity to remove myself from the poverty that dominated my childhood. The amenities offered by the navy, which included an expanded worldview, a monthly salary, health care, and access to the GI Bill, were a welcome relief while also serving as a springboard for future success. Indeed, the latter benefit and my continued participation in the USNR were instrumental in funding my pursuit of a bachelor's degree and a doctorate, both in U.S. history, with a specialization on the American Southwest.[1]

Other factors included my awareness that as a Mexican American, I was somehow different, culturally and racially, which placed me outside of the American mainstream.[2] I endeavored to strengthen my claim to American citizenship through military service, an effort that dovetailed with the patriotism I expressed as a young man. My mother's approach to child-rearing and her emphasis on patriotism, education, a strong work ethic, and an English-only upbringing, enhanced my patriotic fervor and fascination with the U.S. military, despite the lack of any significant veteran influence in my immediate or extended family. In fact, as a young teenager, I eagerly anticipated my opportunity to enlist as I played make-believe war games and watched Hollywood war movies. Furthermore, I struggled to establish a masculine identity while reared by my mother and grandmother. Try as they could, their loving presence and many sacrifices could not help me navigate the cultural expectations often associated with Latin machismo. While negotiated on an individual basis, more conservative interpretations of machismo have cast a large shadow over many Mexican and Mexican American men coming of age. It has influenced a wide array of behaviors, including exaggerated forms of masculine prowess, while also promoting military service as a stepping-stone into manhood. Such naïve romanticism was especially appealing for me, and thus, it seemed quite clear to me at an early age that part of my civic and masculine responsibilities included a tour of duty in the U.S. military, which also offered the possibility of social and economic mobility.

My personal story outlined here is not unique. Many communities marginalized on the basis of race, ethnicity, class, gender, and sexual orientation have viewed military service as a type of social contract, one that offered avenues toward social and political equality and economic advancement.[3] Take, for example, the "Double V" campaign of the Second World War. Originally coined by African Americans to depict their struggle for a double victory over the Axis powers abroad and for civil rights at home, this concept celebrated the opportunity provided by World War II to secure full citizenship through dedicated military service. By comparison, the story of Asian veterans is equally compelling. Following America's entry into World War I, almost 24 million men registered for the Selective Draft Act of 1917. Of these, approximately 16 percent were noncitizens, prompting the U.S. government to provide for their naturalization in May 1918. As historian Lucy Salyer describes it, while the "government not only allowed, but actively courted and cajoled, European alien soldiers to become American citizens; Asian soldiers had to make their own case for citizenship again and again."[4] The 1922 Supreme Court cases *Ozawa v. United States* and *United States v. Bhagat Singh Thind*, in addition to the 1925 case *Toyota v. United States*, illustrate the pursuit of U.S. citizenship by Asian veterans using their military service as proof of their worthiness. All three plaintiffs were nevertheless denied citizenship on the basis that they did not meet the proper racial classification for naturalization.[5] Tragically, the Japanese American community would again suffer civil indignity with their 1942 internment under Executive Order 9066. Once again, military service was used to demonstrate fealty toward the United States. Over 33,000 second-generation Nisei men would serve in units such as the 100th Infantry Battalion and the famed 442nd Regimental Combat Team, which became the most decorated unit in U.S. military history, owing to its size and length of service.

This linkage between military service and citizenship was equally apparent to the Mexican American community in its own struggle for civil rights. Legally classified as white, Mexican American servicemen were spared the indignity of serving in segregated units endured by other marginalized communities.[6] Nevertheless, discriminatory treatment often associated with racialized "others" remained the de facto reality for the community, producing a generational perception among many young Mexican Americans from 1940 to 1975 in which warfare represented a social contract toward the acquisition of full citizenship rights. It was further influenced by traditional notions of masculine honor and behavior often associated with machismo. As literary critic George Mariscal has argued, a type of "warrior patriotism" has typified the Chicano drive to assimilate into the American mainstream, with historical antecedents in masculine codes of conduct within Mexico that celebrated the willingness to die in defense of *la patria* (fatherland). When transferred to a modern U.S. context, the combination of poverty, segregation, poor educational opportunities, and the perceived need to prove one's loyalty and manliness motivated significant numbers of Mexican American youth to enlist or accept their draft notice for service in World War II, Korea, and Vietnam.[7]

This tradition of martial citizenship is the basis for this book. Drawing on several fields that include Chicano and Latino history, critical men's studies, war and society, and oral history methodology, I examine the participation of Mexican American males in the U.S. military from 1940 to 1975. Not to be overlooked is the Mexican American contribution to the Korean War, a conflict that is largely overshadowed by World War II and the Vietnam War. Indeed, this book represents the only known attempt to bridge all three conflicts. In what follows, I investigate the military's transformative potential with a particular focus on socioeconomic mobility, gender identity, and postwar political activism across three generations. In this approach, I am influenced by recent trends in the study of warfare that move beyond the battlefield to examine the social, cultural, and gendered dimensions of military service.[8] Furthermore, my objective here is not another hagiographic effort that glamorizes the U.S. military while providing a celebratory assessment of military service. For example, the ongoing utilization of celebratory rhetoric and imagery to discuss the accomplishments and ultimate victory of the "Greatest Generation" perpetuates a hagiography of the Second World War. Rather, I am interested in the diverse outcomes associated with the armed forces, which include minimal upward mobility, anger and disillusionment, and other negative and tragic consequences in addition to positive gains experienced by individual servicemen.

The complicated intersection of these positive and negative consequences is underscored by the differing nature of military service during this thirty-five-year time period. The national collective effort characteristic of World War II and the Korean War differed sharply from the highly divisive nature of American involvement in Vietnam. Mexican American veterans of the former two conflicts generally pursued a precisely defined agenda that linked their military service with civil rights activism. The integrationist policies of the American GI Forum, and its founder and World War II veteran, Dr. Hector P. Garcia, offers a powerful example. First established in 1948 to aid Mexican American veterans in securing GI Bill and other entitlements in a timely manner, the American GI Forum was propelled in the following year to the forefront of civil rights activism following a white mortician's refusal to bury the returned remains of Private Felix Longoria in his hometown of Three Rivers, Texas. By contrast, as national support for the Vietnam War steadily decreased, it was exacerbated within the Mexican American community by the burgeoning Chicano movement and its emphasis on social justice and ethnic empowerment. These contrasting characteristics are further complicated by empirical evidence that demonstrates the one-sided involvement of draft-eligible males for service in Vietnam, with class serving as the major criteria for induction into the military. Unable to take advantage of the class-based possibilities for deferment made available during the war—namely, the student deferment program—Mexican American youth proved to be highly vulnerable to the military draft.

Thus, for Mexican Americans, military service produced a wide range of ideological reactions, the ideals of each often being in opposition to the others. For some veterans, most notably those that served in Vietnam, inconsistencies in American society produced various levels of disillusionment and outright anger that called into question their very identity as American nationals and the venerable tradition of military service expected of young Chicanos since World War II. My use of the phrase *Soldado Razo* (Common Soldier) as part of this manuscript's title, which I borrow from Luis Valdez's famous antiwar play of the same name, is indicative of this critical mind-set and politically engaged ethnic identity that increasingly emerged during the course of the Vietnam War.[9] For other veterans, however, their dedicated service was an opportunity to showcase fealty and provide proof that the Mexican American community had indeed earned the rights of first-class citizenship. Activism followed, but a type that emphasized patriotism rather than critical inquiry. Ultimately, it is my contention that a critical thread connecting these disparate outcomes was a redefined sense of self and proud minority identity willing to engage in individual and collective action to secure first-class citizenship. This politicized aftermath of military service, which serves as the central argument of this manuscript, must be seen as the most prominent legacy of military service for the Mexican American community from 1940 to 1975.

The U.S. military also provided an arena in which a preexisting emphasis on conventional forms of masculine and sexual behavior paralleled, and often reinforced, more orthodox notions of machismo, including idealized notions of the warrior. However, defining the Mexican macho, and the machismo of their Chicano brethren to the north, is no easy task. Sensationalized passages utilized by a number of early scholars have emphasized an aggressive form of masculine and sexual posturing, typified by infidelity, alcoholism, and a willingness to go to one's death "smiling."[10] Perhaps no author better exemplifies this exaggerated view of masculine and national identity within Mexico than Octavio Paz—a noted, yet controversial, member of the Mexican intelligentsia. According to Paz, at blame for such behavior is a tremendous sense of inferiority stemming from the intermixture of Spaniard and indigenous peoples through violence, and furthered by territorial conquest and economic subjugation at the hands of the United States. A form of defensive masculinity and warrior fatalism was the inevitable result.[11] Furthermore, Mexican nationalist ideology championed an intense form of exaggerated masculinity in literary and cinematic productions in the decades following the Mexican Revolution (1911–17), one that reinforced many of the popularized character traits associated with machismo.[12]

This scholarship similarly depicted the Chicana/o community as heir to a cultural heritage obsessed with machismo and hierarchical gender relations. Indeed, the assertion of manhood by Mexican immigrants in the United States was a recurrent theme in early Chicano literature.[13] Caught between two worlds, Mexican and American, machismo offered emotional support for young Mexican Americans coming of age in the United States as they struggled with overt racism and socioeconomic marginalization. In the struggle to assimilate in the modern U.S. context, the perceived need to prove one's manhood and loyalty as an American citizen—what Mariscal describes as the notion of warrior patriotism—provided added incentive to serve in the U.S. military. The period from 1940 to 1975, encompassing World War II and the conflicts in Korea and Vietnam, offered ample opportunities to do so, reaffirming for many a connection between machismo and conventional manifestations of male sex role behaviors, including the pursuit of masculine honor through warfare.

This distorted and sensationalized discourse largely remained unchallenged in scholarly and popular conceptions of machismo until the emergence of critical men's studies in the 1980s and 1990s. Initially, the emphasis in this new literature within the U.S. and European academy was on the multiple masculinities of European males and their American counterparts, but more recently a steady and more nuanced stream of scholarship has emerged, led by the behavioral and social sciences, that has examined men and masculinities in Latin America, the U.S. Latina/o community, and the migrant streams between the two.[14] This rich body of scholarship has ultimately highlighted a series of themes in the construction of masculine identity. First, male gender develops in relation to sets of "others." These include women, other men, larger marketplace forces, and social structures of power, such as racial and class privilege. Second, notions of manhood evolve, are contested, and thus are in a constant state of flux. And third, there are multiple masculinities, each defined contextually. While a dominant, or hegemonic, form of masculinity exists, as Raewyn (R. W.) Connell asserts, it "is not a fixed character type, always and everywhere the same. It is, rather, the masculinity that occupies the hegemonic position in a given pattern of gender relations, a position always contestable."[15]

Utilizing the critical lens put forth by Connell, and in keeping with the nuanced scholarship mentioned earlier, I offer a revisionist interpretation that challenges the tendency to view machismo as immutable and inherently obsessed with gender hierarchy. Rather, my analysis will demonstrate that the homo-social milieu fostered by the U.S. military's all-male environment played a critical role in cultivating a gendered process that was anything but fixed and conventional, allowing for alternative masculine behaviors, both homosexual and heterosexual, despite the military's focus on strict regimentation and compulsory heterosexuality. For example, clearly evident is a noticeable evolution from one generation to the next. Generally, military service and machismo were mutually reinforcing in World War II and Korea, while that connection, and martial manhood overall, was challenged more by some veterans of the Vietnam War. This is not meant to suggest that all World War II–era veterans were aggressively macho or that all Vietnam veterans pursued alternate forms of masculine identity. It just means that shifting notions of manhood impacted the Mexican American community and its relationship to conventional displays of machismo. Furthermore, I endeavor to convey a broad range of combat and noncombat military experiences in order to demonstrate that the "link between masculinity, violence, and the military is more complex than the image of 'man the warrior' might suggest."[16] However, the preponderance of combat stories within this study does call into question whether or not combat veterans have a different and more complex relationship to machismo than those who served in noncombat positions.

Another key factor in the decision to enlist was the potential for upward mobility and the desire to leave behind difficult economic circumstances. For many Mexican American families, from 1940 to 1975, poverty remained a constant reality in urban barrios and agricultural labor camps, and the promise of regular wages, military training, and access to health care was a welcome relief. A tour of duty also provided access to the various entitlements associated with the GI Bill, including low-interest loans, educational assistance, and unemployment compensation. This capacity to serve as a "bridging environment" that can nurture improved socioeconomic status has remained one of the more powerful points of debate in connection with the armed forces. Furthermore, veteran status for socially marginalized groups would seemingly enhance this bridging process as a result of their less advantageous position.

Yet not all veterans encountered social mobility after their tours of duty. Provided with few transferable skills and unwilling or unable to utilize their GI Bill and other entitlements due to discriminatory practices and other logistical issues within the Veterans Administration (VA), many Mexican Americans returned to unskilled manual labor or migrant farm work in the civilian sector. Furthermore, the tangible benefits associated with the GI Bill fluctuated considerably from 1940 to 1975, leaving Korean and Vietnam War veterans with fewer benefits from which to draw. In addition, I will also highlight the uneven implementation of the direct forms of assistance provided by the 1944 Servicemen's Readjustment Act, which also prompted calls for reform and influenced civil rights activism. Recent scholarship has at last turned its attention to the original bill's many limitations and outright exclusions based on race, gender, and sexual orientation.[17] My analysis will be the first to do so vis-à-vis the Mexican American community.

Further complicating reentry into the civilian sector were the many physical and emotional scars acquired while in uniform. A variety of ailments, ranging from tropical diseases common to the battlefields of Southeast Asia and the Pacific, alcoholism, exposure to Agent Orange during the Vietnam War, and post-traumatic stress disorder (PTSD), have plagued the lives of returning Mexican American veterans. In fact, the physical and mental health of returning Vietnam veterans became a subject of intense scrutiny for the behavioral and social sciences in the 1970s and 1980s—an effort that extended a modicum of coverage to the Mexican American community.[18] And so, the psychiatric and medical services provided to wounded GIs under Title IV of the GI Bill's appropriations, and administered by the Veterans Administration, would play a vital role in the physical and mental health of returning veterans. However, critiques and outright anger toward the health-care practices of the VA produced a disturbing indifference to such services while also prompting calls for reform in a manner similar to the uneven implementation of the bill's direct benefits. Indeed, an examination of the VA as a health-care system also provides a rich opportunity to underscore the connection between health care and political activism.

These vast experiences encompassing the Mexican American military experience produced a proliferation of much-needed scholarly analysis and publications in the 1990s and the following decade. For too long, existing scholarship was dominated by the aforementioned psychiatric studies, along with the 1963 publication of *Among the Valiant: Mexican Americans in World War II and Korea* by Raúl Morin. In the case of World War II, the connection between military service and the struggle for first-class citizenship was forcefully made, with a particular focus on the Longoria affair and the subsequent activism of the American GI Forum.[19] A vital component of this effort has been the remarkable achievements of Maggie Rivas-Rodríguez, associate professor of journalism at the University of Texas. Her three anthologies, which first appeared in 2005, serve as a valuable resource for an audience interested in the civilian and military contributions of Mexican Americans and the larger Chicana/o community to World War II.[20] This undertaking stems, in part, from her ongoing project, the U.S. Latino and Latina World War II Oral History Project, launched in 1999. Over eight hundred interviews have been gathered, culminating in the 2006 release of *A Legacy Greater Than Words: Stories of U.S. Latinos and Latinas of the WWII Generation*, based on 425 of these narratives.[21] Such work stands in stark contrast to the glaring omission of the Latina/o community in the 2007 release of *The War*, Ken

Burns's World War II documentary, despite his inclusion of African Americans and the interned Japanese American community.[22]

Meanwhile, with veterans at the forefront, an emerging literature began to document the Mexican American experience in the Vietnam War, an effort that coincidentally highlighted the divisive nature of U.S. involvement in Vietnam and the contradictions faced by Chicano servicemen. At one end of the spectrum are the tales of heroism and patriotic discourse offered by Everett Álvarez Jr. and Roy Benavidez.[23] The former was a naval aviator, held as a prisoner of war for eight and a half years in North Vietnam; the latter was an Army Special Forces soldier and Medal of Honor recipient, the nation's highest award for valor on the battlefield.[24] This perspective differs sharply from more critical analyses, including the tragedy and trauma associated with combat, generated by other veterans and scholars.[25] In particular, the publication of compelling oral history collections emerged as an effective tool in the dissemination of this more strident point of view.[26] Finally, the Mexican American contribution to the Korean War has received far less attention. The work of the renowned writer and professor Rolando Hinojosa-Smith remains the notable exception.[27]

The published oral histories dealing with the Vietnam War allowed for a comparative analysis of major themes and concerns that inspired my own use of oral history methodology. While I employ a variety of different resources—including archival material, newspapers, and census data—this manuscript is primarily an oral history venture. I acquired a collection of sixty-four narratives utilizing a "snowball" methodology of locating interviewees, in which each veteran provided contact information that led to another, culminating in forty-seven interviews conducted in various Southwestern locations, sixteen in Michigan, and one in Virginia.[28] The demographic environment in Southern California, where I pursued my graduate studies, provided an abundant supply of Mexican American veterans, and my five-year tenure as an assistant professor of history at Grand Valley State University in Grand Rapids, Michigan, afforded me the opportunity to expand my collection of oral histories into the Upper Midwest. This latter sample will extend my analysis of Chicano soldiering beyond the American Southwest and will demonstrate that the blurry, often contradictory nature of claims to national belonging and other consequences associated with military service were not specific to the Chicano community residing along the U.S.-Mexico border.[29] This larger national story thus continues the more recent process of decentering Mexican American and Latina/o Studies away from the Southwest. Indeed, as the Chicana/o and Latina/o population continues to grow at an exceptional rate—it currently comprises one-sixth of the U.S. population—new geographic spaces, such as the Midwest and the South, have become more central to the study of U.S. Chicanos and Latinos.

The sixty-four interviews represent a diverse range of domestic and wartime experiences.[30] The majority of these veterans experienced impoverished and working-class lifestyles in rural and urban locations, and all were born in the United States or arrived at an early age from Mexico or Puerto Rico.[31] Twenty-two narrators were drafted, thirty-five enlisted, eight were drilling reservists when mobilized, and one was recalled to active duty following the completion of his initial tour of duty.[32] They served in all four U.S. military branches, with the majority serving in the army and the marines. An overwhelming majority, fifty-two, experienced varying degrees of combat, and enlisted men, fifty-nine total, predominate. Their attained rank ranges from E-3 to E-9 based on an enlisted ranking system that ranges from E-1 (private) to E-9 (sergeant major). By comparison, there exist only five officers within this sample—one chief warrant officer and four commissioned officers.[33] The rank attained by the latter ranges from O-2 to O-5 based on an officer ranking system that ranges from O-1 (second lieutenant/ensign) to O-10 (general/admiral). There are also seven retirees—three officers and four enlisted personnel. Finally, all interviews were based on a standardized set of thirty-three questions that were influenced by my own experiences in the U.S. Navy.[34] While these served as a guiding rubric, to varying degrees, each interview contained a nonstructured exchange of information. I remained always prepared, as described by renowned oral historian Donald A. Ritchie, "to abandon carefully prepared questions and follow the interviewee down unexpected paths."[35] Individual struggles influenced the questions posed in each interview, yet larger cultural and social issues as members of the Mexican American community and the U.S. military also played a prominent role.

Admittedly, some scholars continue to doubt the value of first-person testimonies as a valid method of historical inquiry. From this perspective, oral history is viewed as far too subjective and shaped by memory lapses and a multitude of individual emotions and social concerns that may attempt to portray historical events, the narrator, and their community too positively. Ronald J. Grele offers the following perspective, "marching in a commemorative parade not only refreshes the memory of the event being commemorated and the mythic heroes at the center of that event, but it also reaffirms one's position in the hierarchical world in which that commemoration and those heroes have meaning."[36] More specifically, another potential issue within this study is the overrepresentation of enlisted personnel that has produced a working-class profile of my narrators. Indeed, their dire circumstances as children and young adults, which take center stage in the first two chapters, influenced my analysis and conclusions. Yet another potential bias is the substantial number of vignettes by combat veterans discussed earlier. All in all, my sixty-four narrators certainly cannot convey a complete and unbiased picture of the Mexican American military experience from 1940 to 1975. Nevertheless, I employ their narratives because they provide a deep understanding of individual experience and because they suggest larger patterns in terms of Mexican Americans veterans and their service in World War II, the Korean War, and the Vietnam War.

Grele's commentary also highlights the joint nature of an oral history interview, what Michael Frisch has termed a "shared authority" that involves the narrator, the interviewer, and external stimuli in a complex exercise meant to reconstruct historical events.[37] It provides for a type of mutual exchange between narrator and researcher that allows the latter to draw upon shared experiences with the former in the production of new knowledge. I firmly believe that my status as a fellow Mexican American veteran provided me with this shared identity described by Frisch that served as a kind of "cultural capital," which fostered a level of solidarity and, arguably, a more frank disclosure of information by the interviewees. Nevertheless, my efforts to find and interview veterans were not free of difficulty. For example, while narrators typically shared their stories willingly, hesitation and outright refusal were also possible. In particular, the requirement that interviewees sign a release form provided some suspicious reactions. In addition, for some, our one-on-one dialogue represented their first significant exchange of memories long kept hidden, often reopening old wounds in the process. These difficulties aside, a lack of resources that would allow for an examination of masculine identity and the transformative potential of military service from the vantage point of institutional records is a key reason to use oral history. As I argue, it is the use of oral history that allows us access to the more fluid and complex consequences of military service and gender behavior that are central to my analysis.

This book is organized both chronologically and thematically. The first two chapters examine my narrators' lives prior to their entrance into the armed forces. Chapter 1 examines the post–World War I formation of Mexican American communities, both rural and urban, across the American Southwest and the social, political, and economic barriers that confined large elements of the community to a working-class or impoverished status well into the Vietnam War era. However, at the same time, a strong work ethic, spiritual and cultural steadfastness, and a commitment to family characterized the formation of these communities. For many Mexican American men, these values, as well as the lessons learned and fortitude gained from their hardships, often eased the transition to military life. Chapter 2 conducts a similar examination of Mexican American communities in Michigan, with a particular focus on Saginaw, located in eastern Michigan at the crossroads of the fertile Saginaw Valley and the industrial zone that encompassed Detroit.[38] Special emphasis is given to the process of arrival, migrant field work throughout the state of Michigan, and foundry work associated with the booming automobile industry, particularly in Saginaw's Grey Iron Foundry, a subsidiary of General Motors.

The next three chapters chronicle my narrators' entrance into the U.S. military. For many, their encounters with the pay and amenities associated with military service were a welcome relief from poverty and other substandard conditions. This was especially true for the World War II and Korean War cohorts that lived through the Great Depression. Following the completion of basic training, a universal process meant to rebuild recruits in the image of military doctrine, Mexican American servicemen served in a variety of overseas and domestic locations. Chapter 3 offers a sampling of these combat and other military experiences in Europe and the Pacific during World War II, while chapter 4 examines Mexican American contributions to the Korean War, including some of the battlefield conditions and tactics they encountered, such as human-wave assaults and freezing winters.

In chapter 5, I begin my analysis of the Vietnam War by placing initial emphasis on Cold War rhetoric, popular culture, and the memory of World War II and Korea in motivating young Mexican Americans to join the U.S. military. I then showcase how military participation by draft-eligible males did not occur equitably across American society due to class-based exemptions made available by the Selective Service, most notably through student deferments. Moreover, local draft boards all too often mirrored federal policies in maintaining class distinctions within the U.S. military by channeling the working class and racial minorities, including the Chicano community, into the military at an increased rate. A subsequent examination of military experiences in Vietnam will then highlight the tenacity of North Vietnamese soldiers and Viet Cong guerrillas, the invasion of Cambodia, and the distrust of South Vietnamese soldiers by U.S. military personnel.

The final four chapters provide a focused examination of the impact of military service on Mexican American veterans in what concerns the aforementioned topics: masculine identity, socioeconomic mobility, and postwar political activism. Chapter 6 explores masculine identity by utilizing the insights developed by the emergence of critical men's studies to examine the contested nature of military service from 1940 to 1975. My objective in this chapter is an examination of machismo that challenges conventional forms of masculinity, including heterosexuality. I do this through an expanded discussion of gender identity that illustrates a diverse range of masculine and sexual behaviors by Chicano servicemen once they were inducted into the U.S. military. Chapter seven follows with a critical assessment of the GI Bill in promoting a "bridging environment" to improved socioeconomic status that will contrast its many positive benefits with potentially negligible outcomes. This chapter explores the bill's education and training benefits, while the health-care services provided by the Veterans Administration under Title IV of the bill's appropriations are the subject of chapter 8. In the ongoing debate over the bill's many limitations and outright exclusions, the latter resources have been overlooked in favor of the more celebrated forms of direct assistance. Chapter 9 delves into the military's capacity to foster a politicized consciousness among Mexican American veterans. I begin by analyzing the post–World War II and Korean War generation that struggled to overcome institutionalized discrimination by linking civil rights activism with their military service. The integrationist and anti-Communist policies of organizations such as the American GI Forum receive special attention. This chapter then proceeds to examine the highly divisive nature of American involvement in Vietnam. The failure to reach victory, in tandem with the Chicano and antiwar movements, produced a diverse range of reactions and political activism among Chicano veterans, often challenging the patriotism expressed by an earlier generation. For other veterans, however, time spent in Vietnam further solidified their patriotism and pride in their military service.

In the case of my narrators, voter registration drives, lawsuits meant to combat segregated facilities, participation in demonstrations, or voluntary exile abroad are but a few examples of the many activities employed by the veterans I interviewed that illustrate this transformed subjectivity. Furthermore, a tour of duty reaffirmed for many veterans a more traditional masculine identity while simultaneously allowing others to push boundaries and craft their own definition of manhood. Moreover, tangible material benefits, such as the GI Bill, played a key role in fostering more lucrative careers as lawyers, writers, and professors for a select number of individuals within my sample. More prevalent, however, were the many trade skills acquired through vocational training, producing a middle- and lower-middle-class lifestyle. Still other veterans experienced little to no socioeconomic mobility, and a return to unskilled labor and migrant farm work characterized the post-military careers for a handful of the narrators I interviewed. Such contradictions reinforce the need to move beyond mere celebratory assessments of the U.S. military. Rather, the matrix between military service, citizenship, and manhood produced a redefined sense of self willing to engage in individual and collective action to confront the inequalities present in American society.

1

NORTHWARD FROM MEXICO

"Every time [the attendant] opened the gate for the white boys to go in swimming, I would stick my dime out and the attendant would say, 'Sorry, but I can't.' So then I'd sit down back on the ground next to the gate."

"I remember my senior year in high school I went to my counselor and said, 'You know, I think I'd like to go on to college.' She told me to forget it. I'd never make it."

TURN OF THE-CENTURY NATIVIST LEGISLATION that banned traditional sources of cheap labor from Europe and Asia in tandem with disastrous economic policies within Mexico increasingly pushed Mexican migrants northward prior to the Great Depression. Although estimates vary, from 1900 to 1930, roughly 1.5 million Mexicans arrived in the United States, where settlement occurred in migratory labor camps or in urban barrios. This thirty-year "Great Migration" produced the first sizeable Mexican immigrant communities in the United States, and although more than a few thousand served in World War I, most notably from Texas and New Mexico, there existed no longevity of military service in large parts of the Mexican American community before World War II. Rather, by 1930, the U.S.-born children of this migrant Mexican workforce increasingly embraced American consumer culture while confronting discriminatory policies and harsh economic difficulties that foreshadowed their entrance into the military. Such was the case for the majority of my narrators, and their following testimony relates, in poignant terms, their haphazard contact with the American mainstream that continued well beyond the Second World War. The community life that emerged was largely defined by participation in a family economy, a bilingual and Catholic upbringing, and nascent forms of advocacy in the pursuit of social and political equality, a process that was galvanized by their dedicated military service.

THE FAMILY ECONOMY

Mexican immigration to the United States has its origins in the late nineteenth century—in particular, the economic policies of Mexican president Porfirio Díaz during his thirty-four-year tenure (1876–1910). The underlying intention was to modernize Mexico, yet the impact on the Mexican peasantry was disastrous. As described by historian George Sánchez:

> The Díaz administration followed a land policy which encouraged the growth of large haciendas at the expense of small farmers and communally owned lands, or ejidos . . . Previously independent peasants were forced into debt peonage or into joining the growing migratory labor stream. At the same time, the shift to export crops severely decreased the production of maize, the staple food in the Mexican diet. Along with other governmental policies, this decline in production boosted the cost of living . . . By the time of the Revolution of 1910, these factors had combined to bring the rural masses of Mexico to the brink of starvation.[1]

The subsequent Mexican Revolution (1911–17) further destabilized socioeconomic conditions in Mexico, ultimately producing swirling patterns of internal migration by these landless peasants that was characterized by movement toward urban centers and northern border towns where employment in mining activity and railroad construction was readily available.[2] Already part of a migratory process, many individuals ventured further north into the United States where cheap labor in various industries was in high demand. This large influx of Mexican immigrants spurred American industries, notably commercial agriculture, to increasingly turn to these low-wage laborers. A combination of labor agencies, word of mouth, and advertisements spread the news of such opportunities, including the following excerpt for the cotton industry in California's San Joaquin Valley:

> The Pay Is Magnificent!
>
> The conditions are superb and the work season is very long.
> Come to the Government Employment Office at ________
> and ask for Don FRANCISCO PALOMARES, representative
> of the AGRICULTURAL LABOR BUREAU of the SAN

JOAQUIN VALLEY; he will be pleased to give you all the
Information.[3]

The demand for labor in various Southwestern industries was magnified by anti-immigrant legislation such as the Chinese Exclusion Act of 1882, the 1908 Gentleman's Agreement with Japan, and the 1917 National Origins Act that severely curtailed the availability of cheap labor from other immigrant groups. In particular, the latter piece of legislation, modified in 1921 and 1924, provided for literacy requirements, a head tax, a medical examination, and, most notably, a mathematical quota system, which capped the number of immigrants allowed to legally enter the United States from any given country. These restrictions, however, did not apply to the Western hemisphere, and the flow of Mexican immigrants continued unabated. As described further by Sánchez: "both American officials and entering aliens understood that it was the labor needs of the American Southwest that defined Mexican migration to the United States and not laws drawn up in Washington."[4] Upon arrival, these migrants often combined an itinerant lifestyle in commercial agriculture with urban residence and employment in a variety of odd jobs, including seasonal participation in agricultural migrant streams. Against this backdrop, the labor power of the entire family unit became a critical source of additional income.

In the case of World War II, Jesse Ybarra, born in San Antonio in 1916 and drafted into the army in 1943, began working a variety of odd jobs at the age of ten, often loading and unloading newspaper trucks at 3:00 a.m. in order to help his mother and two sisters. The family's dire predicament was compounded by the death of Jesse's father in 1920 in a coal mining accident. Left alone with few marketable skills and no English proficiency, his mother suffered terribly in her efforts to provide for her children. As Jesse described, she "had a hard time bringing us up . . . My mother didn't have . . . the language to find employment, [so] she had to do housekeeping . . . We were real poor."[5] As a result, the entire family would often shell pecans: "At that time . . . that was one means to sort of help us supplement our income."[6]

Furthermore, the constant need to uproot themselves due to an inability to afford monthly rent also hampered Jesse's ability to continue his education. As he stated: "I had . . . to drop out because I didn't have the clothing. I dropped out at the eighth grade."[7] Alfred Bablot, born in the Jerome, Arizona, in 1925 but raised in the Mexican American barrio of East Los Angeles after moving there with his family in 1935, offered a similar account of his mother's desperation and subsequent work ethic: "In grammar school, in order for us [children] to get something to eat . . . my mother would have to go wash some of the pots and pans [at the school cafeteria]."[8] His entrance into the army as a draftee sometime in 1943 provided himself and his family with immediate financial relief.

John Sótelo, born in Riverside, California, in 1925, fully remembers the impact of the Great Depression on his family. It meant the loss of his father's grocery store because the customers to whom he extended credit failed to pay. His family soon joined a growing stream of itinerant farm workers harvesting crops throughout California. He elaborated further: "the navel oranges in Riverside would start in late November . . . 'til May; the Valencias came in early May . . . 'til June. And then . . . a lot of [farm workers] took off, as my mom did with [her] children . . . Some went to [the California city of] Hemet 'cause Hemet was [the] apricot center in the area . . . From there . . . we went to pick grapes in the Fresno area . . . and then we would go . . . to San Jose to pick prunes."[9] Meanwhile, Raúl Medina, born in El Paso, Texas, in 1925 but raised in Fresno, California, suffered considerable economic hardship living in an extended family that numbered twenty. Prior to being drafted into the army in 1943, he remembered his childhood as "definitely poor, [very] poor."[10] He dropped out of school at the age of fifteen in order to find employment: "We didn't have any clothes . . . There was always a shortage of food."[11] A similar turn of events characterized the childhood of Carlos Santillán, who was born in Tampico, Mexico, and crossed the border at El Paso, Texas, with his parents in 1927 at the age of four. In his recollection, he equated the need to earn a living with a perceived masculine responsibility to do so: "The Mexican people always believe . . . to make an hombre [man], he should learn young to earn his living . . . Never mind going to school. The thing is to 'to be a man.'[12] One of his many odd jobs before being drafted in 1943 included helping the local milkman along his route, with free milk as his pay.[13]

The parents of veteran Joe B. Medina, from the Mexican state of Chihuahua, settled in a small farming community in southeastern Colorado, where Medina was born in 1924. Ultimately drafted into the army in 1943, he recalled a simple upbringing that was not desperately poor, largely due to his father's tireless efforts to provide for the family: "My father had three jobs. He usually worked for the hay mill, hauling alfalfa, and occasionally he would unload boxcars . . . The third job [was] helping farmers with their duties . . . The farmers didn't have any money so they would pay him [with] a big leg of lamb or a big piece of pork or beef. So we were never hungry [and] we had a big garden and we had a cow [for milk]."[14] Medina, however, did witness the devastating consequences of the Great Depression as a child; moreover, as he described, his parents responded with considerable humanitarianism:

> We lived not too far from the railroad tracks [and] almost constantly, big trains would stop . . . and the poor guys riding the trains would come over to our house and ask my mother [for food]. My mother would tell me in Spanish [to] keep an eye on him and she would . . . make a nice big long burrito . . . They didn't know what it was, but they ate it . . . My parents never turned anybody down.[15]

Fortunately, the often difficult economic circumstances encountered by these veterans were partially offset through participation in various New Deal programs. Arguably, the program with the most appeal was the Civilian Conservation Corps (CCC), which offered unemployed young men between the ages of eighteen and twenty-five a monthly stipend of $30, as well as room and board, in exchange for their manual labor in various environmental conservation projects. As historian Maria Montoya notes in her study of the CCC in northern New Mexico, "in the Civilian Conservation Corps the Roosevelt Administration believed it had found a partial solution for the two overwhelming problems of youth unemployment and environmental deterioration."[16] Such aid was a welcome relief for many families, including Jesse Ybarra. As he recalled: "At that time the government would give my mother $25 a month and I would get $5 for my own personal use."[17] U.S. Army veteran, William Sánchez, served six months in 1939, while Alfred Aguirre, also an army veteran, remembers building dams and planting trees throughout most of 1938. Aguirre also credits the CCC with providing him a more cosmopolitan outlook: "I was more Americanized because I lived with people from all walks of life."[18] Moreover, these camps, administered by the U.S. Army, provided future veterans with their first contact with a bureaucratic system, as well as exposure to military-style discipline and drill formations, characteristics that would be of use during their time in the military.

As for the above veterans of the Second World War, difficult economic circumstances and the Great Depression also loomed large for many of my narrators that served in the Korean War. In the case of U.S. Navy and Marine Corps veteran Ruben Moreno, the death of his father soon after his birth in 1927 in Tucson, Arizona, plunged his family into dire financial circumstances. He remembered that his mother worked tirelessly to support him and his two siblings.

As he stated: "After she lost my father, she took in laundry, cleaned houses, and the like, to put food on the table. She didn't get paid much, but then it didn't take much to eat either . . . $5 worth of groceries would feed us for two weeks. But, of course, it was mostly beans and tortillas."[19] Given these circumstances, Moreno and his siblings also worked as youngsters: "We were always looking for something [such as] collecting bottles, shining shoes, or selling papers. All of that helped."[20] A similar set of circumstances emerged for David Carillo. Born in Riverside, California, in 1930, Carillo and his family moved to East Los Angeles in 1934, where he and his seven siblings soon joined their parents in the migrant stream harvesting crops in the fields adjacent to Los Angeles. He described their efforts succinctly: "We followed the season[s] of picking grapes and prunes and whatnot."[21] In such efforts, his father set a powerful example: "We had a lot of respect for my father . . . I've never seen such a hardworking man."[22] The work ethic instilled in him at such a young age by such arduous employment would ease his transition into the army in 1947.

Similarly, Ray Gómez and his seven siblings picked cotton as youngsters in the fields surrounding Anthony, New Mexico, adjacent to El Paso. Born into impoverished conditions in 1931, Gómez remembered a childhood filled with constant toil, which left little room for a proper education, and Gómez only completed the fifth grade. Such poverty, in tandem with the tragic death of his parents, left Gómez with little recourse but to lie about his age and enlist in the army in 1948 at the age of sixteen. He offered the following motivation for doing so: "I needed a place to live. We were so poor . . . I found a home in the army as far as I'm concerned."[23] His childhood friend, José Domínguez, born in Las Cruces, New Mexico, in 1930 but raised in Anthony, also joined his siblings in picking cotton at a young age, and he sporadically attended school past the fourth grade. He was convinced at an early age that a tour in the military was better than the boredom and limited opportunities present in the town. As he explained, "My mind was made up since I was a little kid that I wanted to be a soldier."[24] And so, upon turning eighteen in 1948, Domínguez enlisted in the army along with Ray Gómez and other childhood friends. He recalled, "That's the first thing we went to, the army recruiting officer in El Paso [Texas]."[25] By comparison, the economic difficulties encountered by Eddie Trujillo in Silver City, New Mexico, after his birth in 1931 deteriorated further at the age of fourteen with the death of his mother. Her loving presence stood in stark contrast to his abusive, alcoholic father, and Trujillo was left with no option but to leave home. As he described, he suffered immensely: "Sometimes I would go two [or] three days without eating."[26] Lacking any formal education, unable to read and write, and already a seasoned drinker, Trujillo lied about his age and enlisted in the army in 1948 at the age of sixteen. As he elaborated further, he literally found a home in the military: "I was on the streets just roaming around the town and [eventually] some guy came with the idea to enlist in the army."[27]

Comparable circumstances extended well beyond the Second World War to include the Mexican American generation that served in Vietnam. Once again, childhood poverty was an everyday reality for several interviewees, requiring them to work for wages to survive. For example, Alfredo Vea vividly recalls the dilapidated housing conditions that dominated his childhood, which included makeshift lean-tos, Quonset huts, and automobiles. Born in a migrant labor camp outside of Phoenix, Arizona, in 1950, Vea was raised by his grandmother after being abandoned by his mother. He ultimately struck out on his own in his early teenage years and worked as an agricultural worker up and down the West Coast before being drafted into the army in 1967. Such constant migration made the pursuit of a formal education somewhat difficult, yet he endeavored to remain a student despite having a normal school day sandwiched by constant work in the early morning hours and late into the evening. Benevolent high school teachers in Livermore, California, provided some guidance; however, his dire circumstances, made painfully obvious in the clothes he wore, elicited harsh reactions from fellow students. As he explained, "I felt so embarrassed . . . because I used to wear my Levis and my knee pads with my grape knife [to school]."[28] Victor Ramírez, born in Del Rio, Texas, in 1941, joined his family in migrant streams throughout Texas and California. He stated: "We picked cotton [in Texas and] we [went] to California to pick fruits."[29] Moreover, in a manner similar to José Domínguez, Ramírez and his two older brothers resolved at an early age to join the U.S. military, and he enlisted in the air force in 1960, offering the following rationale: "Myself and my brothers, we worked so hard in the fields and were so poor that our mentality was always to join the military . . . I was eight years old, I was pickin' cotton . . . [We also] used to go and caddy . . . at golf courses [and] get a little [more] money like that."[30]

Born in Texas in 1943, Joe Rodríguez performed a variety of odd jobs in Hawaii, where his family settled after his father completed his career in the U.S. Navy. His father's inadequate retirement income coupled with his alcoholism did not meet the bare needs of the seven-member family. This constant struggle to survive was etched in Rodríguez's mind as he entered early adulthood and began a family of his own. Finding himself heading down the same path of poverty, he relinquished his status as a naval reservist and volunteered for active duty in 1965. Basing his decision on the pay and benefits that military service offered, he likened his decision to an unfortunate, but necessary, deal with the devil. He offered the following vivid recollection:

> The service to me was a way to get up and to get out [of poverty]. I can remember what it's like to go to bed hungry and I can remember being in a community where people didn't have money . . . It effects the way they think and I didn't want to be that way. I wanted out. And so I used the military . . . In a certain way I was a mercenary. It's one of those Faustian bargains.[31]

Meanwhile, Jesus Barragan, born in the Phoenix suburb of Glendale, Arizona, in 1944, suffered considerable financial hardship following his parents' divorce. Enrolled in the fourth grade at the time, he and his four siblings joined his mother in California's migrant streams, where his diminutive size initially restricted his availability. As he stated, "I was too small to pick [other crops], so I would cut apricots."[32] After settling in San Jose, and prior to his enlistment into the U.S. Naval Reserve in 1965, Barragan continued in his capacity as a farm worker, although with some difficulty: "In San Jose, I also continued . . . [as] farm labor. I picked string beans, cotton, cherries, and apricots. [However,] I remember getting fired from the cherries 'cause I was picking too slow."[33]

In contrast to the previous harsh conditions, several other narrators from all three generations experienced a more solid working-class lifestyle. They were nevertheless required to work as youngsters in order to generate additional income. A case in point is naval aviator Everett Álvarez, born in Salinas, California, in 1937 but raised largely in San Francisco, where his father worked as a welder during World War II. As a youngster, Álvarez worked a number of odd jobs that extended into his college years at two-year Hartnell College and Santa Clara University until his graduation in 1960. As he recalled: "In high school, I was a dishwasher. In junior high [school], I was picking strawberries. In college, I worked in a warehouse, I worked as a store clerk, [and I] drove a school bus."[34] He subsequently completed Officer Candidate School (OCS) and was commissioned an ensign in the navy in 1960. Born in Riverside, California, in 1948, Raymond Buriel often worked alongside his father in his capacity as a gardener and landscaper for affluent white residents of Riverside. Before volunteering into the Marine Corps in 1967, he can remember instances where his fellow classmates sat poolside while he helped his father perform his duties.

Jesse Salcedo, born in Hollister, California, in 1948, and drafted into the army in 1969, found steady employment and fair treatment at the same ranch that employed his father, a Mexican immigrant from Chihuahua, Mexico, for approximately forty years. Salcedo recalled this family commitment to the ranch and his father's work ethic: "He [was] a hard worker . . . He set the pace for me and my siblings . . . We used to pick grapes, and walnuts, and pears."[35] Lastly, in San Diego, California, U.S. Air Force veteran Gene García clearly remembered a united family approach to financial well-being. Born in 1932, he performed a number of odd jobs throughout his adolescence, transferring his earnings to his mother who managed the family's finances. As he described: "I usually just turned my money over to my mom and she would allocate so much for school, clothes, and stuff like that."[36]

STRUCTURAL RACISM

These difficult economic circumstances were exacerbated by the rampant discrimination and segregation that typified race relations throughout the United States, which further reinforced a second-class existence for the Mexican American community despite its de jure classification as white citizens. Indeed, the overwhelming testimony provided by my narrators offers numerous glimpses of discriminatory treatment in housing and public facilities throughout the Southwest. In Fresno, for example, Raúl Medina clearly remembered a racially divided city where "Chinese, Japanese, blacks, Mexicans . . . [and] any [other] minority was on the west side."[37] Ray Gómez offered a similar assessment of Anthony, New Mexico, where segregation dominated the daily lives of the town's Mexican American inhabitants: "There were very few white people . . . Of course, they didn't like the Mexicans at that time."[38] Ruben Moreno also recalled the racial divide that separated the Mexican American and African American communities from Tucson's white residents in the following account: "In Tucson, there was a definite division. South of Congress Street and west of Stone Avenue was all [a] Mexican barrio."[39] Eddie Lovio, born in Tucson in 1932, and a volunteer into the Marine Corps Reserve in 1949, offered similar commentary: "The north side [of the city] didn't like Chicanos . . . We knew not to go there or else we'd get into trouble. Swimming pools were [also] segregated."[40] So too, did Jesus Barragan in relation to Glendale, Arizona: "The main avenue [was] Glendale Avenue . . . All the Mexican folk lived on one side of Glendale Avenue and all the white folk lived on the other side. And all the better businesses were on the other side."[41]

Born to a miner in Miami, Arizona, in April 1925, Marine Corps veteran Robert L. Castro provides a powerful portrait of the discriminatory apparatus that dominated the mining communities of southern Arizona, including the town of Ray:

> Ray, Arizona, had four communities. One was [for] the Anglos. Of course, I'm talking about . . . engineers and administrators . . . Lower-class Anglos . . . that worked also in the mines, they lived in [another] area . . . The Mexicans, they lived in a town by the name of "Sonora." And then there was another residential area by the name of "Barcelona," where the Spaniards lived.[42]

Castro also offered stark commentary on the town's segregated public facilities: "They had basketball courts, we had none. They had a swimming pool . . . [with] grass all the way around [it] and changing rooms . . . We had nothing but a cement square with a wire enclosure around it."[43] As he continued, wage differentials were also the norm: "If a [Mexican] miner [earned] $4 an hour, the Anglo [miner] . . . earned $1 to $2 more an hour."[44] Not surprisingly, the educational facilities of Ray were also affected: "School was segregated through grammar school. High school was integrated."[45] Once he reached high school, Castro described the race relations on campus: "We got along, but we knew there was a difference."[46]

Segregated public facilities, however, could also be sites of contention. An example is offered by John Sótelo in Riverside, where the swimming pool located on the city's east side remained segregated. He nevertheless displayed a passionate commitment in his efforts to allow Mexican American kids access to the pool. As he stated in this chapter's epigraph, "Every time [the attendant] opened the gate for the white boys to go in swimming, I would stick my dime out and the attendant would say, 'Sorry, but I can't.' So then I'd sit down back on the ground next to the gate [and await another opportunity]."[47] Historian María Eva Flores offers commentary on a similar process in Fort Stockton, Texas, that further highlights the contested nature of public facilities such as swimming pools and the concerted efforts of elected officials to maintain segregation. In 1935, Pecos County officials applied for and received funds from the Works Progress Administration (WPA) to improve the local swimming pool and adjacent park that, coincidentally, were off limits to the county's Mexican American inhabitants. In this application to the WPA, the county also proposed building a separate bathhouse for them. However, with no such facility to speak of, seven years later, on July 6, 1943, Corporal Jesse García attempted to gain access to the pool while in uniform. He was denied and left after a heated exchange, ultimately taking his case to the local chapter of the League of United Latin American Citizens (LULAC).[48] The following day the directors of Water Improvement District #1, which supervised the waters of Comanche Springs that fed the pool, brought into focus the reality of segregation in west Texas. They issued the following directive:

> That the property set out in said lease contract . . . is owned by said district, and partly by Pecos County, and being a stone bath house near the waters of Comanche Chief and Government Springs, and the water from said springs and water that may flow into the swimming pool from said springs, and all of said property now being in use for bathing purposes be used solely by the Anglo-American people, and that no person or persons of the Latin-American race shall be permitted to use said property for swimming, bathing, drinking or for any other purpose.[49]

Another barrier that maintained socioeconomic marginalization was public education, where perceived deficiencies in the English language provided the intrinsic rationale for the segregation of Mexican American schoolchildren into "Mexican" rooms or separate "independent schools" through elementary and middle school.[50] For instance, Mike García, born in Los Angeles County in 1925 and drafted into the army in 1944, was raised in the northern suburb of Simi Valley, where he encountered a segregated public school system. He explained: "At that time, the Anglo-Saxons separated us [Mexican Americans] at school . . . They got us together when we were going to high school, but grammar school was all segregation."[51] Moreover, racial epithets and fighting with white students were a common experience for García in this charged environment. Alfred Aguirre also encountered a segregated school system in Placentia, California, through the eighth grade before enrolling in the local integrated high school, where he was similarly required to defend himself on more than a few occasions.[52] He proudly stated: "They [white students] were afraid of us. We Chicanos, we're fighters, you know."[53] In Tucson, Ruben Moreno toiled in an oppressive educational system: "We had a school system . . . that would spank us for speaking Spanish, and most of us [Mexican American students] didn't know a word of English before we started school . . . And in grammar school

I don't remember seeing any Anglos in my class."[54] In San Diego, Gene García also recalled a significant degree of racial hostility. Oddly enough, however, Mexican cuisine provided an avenue for greater interaction. He described the process: "At that time, the Caucasians . . . were not receptive to the Mexicans . . . The thing that kind of brought us together . . . [was when] we used to take taquitos and burritos [for lunch] . . . Pretty soon it got to the point where they wanted to trade us their lunch for our lunch."[55]

In the case of Mexican American veterans of the Vietnam War, a more diverse picture emerges. As the beneficiaries of desegregation efforts in the late 1940s and '50s, segregated schooling and public facilities increasingly became a hit-or-miss proposition; nevertheless, the practice did not entirely disappear. An illustrative case is provided by Victor Ramírez in the border town of Del Rio, Texas: "When we were growin' up . . . [until the] 1960s, it was segregated. [We went to] what [was] called an independent school . . . The white people that lived there were all ranchers. They controlled the whole town. They had all this land [and] cattle [and] were very wealthy."[56] Born in Hanford in 1949 but raised in nearby Corcoran, in California's San Joaquin Valley, Charley Trujillo provides a general overview of the discriminatory environment he and his father encountered before he joined the army in 1967: "Discrimination was so hard. It was very difficult to have socioeconomic mobility . . . There were many barriers."[57] Furthermore, as with previous generations, hostile encounters with school officials and white students remained an everyday reality for many Mexican Americans that attended an integrated school. For example, Marine Corps veteran Eddie Solís, born in Texas in 1944 but raised in Riverside County after moving there with his family at the age of seven, remembers numerous displays of racial epithets and constant fighting between white and Mexican American students. As he recalled, it was a process that occurred "on both sides . . . There was fights all over the place."[58]

In Riverside County, Raymond Buriel and his brother initially attended an elementary school designated for Mexican American and African American communities. Spurred by a note from the campus administration that depicted his brother as intellectually incompetent, Buriel's parents withdrew the two and enrolled them in parochial school in the fourth grade at considerable cost.[59] Here, he encountered an integrated student population and a teaching staff that placed far greater emphasis on Catholicism rather than on racial profiling.[60] His cousin, Tony López, also began at a segregated grammar school in Riverside County before entering parochial school. He attended Catholic institutions throughout the remainder of his academic career, which culminated in a bachelor's degree from the Franciscan-affiliated University of San Diego in 1964. He then successfully completed OCS, becoming a second lieutenant in the Marine Corps. This parochial experience offered protection from further segregation and the concomitant racism that frequently prevailed in public institutions. As López stated, it also provided the basis for future academic success: "As I look back . . . I think, the parochial school [system] gave us a pretty well-rounded education and motivation to pursue our studies."[61]

While integration at the high school level was the norm for public school districts in the Southwest that had a Mexican American student population, the need to contribute to a family economy in tandem with poor facilities, uncommitted teachers, the forced repetition of grade levels, and a significant emphasis on vocational training ensured large drop-out rates prior to reaching high school. The latter characteristic emphasized industrial occupations for boys and home economics for girls. A typical scenario is provided by Alfred Bablot, who witnessed vocational training firsthand. As he recalled, "At that time, [school officials] were more or less channeling [Mexican American students] into wood shop, auto shop, and so forth."[62] Coincidentally, John Sótelo remarked on strikingly similar circumstances: "At that time [as a boy], you were . . . a mechanic [apprentice] . . . and women would [learn] household [duties], and that's what they encouraged us [to learn] as youngsters."[63] Jesus Barragan also recalled being tracked into less than challenging classes: "A lot of my classes . . . were these off-the-wall bonehead [courses]. For example, in high school, I never had a math class. My last math class was in the ninth grade."[64] To conclude, Jesse Salcedo offers one final chilling example: "In my senior year, I took wood shop first and second period, I had auto [body] shop third and fourth period, and then fifth period I had P.E. (physical education). In sixth period I had general U.S. history."[65]

YOUTHFUL RESPONSES, YOUTHFUL HAZARDS

These structural limitations that enforced socioeconomic marginalization, however, did not prevent second-generation Mexican American youth from creating their own cultural spaces. Historian Vicki L. Ruiz has termed this process a "cultural coalescence," where immigrants "pick, borrow, retain, and create distinctive cultural forms. There is no single hermetic Mexican or Mexican American culture, but rather permeable cultures rooted in generation, gender, region, class, and personal experience."[66] In particular, young boys and girls increasingly embraced popular music, such as jazz, the latest trends in fashion, and other commodities and forms of entertainment that characterized the growth of consumer culture in the United States, which also increasingly led to generational tension with Mexican parents who feared changing dynamics in terms of family, gendered norms, and culture. For example, the flapper of the 1920s, encompassing bobbed hair, short skirts, and cosmetics was followed by the zoot suit of the mid- to late 1930s and early '40s. Indeed, clothing took on a politicized nature, providing youngsters with the ability to display disaffection with their status in American society. According to historian Edward J. Escobar, the "symbols of this youthful rebellion were the zoot suits worn by many youths, the distinctive argot they spoke, and the general attitude they displayed that demonstrated both hostility toward and scorn for white society."[67] This also provided for increased levels of attention from law enforcement and society at large, an aspect enhanced by a small but visible minority of juvenile delinquents known as pachucos, forming for many a link between the zoot suit and criminality. A derisive term, "pachuco was not a badge of honor; it was meant to evoke shame and, more important, fear."[68] Within my collection of narrators, Raúl Medina was the only self-admitted pachuco. While fights with other gangs were common in Fresno, he admits to no legal issues with the police. He also fondly remembered the allure of the zoot suit: "The fascination was . . . the dress. We liked it and I used it until I went into the service . . . When the war [World War II] broke out it just disappeared because guys like me were drafted."[69] By contrast, John López, born in Mexico in 1923 and drafted into the U.S. Army Air Corps in 1943, was raised in East Los Angeles after arriving there with his parents the following year. He clearly recalled his father's forceful warnings: "I don't want to see you dress like that, speak like that . . . ever."[70]

The challenging circumstances that confronted many in the Mexican American community also fostered various levels of juvenile delinquency that extended well beyond the Second World War. An example is offered by Victor Ramírez, who confronted repeated overtures by neighborhood pachucos in Del Rio, Texas, to engage in criminal behavior and a burgeoning drug culture. A brush with the law at age fifteen initially forced Ramírez to relocate to San Angelo, Texas, and ultimately factored into his decision to enlist in the air force in 1960. He considers his decision to do so a fortunate one given the opportunity for further mischief that lay readily available. As he recalled: "You know, it was very hard to stay clean [at] that time. They [pachucos] had weed, they had drugs . . . I was fortunate that I was able to stay clean."[71] The rough-and-tumble environment of East Los Angeles also presented hazardous conditions, as encountered by David Carillo: "In East Los Angeles, you had to learn how to fight, or run, and I wasn't a very fast runner."[72] By comparison, an undisclosed legal incident prompted Eddie Solís to enlist in the Marine Corps in 1962 at the age of seventeen when given the choice between military service and incarceration by the judge that presided over his case.

John Rodríguez also encountered legal troubles as a youngster. Born in San Jose, California, in 1950 and raised in a Mexican American barrio adjacent to the city of Mountain View, Rodríguez encountered a harsh street culture on an everyday basis. He offered a chilling reminiscence: "You walk out [into] the streets, you're fighting. There's no way around it . . . You could be as gentle as possible, but you had to defend yourself . . . And I learned it well."[73] He offered additional commentary on his decision to join a gang as a youngster: "Gang to me at that time was . . . a group of guys getting together and you're looking up [to] your teenage uncle and [his] friends and all the things that they were doing, and you wanted to be a part of that."[74] Following his conviction after a violent confrontation, Rodríguez was offered a chance to eliminate the remainder of his probation through military service, prompting his decision to enlist in the U.S. Army in 1969 at age nineteen. As he recalled: "I was on probation and the [civil authorities] were allowing those who were on probation to go to the service as part of their [attempt to] lessen [their] probation."[75]

Sal Martínez, the lone individual of Puerto Rican ancestry within my cohort, encountered similar difficult circumstances in New York City. Born in Puerto Rico in 1941, he arrived in the United States as a nine-month-old infant with his parents as part of a larger wave of Puerto Rican migration during World War II. Raised in impoverished conditions in the city through junior high school, Martínez detailed the heterogeneous mixture within his neighborhood: "I lived and [was] raised in tenement buildings just north of Harlem and it started to grow rapidly into a split community between Irish and Puerto Rican. And then African Americans started moving in."[76] A self-described "marginal punk," Martínez encountered numerous opportunities for mischief. He looked backed on his father's decision to relocate the family to a much smaller farming community outside the city a fortuitous one. He revealed a harrowing daily existence: "I suspect that if we had not moved out of New York City, you and I wouldn't be talking today . . . probably because I may have wound up like many of my friends. The youngest man in New York to be electrocuted . . . was a very close friend of mine. He was part of our little group. He killed two policemen . . . That was the environment I grew up in. It was a rough neighborhood."[77] These experiences played a factor in his decision to enlist in the Marine Corps at age eighteen within a month following his high school graduation in Middleton, located in New York's Catskill Mountains.

Inner-city environments could nevertheless be sites of tremendous multiculturalism that fostered varying degrees of cultural and social interaction, especially so for youngsters who often attended school together. An illustrative example is provided by several of my World War II narrators that lived in Los Angeles' Eastside—in particular, the neighborhood known as Boyle Heights—where Japanese, Italian, Jewish, and a variety of Eastern European residents lived together with rising numbers of Mexican immigrants and African American sharecroppers from the South. As documented by historian Josh Sides in his study of African American migration to Los Angeles, the communities of Boyle Heights and East Los Angeles were ethnically diverse prior to World War II, with Little Tokyo serving "as the port of entry for new black migrants. Located just south of Union Station, where the Southern Pacific [Railroad] ended its route from New Orleans and Houston, 'Bronzeville' . . . became the center of the black migrant community."[78] For historian Douglas Flamming, the "striking thing about the Eastside was not simply its ethnic diversity but also that the racial and ethnic groups lived interspersed with one another. Despite references to the Mexican Plaza, Little Tokyo, and the black belt, these ethnic groups lived side by side throughout the Eastside."[79] Similarly for George Sánchez, "the most striking aspect of Mexican residential distribution in Los Angeles between 1900 and 1940 . . . was not intense segregation; rather, it was the widespread dispersal of Mexican homes throughout central and eastern Los Angeles."[80]

Born in Boyle Heights in 1925, George Castrueta remembers his childhood as one "that was very multi-racial, and so were our student bodies in our schools . . . For example, in my high school, 45 to 50 percent of the student body was Jewish. We had a large segment of Japanese kids, another large segment of Russians . . . and then we had a smattering of other people [such as] Armenians, Greeks, Italians, and, of course, Anglos. And we mixed very well and I think it was very advantageous for us to be raised in that fashion. But after school, we resorted back to our barrio."[81] This barrio, named La Purisima (The Most Pure) after the local Catholic church, encompassed a seven-block area of Boyle Heights that catered to the community's spiritual needs while also providing a variety of social services. As he briefly stated, the church "was our [central] focus [in] the social structure of our community."[82] Spanish remained the language of choice at home, but he learned English at school and through his interaction with other neighborhood children. Before being drafted into the Navy's Armed Guard in 1943, he sold newspapers and shined shoes in order to supplement the family's income, a domestic setting that he described as poor but not overwhelmingly so, due to his father's tireless efforts to secure employment. As he recalled: "My father was an extreme[ly] . . . hard worker. He was a tailor, and during the lean times he hustled work . . . throughout . . . the area."[83]

Richard Domínguez, born in Boyle Heights in 1924, offered a similar recollection of the significance of La Purisima to the area's inhabitants: "Our lives . . . [were] centered around the church."[84] Domínguez described the social environment present within the neighborhood as very tight-knit. As he stated, "You knew everybody in your block, everybody in the surrounding blocks. The [other] families knew who you were, knew that you were a Domínguez, and they knew where you lived. And you knew the people by seeing 'em in church or greeting them on the street [or] seeing them in stores."[85] Prior to being drafted into the army in 1943, Domínguez also recalled a tremendous degree of social interaction with other ethnic groups, especially while enrolled at Roosevelt High School, where he encountered a diverse student body. While Spanish remained the primary language spoken at home, English was the language of choice out in the community. Moreover, as an additional source of income, his father, José Domínguez, first started as an extra earning $5 a day in a variety of Hollywood films during the silent era.[86] Soon Domínguez and some of his nine brothers also began working in crowd scenes as extras, usually in a typecast fashion. As he described, "We could pass as Indian . . . as Arab . . . [and] Egyptian."[87]

David Fuentes also remembered a multicultural milieu in Boyle Heights, his birthplace in 1925. As he recalled, the neighborhood kids and fellow classmates at Belvedere Junior High School and Roosevelt High School were "mostly Jewish really. A lot of Japanese . . . a few blacks . . . [and] Russians . . . [and] Slavs."[88] Fuentes was also a childhood friend of Guy Gabaldon, an impoverished local street tough raised by a Japanese family who taught him to speak Japanese.[89] Fuentes and his family were parishioners at another Catholic church, Our Lady of Assumption; however, he interacted with many of the neighborhood kids of La Purisima. In a similar manner, Fuentes also spoke Spanish at home and learned English in school and in the surrounding neighborhood. Ultimately drafted into the army in 1944, he experienced a lower-middle-class standard of living, largely due to his father's tireless efforts as a musician and furniture salesman, while his mother worked as an occasional caregiver for foster kids. As he described, "He used to . . . work daytime in furniture and at nighttime he'd always play. [On] weekends he would always play, so we never suffered."[90]

These reminiscences also highlight the significance of Catholicism in the social and religious makeup of the majority of the veterans that comprise my collection. Nevertheless, Protestant religious experiences were certainly possible, as illustrated by Nick "Nicho" Salazar. Born in the coastal California city of Long Beach in 1923 but raised in Boyle Heights from age nine or ten, Nicho and his family were Baptist converts. Indeed, white Baptist missionaries exerted considerable influence on young Nicho's life. As he related, "I had a good experience when I was a kid. I knew a lot about the world . . . so I was happy to be raised by the [Baptist] missionaries."[91] As he continued, he also endeavored to convert local neighborhood friends: "I used to take some of my Catholic friends with me to the Baptist church."[92] Such efforts, however, were largely futile. Services provided by the missionaries included various social clubs and classroom instruction meant to improve literacy and English-language skills, as well as an overall emphasis on proper hygiene and acculturation into mainstream America.[93] As a result, English became Nicho's primary language. Ultimately, however, Nicho's parents, despite their own conversion, lamented the perceived cultural loss suffered by their children. Their response was to secretly send Nicho to the Mexican consulate in downtown Los Angeles in an effort to learn the Spanish language and the customs and traditions of Mexico. He offered the following: "I hardly spoke any Spanish at all, so when I was nine years old, [my parents] sent me to Third [Street] and Broadway [Avenue], at the Mexican consulate, for three years to learn Spanish."[94] By comparison, Ruben Moreno, initially a Methodist convert and subsequently a member of the local Baptist church in Tucson, Arizona, experienced numerous hostile encounters with local Catholic youth. As he explained, "I suffered for it because everybody was Catholic as far as the [Mexican American community] was concerned . . . I was the 'hallelujah' in the crowd."[95]

CONCLUSION

The approximately 1.5 million Mexicans that arrived in the United States between 1900 and 1930, and their U.S.-born children, experienced a variety of political, economic, and educational contradictions that extended well beyond the Second World War. Thus, the allure of social and political equality for my narrators and the desire to overcome their socioeconomic marginalization represented key motivating factors in their decision to enlist or readily accept their draft notice for service in World War II, the Korean War, and the Vietnam War. Charley Trujillo, for example, listed a variety of factors for enlisting at age eighteen. Chief among these were "patriotism, loyalty to the country, [to] fight communism . . . and socioeconomic mobility."[96] Victor Ramírez was driven by a similar desire: "My attitude was to serve my country, but at the same time, get an education."[97] However, at the same time, a strong work ethic and a commitment to family and cherished cultural attributes characterized the formation of Mexican American communities, both rural and urban, across the Southwest, and for many young Mexican American males coming of age, the fortitude gained from their hardships often eased the transition to military life. Meanwhile, across the nation, a similar process would unfold in Michigan, where a variety of employment opportunities in the Great Lakes region, including sugar companies and manufacturing industries, first pulled Mexican migrants northward from Texas and Mexico during the First World War.

2

AL NORTE

Mexican Migration to Michigan

"We came with a [family] friend of ours. The [Mexican workers] were coming here [to Michigan] to work sugar beets . . . The [sugar companies] would give you transportation . . . You sign up with . . . sugar companies . . . [For example,] the Michigan Sugar Company of Saginaw."

"At the time [in the 1920s], the automotive industry was really taking off. The Chevrolet foundry here in Saginaw was hiring a lot of people . . . They were hiring just anybody and everybody."

AS THE MAJORITY of Mexican migrants and their U.S.-born children developed communities along the U.S.-Mexico border, migratory labor streams also pushed some northward into Michigan and the Upper Midwest before and well after World War II. One destination was Saginaw, located at the crossroads of the fertile Saginaw Valley and the industrial zone that encompassed Detroit, because it offered easy access to agricultural labor and foundry work associated with the booming automobile industry. The latter possibilities, in particular, offered regular employment and better wages compared to migrant farm work. Other destinations included the cities of Muskegon and Grand Rapids in western Michigan. At diverse sites of exchange in these locations, these migrants developed a robust work ethic and a strong sense of permanence and place within a new geographic space that offered fewer of the social and cultural support systems typically present within the Southwest. Indeed, these migrants were required to build such networks entirely from the bottom up as they confronted a variety of discriminatory practices at work and in society at large. As they did so, such resilience gave rise to their Americanization and commitment to the American Dream that ultimately facilitated their entrance into the armed forces across several generations.

FACTORIES IN THE FIELDS

As the consumption of sugar skyrocketed in the latter part of the nineteenth century and into the twentieth, several distinct zones of sugar beet production emerged in an effort to meet demand. According to historian Dennis Valdés, the most important areas for sugar beets were throughout Michigan, particularly the Saginaw Valley, as well as northern Ohio, Wisconsin, and Indiana.[1] This labor-intensive crop, which required several cultivation tasks beginning in May and ending with the crop's harvest in late September and early October, relied on a vast pool of cheap labor. By World War I and the decade following, an initial reliance on European immigrants by sugar beet growers necessitated a new source of labor as the former became part of the urban industrial proletariat with varying degrees of upward mobility. Thus, the recruitment of Mexicans and Tejanas/os began, a transformation documented by George T. Edson, an investigator for the Bureau of Labor Statistics. From 1926 to 1927, Edson was assigned to investigate the work and living conditions of Mexican labor in the north-central states, a broad region that included the Upper Midwest.[2] As he stated:

> Mexicans are largely replacing the Belgians and German-Russians formerly used as laborers in the sugar beet fields of Ohio, Michigan, Iowa, Minnesota, and North Dakota and now comprise from 75% to 90% of this class of agricultural workers . . . When the shortage of field laborers became acute in 1917 and 1918, the producers of sugar beets followed the example of the Colorado growers and shipped in a force of Mexicans. Year by year the number of Mexicans coming into the beet country increases as the number of other nationalities decreases. A large proportion of the Mexicans are hired in San Antonio and Fort Worth, Texas, at the agencies of the large sugar producing companies.[3]

Families and single men were recruited, although the former were more highly prized due to the increased production levels they represented. As described by Valdés, these families were "typically composed of young Mexican-born parents in their twenties and thirties with only weak ties to Texas. Most families were small nuclear units with both parents present."[4]

As in the Southwest, a combination of labor agencies, word of mouth, and advertisements, often written in Spanish, spread the news of opportunities in

FIGURE 1. Menominee River Sugar Company advertisement, 1926–27. (Source: File Folder 12.3, Paul Taylor Collection, Bancroft Library, University of California Library.)

Michigan and throughout the Great Lakes region. For example, one advertisement (see fig. 1), produced in 1926 or 1927, describes the "need for families and single men to work in the agricultural and beet fields of Menominee River Sugar Co., Menominee, Michigan." The company paid "$23.00 per acre" and, "as a bonus," guaranteed "travel money to get there as well as a house and land for vegetable gardening." Another added bonus seemingly included the opportunity to "get yourself and your family out of the smoke of the city to the fields and pure air."[5] The processing plants were located in Michigan and Wisconsin, and the company's contact office was in Chicago. By comparison, an excerpt taken from another advertisement for the Michigan Sugar Company in Saginaw, dated October 22, 1926, offered the following "to our friends from Texas":

> We welcome you to Michigan to assist our farmers with their beet harvests. A great number of you have been coming for many years and we are pleased that you have found pleasurable, and profitable, working for our beet farmers.
>
> For all you who are making your first trip here, and also to our old friends that find themselves among you, we wish to extend every possible assistance within reason, and help you to be happy.
>
> For those of you who need household goods, the Michigan Sugar Company will supply them to you at a price equivalent to their cost, and when these goods have been returned to the company in good condition, you will be given credit for everything you have returned; the company requires that you pay for all articles that you loce or breák.
>
> You will find that going to work early in the morning and working late during the day, during the thinning, clearing, and covering seasons, by doing this you and your family will be able to earn an excellent salary.[6]

Such recruitment efforts provided crucial incentive for those willing to move northward in the pursuit of a better life, and, by the 1920s, preexisting migrant networks from Mexico through Texas expanded into the Upper Midwest.

Among those answering the call was young Maria S. Montano, who crossed the border into Texas in 1920 and made her way to San Antonio. As she described it, "One day as we walked along West Commerce St., we saw a big blackboard advertising in white letters, a trip to Michigan with the 'Michigan Sugar Company,' with headquarters in Saginaw, Mich." Leaving on May 10, 1920, with several family members, they "rode five days and five nights" and "at last the conductor said 'Kinde, Mich.,' and as soon as possible we alighted from the train and met a young man who said he was going to take us to the farm."[7] These train rides, sponsored by the Michigan Sugar Company, began during World War I, according to Edson, and by "1924 they shipped up about 2,600. In 1925 they brought 2,200. This year [1926] they brought 3,048." Unfortunately, despite the advertised promise of free transportation and $23 an acre, "for those Mexicans transported from Texas a fee of $5 an acre is deducted, making it $18 an acre."[8] An affidavit provided by Javier Tobar, an employee of the Ford Motor Company and a resident of Detroit for four years, offers additional commentary on the misleading practices encountered by Mexican migrants throughout the recruitment process:

> At the border they are signed up by the enganchista [recruiter]. The latter asks him if he can read. "No." Then he proceeds to read the contract the Mexican is signing. Not what's there but some very absurd things. They promise him transportation to and from the border. Also to a nearby large city. They promise them good wages, free fuel, food and housing. [However,] when they get up here, it is entirely different and they abandon their contracts by the score.[9]

These recruitment efforts were nevertheless effective in pulling migrants northward, including the father of John López, an air force veteran of the Korean War, who fled the ravages of the Mexican Revolution (1911–17) in 1915 and worked throughout Texas until approximately 1923. He moved his family to Michigan, where López was born in Tuscola County in 1929, before ultimately settling in Saginaw in 1943. He offered the following rationale for his father's decision to leave: "They [sugar beet growers] were recruitin' people to come up here [and] work in the farms and the fields . . . They were payin' more money than, say, down there pickin' cotton."[10] Indeed, the prospect of better pay and less overt discrimination than in Texas served as additional motivation to head north. Born in Texas in 1927, George Castaneda clearly remembered the harsh reality of sharecropping: "You do all the work and everything, and the owner of that farm, you have to give 'em half of [the] profits."[11] And so the family responded to the recruitment efforts by Michigan sugar companies. As Castaneda described, "We came with a [family] friend of ours. They were coming here to work sugar beets . . . They [sugar companies] would give you transportation . . . You sign[ed] up with . . . sugar companies . . . [like the] Michigan Sugar Company of Saginaw."[12] His first trip north occurred during the summer months of 1939, with subsequent visits aided by the family's purchase of a pickup truck that enabled them to expand their search for employment throughout Michigan. Castaneda explained this constant migration through many of Michigan's smaller towns and communities:

> The [sugar] beets [were] only temporary . . . but when they're out [between cultivation tasks] then the cherry crop started . . . In Traverse City, there's a lot of cherries, so we went to work in Traverse City . . . But that was only temporary

> too. And when we got done with cherries, we went south to New Haven and Muskegon. They [grow] peaches, apples, and they got some cherries too . . . In Holland, Michigan, they got a lot of Hispanic people that live there . . . and we worked there, only temporar[ily] . . . And then when it got cold . . . we'd go back to our home out in Texas.[13]

Despite the cold weather, after several years of back and forth migration, the family purchased a home and settled in Saginaw sometime during World War II. In 1948, Castaneda volunteered and served as an army paratrooper.

Born in 1931 in Henrietta, Oklahoma, and drafted into the army in 1950, Frank Ornelas and his family were also part of the seasonal trek northward. He offered the following recollection: "In 1939, we came to Michigan as migrant workers with other families . . . We were picking anything that was available, tomatoes, potatoes, pickles, cherries . . . sugar beets also . . . We were all working."[14] Such constant migration in search of better opportunities spread the births of himself and his nine brothers and sisters "all over the country . . . I have a brother born in North Dakota. My other sister in Henrietta, Oklahoma. Some in Texas, some in Michigan [and] two of 'em in Mexico."[15] Meanwhile, Arnulfo "Arnif" Nerio's family also decided to head north soon after his birth in San Antonio, Texas, in 1923. The family initially left for Thornbill, Minnesota, in the mid-1920s and then "my dad went down to [the] Twin Cities and he bought a little Ford . . . It was good enough to get us to Michigan."[16] Nerio's father found employment at the Buick plant in Saginaw; however, the Great Depression found the family once again involved in migrant farmwork. As he described, "We worked . . . outside of Bay City pickin' tomatoes. We worked pickin' beets . . . That was long work there. It took about all summer."[17] Nerio was able to join the Civilian Conservation Corps (CCC) in 1939 at age seventeen in order to help the family's financial situation and acquire some vocational training. He was also the only Chicano in his CCC camp in Iron River, Michigan. He recalled: "I got in pretty well with the guys there . . . They showed us how to [fell] trees, how to spring wire."[18] Furthermore, much like William Sánchez and Alfred Aguirre discussed earlier, the militarized daily regimen of the camp provided valuable experiences that served him well in the army after being drafted for service in World War II.

Salvador Marez was born in Corona, Michigan, in 1925, while his parents were employed in seasonal migrant farm work before returning to their hometown of Austin, Texas, where Marez was raised. Forced to drop out of school in the eighth grade due to the family's impoverished circumstances, Marez clearly remembered a childhood filled with constant employment in Texas and the midwestern states of Michigan, Ohio, and Indiana before his family's permanent move to the Upper Midwest sometime in 1942, just prior to his entrance into the navy the following year: "I worked full time in Texas until we moved up here . . . We came up to Ohio and we worked in the fields . . . We worked the sugar beet fields . . . sweet corn . . . pickin' tomatoes. Anything that needed [to be] done."[19] Similar poverty also forced Martin Morales to leave home at the tender young age of nine years old. Born in Rio Grande City, Texas, in 1928, he offered the following recollection: "Well, it was grinding poverty. I phrase it 'grind' because that's what it was. Nothing to eat, sleepin' outside . . . It was just plain poor."[20] Morales also joined the itinerant streams throughout the Upper Midwest, and as he reminisced, he marveled at the work ethic of his fellow migrant workers: "The Mexican is the Cadillac of the labor industry."[21] These dire circumstances would facilitate Morales's entrance into the U.S. Army Air Corps in 1943 at the tender age of fifteen.

These experiences during the Great Depression correspond to the tragic socioeconomic hardships endured by my narrators in various locations throughout the Southwest. Moreover, the repatriation drives that intended to remove the Mexican population residing in the U.S. expanded into the Great Lakes region.[22] Denied access to relief programs, many unnaturalized Mexicans left voluntarily (and in some cases were forcibly removed), often taking their U.S.-born children with them, including Vincent Pardo Jr., born in Saginaw in 1931. His father worked at the local foundry, but "when the Depression came . . . everything closed down. My dad lost his job, and my dad decided to go back to Mexico where his family was."[23] Young Pardo was approximately one year old and would not return to the United States until 1944, and was ultimately drafted into the Marine Corps in 1952. By comparison, the birth of Salvador Marez and his four siblings in the United States prevented the family's deportation to Mexico despite his parent's unnaturalized status. He clearly remembered the keen interest of Austin city officials in the family's possible removal: "The only thing that helped [us] to stay here [in the U.S.] was us [children]. All of us [were] born here. They couldn't kick [my mother] out of here without kicking us out too . . . [City officials] talked to us about that [possibility]."[24]

Trainloads of other Mexican migrants nevertheless departed the Upper Midwest for the Mexican border, a process often documented in local newspapers, as in the case of Saginaw. For example, in 1932, the *Saginaw Daily News*, under the headline "470 Mexicans Leaving Today," described how "220 Saginaw Mexicans and 250 to 270 from Mt. Pleasant, Bay City, Sebewaing, and other places in this vicinity were scheduled to leave late this afternoon on their long journey back to their ancestral home beyond the Rio Grande."[25] Another article offered a more blunt assessment and the perceived benefits for local taxpayers: "Saginaw's Mexican population is believed to have been decreased by approximately 300 persons . . . In reducing the city's population . . . a real service is being extended to the people of the city, for all of these people have little to contribute to a community and frequently take much from it."[26] The impact of such efforts on midwestern communities was catastrophic, decreasing Saginaw's Mexican and Tejana/o population from a listed total of 2,085 in 1930 to 455 in 1940.[27] And yet, by 1938, Mexicans and Tejanas/os were once again being recruited northward. Under the headline "Sugar Beet Farm Hands Arrive Here, City's Unemployed Not Suited to Task—Officials Puzzled," the *Saginaw News* announced in May 1938 that two hundred families had arrived "despite the fact that many Saginaw men are unemployed or are working on government relief projects . . . Farmers . . . say they would rather hire local labor, but that a city man will 'take one look at a beet field and walk away.'"[28]

Indeed, the inability to acquire a local labor force, an aspect of migrant farm labor duplicated in countless rural counties, contributed to the continued reliance on Mexican and Mexican American agricultural workers well beyond the Great Depression and World War II. In the late 1940s, after his return from Mexico, Vincent Pardo would finish his school year and then move immediately into migrant field work. As he recalled, "In the summertime, during vacation, we worked in the fields. We had farmers that would hire us . . . We worked [sugar] beets . . . We would go to a place called Traverse City and pick cherries. We'd stay there for about three weeks . . . and then we'd pick potatoes."[29] Working during the summer months to earn additional family income was a common experience shared by many Mexican American schoolchildren. Gilbert Guevara, born in Saginaw in 1942 and a Vietnam War army veteran—he was drafted in 1967—described this seasonal farm work with his family in the 1950s: "We picked cherries for ten years. We used to go up to Traverse City and we were there by the Fourth of July and we were up there maybe five weeks . . . I remember coming home [and] we probably had two weeks and then we were in school."[30]

John Sánchez, born in 1945 in Alma, Michigan, followed the same schedule through the early 1960s prior to his enlistment in the army in 1966. He stated: "I worked off and on since I was seven . . . in the fields doing various things . . . I went to school throughout the fall and winter . . . but [as] soon as we all head out for summer break, we went straight to the fields."[31] Despite the difficulties involved, he fondly remembered the work ethic that brought family members together:

> I picked pickles and in Saginaw, we picked potatoes . . . During the day I would work in the fields with my mother . . . and at night . . . I wanted to be with all [of] my cousins . . . All the young men worked in the pickle stations. And those ran all night long, and the lights and the music . . . so I'd go home, wash up, and then go work at the pickle station.[32]

For U.S. Navy veteran Raúl Mosqueda, born in Benton Township, Ohio, in 1948, summer employment in Michigan required a lengthy journey with his family from La Pryor, Texas, where his family maintained their permanent residence. As he described, "In Michigan we would come to do sugar beets early in the season . . . [and to] clean and hoe beans . . . [in] early May . . . Every year we'd start the same kind of . . . cycle."[33]

Born in Muskegon, Michigan, in 1947, and a Marine Corps volunteer in 1965, Guadalupe "Lupe" Alviar offered similar commentary of his extended family:

> My mother had seven brothers and I had a lot of cousins. And all of my cousins went up to Oceana County [in western Michigan] in the summer, and they all worked the fields with my aunts. My uncles would work in the [local] factory, Monday through Friday, [and on] Friday night they'd go up to the farms, pickin' cherries . . . apples, whatever crop.[34]

Fred Medel, born in Saginaw in 1951 and an army volunteer in 1969, also remarked on this powerful work ethic that was necessary for survival:

> We were crop pickers . . . string beans, potatoes, tomatoes, pepinos, strawberries, whatever was in season at the time. And then we always ended up in Traverse City . . . pickin' cherries . . . that's how we survived. We all pitched in. That's the way of the family unit . . . All the Mexican families . . . were all the same way.[35]

As the aforementioned stories illustrate, a powerful motive driving Mexican families northward was the constant availability of migrant farm work throughout the Great Lakes region. An active effort by the sugar beet industry to recruit workers in Texas inevitably dovetailed with the harvesting of a multitude of different crops. Of particular note was the cherry harvest in Traverse City, which occurred in July during an interlude in the sugar beet harvest cycle and afforded families additional opportunities for extra income. The work was brutal and often exploitative; as John Sánchez stated, "We always had to watch how we were paid . . . and to make sure we were not short-changed."[36] And yet, through their strong work ethic, the path to improved socioeconomic standing emerged for many families, as was the case for Frank Ornelas. As he recalled, "The money that we saved from working out in the fields, we were able to buy a house [and] to put a down payment of five thousand dollars cash . . . dollars and quarters and nickels."[37] Moreover, a critical factor in this pursuit was an expanded worldview that increasingly viewed industrial labor as more dignified and a more dependable route to upward mobility. Thus, the foundries and auto manufacturing plants of eastern Michigan beckoned as they had for European and other immigrant groups prior, and Mexican Americans began to answer the call.

THE MEXICAN AMERICAN INDUSTRIAL CLASS

When asked what brought his family north to Michigan, U.S. Army veteran Guadalupe "Lupe" Ortega simply stated "the plants, General Motors."[38] His family moved from Texas, where Ortega was born in 1921, and his father and two older brothers found immediate employment. Recruitment efforts ranging as far as California also lured Frank Gonzales's father, who arrived in Saginaw sometime in the late 1920s. Born in Saginaw in 1930, and a navy volunteer in 1949, he recalled that "at that time, they were recruiting laborers [for] the auto industry here . . . My dad saw an opportunity . . . so he joined a group of laborers . . . and they got a free train ride from California all the way to Michigan . . . That's where he ended up."[39] According to Tony Moreno, born in Saginaw in 1948, and an army draftee in 1969, "at the time, the automobile industry was really taking off. The Chevrolet foundry here in Saginaw was hiring a lot of people. They were hiring just anybody and everybody."[40] And George Castaneda's commentary sheds light on one of the more popular hiring practices often employed by management: "The bosses in the morning, they would stand out in the gate out in the street . . . and look at all the people that wanted to work, and they said, 'you and you . . . and you. Come on in, we got a job for you.'"[41]

Arguably, factors such as race and ethnicity played a role in this selective process; nevertheless, as George T. Edson discovered, Mexicans and Mexican Americans were noticeably present as industrial workers, including in the city of Saginaw:

> The largest single employer of Mexican labor is the Saginaw Products (Grey Iron Foundry), a division of the General Motors Corporation. This concern has about 550 Mexicans out of 2,900 employees, and the number has been increasing since 1919 when it first sent for a bunch . . . Last year the company shipped in about 125 from Kansas City, and many others came of their own initiative. The men work 10 hours, on an average, and make around $6.50 a day on piece work. The minimum wage, the employment manager said, is 45 [cents] an hour . . . About 10% of them are engaged in core making and other semi-skilled work. The company finds them desirable and shows a preference for them in foundry work.[42]

Edson also discovered sizeable Mexican colonies in the nearby towns of Pontiac and Flint, as well as Detroit, one hundred miles to the southeast. Of the migrants located in this latter city, he offered the following: "The great majority of wage earners are employed in foundries and metal work. The Ford plants have 1,200, the Briggs Manufacturing Company has around 400; Dodge Brothers has close to 300; the Detroit Copper & Brass Rolling Mills has quite a number, and a good many are used in groups of from 10 to 50 in a dozen or two other motor car and machinery plants."[43] Including Saginaw, the major employer of Mexican labor in all four locations was the auto industry, which experienced a massive boom cycle during the 1920s, requiring an enormous labor force for the over 20 million Model T and other vehicles, trucks, and tractors produced between 1919 and 1929.[44] Ford Motors clearly hired the most Mexicans, almost 4,000 in 1928, in three major plants—Highland Park, River Rouge, and Fordson.[45] Despite the impact of the Great Depression, this Mexican and Mexican American presence in the auto industry would continue to thrive and expand after World War II.

Within this world of manufacturing, the work was brutal, dirty, and often performed under intense heat. For example, Vincent Pardo, who often carried his father's lunch and sat quietly as his father ate his meal, clearly remembered his father's grimy face and two large circles around his eyes where his goggles had been. Gilbert Guevara, whose father also worked at Saginaw's Grey Iron Foundry, recalled a similar episode in his effort to secure employment at the foundry after his high school graduation in 1960:

> He said, "I want you to be at the gate at eight o'clock in the morning. Have some work clothes on." And I thought, "oh boy." So I stood at the gate and I saw my father in this long leather apron . . . goggles on top of his head over his hat and around where his goggles were, the rest of his face was dirty. And he was walking

> with this little white man who had a white shirt and glasses . . . And they stood at the gate and my dad pointed at me, and then that white man . . . said, "Hey you, come here" . . . "I want you to go in here and get registered and go to personnel" . . . So I did and the next day I got hired . . . to my displeasure.[46]

Guevara lasted six months before leaving to enroll at nearby two-year Delta College with the money he earned while employed at the foundry. By comparison, Arnif Nerio returned from military service in World War II to find a job at Grey Iron waiting for him. As a grinder and lead machine operator, his work involved constant heavy lifting: "I had a heavy job. I was pickin' up ten pounds in each hand and puttin' it on the machine, all day."[47] Such intense labor requirements factored into his early retirement in 1974 at the age of fifty-four, after thirty-one years of employment with General Motors. Like Nerio, George Castaneda also worked under similar strenuous conditions: "I worked all [of] them jobs like pouring iron. That was a hot job, and making molds."[48]

Discriminatory policies toward Mexican American and African American workers often added to the grueling nature of foundry work. For example, Frank Ornelas clearly remembers his first job: "The first time when I was hired, they hired me on the third shift cleaning the place up, in maintenance. That was bad [and] dirty."[49] George Castaneda offered a similar critique of the types of unskilled labor assigned to nonwhite employees: "They didn't have no Chicanos [among] the mechanics. And no black guys . . . They would give you the bad jobs like shoveling dirt . . . hard jobs, dirty jobs."[50] Such conditions, which Lupe Ortega encountered through his father's and brother's experiences, were enough to keep Lupe away. As he recalled: "I wouldn't work for them . . . I felt that the work in the plants at that time was dirty. And the black people and the Mexicans got the dirtiest jobs all the time. And I wasn't gonna be a part of that."[51] Edson noted similar complaints by local Mexicans in his study of Saginaw, writing that "the work is hard and long. They had seen men go into work at 5 in the evening and not come out again till 5 in the morning, at 45 cents an hour. Others have worked from 7 in the morning until 10 at night, with no extra pay for overtime. In the hot summer days the Mexican boys frequently faint at their task. [And] the Italian foremen 'give them hell.'"[52] These latter authority figures, with the ability to harass and arbitrarily fire individuals, personified the abusive nature of the automotive industry and were constantly viewed with hostility and fear.

A related form of discrimination was the inability to win promotions or gain acceptance into skilled occupations. Frank Gonzales often eavesdropped on his father's conversations on this very subject. As he recalled: "My dad . . . realized that there were no opportunities for him or for a lot of other Mexicans to go into higher position[s], such as foreman . . . I could hear him say that when he was talking to other people."[53] As an electrician, Vincent Pardo encountered very few nonwhite skilled tradesmen in his thirty-three years at General Motors: "The only thing that I did consider close to discrimination was the non-acceptance into the technical fields or the skilled trades [of] minorities."[54] Meanwhile, Gilbert Guevara decided to return to the Grey Iron Foundry in Saginaw in order to accumulate additional savings for his tuition. His new position as an inspector was somewhat fortunate as "an inspector was a good job for anybody that could get it, 'cause most of the inspectors were basically white men."[55] This new job also prompted the following reminiscence by Guevara's father, which he recounted: "Back when he worked, his story to me was that there were a lot of Mexicans working there . . . [And] all these men were laborers . . . There were no foremen, there were no assistant foremen, there were no skilled tradesmen."[56] Furthermore, Tony Moreno, in his capacity as senior management for General Motors, also discovered wage disparities after the department he supervised conducted an investigation in the late 1980s. He also encountered a more favorable climate willing to address these disparities:

> When we did an analysis, we found out the Hispanics at our plant were being . . . discriminated because they had the same amount of education, if not more, and in some case[s], they had more service than their Caucasian counterpart, and yet, the pay was much lower . . . The corporation sent money to our plant to address the issues.[57]

Ultimately, however, the prospect of monetary gain was not lost on Mexicans and Mexican Americans, and many rushed to take advantage of the financial opportunities offered by the auto industry. As John López stated, "The money was good, we worked a lot of overtime . . . The foundry here . . . employed around ten thousand people . . . Anybody could go in there and they'd hire you. No background, no college education, no high school education . . . You just went in there. You didn't even have to speak English . . . I'd be working seven days a week, ten, twelve hours a day."[58] López eventually retired from General Motors after thirty years of service. At times, dedication and hard work could overcome discriminatory practices and were often key factors in promoting occupational mobility and seniority. Frank Ornelas, who retired from General Motors as a supervisor in the quality control department after twenty-seven years of employment, recalled: "I did pretty good, from a sweeper to a supervisor."[59] Tony Moreno began as a junior accountant and eventually became an administrator for human resources for international operations, retiring after thirty-five years. Meanwhile, Vincent Pardo applied for and was accepted as an electrician apprentice and received training at the General Motors Institute in Flint. As he stated, "I got assigned as an electrician apprentice in training . . . then afterwards, I was assigned as a journeyman electrician and an instrument repairman."[60] Such training made Pardo a natural candidate to help lead the transition to front-wheel drive as this new automotive technology began to appear in the 1970s.

These tangible results are clear evidence that the structural limitations caused by racist hostility and abusive work conditions did not entirely curtail the range of opportunities available to Mexican auto workers and their U.S.-born children. Discriminatory practices were but one reality in a vast array of experiences for the industrial working class. Overall, it offered regular employment and better wages compared to agricultural labor, and it enabled these workers to enter the ranks of the middle class across several generations. Other intangible, yet equally important, results included a transformed sense of self that took pride in their participation in such a vast enterprise. Salvador Marez, for example, fondly recalled his twenty-six years of employment at Wolverine Brass in Grand Rapids, Michigan, and the high-quality plumbing ware he helped produce. As he stated, the products were not available to the general public: "Our company did not sell to . . . just anybody [that] wanted to buy the Wolverine product. You had to go through a master plumber to get it, and they would [install] it for you."[61] This accumulation of hard work and increasingly empowered consciousness enabled individual workers to define success on their own terms, a process within the world of employment that set the stage for similar endeavors in public settings. Indeed, wage labor would become an impetus for community formation and the pursuit of social integration and acceptance by the mainstream.

COMMUNITY BUILDING ALONG THE SAGINAW RIVER

As agricultural and urban industrial labor increasingly lured Mexican and Tejano workers northward, these migrants developed permanent settlements that afforded them the opportunity to take advantage of such urban amenities as better housing and regular schooling for their children. Segregated residential development, while not as severe as de jure segregation found in Texas and throughout the South, could nevertheless typify residential neighborhoods in the Upper Midwest. In the case of Saginaw, the city's First Ward emerged as the primary location for Mexican American and African American residents. However, the presence of working-class whites, though few in number, created an urban space with some degree of racial and ethnic diversity. As Edson reported in 1926:

> Nearly all the Mexicans live in one quarter of the city, all comprised in the First Ward, lying several blocks on the north and south sides of the Pere Marquette railroad tracks, from Washington Avenue east four or five blocks. The business center of this colony is along Potter Street, east from Washington, parallel to and facing the railroad tracks and station. This street is essentially Mexican, for although they themselves have only four businesses here, not counting boarding houses, the other businesses count largely on Mexican patronage. The Mexican businesses consist of a tailor shop, two restaurants, and a pool hall. On Washington Street about a block west is another Mexican pool hall. To the north of Potter Street the poorer Mexicans live, intermingled with Negroes and Balkan peoples, and to the south of Potter Street the better element reside, in a neighborhood verging into respectability as it nears the main business section of Saginaw.[62]

Frank Gonzales emphasized such diversity in his recollection of his childhood in the First Ward leading up to his high school graduation in 1948: "I grew up in a mixed neighborhood [that] was very diverse . . . blacks, whites, and a few Mexicans where I was living."[63] By contrast, Tony Moreno offered a different assessment of the First Ward life in the 1950s and 1960s: "We grew up in a neighborhood [that] was mostly blacks, Hispanics . . . The eastside of Saginaw was mostly minority populated."[64] Gilbert Guevara agreed: "Living in the First Ward . . . you were either black or Mexicano."[65] Perhaps the area's demographics changed in the decades following Gonzales's youth to reflect a less diverse community; nevertheless, these opposing viewpoints of life in the First Ward remind us that lived experiences and the memories that are produced seldom reflect a monolithic picture. Rather, as in the case of Gonzales, they reflect the minutiae of the individual subconscious—a process that is fraught with conflicting opinions and recollections.

As early as 1926, the steady influx of Mexicans and African Americans was cause for concern for local white residents of the First Ward. Under the headline "Negroes, Mexicans, Cause of Protest," the *Saginaw News Courier* described how "a delegation of 15 residents of the First Ward attended the [city] council . . . asking for relief because of the influx of certain workers . . . that were claimed to be undesirable."[66] Moreover, such residential antagonism was accompanied by other discriminatory behaviors in a variety of public settings. As Vincent Pardo described, "You [went] to the bus station and the whites would be on one side, here in Saginaw. And the bathrooms, everything was separated. You were not allowed to . . . sit [at] the ice cream bar."[67] Furthermore, as Fred Medel remembered, these residential and public boundaries were often enforced by fears of violence: "You had to watch where you were walking. You couldn't walk through a white neighborhood."[68]

Within the educational system, Mexican American children could often encounter benevolent teachers, as did Vincent Pardo: "The teachers that we had were very understanding. And we were treated just like the rest of the students."[69] Nevertheless, prejudicial practices were commonplace, including the institutional effort to maintain a steady supply of workers for local industries. According to Edson, "The public schools in this section are conducted according to the interests of the beet growers, as would be natural. They open early and then, when the beet harvest begins, they have a 'sugar beet vacation' so the children may help in the beet gathering for a couple of weeks."[70] Gilbert Guevara recalled a similar concern expressed by his biology teacher while enrolled at Saginaw High School on the city's east side from 1957 to 1960: "Ken Gray was my biology teacher and I wasn't doin' too well . . . and he stated after class . . . 'Maybe you need to go to the plant, get a job, and work and help your family out.'[71] Fellow classmates often intensified this discriminatory educational process, as described by John López, who recalled classmates using the term *wetback*, but explained, "I remember discrimination in grade school, but it wasn't something big . . . a few kids that always picked on somebody."[72]

Such discrimination, however, did not dampen the drive to secure financial security and promote the interests of the Mexican American community. Proof of these efforts in the First Ward can be found in the number of commercial endeavors aside from migrant farm work and urban industrial labor. According to Gilbert Guevara, "My dad had a business. There were Mexican businesses in the First Ward [and] there were some black businesses."[73] John López also remembered a thriving community of small businesses: "Sixth Street . . . and Farwell [Street], they used to have grocery stores, barber shops, drug stores, pool halls. Everything was there for the Hispanics."[74] Other, more informal methods of commercial activity included selling Mexican street food, as Frank Gonzales did as a youngster. He recalled how "Ma would make . . . tostadas. And she'd put 'em in a little box . . . for my brother and myself and we'd go up and down the streets selling them. I'd go into pool halls . . . because a lot of people were there playing cards."[75] Meanwhile, Vincent Pardo's grandmother also cooked Mexican cuisine that his grandfather sold to eager customers during lunch hour at the Grey Iron Foundry. He offered the following possible rationale for the popularity of his grandmother's food: "At that time, Mexican food was kind of rare . . . for [white] people."[76]

To meet their spiritual needs, the growing Mexican and Tejana/o population began attending St. Joseph's Catholic parish on North Sixth Street in the First Ward, despite its segregated seating arrangements.[77] John López noted that "the Mexican community used to live there in that area, St. Joseph's parish . . . all Hispanics went to church there."[78] Religious organizations eager to promote Mexican customs, traditions, and religious practices were soon established. One organization in particular, Las Damas de Guadalupe (The Ladies of Guadalupe), was formed in 1931 in honor of the Virgen de Guadalupe (Virgin Mary), the official patron saint of Mexico. This small women's group initially conducted their religious services in private homes until the arrival of Monsignor Harold Bolton in 1944 put an end to the church's discriminatory practices, enabling the group to move into the church. In addition to its religious mission, it also performed other communal responsibilities. Beatrice Valle, president of the Damas in 1979, offered the following reminiscence of the group's activities: "They conduct fundraisers throughout the year such as food sales after Mass, bingos, etc. Also, they visit the sick, help the poor, help the migrant workers with food and clothing, and at times have helped students."[79] Protestant experiences were also possible, as documented by the *Saginaw Daily News* in 1934, under the headline "Mexican Mission Five Years Old": "The Mexican Baptist mission of Saginaw was started by Rev. Mr. [Ramon A.] Tolosa in 1929 and the congregation was formally organized on April 27, 1931."[80] Invited to the area by the Michigan Baptist Convention, Reverend Tolosa catered to the Mexican migrant community in Saginaw and nearby cities. For John Sánchez, a religious divide developed at home, yet Protestantism was seemingly the clear winner: "My mother was a very staunch Baptist. My father was Catholic, but we grew up in a Baptist home."[81]

Such efforts are a clear indication that no single religious experience characterized the formation of migrant Mexican communities in Michigan and throughout the Upper Midwest. Traditional cultural and religious practices could ease the process of assimilation by providing moral support and other forms of assistance. Nevertheless, these migrants eagerly embraced new challenges and new sources of spiritual comfort as a family or on an individual basis.

CONCLUSION

Clearly, the experiences of the Mexican American community are not specific to the Southwest, and resistance to an apparatus of social oppression in the creation of ethnic spaces, both rural and urban, must be examined on a national basis. In the case of Michigan and the Great Lakes region, such communities date back to World War I, when Mexicans and Tejanas/os first began migrating northward in search of a better life. Wage labor, both agricultural and industrial, emerged as a defining characteristic of these expanded migratory networks. And while the majority of these migrants and their U.S.-born children did not attain material equality with mainstream society, to strictly focus on limitations and other forms of social inequality overlooks the strong work ethic that enabled them to embrace their new homes on their own terms. Moreover, various cultural performances, community activities, and a fledging display of social activism also emerged that simultaneously valued the promises of the American Dream and their Mexican heritage. A similar process unfolded in Mexican American communities throughout the Southwest, and this nascent activism would be galvanized by military service in World War II (and the Korean and Vietnam Wars). Having championed democratic principles abroad, these returning Mexican American veterans and the community at large would accept nothing less than first-class citizenship at home. First, however, the many wartime hazards of military life awaited them, and they departed to an uncertain future.

3

WORLD WAR II AND THE MEXICAN AMERICAN CONTRIBUTION TO THE GOOD WAR

"My life turned upside down when I was drafted . . . It just changed my whole life."

"When I went to war and I fought for this country, as well as others . . . I figured that [U.S.] flag was mine."

PRIOR TO HIS DEATH at the hands of a Japanese sniper in April 1945, World War II correspondent Ernie Pyle attracted an immense following for his intimate and folksy writing style, a prose often written from the perspective of the common soldier. His descriptive accounts focused on the out-of-the-way places he visited and the daily ordeals endured by American servicemen overseas, ranging from the dangers associated with combat to the lack of hot meals and proper shower facilities. His interest on the mundane and routine also highlighted the ethnic composition of the rank and file in the U.S. military. For example, in the summer of 1943, while serving in the Sicilian campaign with the 120th Engineers Battalion of the 45th Infantry Division, Pyle made the following observation:

> The 120th was made up of Spanish Americans, Indians, straight New Mexicans, and a smattering of men from the East . . . A large percentage of the battalion spoke Spanish, and occasionally I heard some of the officers talking Spanish among themselves, just to keep in practice, I suppose. That New Mexico bunch missed more than anything, I believe, the Spanish dishes they were accustomed to back home. Their folks occasionally sent them cans of chili and peppers, and then they had a minor feast.[1]

This report from Sicily confirms the presence of Mexican Americans (and other Latinos) in the U.S. military during the Second World War. Overall, an estimated 250,000–500,000 served in the war, representing a range of 2.5 to 5 percent of U.S. Armed Forces personnel.[2] Upon completion of basic and other specialized training, they participated in numerous military campaigns in Europe and the Pacific in a variety of military occupations following the Japanese attack on Pearl Harbor. The rigors of military life were partially offset by the pay and amenities provided by the U.S. military, which were often a welcome relief from the substandard conditions many endured prior to World War II. Unfortunately, military service also meant continued exposure to discriminatory practices and segregated facilities at domestic military bases despite their de jure whiteness that spared Mexican American servicemen from having to serve in segregated units endured by other racialized communities. Such hostility also extended into society at large, and in the case of the 1943 Zoot Suit Riots, domestic hysteria violently targeted Mexican American youth on the streets of Los Angeles. Nevertheless, Mexican Americans served with honor and distinction, and as the epigraphs highlight, an expanded worldview accompanied these overseas deployments to defend freedom and democracy, demonstrating the transformative potential of military service in sociopolitical and ideological terms.

THE INTERWAR YEARS

Despite the pay and benefits associated with military service, a stint in the armed forces in the interwar years was an option seldom entertained by a clear majority of the individuals I interviewed. The lone exception was William Sánchez, who enlisted in the army in September 1940 at the age of twenty-two, becoming the only narrator to join the military before the United States entered the war. Motivated by the recently established draft (discussed later) and the opportunity for overseas travel, Sánchez recalled the sales pitch of the local recruiter: "I went to the recruiting sergeant and he told me . . . 'If you will serve overseas, in two years you [can] fulfill your [military] commitment.'"[3] Sánchez chose the Philippines over other international locations, arriving in October 1940, where he completed his recruit training in six weeks. He fondly recalled his first official pass and review at the completion of his training, yet he was adamant in his overall objective: "I was gonna put [in] my two years, come home, and forget about the army. I wasn't there for a career."[4] In addition to Sánchez, the military did have some appeal for Richard Domínguez, who joined the Junior Reserve Officer Training Corps (JROTC) at his local high school in Los Angeles. As he stated, "I liked the military and that helped me later on . . . when I went into the service . . . knowing some of the basics."[5] In San Antonio, Francisco Vega also joined the JROTC: "The military appealed to me because of the discipline."[6] Meanwhile, the other narrators established no connection to the U.S. military prior to America's entry into the Second World War, as epitomized by Nick "Nicho" Salazar, who simply stated: "I never thought about the army."[7] Changing world events, however, would alter this mind-set.

Following Adolf Hitler's appointment as chancellor of Germany in 1933, the road to war in Europe progressed steadily throughout the 1930s as Germany rebuilt its military and industrial capacity while disregarding the mandates laid out by the Treaty of Versailles (1919). Obsessed with the reunification of a greater Germany dismembered after World War I, Hitler demanded the return of ethnic German enclaves scattered throughout Europe. German demands to one such location, the Czech Sudetenland, were met at the Munich Conference in March 1938, where a policy of appeasement was utilized by the Allies in their approach to Nazi Germany. Later that same year, anschluss with Austria occurred, while the following year Germany occupied all remaining Czech territory. The subsequent invasion of Poland on September 1, 1939, was the final provocation for Great Britain and France, and both declared war on Germany two days later. The Second World War had officially begun.[8]

On the other side of the world, a growing state of militarism and conquest also typified the island nation of Japan. The invasion of China's northwestern province of Manchuria in 1931 was followed by an outright attack on the Chinese mainland in 1937, where Japanese atrocities against Chinese civilians occurred with alarming regularity. Japan's subsequent incursion into the northern provinces of French Indochina following Germany's invasion of France in June 1940 was met with an American embargo on exports of aviation fuel and all grades of iron and steel scrap. The complete takeover of Indochina in July 1941 produced more U.S. sanctions—most notably an embargo on oil, which threatened the Japanese economy considerably since they were especially dependent on fuel imported from the United States. The assumption of the Japanese premiership by the militarist General Hideki Tojo later that year finalized the road to war with the United States, culminating in the sneak attack on the U.S. Pacific fleet at Pearl Harbor on the morning of December 7, 1941.[9] The United States declared war on Japan the following day and, in response, Germany and Italy honored their treaty obligations established by the 1940 Tripartite "Axis" alliance with Japan. The United States was now one of three major Allied powers, along with Great Britain and the Soviet Union, in a global struggle against the Axis powers.

The U.S. military was in no condition to fight a major conflict, however. In terms of preparation, the National Defense Act of 1920 was the basis for the U.S. Army's organization between the two world wars. Among its more notable stipulations were the increased coordination between the military and leaders of business and industry, the requirement that the army conduct strategic planning in preparation for future conflicts, and the enhanced role of reserve components and the National Guard. It also created the ROTC, which solidified its presence at universities across the nation.[10] Ultimately, the regular army suffered from neglect and poor funding during the interwar years, as described vividly in the following excerpt provided by Victor Vogel, an army enlistee in 1934 who would retire in 1955 as a lieutenant colonel:

> The maximum authorized strength of the regular army was set at 17,717 officers and 280,000 enlisted men, but it was never that large until 1940 . . . and until 1939 the actual strength . . . never exceeded 12,000 officers and 118,750 men . . . The dismantling of the army after World War I, the failure to fund the forces authorized by the National Defense Act of 1920 . . . left the army stripped to the bare bones as a fighting force . . . Weapons, uniforms, and equipment were the same as those used in World War I . . . There was no increase in pay between 1922 and 1942. It was only when war began in Europe in 1939 that changes were made to modernize our forces, and these came gradually.[11]

Such indifference operated in tandem with the ravages of the Great Depression and a spirit of isolationism that produced a powerful aversion to foreign entanglements. German victories in Europe and Japanese aggression in the Pacific, however, stirred President Roosevelt to begin preparations for war, which included the passage of the Selective Training and Service Act in September 1940, which established the nation's first peacetime draft and also mobilized certain National Guard units.[12]

The 200th Coast Artillery (Anti-Aircraft) regiment from New Mexico was one such outfit. Along with other mobilized National Guard units, its 1,800 personnel arrived in the Philippines in October 1941 to bolster the island's defenses against a possible Japanese attack.[13] As documented by author Dorothy Cave, upon the unit's arrival on the main island of Luzon, the strong Mexican American presence made an immediate impact: "As the men debarked . . . a band greeted them, and, hearing as much Spanish as English among the regiment, the musicians burst into 'South of the Border' and asked what Mexico was doing in this war."[14] William Sánchez also recalled this strong Mexican American contingent: "All these guys from New Mexico could speak Spanish, so I was no longer a novelty."[15] His capacity as a plotter for one of the island's coastal artillery units provided Sánchez with additional communication with personnel from the 200th, which he described as jovial. As a matter of fact, Sánchez fondly recalled his year in the Philippines prior to the Japanese attack, especially due to the fact that his meager $21 monthly salary packed a considerable punch in the local economy.

This changed on December 8, 1941, when the Japanese began a continuous air bombardment of the island's defenses, ultimately landing troops two weeks later on December 22. U.S. forces and colonial Filipino troops, with little hope of obtaining reinforcements from the United States, began a fighting retreat, making a last stand at the Bataan Peninsula before surrendering on April 9, 1942. A few remaining troops, including Sánchez, who manned a machine-gun nest, continued the struggle for another month from the fortified island of Corregidor, which ultimately succumbed to Japanese forces on May 5. Upon surrender, Sánchez was given the responsibility of shredding his unit's American flag. As he recalled, he received help with this dismal task:

> As I was doing that, a Lieutenant Cullen, a West Point officer said, "Can I help you?" I said, "I need all the help I can get." As we were doing that, he was crying, and I said, "Lieutenant, let's just hope that never again in the history of our country, someone will have to do what we are doing."[16]

Inhumane treatment by the Japanese began immediately, and Sánchez found himself in a working party piling up American and Filipino dead. As he stated, total confusion reigned: "The chaos after the capture was bad. We were just sleeping outside . . . no facilities, nothing."[17] Transferred to Manila and forced into overcrowded boxcars, he and other U.S. personnel were transported to a railroad junction, where they encountered U.S. and Filipino survivors of the Bataan Death March, a sixty-mile forced march that was characterized by unbearable conditions and severe abuse.[18] This combined force of prisoners was subdivided and marched to their designated prisoner of war (POW) camp. Arriving at Cabanatuan, Sánchez estimated the death rate at approximately one hundred per day, including his good friend, Frank Domínguez. Unspeakable horrors, disease, and brutality were an everyday occurrence. And yet, the situation for Sánchez grew worse. In October 1942, he was transported by ship to Japan to be used as forced labor. The journey lasted thirty three days, and his group arrived in Japan after stops in Formosa and Korea. He described one harrowing incident with a U.S. submarine: "I saw one torpedo that fizzled out right before it got to the bow [of the ship]. I said, 'thank God.' I was rooting for the Japanese navy!"[19] Upon arrival, his daily life was characterized by more forced labor and brutality.[20] His improved ability to speak Japanese also brought him into contact with kamikaze pilots prior to their suicide bombing runs against U.S. warships. Sánchez described one surreal encounter with one such pilot during the U.S. invasion of Okinawa in April 1945:

> They would . . . bring 'em and say, "This is what you're fighting [against]" . . . One young fellow sat down with me [and] he gave me a cigarette . . . We talked and he said to me, "What are you going to do after the war?" . . . I said, "Boy, I'm going home and enjoy life." He [said], "Yes, but you've insulted the family name" . . . I [said] "I haven't insulted anything . . . Look at you, you're leaving for Okinawa [and] you're not . . . coming back." He [said], "Yes, but I have the privilege of dying for the emperor."[21]

The harsh ordeal of Sánchez underscores the brutal nature of the Pacific campaign. The island-hopping strategy of U.S. forces was met with ferocious Japanese resistance. Imbued with the code of Bushido, "a spiritual shield that gave each soldier the strength to fight to the limits of endurance and self-sacrifice, even against overwhelming material odds," Japanese soldiers preferred death to the dishonor that accompanied surrender to U.S. and Allied forces.[22] Furthermore, given these tactics, the attack on Pearl Harbor, and decades of racial antagonism directed toward Asia and their migrants to the United States, American forces appeared all too willing to annihilate Japanese troops. According to historian John Dower, the brutal nature of the Pacific theater and the overall perception of the Japanese was "surely, in large part racial . . . German atrocities were known and condemned from an early date, but in keeping with their practice of distinguishing between good and bad Germans, Allied critics tended to describe these as 'Nazi' crimes . . . In the Asian theater enemy brutality was almost always presented as being simply 'Japanese.'"[23] As the nation mobilized in the aftermath of Pearl Harbor, U.S. personnel departed for this cauldron of racial animosity and brutal island-hopping in the Pacific, as well as the war in Europe, a mobilization that included the Mexican American community and the narrators present within this study.

INTO THE MILITARY

Newly married and drafted into the U.S. Army in late 1943 at the age of eighteen, Raúl Medina clearly remembered the amenities that were a welcome relief from the poverty that dominated his childhood in Fresno. As he described, the abundant food ration was a godsend: "Food galore . . . More food than I had ever seen in all my life . . . There was some things that the other [soldiers] didn't like, like dehydrated eggs. I loved 'em."[24] While the lack of traditional Mexican cuisine often provided a rude cultural shock to Mexican American servicemen and, conversely, promoted assimilation and cultural homogeneity, impoverished circumstances outweighed these awkward moments, as Medina clearly indicated. To earn additional income, he also served as his unit's barber, allowing him to send an allotment home to his wife and newborn child. Assigned to the 48th Infantry Division as a scout, Medina experienced extensive combat while serving in New Britain and in Leyte and Luzon during the U.S. invasion of the Philippine Islands that began in October 1944. Asked to recall whether he endured the loss of friends, he somberly reflected without providing additional information: "Yeah. Oh, yeah."[25] Despite lingering issues with post-traumatic stress disorder (PTSD), Medina summed up the significance of his military service with the following statement:

> Having dropped out of school at fifteen and working on a farm, and then drafted at eighteen, I didn't see the world. I didn't know anything about the world . . . In the service, you [had] all these guys from Texas, from Arizona . . . and they'd talk, and I would listen. They'd talk about their home [life] . . . When I was discharged, I knew that there was a better way of making a living other than working in the fields.[26]

Meanwhile, Darío Villegas, brother to Medal of Honor recipient Ismael "Smiley" Villegas, also served in the Philippines, specifically the island of Negros, as an army paratrooper with the 503rd Parachute Regiment.[27] He offered no explanation for his decision to volunteer for airborne training other than to intimate that the $55 supplement to his monthly salary provided motivation to do so.[28]

Upon arrival in Negros in 1945, he experienced six months of continuous combat until the war's end. He somberly recalled the friends that did not survive: "I lost a lot of friends . . . [We] went to training together and everything."[29] Villegas subsequently redeployed to Japan as part of the U.S. occupation force; he received his honorable discharge in March 1946. As he remembered, he was eager to leave: "I didn't want to stay in [the army] . . . I had [had] more than enough [of military life]."[30]

When World War II began, Richard Domínguez was "anxious to go. Most of my friends had already left . . . the guys I grew up with in high school."[31] Airborne training also appealed to him after being drafted into the army in June 1943. As he recalled, he volunteered to be a paratrooper for a number of reasons: "They did pay an extra [$50] bonus . . . that would be one [reason]. I think, also, the dress [uniform]. They were able to wear the jump boots and blouse . . . And [it was] a little prestigious thing [for me] . . . When they trained you, they said you were better than all the rest."[32] Extensive training in the United States delayed his departure for the Pacific, and Domínguez would not arrive in the Philippines until July 1945, where he experienced no combat. He offered the following statement, "I was fortunate, I guess, overall . . . that I moved around from one . . . camp to another, and I didn't get overseas until the final months [of the war]."[33] Upon arrival, he joined a battle-hardened airborne unit that contained a large Mexican American contingent: "In the Philippines I joined the 11th Airborne Division . . . There was quite a lot of [Mexican Americans] there."[34] Domínguez subsequently arrived in Japan, where he served as part of the occupation force until his honorable discharge in March 1946.

By comparison, Alfred Aguirre provided critically needed labor in the war industry rather than immediately enter the armed forces. He stated: "When the war started, I got a job at Voltee Aircraft in Downey [California]. They were building . . . parts for the B-24 bombers. I worked there for a year and a half."[35] Despite being drafted into the Army Air Corps in July 1943, Aguirre returned to Voltee in October due to his valuable expertise. His superiors provided the following rationale: "You're needed more where you were working before than you are here . . . your [former] department is lacking production and it takes a long time to train a man to do your job."[36] Recalled into the army in July 1944, Aguirre was reassigned to the 1901st Engineer Aviation Battalion, which participated in the invasion of Okinawa on April 1, 1945. As he described, the beachheads were not contested by the Japanese, unlike previous engagements: "They were waiting for us up in the hills about four [or] five miles inland."[37]

Aguirre, therefore, experienced no direct encounters with Japanese forces while assigned to the reconstruction of Kadena Airfield. However, his unit was constantly harassed by enemy snipers and artillery bombardments: "We start[ed] getting artillery shelling 'cause they were trying to hit the airfield. And we had artillery shelling off and on for two [or] three weeks until their guns couldn't reach us anymore."[38] Aguirre described the lingering effect of one close encounter: "I started getting pains in my back . . . I started getting pains in my head, too. Sharp pains."[39] Ultimately diagnosed with shell shock, Aguirre was hospitalized in various locations in the Pacific and the United States before receiving his honorable discharge in December 1945.

John Sótelo joined the navy at the age of seventeen in June 1942, and much like Raúl Medina, he welcomed the accommodations and cuisine the navy had to offer despite its unfamiliarity. Moreover, his commentary also hints at the capacity of these amenities to engineer cultural hegemony: "The living conditions in the Navy were better than what I had at home and [the] food was different . . . than I was used to, but I learned to adapt."[40] In choosing the navy and his specific occupation, Sótelo offers fascinating insight into the capacity of an inductee to influence the parameters of his military service. As he recalled, he deliberately wanted to differentiate himself from other neighborhood friends: "Most of the Mexican American friends [I] had wound up in the army and the infantry divisions, so I didn't want any part of that."[41] Moreover, Sótelo enlisted in an effort to exert greater control over his occupational assignment in the navy: "I was gonna be drafted anyway . . . [By enlisting] I had a chance to [choose] what I wanted to do."[42] He chose the navy's Motor Machinist (MM) rating, with a specialization in hydraulics, a decision he credits in part to the vocational training he received during his childhood education. Sótelo largely served in rear areas of the Pacific theater on two submarine tenders that provided support and repair facilities for U.S. submarines. He received his honorable discharge in May 1946.

Initially declared unfit for military service by his local draft board in Los Angeles, Mike García was eventually drafted into the U.S. Army in September 1944.[43] Upon receiving his notification, he recalled some initial hesitation: "I didn't have to go. I could have gone across the border [into Mexico] . . . but then so many of my buddies were going. And then during that period, my mother died that adopted me and I was all by myself . . . so I decided I'd rather go to the service."[44] Arriving as an infantryman in the Philippines, García's exposure to combat was limited. What he clearly remembered, however, was the rampant discriminatory behavior of his immediate superior, an unnamed second lieutenant: "Most of us Chicanos would hang together. We had a couple of guitars . . . Five or six of us would hang together [and] he didn't want us to speak Spanish."[45] As he related, the Spanish language came naturally to the unit's Mexican American personnel; moreover, a Mexican national that had joined the army spoke no English whatsoever, requiring García and others to translate for him. As he continued, it was clear that a boiling point had been reached: "He was lucky that we didn't go to battle that [particular] night because we [Mexican Americans] already had it figured [out]. He would have got[ten] killed."[46] García subsequently arrived in Japan in September 1945 as part of the occupation force, and he received an honorable discharge one year later. He summed up his military experience with the following reflection: "I didn't care for the army. I didn't care for the service."[47]

Drafted into the navy in May 1943, George Castrueta was provided with some leave time the following month while he attended basic training in San Diego as the Zoot Suit Riots raged in his hometown of Los Angeles. Despite traveling restrictions imposed on military personnel, he decided to head home in his uniform, but as he soon discovered, his Mexican ancestry did not provide safe passage through his old neighborhood. In fact, Castrueta's following reminiscence complicates the classic narrative of the riots as a fight strictly between Mexican American youth and white servicemen. Rather, Mexican Americans in uniform were also caught in the crossfire and viewed no differently by local youth:

> I was in boot camp in San Diego. We weren't supposed to leave the area . . .'cause we had a fifty-mile quarantine [zone]. Living in L.A., I [went home] anyway . . . Within, maybe, three blocks from my home . . . I saw what appeared to be a 1934 Ford two-door Sedan, packed with paisanos—or, in this case, Mexican guys. And they looked at me in a sailor's uniform and said, "Hay va uno" (There goes one) . . . You know, I was a track man in school and in great shape coming out of boot camp and I knew every inch of that neighborhood. I ran through alleys, backyards, jumped a fence, [and] I got home, panting.[48]

As discussed previously, a presumed link between the zoot suit and criminality generated a disproportionate level of scrutiny by law enforcement, the penny press, and society at large that bordered on hysteria. Increasingly racialized commentary against Mexican American youth, and indeed the entire community, was exacerbated in August 1942, when José Díaz was found mortally wounded near the Sleepy Lagoon, a watering hole in the eastern suburbs of Los Angeles that produced a dragnet by the Los Angeles Police Department (LAPD).[49] Public hysteria continued as confrontations escalated in the spring of 1943 between local youth and sailors stationed at the naval training center near the barrio of Chávez Ravine.[50]

This volatile situation finally exploded in June, and sailors, marines, and civilians searched for and assaulted Mexican Americans wearing a zoot suit. By week's end, all distinctions were lost, and mobs of military personnel ventured across the Los Angeles River into Boyle Heights in the pursuit of Mexican American youth.[51] George Castrueta remembered the negative publicity and the riots with a profound sense of disillusionment:

> The Zoot Suit [Riot] was more or less brought about by some bad journalism that gave the Mexicano boys a bad name. So consequently, some of the military . . . [when] they read about us, it really incited them, and they would get the . . . Mexican kids uptown [and] just because they were dressed [in a zoot suit], or even not dressed [in one] . . . they would abuse 'em something terrible. In some instances they [would] take off their clothes and whip 'em [and] beat 'em up. Even the police got involved . . . The sorry thing is, the majority of those fellows that got beaten up, they later went into the military to defend the rights and the liberties of this country.[52]

After completing basic training, Castrueta was based in San Francisco, where he served onboard liberty ships in the Armed Guard ferrying troops and supplies throughout the Pacific theater. A fair amount of discriminatory behavior existed onboard that targeted the crew's Mexican Americans and African Americans, and according to Castrueta, one method of reprisal lay in boxing, which he enjoyed: "It was something to do and you let out steam."[53] During his second deployment, he also participated in a world tour that began in late 1944, stopping at various port cities in the Pacific, Indian, and Atlantic Oceans before reaching New York City the day after V-E Day in May 1945.[54] He celebrated V-J Day in Portland, Oregon, and was honorably discharged in April 1946.

Unable to secure a manufacturing job in eastern Michigan, Arnulfo "Arnif" Nerio was immediately hired by General Motors in Saginaw following the Japanese attack on Pearl Harbor. He stated, "The war broke out . . . [and] the plants start[ed] hiring left and right."[55] Drafted into the army in December 1942, Nerio attended basic training in the South, where he encountered a brutal discriminatory environment: "I went down to Little Rock, Arkansas, and there [was] nothing but rednecks down there. They didn't like the Mexicans."[56] He recalled one occasion when room assignments were being determined: "I sat down and took my [field] pack off and my rifle and laid it on the bed . . . [but] nobody would come in [and share the room with me]."[57] When forced to by the ranking sergeant, Nerio's white roommates nevertheless ignored him: "They wouldn't talk to me because I was a Mexican."[58] However, on another occasion when Nerio made the beds for two of his roommates, which enabled them to pass morning inspection, he earned their gratitude: "From there on they talked to me all the time. I broke the ice that way."[59]

After additional training at various domestic locations and in Hawaii, Nerio arrived in New Guinea in early 1944 as an infantryman assigned to the 6th Infantry Division. He explained their daily routine and the inherent danger involved: "We used to get in columns of twos . . . Sometimes a buddy would get hit . . . And all of a sudden . . . he'd be dead by snipers. And then we had to wait till we cleaned out the snipers and then we moved again."[60] Using this approach, his unit traveled a considerable distance over six months: "We marched from . . . the southern part of New Guinea all the way up to the north part of New Guinea."[61] Nerio was ultimately wounded by Japanese artillery in one engagement, which he described: "All of a sudden, I heard Zoom! Zoom! . . . [The explosion] threw me up against a coconut tree [and] I thought I broke my ribs . . . I looked around and some of [the] guys were laying there and it looked like somebody took [sledgehammers] and knocked their legs off."[62] Hospitalized at various locations, Nerio was provided with a thirty-day furlough in Miami Beach in the winter of 1944, which he fondly recalled: "All I did was lay around and go eat and go dancing. I had it easy there."[63] Subsequent assignments included a brief tour as an instructor at Camp Wolters, Texas, as well as guarding the entrance to Puget Sound before receiving his honorable discharge in October 1945.

Joe B. Medina, from southeastern Colorado, joined the army in late 1943 after his high school graduation and was soon assigned to Officer Candidate School (OCS) at North Dakota State University after an extensive battery of examinations. He detailed his daily routine at OCS, which lasted a few months: "We'd go to school at eight o'clock in the morning until noon [and] back at one until five [and] back at seven until nine. And we could not do homework after nine o'clock because the lights would be out, so the only homework we could do would be in the men's latrine . . . 'cause that's the only place where they had lights."[64] As a newly minted second lieutenant in the army's support forces, Medina participated in the invasion of the Philippine Islands and Okinawa, offering few details other than to list a few close encounters with death, including the following incident on the island of Leyte: "Right on the beach, I was knocked out of a foxhole . . . by a concussion bomb . . . but I was okay."[65] Assigned to the Far Eastern Air Force intelligence group based in Tokyo, Medina described his subsequent assignment after the war: "I was doing research work on . . . the Japanese version of the jet plane that they never had a chance to perfect . . . We were recovering all these blueprints [and] textbooks, most of them from Germany [and] we were making reports and they were sent to Wright Field, Ohio."[66] Honorably discharged as a first lieutenant in mid-1946, he offered this final somber reflection on his military service: "We won the war that I was in, but everybody loses in a war . . . But I'm not bitter about it."[67]

Medina's final commentary underscores the tragic consequences inherent to warfare that often plagued the lives of veterans long after their discharge from active service. The brutal nature of the fighting in the Pacific against a foe often willing to fight to the death readily produced such physical and emotional scars. Of course, the European campaign also gave rise to lingering aftereffects for returning veterans. Unlike the Pacific theater, however, the war in Europe encompassed a more conventional emphasis on maneuvering and flanking movements across large geographic spaces. An exception was the Italian campaign, beginning with the successful invasion of Sicily in July 1943 and the September invasion of the mainland, which provided a combat environment that was reminiscent of the close-quarter fighting in the Pacific. Adept in the art of defensive fighting despite the fame attached to blitzkrieg warfare, German forces skillfully utilized the terrain of central Italy, dotted by successive mountain ranges, to impede the Allies' advance northward through the Italian Peninsula. One army division that confronted these German defensive positions was the 36th Infantry Division of the Texas National Guard, which had been mobilized in November 1940 as part of the Selective Service Act.

One unit within the division, noted for its all-Tejano personnel, was Company E, 2nd Battalion, of the 141st Regiment.[68] World War II veteran Raúl Morín offered the following description of the company:

> The entire company was made up of Spanish-speaking soldiers. They included Mexicans, Mexican-Americans, and the so-called Latin-Americans. Many of the enlisted men spoke limited English. All of the non-coms and platoon officers were Americans of Mexican descent. Most of its members were former citizens

> of El Paso and nearby points who were in the original E company of the Texas National Guard. These were supplemented by other Spanish-speaking G.I.'s who later were drafted or volunteered into wartime service.[69]

Employing the slogan "Remember the Alamo," Company E suffered heavy casualties during the unsuccessful forced crossing of the Rapido River in January 1944. Employed as the lead assault unit against strong German defenses, only 23 men survived out of a company strength of 187 soldiers.[70] Overall, the division suffered over 27,000 casualties, the third highest of any division that served in World War II. Continually resupplied with replacement troops, the 36th participated in the invasion of the South of France in August 1944 and crossed into Germany in March 1945.

Operations in the Mediterranean were of secondary importance, however, since the defeat of Germany ultimately required a cross-Channel invasion of France, which occurred on June 6, 1944, a day that has since been immortalized as D-Day. Francisco Vega participated in the invasion; however, his initial efforts to enlist into the military in the wake of the Pearl Harbor attack were thwarted, and he offered the following explanation: "I went to the [Army] Air Corps . . . I went to the navy. I went to the merchant marines. I went to the Marine Corps . . . I went to enlist, but they told me, every one of 'em said, 'We were not taking Mexicans at this time.'"[71] Vega eventually joined the army in October 1942 and was assigned to various locations throughout the United States before arriving in England as a replacement soldier on May 15, 1944, onboard a passenger liner. As he described, the voyage across the Atlantic came at a heavy cost: "All of a sudden, one of the ships was hit . . . You could hear the explosions . . . And it went down . . . by the [German] submarines. This was happening all the time. There was a number of ships that were sunk."[72]

His excellent typing skills earned him a job with the 1st Signal Service Battalion, where Vega transmitted and received classified messages in mobile teletype stations carried on the back of trucks. Unfortunately, however, this unit was assigned to Omaha Beach, the deadliest of the five Allied beachheads established on D-Day. He offered amazing and vivid testimony of the assault, as troops embarked on landing craft that immediately sailed for the beach, where they were greeted by intense enemy gunfire. As Vega recalled, it was a day filled with constant profanity, tears, and prayer:

> Pretty soon, we get a landing barge. It comes up next to us. It was the kind that the front could drop [down] . . . They dropped a net over the ship and we started

> goin' down. What was not in the training was that this ship was rockin' . . . [and] the net was short by about eight feet . . . The guys that were [controlling] this landing barge . . . [were] yellin', "Jump! Jump!" Well, many of 'em never made it . . . They were being smashed [between the barge and the ship] . . . The sea was just red [with blood] . . . I . . . landed at Omaha Beach . . . Even before we got there, there was pieces of bodies just floating all over the place . . . And there's a lot of fire . . . [The Germans] were shooting at us from up high and they're in bunkers . . . [and] they [were] just raking the beachhead. . . . [There] was one heck of an explosion and then another one . . . And the next thing I know, I'm on the beach in the sand. I'm face down . . . I felt my arms. I felt everything . . . And just about that time . . . [another soldier] came and fell right next to me . . . And the next thing I heard [was] "thunk!" I looked down [and] right through his helmet, he had a [bullet] hole.[73]

Vega's unit was part of the subsequent Allied offensive across France, encamping in Chantilly in August 1944, where Vega handled a considerable flow of message traffic. His unit continued into Germany the following spring, and Vega remembered the weary and demoralized nature of the German inhabitants as well as the concentration camp they encountered, which he described as grotesque and bizarre: "I remember seeing [the inmates] in groups, all starving . . . Skin and bones some of 'em."[74] He remained in Germany before departing for the United States onboard a liberty ship, which was followed by a train ride to San Antonio, where Vega was honorably discharged at Fort Sam Houston in December 1945.

Jesse Ybarra welcomed his entrance into the army after being drafted in January 1943: "I figured out . . . I had [to be] worth more dead than I was living because then 'Uncle Sam' could support my family, so I was ready to go when they called me."[75] He also insisted that his childhood poverty in San Antonio provided him with a work ethic that steeled him to the tasks expected of him: "I did [work] without question. Most of the other guys would bitch and complain and I didn't . . . [Work] had to be done and I might as well do it without complaining 'cause otherwise it won't do me any good. I learned that [lesson] real early in life."[76] Moreover, his time in the Civilian Conservation Corps prepared him for basic training and the daily routine of army life: "The CCC had me trained and ready, so I fell in just perfect . . . I was ready to follow instructions."[77]

Trained as a medic, Ybarra was assigned to the 341st Medical Detachment of the 86th Infantry Division that crossed into Germany in early March 1945.

Following the forced crossing of the Rhine, the 86th fanned out into the German interior, and along with other American units, enveloped the remnants of organized German resistance in the west. Ybarra and his unit experienced nonstop action, and in one engagement, under intense enemy fire, Ybarra was awarded the Bronze Star for his care of the wounded: "In the Ruhr Pocket, we were pinned down . . . They were [firing] at us artillery, mortars, and machine guns. So, under that fire, we were taking care of the wounded."[78] He was also wounded himself, which he described: "The Germans [ambushed] us . . . We were going so fast [in a jeep] and [we flipped] over . . . I had five vertebrae hurt."[79] Miraculously, he remained with his unit, which fought its way into Austria when Germany surrendered in May. Subsequently, the entire division, including Ybarra, was redirected to the Philippines, arriving in August when the atomic bombings occurred. His family situation, which included care for his mother, wife, and newborn child, expedited his release from active duty, and he was honorably discharged in December 1945.

Working San Francisco shipyards, where he slept in a car while dormitories were built for the workforce, Carlos Santillán was not an American citizen when he was drafted into the army in February 1943. He earned his citizenship the following July at Fort Benning, Georgia, while undergoing airborne training. He recalled, "A bunch of us guys, they just took us to court, [and] raised [our] right hand . . . There was a lot of Latinos."[80] Furthermore, his decision to volunteer as a paratrooper was a combination of youthful bravado and monetary gain: "I felt that it was better than being just a foot soldier, and they get more money, too."[81] Arriving as a replacement soldier in Oran, Algeria, Santillán was assigned to the 504th Paratroop Regiment in the famous 82nd Airborne Division. His first exposure to combat occurred at the Anzio landing in January 1944, which was intended to outflank German forces and enable an attack on Rome. Santillán offered a glimpse of the difficulties that day: "It's just like you see in the movies when they strafe the water. That's the way the German [planes] came down strafing the ships and everything . . . [I was] heavily loaded with [my] own bag . . . Your uniform is all wet. You could hardly move [on the beach]. You know, you're soaking, your rifle and everything."[82]

Placed on reserve in the United Kingdom for the D-Day invasion, the 504th participated in Operation Market Garden, a failed attempt in September 1944 to gain control of key bridges in the Netherlands. Subsequent engagements included the Battle of the Bulge and the Ruhr Pocket, culminating in a week of rest and recuperation in the French Riviera. As he explained, "Word came down that so many soldiers [were] to get a vacation. So I was one of the lucky ones . . . and I stayed there seven days. It was real nice there."[83] Assigned to garrison duty, Santillán described the profitable black market that emerged: "We used to get passes to go to Berlin . . . There was a black market [and] you could sell anything there . . . The Russians would buy anything . . . I was able to send [a lot of] money home."[84] Santillán ultimately received an honorable discharge in November 1945, summing up the significance of his two and a half years in the army as enabling him to "stand up and think for yourself."[85]

CONCLUSION

Santillán's overall assessment is indicative of the profound sense of pride, patriotism, and accomplishment that largely typified the reminiscences of these veterans. Jesse Ybarra's sense of being "more of an American than I was before," provides another example.[86] So does the following observation by Darío Villegas, that military service in World War II "made me more strong . . . It made [me] more tough, more proud."[87] Raúl Medina also reflected on the war's impact on the Mexican American community: "I think [World War II] lifted us as Hispanics. It brought us up . . . We proved ourselves."[88] Indeed, the institutionalized discrimination so prevalent before the war largely remained intact, and returning Mexican American veterans, having championed democratic principles in helping the Allied effort, expected full access to America's promises. The Mexican American community became emboldened by this activist spirit that these veterans provided and by the hope that meaningful victories would be accomplished (discussed in chapter 9). As described by Maggie Rivas-Rodríguez, "World War II, then, imbued the ongoing Mexican American civil rights movement with new leadership and a new attitude of entitlement . . . now it was time to reap the benefits of full citizenship rights."[89]

An additional concern, however, in the Cold War environment that followed World War II, was the added scrutiny that was placed on the flow of undocumented immigrants from Mexico. As this hysteria unfolded, the ongoing "Red Scare" enabled a concurrent "Brown Scare" that increasingly highlighted the need to distinguish between citizens and criminal outsiders in the form of unwanted immigrants as well as perceived Communist infiltrators in the shadows of American society. The inevitable result was Operation Wetback, a multiagency effort launched in 1954 in an effort to round up and deport undocumented immigrants. Such efforts at immigration restriction, as described so eloquently by historian Mae M. Ngai, "produced the illegal alien as a *new legal and political subject*, whose inclusion within the nation was simultaneously a social reality and a legal impossibility—a subject barred from citizenship and without rights."[90] Within this debate over citizenship during the Cold War, large elements of the Mexican American community dissociated themselves from those recently arrived from Mexico in order to establish their credentials as legitimate and patriotic American citizens. Moreover, military service once again became a litmus test for showcasing fealty toward the United States, as it had during World War II, and the police action in Korea offered the community the opportunity to serve as "committed Cold Warriors ready to serve their country again."[91]

4

THE KOREAN WAR

"They call it a police action. It wasn't a police action because . . . when somebody's shooting at you, I don't care where you're at, it's war. You know, war is war."

"I have never been able to comprehend why they refer to Korea as the 'forgotten war' because we lost thousands and thousands of people. It was not a police action."

ON JULY 5, 1950, a hastily assembled force of four hundred American soldiers sat in their foxholes awaiting the arrival of the North Korean People's Army (NKPA). Task Force Smith, under the command of Lieutenant Colonel Charles Smith, would be the first American unit to confront the NKPA following its invasion of South Korea on June 25. The U.S. military, however, was but a shadow of the formidable war machine that had achieved victory in World War II just five years earlier. According to historian Max Hastings, "By the summer of 1950 the American armed forces . . . had shrunk from 12 million men in 1945 to 1.6 million. Spending was down from $82 billion to $13 billion . . . Nearly every unit in the army was understrength, undertrained, and underequipped."[1] The inexperienced troops of Task Force Smith, fresh from occupation duty in Japan, epitomized these deficiencies as they awaited the battle-tested soldiers of the NKPA. The subsequent rout of the task force and the Battle of Pusan Perimeter foreshadowed the difficult struggle to save the Republic of (South) Korea (ROK) over the next three years. This police action against North Korean and Chinese forces was also an effort to contain the perceived monolithic threat posed by the Soviet Union and the forces of communism. The domino theory lay at the heart of the Cold War policy of containment that dominated U.S. foreign policy, which the "loss" of China to Mao Zedong in 1949 further reinforced.

This rationale drove the United States to commit to the defense of South Korea as it would a decade later in South Vietnam.[2]

The Korean War was also the first test case for integrated units, and personal encounters with discriminatory behavior remained a common occurrence for Mexican American servicemen. Additionally, the pay and benefits associated with military service were again a welcome relief for many, but more importantly, for many young men, including my narrators, the tradition established by older brothers and other family members that served in World War II motivated their entrance into the military in a manner comparable to the young men that came of age during the Vietnam War. Thus, service in Korea built upon the sense of Americanness and the tradition of military service first established in the Second World War that promoted a Mexican American culture and identity willing to reaffirm its patriotism through dedicated military service.

SOLDIERING IN THE SHADOW OF THE GREATEST GENERATION

Born in 1929 in the border town of Mercedes, Texas, Rolando Hinojosa enlisted into the U.S. Army in August 1946 at the age of seventeen after completing high school. He served an unspectacular eighteen months at Fort Eustis, Virginia, in a variety of administrative positions until he received his discharge in December 1947. More importantly, his tour of duty entitled him to twenty-four months of educational benefits under the 1944 GI Bill, which he used to enroll at the University of Texas for the following spring semester. He explained: "Because I'd gone in before Korea, I was still eligible under World War II [entitlements], which didn't end until 1949."[3] His undergraduate schooling was interrupted, however, when Hinojosa was recalled to active duty in November 1949. He stated, "I was very disappointed, to put it mildly. But then I remembered that I had the [eight year] obligation."[4] Assigned to Japan as a radio disc jockey, Hinojosa was reassigned to Task Force Smith, which arrived in Korea on the Fourth of July. He offered vivid testimony of the unit's catastrophic defeat the following day:

> This was the very first battle for all of us, except for the old sergeants and for the officers [who] were World War II vets. Now, a lot of [our] guys cut and ran . . . They fought as well as they could, then they ran because even though there was

> no infantry of the NKPA, [the] North Korean People's Army, they had tanks. And a lot of [our] guys . . . wound up in the rice paddies . . . They abandoned their uniforms. Some lost their boots [and were] walking around and running around in shorts . . . We had to go around driving in the trucks . . . picking up the guys and driving 'em out of there. It was pretty bad.[5]

After this victory, the NKPA continued southward, trapping remaining U.S. and ROK forces in the southeastern coastal city of Pusan by the end of July. Despite repeated efforts by the NKPA to break through, a dogged defense of the Pusan Perimeter supported by U.S. reinforcements prevented a total collapse. Additional military and logistical support was also provided by a number of countries operating under the aegis of the United Nations (UN).[6] The September 1950 amphibious landing at Inchon to the rear of NKPA forces, in tandem with a breakout from Pusan, turned the tide of the war. With the NKPA in full retreat, the decision was made to proceed across the 38th parallel in an effort to reunify the peninsula with a friendly government elected under UN auspices. Crossing into North Korea and approaching the Manchurian border, however, posed a direct threat to Communist China, and despite repeated warnings, UN forces were within reach of the Yalu River in November when the Chinese responded with overwhelming force. This winter offensive dashed all hopes of securing a unified, democratic Korea. A strategic impasse developed and, as Hastings stated, "the United Nations' objectives from the spring of 1951 to the end in 1953 were plainly limited. At an acceptable cost in casualties . . . Ridgway's forces sought to kill sufficient Communists and defend sufficient real estate to secure peace."[7] As mentioned, however, the troops pulled from occupation duty in Japan proved woefully inadequate, and a more extensive utilization of the armed forces, including mobilized reservists and guardsmen, would be needed. This mobilization ultimately included my narrators, and during the Korean War era they participated in a variety of combat and noncombat experiences. Among the former were human-wave assaults, freezing winters, and the fear and uncertainty that accompanies soldiers into battle.

Ruben Moreno was influenced by his two older brothers to enlist in the U.S. Navy in 1946 for a two-year term. Both were World War II veterans, and Moreno was eager to follow in their footsteps: "I could hardly wait to join . . . because both of my brothers had done it."[8] As he laughingly recalled, the pay and amenities provided an immediate and rather incredible impact: "I gained about twenty-five pounds right out of boot camp!"[9] An allotment to family members back home was also necessary: "[I earned] more money than I ever had . . . They were feeding me and [giving me] a place to sleep . . . And [I had] a little left over to get drunk on . . . So I sent most of my money home."[10] In 1949, soon after receiving his discharge from the navy, Moreno decided to enlist in the local Tucson-based Company E, 13th Infantry Battalion, of the U.S. Marine Corps Reserve (USMCR) in order to supplement his monthly income, as well as the potential for camaraderie with other Mexican American reservists.[11] When the entire company was mobilized on July 10, 1950, for service in Korea, Moreno felt no alarm. As he stated, "[I was] young and stupid. You don't think that you're the one that's gonna get killed."[12]

Initially assigned as an ammunition carrier, Moreno landed with the 1st Marine Division at Inchon and was quickly promoted to a machine gunner, an assignment he would occupy for the remainder of his deployment. He offered the following explanation: "By the process of elimination, four days after we had [landed in] Inchon, I was a gunner because they had killed our gunner and pretty badly wounded our assistant gunner. So, I took over the gun [and] kept it all the time I was over there."[13] Moreno offered the following overview of his nine-month tour in Korea, beginning with the division's epic retreat through the Chosin Reservoir in the winter of 1950 following China's entrance into the conflict:

> Of course we had to fight our way out of there. Then we regrouped . . . and got some replacements and started fighting our way back to the 38th parallel . . . Most of the time I was out there [in Korea], we were in combat. They put us behind the line to take a respite [and] get resupplied. And then we'd have to go plug a hole because the [U.S.] Army or South Koreans had given way.[14]

After rotating back to Camp Pendleton, California, and marrying his fiancée, Moreno was demobilized with a 10 percent disability rating in the summer of 1951. As he recalled, however, he was left with the following choice in order to remain in the USMCR: "In order to [remain in] the reserves, I had to forgo the 10 percent disability, and I figured, if that arm gets any worse, I'm gonna need [financial] help, so I'd better just stay out. Besides, I [had] enough of that already."[15]

In a manner similar to Ruben Moreno, David Carillo was influenced by his older brother, a paratrooper in World War II, to enlist in the army for six years immediately following his graduation from high school in 1948, and to volunteer for airborne training. Such enthusiasm for military service had manifested itself at an early age for Carillo. He remembered his favorite childhood pastime: "We [neighborhood kids] used to go to the dump and we used to get a lot of stuff from World War II . . . that [was left] at the dump, and we'd bring it home and we'd put it on . . . I had all the kids in the neighborhood marching up and down the street."[16] When the Korean conflict began, Carillo volunteered for reassignment to Korea, arriving as a paratrooper in August 1950. He remarked, "I wanted to go fight for my country. That's why I joined the service. In case there was a war, I'd go fight for my country."[17] He offered compelling testimony of the human-wave assaults he encountered soon after his arrival:

> They just kept coming at you. I don't know where . . . they got so many people. The first wave normally didn't have weapons. They just came at us so we could expend our ammunition . . . and we just literally blew them away.[18]

Redeployed to Japan with his unit, Carillo refused an opportunity to rotate back to the United States in order to remain there. As he explained, it was a decision with adverse consequences: "I figured, well, I'm having a good time here in Japan, why go home? So I waivered my rotation. Two weeks [later], we went back to Korea."[19] This increased his tour to approximately eighteen months before rotating back to the United States in the spring of 1952. Rising to the rank of sergeant first class (E6), Carillo was honorably discharged in 1954 after fulfilling his six-year tour of duty.

Gene García also recalled the powerful impression of his older cousins that served in World War II: "When they came back from the service . . . they were more mature."[20] Intent on enlisting, yet eager to further his education, García decided to join the U.S. Air Force (USAF) in July 1951 at the age of nineteen. He offers a powerful example of an individual who clearly intended to navigate the military's many occupational specialties in order to avoid a career in the combat arms. He stated: "At that time, I had just started going to junior college and I saw an opportunity that, if I went into the Air Force . . . there was a better chance of continuing college after I got out of there . . . I just kind of had a feeling that when I joined the Air Force, there was more opportunity to learn, instead of carrying a rifle and pulling a trigger."[21] After multiple stops at several bases, García was ultimately stationed in Cheyenne, Wyoming, as a clerk typist, where he provided a variety of administrative services. As he described, however, he was hoping to broaden his experiences further: "They were looking for guys to volunteer to go to Korea, so I was one of the volunteers . . . I wanted to get out of [Cheyenne] because I wanted to see more. I wanted to be able to go somewhere else."[22] Arriving after the armistice, which had been signed in July 1953, García served a one-year tour with the 6147th Tactical Control Group at Chun Chan Air Base, where minor cat-and-mouse encounters with enemy reconnaissance planes were the primary source of disturbance. García was subsequently reassigned to March Air Force Base in Riverside, California, where he completed his four-year term. He was honorably discharged in July 1955 as a staff sergeant (E5).

Frank Gonzales provides another example of a recruit who was not driven by a desire to participate in the military's combat arms. In fact, he was rather adamant that his four-year navy enlistment in 1949 was strictly governed by the increased likelihood of a noncombat assignment: "The little bit that I knew about the navy was that I knew that I wasn't gonna be in a foxhole in strange terrain. I was gonna be on a ship and I was gonna . . . be able to take a shower. And I was gonna get a good meal."[23] In addition, he was also hoping for some overseas travel and an expanded worldview: "I joined to see the world. I thought that I wanted to see something besides Saginaw [Michigan] . . . That was my key motivation."[24] Gonzales spent two years onboard the aircraft carrier USS *Bonhomme Richard* as a navy hospital corpsman, where he participated in two deployments off the coast of Korea. As he fondly recalled, sixty-day stretches out at sea, which included combat sorties by the carrier's air wing, were followed by rotational visits to Japan: "I liked Japan . . . I enjoyed myself going there . . . We'd go there for so many days . . . Then we'd go back out to our task force."[25] He continued by providing details of the flotilla's composition: "We got over there [to Korea] and meshed with two other carriers, the [USS] *Kearsarge* and the [USS] *Essex*. And then the [USS] *Boxer* [joined us]. So there was a contingent of carriers out there and battle[ships] . . . And we had destroyers and [destroyer escorts] . . . We were Task Force 77."[26] After rotating back to the United States, Gonzales ultimately received an honorable discharge as a petty officer, third class (E4) in 1953.

For Mike González, having two older brothers that served in World War II did provide partial inspiration for his decision to enlist in the army in 1947 at the age of seventeen. He insisted, however, that his primary motivation for doing so was the constant harassment from local gang members in his hometown of Los Angeles: "I wanted to get away from all the pachucos that were trying to bust my chops."[27] He also successfully completed paratrooper training, offering the following reason for his interest: "It [was] something exciting [and] more than just regular infantry."[28] Moreover, the supplement to his monthly salary, which had remained fixed at $50 since World War II, enabled an allotment home to his mother. Arriving in Korea in October 1950 with the 187th Regimental Combat Team, González experienced extensive combat throughout his tour, including human-wave assaults. He described the following encounter in a manner that referenced Japanese suicide charges in World War II: "They pulled a 'banzai' on us . . . They were all young kids . . . And so we [were] . . . knockin' them off like flies . . . But we didn't go after them 'cause a lot of times that's what they want[ed] you to do."[29] It was also rather obvious through the following reminiscence that González was a natural-born leader: "When I was in Korea, I was always put in charge of a detail. [If] a patrol would go out, I'd take it out. We'd go out in[to] no-man's-land and I was responsible for all our guys. A couple of times we got ambushed, I lost a couple of guys. Another time . . . I lost my assistant gunner. He was just a little guy; he was sixteen years old."[30] González was eventually removed to Japan sometime in late 1951, and to Fort Ord, California, in March 1952, where he was honorably discharged as a staff sergeant (E6) after five and a half years of military service.

George Castaneda also served as a paratrooper for four years in the 187th Regimental Combat Team after enlisting in Saginaw, Michigan, in 1948. He fondly remembered the additional stipend for successfully completing airborne training: "They used to pay us $50 more for parachuting out of the airplanes."[31] Like Mike González, Castaneda accumulated extensive combat experiences with the 187th, including the following encounter during the Chinese winter offensive:

> One time . . . I got in a foxhole and my buddy . . . was with me . . . I [saw] them Chinese or North Koreans [and] they were coming straight at me . . . I had a [Browning Automatic Rifle] . . . and I had thirteen magazines in my belt . . . I [pointed] my B.A.R. straight at 'em and I opened up, full automatic . . . and I dropped 'em.[32]

Having been shot in the leg in late 1950, Castaneda was removed to Japan, where he recovered for two or three months. Much to his dismay, however, he was sent back to Korea: "I was mad because they didn't send me home . . . [I was sent] straight back to the battlefields. So I wasn't really happy about that."[33] On another occasion, he participated in a mission to rescue U.S. prisoners, which he described: "They were taking them to China. But we parachuted and [saved] most of them."[34] After serving approximately eighteen months overseas, Castaneda was honorably discharged in April 1952 as a sergeant (E5). He returned to Saginaw, and as he recalled, difficult economic circumstances almost pushed him back into the army: "I couldn't get no job . . . I was getting ready to reenlist . . . But I get a job [at General Motors], so I stayed."[35]

By comparison, William J. Fisher offered a somewhat comedic reminiscence on his decision to enlist in the navy in August 1945 for three years: "My girlfriend said I look[ed] real cute, which I did, in a navy uniform."[36] Born in Wylmar, California, but raised in Tucson, Arizona, Fisher was discharged as a navy corpsman in August 1948. He remained a reservist, and the following year he joined Company E as a combat medic at his brother's request. He explained: "My brother was involved with the Marine [Corps] Reserve . . . and he asked [me], why don't I come in as a corpsman, so I did. I was still in the navy, but attached to the Marine Corps [Reserve]."[37] Following the unit's activation in July 1950, Fisher was immediately deployed to the Pusan Perimeter, arriving in August due to the urgent need for medical personnel. He subsequently landed at Inchon and traveled northward into North Korea. At the Chosin Reservoir, Fisher became one of the first casualties:

> I got shot the 28th of November [and] the Chinese [had] hit us the 27th . . . I gave myself a shot [of morphine]. A couple of guys . . . in a stretcher would carry me off the hill . . . I'll never forget, I was singing [in Spanish], "Ay Jalisco, no te rajes [Be brave. Don't be a coward]," 'cause, man, I could feel it from the top of my head down to my toes, the wound [in the groin].[38]

Evacuated by medevac to Japan to recover, Fisher redeployed to Korea in January 1951 for six months before rotating back to the United States; he deactivated in September of that year. At the behest of Company E's commanding officer, Fisher, who formally transferred to the USMCR in 1953, offered the following explanation: "I figured next time, if I ever have to [serve in combat] again, I'm gonna shoot back . . . so I switched from the Navy [Reserve] to the Marine Corps [Reserve]."[39] Fisher enjoyed a largely uneventful career in the USMCR, eventually retiring in 1976 as a first sergeant (E8) after thirty-one years of combined service.[40]

Born in 1925, Robert L. Castro avoided military service in World War II due to a deferment while employed as a miner. Finally drafted in June 1946, Castro recalled his choice of the Marine Corps rather than the army or the navy: "I heard that they were a hard unit and I liked the uniform."[41] Released from active duty in August 1947, he joined Company E the following year and was mobilized with the unit in July 1950. After several months of training, he deployed to Korea in October, where he volunteered for motor transport duties. Assigned to the 1st Motor Transport Battalion as the 1st Marine Division traveled northward, he offered another perspective on the Chosin Reservoir:

> We took the 5th Marine Regiment [located] to the right of the [Chosin] Reservoir . . . and we moved [them] up close to the . . . Manchurian border. Then we came back to our base of operations, which was at the bottom of the hill . . . We were ambushed on the sixth or the seventh of December and we lost . . . eight or nine people [after being] ambushed by the Chinese.[42]

Castro rotated back to the United States in July 1951 and was simultaneously demobilized. By the following year, however, he decided to return to active duty—he offered the following rationale for doing so: "I came back and I started working [in] the mines again . . . And then in 1952, I joined the regular Marines because I felt that due to my father's death [from] miners' consumption . . . I did not feel I wanted to follow in his footsteps and be a miner."[43] Castro rose steadily through the ranks, becoming a master gunnery sergeant (E9) before ultimately retiring from active duty in 1983 with thirty-five years of military service.[44]

Returning to Rolando Hinojosa, he was assigned to a tank reconnaissance unit for approximately eighteen months following the defeat of Task Force Smith. He described his initial experiences: "After we got the heck beat out of us, we fought delaying actions . . . all the way back to Pusan."[45] Part of the breakout and offensive northward, Hinojosa also commented on the impact of the Chinese offensive, including the dreadful winter: "It was on a Friday the day after Thanksgiving. It was very cold. One of the coldest winters [Korea] had that century."[46] He would commemorate many of his experiences in future writings, including the following poem, which provides an overview of the first six months of his deployment:

June-December 1950

The Pusan Perimeter. Breakout.
Crossing the 38th Parallel. The
Drive North. Encounter With

> the Chinese. The Rush South.
> Caught in the Pass. Defeat of
> the Eighth Army. Holding and
> Delaying Actions. The 3000
> Casualties of the Second
> Division. Pyongyang Afire. Brief
> Stand at the Taedong. Loss
> of Seoul. Back to Pusan for
> Reorganization. First Rest
> and Recuperation.[47]

As he narrated further, Hinojosa was grateful for the few respites that interrupted his extensive exposure to combat. He stated: "You didn't fight every day. You'd go crazy if you fought every day. But we were in [a] combat [environment] all the time. It was a combat unit."[48] He also encountered human-wave assaults, offering a somewhat different perspective: "A lot of that is myth . . . No general wants to waste men . . . What caused a high casualty list on their part was our increased firepower."[49] Honorably discharged as a sergeant (E5) in late 1951, Hinojosa returned to Austin, where he reenrolled at the University of Texas for the following spring semester.

Frank Ornelas received his draft notice toward the end of 1950 while employed at the foundry in Saginaw affiliated with General Motors. Already a seasoned worker with a résumé that also included migrant farmwork and railroad repair, Ornelas assumed an incredible responsibility at age fifteen by becoming the head of household for his ten-sibling family upon his father's death in 1946. As he recalled, the local branch of the Red Cross was concerned with his draftee status: "The Red Cross came to visit us when they knew that I had been drafted. And [the representative] said, 'You know, Frank, you don't have to go . . . You're the sole supporter of your family. You can get exempt from that.'"[50] While sad to leave the following summer, the difficult economic circumstances that characterized his childhood steeled Ornelas to the challenges of life in the army: "Going and living the [difficult] way we did out in the fields and out in the farms . . . I was used to anything."[51] Trained in the field of artillery, Ornelas was assigned to the 398th Anti-Aircraft Artillery (AAA) Battalion, which was tasked with clearing the skies for Allied air sorties.

Upon arrival in Korea in November or December 1951, the unit was shocked to hear enemy radio broadcasts that directly referenced their unit. He described one such incident: "The third day that we were setting up, we had our radios on . . . They were saying, 'Welcome you guys from the 398th AAA Battalion. You shoulda stayed home . . . You may not get to see your home again' . . . So that was scary."[52] On another occasion, he tearfully described the chain of events that transpired when assigned the task of reconnoitering terrain to ensure its safety:

> I was leading a squad . . . to scout [an] area . . . We encountered some gunfire and I had fourteen guys with me. And we knew where it was coming [from] . . . So I got the group together . . . [And] we split [into three smaller detachments] . . . We were able to get 'em . . . Well, I lost a couple of guys.[53]

Such willingness to assume leadership positions led to steady and rapid promotions for Ornelas. He stated, "Within six months I was already a sergeant leading a squad."[54] After approximately fifteen months overseas, Ornelas rotated to Fort Sheridan, Illinois, where he was honorably discharged in June 1953 as a staff sergeant (E6).

Robert Villegas, younger brother of Darío Villegas and Medal of Honor recipient Ismael "Smiley" Villegas, enlisted into the Marine Corps in January 1953 at the age of seventeen in order to escape repeated gang fights that ultimately led to his arrest and probation, which the Marine Corps was willing to overlook. He provided colorful commentary on his decision: "I was starting to go on the wrong path. God was passing out brains [and] I thought he said trains, so I hopped on the wrong trolley."[55] Recruit training, however, provided an immediate sobering effect: "They straightened me out kinda quick [in] boot camp."[56] His two older brothers were also influential, especially Smiley's valor during World War II. Villegas recalled the moment in 1945 when the family received notification of Smiley's death: "It really influenced me once I knew what the . . . Medal of Honor was . . . I was ten years old when my brother got killed . . . We were playing in the backyard and a telegram came to the house and then all hell broke loose . . . My mother was crying."[57] A graduate of basic training in April 1953, Villegas requested a combat assignment to Korea in order to follow in the footsteps of his two older brothers, but was denied. He offered the following explanation: "I graduated from boot camp [on] April 12th and . . . I put [a] request in to [Korea] . . . Little did I know that they won't send you overseas at the age of seventeen . . . On July 20th, I turned eighteen [and] the truce [was signed] on July 27th."[58]

Assigned as a mortarman to the 9th Marine Regiment in the 3rd Marine Division, Villegas recalled the strong Latino contingent within his platoon: "I bet you pretty close to half of the platoon was [Chicano] and Puerto Riqueno . . . [There were] a lot of Puerto Ricans . . . even black Puerto Ricans."[59] Based with the regiment outside of Osaka, Villegas endured constant training and field maneuvers, including the following landing on Iwo Jima:

> In March of 1954, we made a division landing on Iwo Jima, the whole 3rd Marine Division. That was an experience . . . I couldn't help [but] remember the real Second World War landing . . . It was a lot of ash [and] caves . . . We went into this one cave . . . It had to have been a small hospital of some kind because there [were] skeletons still [present].[60]

After fourteen months overseas, Villegas was assigned as a military policeman to the Marine Corps Air Station (MCAS) in Tustin, California, for his third and final year in the Marine Corps. He was prompted to leave with an honorable discharge in January 1956 after an undisclosed incident reduced his rank from corporal (E4) to private (E1): "I didn't want to [reenlist] because I was a buck private and I didn't want to start [from the bottom] again."[61] This painful memory, so different from the tales of bravery and loyalty that are common—indeed, expected—from military service spurred a shameful silence that tarnished the legacy of his three-year tour in the Marine Corps.

In 1949, at the age of seventeen, Eddie Lovio lied about his age in order to join the USMCR's Company E in Tucson. As he provided his rationale, there was little desire to enlist in the active duty Marine Corps. Rather, "it was a neighborhood thing . . . It was a way to make a little extra money and go away for a two-week summer encampment."[62] From a monthly salary of $82.50, one of the first steps for Lovio after the unit was mobilized was to set up a $40 allotment home to his parents. He explained why: "In those days, it was expected. The kids worked and had to chip in."[63] As Lovio recounted, however, he was forced to remain at Camp Pendleton through the following spring after his mother intervened: "My mother sent a letter to the Department of the Navy to tell them that I lied about my age . . . You had to be eighteen to be sent overseas."[64] He also provided vivid testimony of the racial tension that developed on the base with active-duty marines:

> When we got activated, you have to realize that there were about 180 some of us, mostly Chicanos. We landed at Camp Pendleton and it was a culture shock for the Marine Corps because they'd never seen that many Chicanos in one outfit.

So, there were a lot of problems, especially at . . . the beer hall . . . The Marine Corps was pretty lily white at that time.[65]

Lovio arrived in Korea in April 1951, where he was assigned as a forward artillery observer—a job that involved traveling into no-man's-land in order to detect enemy artillery and heavy mortar fire. He offered the following description: "We would set up outposts with one infantry unit . . . and another one . . . We would observe at night, the incoming [enemy fire] and get an azimuth reading from both outposts and triangulate . . . [to] direct [return] fire."[66] On one occasion, while on patrol in October 1951, he was wounded by shrapnel from an artillery blast. He described the surreal chain of events that led to his return to the front after witnessing another wounded marine perform cleaning tasks at the aid station:

> I talked to the doctor. I [said], 'Look, I'm going back to the line. I'm not gonna stay here and mop floors and clean up after these guys.' He [said], 'Do whatever you want. Just tell your corpsman to give you some penicillin for two weeks . . . I went down to the main supply route [and] hitchhiked [on] a truck . . . and went back to the line."[67]

Upon leaving Korea in February 1952 Lovio was simultaneously demobilized; he ultimately left the military as a sergeant (E5) after ten years of combined service.[68]

TO SECURE THESE RIGHTS

Lovio's varied experiences also included an encounter with an all-black unit in Korea that, much to his surprise, remained in operation. He recalled his reaction and his discussion with one African American soldier:

> I was surprised one day . . . We were trying to locate a spot for an outpost and we were surveying the area . . . [And] there was this company [that was] all black. [It was] an army unit. And I said, 'I hate to be nosy, but why in the hell are you guys [all] black?' . . . Well, he said they were from the 24th Infantry Division. . . . and he said we used to be [an] all black [unit] . . . [He said] we were integrating

> [but] they hadn't fully integrated all of us . . . And to me that was really strange and odd.[69]

Lovio's commentary, including his recollection of Company E's reception at Camp Pendleton, underscores the persistence of discriminatory policies and practices within the armed forces despite the passage of Executive Order 9981 in July 1948, which banned segregation in the military. In the post–World War II era, African American organizations such as the National Association for the Advancement of Colored People (NAACP) and other civil rights activists called on the federal government to enact meaningful change (discussed more fully in chapter 9). As historian Lorena Oropeza explained, President Harry S. Truman responded in late 1946 by appointing "a federal civil rights committee to investigate the problem of prejudice. Its report the following year, *To Secure These Rights*, outlined the need for civil rights legislation."[70] One of the committee's recommendations was adopted in 1948 when Truman ordered an end to a segregated U.S. military. Nevertheless, the integration of the armed forces was a gradual process and, as Lovio discovered, all-black units remained in service during the Korean War.[71] Moreover, discriminatory behavior that also targeted Mexican American servicemen continued among the rank and file, and personal encounters with prejudice were a common occurrence for this study's narrators.

For example, Eddie Trujillo insisted that Mexican Americans were singled out and given dangerous assignments. Deployed to Korea in July 1950 as an army infantryman, Trujillo recalled that white noncommissioned officers were largely to blame: "Every time they [had] a real terrible assignment . . . [individuals such as] Trujillo [and] González [would be chosen]."[72] Meanwhile, Mike González encountered some difficulty in acquiring positions commensurate with his recently acquired rank of staff sergeant (E6), which he attributed to his Mexican ancestry. As he recounted, he lodged no formal complaint for fear of possible retaliation: "I felt they'd probably get mad at me and give me all the dirty details."[73] Such hesitation, however, did not restrain González from returning racial epithets to fellow service members: "I used to call 'em wops and what other names I could think of at the time."[74] By comparison, David Carillo was equally defiant but offered a different perspective on name-calling: "In Korea, you couldn't call anybody names, they'd shoot you. You know, you're carrying a loaded gun with you."[75] Frank Ornelas demonstrated that simple restraint could also be utilized when he impassively stated, "Some of them called me names. But that's fine. I learned to live with that."[76]

In a similar manner, Vincent Pardo Jr. also indicated that restraint was the more prudent option when confronted with discrimination. Drafted into the Marine Corps in 1952 for three years, he offered the following: "There was a feeling that sometimes some of the people that had rank over you were pretty prejudiced. Sometimes you felt like retaliating, but of course you couldn't do that."[77] Such efforts included clandestine attempts to speak Spanish with other Mexican American and Puerto Rican Marines: "As soon as the sergeant showed up, we switched to English because they would tell you [to] speak English."[78] Mark Rocha also employed a more cautious approach with fellow shipmates after enlisting in the navy in June 1951 for four years. In particular, he developed few friendships while stationed off the coast of Korea in a naval intelligence ship where he worked as a teletype operator. As he recalled, his poor English-speaking ability was partly to blame, as well as constant rumors of impending hostility: "I started to hear rumors that . . . [sailors] from the South . . . were throwin' blacks overboard at night, and then, three [or] four hours later, hollering 'man overboard.' And that they were [also] thinking about throwing other minorities overboard. So, it kind of put . . . some fear in me."[79]

Robert Castro insisted, however, that dedication to duty and outstanding job performance helped him to overcome the discrimination he encountered. He offered the following explanation:

> I made a point of learning my job and doing it well . . . When I got to the rank of staff sergeant [E6], I saw the importance of knowing your job and conducting yourself in a manner [in] which you would be respected by enlisted [men] as well as officers.[80]

Furthermore, Ruben Moreno firmly believed that machismo partially bridged the racial divide in the Marine Corps when he stated, "We Hispanics got a reputation for being brave, maybe stupid, but they respected that."[81] On the other hand, Moreno also recalled being a young hothead when confronted with prejudicial behavior. He described one particular incident:

> This guy Hernández . . . he was writing to his girlfriend who was an Anglo [woman]. This [white] guy from Oklahoma, he comes by and he [said], "Is this your girlfriend? I can't [imagine] that." And he throws [the picture]. And I was

> sittin' on the other end of the table and I got up and [said], "What the hell do you mean by that?" We tangled . . . They broke us up before we did any damage. Of course, I was boiling.[82]

William Fisher also decided to take a stand against a notoriously racist chief petty officer while stationed on Guam. He remembered the exact phrase he stated one morning after being hassled by the chief: "You know, somebody ought to take a .45 [millimeter pistol] and ram it up your ass and blow your brains out."[83] The subsequent chain of events that followed included a captain's mast and a summary court martial after Fisher was formally accused of misconduct.[84] He stated:

> He was a big Texan and he particularly didn't appreciate Mexicans. So, I got a captain's mast and . . . they were going to give me thirty days [of punishment] . . . I told the captain [that] no, I'd rather have a summary court martial . . . So, I had a court martial [and] that was the charge, threatening a chief petty officer . . . I got thirty days in the brig [and] I got busted to seaman [E3] and loss of pay. But, thirty days later it came back [from higher authority] that it was remitted due to insufficient evidence.[85]

At the same time, Gene García stood by his fellow African American airmen one evening in Shreveport, Louisiana, by deciding to sit with them in the segregated balcony of a movie theater. He described what followed: "Pretty soon somebody shined a light on me . . . And the guy [said], 'Excuse me sir . . . you can't be up here . . . This is the black section.' And I said, 'Wait a minute. These are my friends, and as far as I'm concerned, I can stay here with them.' "[86]

An additional source of anger and distress for Mexican American veterans, in addition to discriminatory encounters, derives from the depiction of the Korean War as the "forgotten war" and a "police action." A case in point is offered by David Carillo, for whom it stirs heartfelt emotions: "What is to forget? All the men—or should I say boys—that we lost over there."[87] Eddie Trujillo is equally disturbed: "I don't like it. I hate that . . . I lost my best friend."[88] Mike González offered an angrier commentary: "I think that sucks. I feel bad about it 'cause there was a lot of good men that were lost there, and I think that we should [have] more recognition because it was a bad war."[89] José Domínguez mocked the notion of the Korean conflict as a police action when he stated: "I think they called it a police action, but I didn't see no cops there."[90] Also recall Robert Castro's reflection in the epigraph: "I have never been able to comprehend why they refer to Korea as the forgotten war, because we lost thousands and thousands of people. It was not a police action."[91] Eddie Lovio simply stated, "It's never forgotten to me."[92] Meanwhile, Rolando Hinojosa offered a sobering reflection that highlights the empathetic bonds forged by men in battle: "I don't think it's forgotten by us who were there."[93] So, too, did George Castaneda: "We [veterans] weren't happy with that . . . We will never forget that war."[94]

CONCLUSION

Despite such heartache over the manner in which the conflict is remembered, all of the narrators nevertheless remain proud veterans in a manner similar to World War II veterans. They overwhelmingly describe their military service as a crucial step in the path toward personal advancement, maturity, and first-class citizenship. Consider the following statement by Gene García: "I think the military helped me a lot to grow up and be independent and be able to do things for myself."[95] David Carillo similarly stated: "It helped to make me a better man . . . It showed me a lot of discipline . . . and, I think, a lot of courage."[96] So, too, did Ray Gómez: "The service made me a man and I learned responsibility."[97] Another case in point is offered by Frank Gonzales: "I'm proud of the fact that I was able to serve . . . I think it's a good learning experience for people."[98] Vincent Pardo Jr. offered the following: "I'm proud I chose the Marine Corps and I'm also very thankful to God that I got through [it] . . . I have no regrets about doing that because I felt that this is my country and we all had to do our part."[99] By comparison, Ruben Moreno felt more of an American upon his return from Korea: "I feel like I earned my stay here in the United States even though I was born here."[100] Meanwhile, Robert Castro indicated that he "would do it . . . all over again in a heartbeat."[101] Simultaneously, for some veterans, such as Eddie Lovio, a willingness to utilize the term *Chicano* in his anecdotes hints at an emerging political consciousness that reflected a more combative and proud minority identity.

As with veterans of the Second World War, the aforementioned sentiments are not meant to suggest a universally positive depiction of the armed forces during these two conflicts. Yet participants of both wars found little room for open displays of discontent given the overwhelming emphasis on defeating fascism and communism. During the Vietnam War, however, deficiencies in stated objectives and the Cold War policy of containment were exposed. This enabled questioning attitudes to emerge among the troops during and after their military service and within U.S. society to an extent never possible during World War II and the Korean War, which the glaring class biases of the Selective Service System exacerbated. Within the Mexican American community, such factors facilitated very public critiques of military service and conventional machismo by a new, younger generation. As Oropeza described it: "Calling themselves Chicanos and Chicanas, they were no longer convinced that the route to equality, liberty, and freedom in the United States should rest on military service, unquestioning patriotism, and devotion to the nation. Instead, they began to argue the opposite."[102]

5

AZTLÁN AND VIETNAM

"Every time I go near the [Vietnam Memorial] in Washington, I can't look at it . . . Spiritually, I am on there."

"The grunt was the epitome of the representation of Latinos in Vietnam as it was for the African American."

THE MEXICAN AMERICAN GENERATION that provided military service during the Vietnam War came of age in a Cold War environment that emphasized national pride and patriotism and was characterized by Hollywood imagery, the wartime memories conveyed by World War II and Korean War veterans, and concern about Communist aggression. Such idealism operated in tandem with structural inequalities that prevented most Chicanos from utilizing student deferments and other class-based exemptions. Approximately 80,000–100,000 Hispanics were inducted into the armed forces for service in Vietnam, and while assignments in the combat arms typically gave rise to an increased level of hardship and danger, the guerrilla warfare that characterized the Vietnam War left no individual safe.[1] In particular, a sampling of combat experiences will highlight the challenges they faced in dealing with the tenacity of North Vietnamese soldiers and Viet Cong guerrillas, a stark reality that increasingly highlighted the ineptitude of American political and military objectives, and also fostered a questioning attitude among growing numbers of U.S. personnel. The Vietnam War was also the first test case for a completely integrated U.S. military, and personal encounters with discriminatory behavior continued as it had for Mexican American servicemen in World War II and Korea. However, Chicano servicemen were also positioned at the center of black and white animosity, a middle ground that offered greater latitude with regard to racial hostility.

THE COLD WAR AS TRAINING GROUND FOR YOUNG WARRIORS

During the Cold War, the domino theory (the belief that nation after nation would fall to communism if the United States did not contain Soviet expansion and influence) emerged as a new cornerstone of U.S. foreign policy. The result was an open-ended, all-encompassing policy of containment that "defined American policy for the next generation and beyond. Whenever and wherever an anti-Communist government was threatened, by indigenous insurgents, foreign invasion, or even diplomatic pressure . . . the United States would supply political, economic, and most of all, military aid."[2] One area of immediate concern was French Indochina, which the French reoccupied after World War II, despite Vietnam's declaration of independence in August 1945 under nationalist leader Ho Chi Minh.[3] A full-scale insurgency erupted the following year, and driven by the policy of containment and China's fall to communism in 1949, American involvement steadily increased. By 1954, as documented by journalist Stanley Karnow, "the United States had spent $2.5 billion to finance the futile French military effort—more assistance than France received in the Marshall Aid Plan from America to rebuild its shattered postwar economy."[4] Following the French defeat at the Battle of Dien Bien Phu in the spring of 1954, Vietnamese independence was secured, and later that year the Geneva Accords provided for the country's division at the 17th parallel pending a nationwide election to be held in the summer of 1956. In the north, the Democratic Republic of Vietnam emerged under Ho Chi Minh, and in the south, the Republic of (South) Vietnam was established under the temporary rule of Ngo Dinh Diem, a Catholic and ardent anti-Communist. These credentials earned him the support of President Eisenhower and, later, President Kennedy, and this proved crucial when Diem refused to allow the stipulated elections to be held. A new Communist insurgency subsequently developed against the South Vietnamese government, which increasingly relied on U.S. support.

Domestically, one powerful source of motivation to combat this perceived monolithic threat was the Cold War rhetoric and call to arms that typified John F. Kennedy's presidency. Famed journalist, writer, and ex-Marine Corps officer during the Vietnam War, Philip Caputo vividly recalled the missionary idealism that Kennedy generated among large segments of the American population, himself included:

> We saw ourselves as the champions of "a cause that was destined to triumph." So, when we marched into the rice paddies . . . we carried, along with our packs and rifles, the implicit convictions that the Viet Cong would be quickly beaten and that we were doing something altogether noble and good. We kept the packs and rifles; the convictions, we lost.[5]

President Kennedy also continued the policy of containment that featured an accelerated arms race with the Soviet Union as well as military and economic aid to non-Communist allies—in particular, the Third World. As he stated to Congress in May 1961: "The great battleground for the defense and expansion of freedom today is the whole southern half of the globe . . . the lands of the rising peoples."[6] On one hand, Kennedy established the Peace Corps, which placed volunteer doctors, teachers, and engineers in impoverished areas overseas. On the other hand, he approved military aid in the form of equipment and advisors, especially in South Vietnam, and by 1963, twelve thousand U.S. advisors were stationed there. The following year, under President Lyndon Baines Johnson, the number of advisors escalated yet again, to twenty-four thousand.

President Johnson also authorized covert operations against North Vietnam by CIA-supported South Vietnamese forces that involved high-speed patrol boats meant to conduct sabotage and gather intelligence. These operations were often supported by specially equipped U.S. naval vessels capable of conducting electronic surveillance from international waters. On one such mission on the evening of August 4, 1964, the USS *Maddox* was attacked (an aggression that has never been verified), which prompted a full-scale retaliatory strike by the U.S. Navy.[7] Furthermore, Congress passed the Gulf of Tonkin Resolution later that month, providing President Johnson with authorization to use armed force in South Vietnam in an effort to defeat the burgeoning Communist insurgency. And so, the introduction of combat troops was inevitable, and it occurred the following spring as marines were dispatched to protect American installations in South Vietnam coming under increased attack by enemy forces. These consisted of regular army units of the North Vietnamese Army (NVA) that traveled southward via the Ho Chi Minh Trail, a supply route from North Vietnam through neighboring Laos and Cambodia, as well as Viet Cong guerrilla forces.

By the summer of 1965, initial defensive measures had become offensive search-and-destroy missions as part of a larger strategy that involved the intensive bombing of North Vietnam through continuous air campaigns and the simultaneous pacification of the South. The latter was to be accomplished through the infusion of economic and nonmilitary aid in an effort to win the hearts and minds of the South Vietnamese peasantry, together with the destruction of enemy forces. This escalation of the war and the emphasis placed on enemy kills produced a war of attrition whereby the enemy body count became the principal measure of progress.[8] In order to prosecute the war more effectively, Vietnam was divided into four military regions. First, or I Corps, was the northernmost zone adjacent to the Vietnamese Demilitarized Zone (DMZ) and IV Corps the southernmost.[9] The aforementioned tactics failed miserably, and the surprise Communist offensive across South Vietnam during Tet in 1968 illustrated the stark reality that the United States was not at all close to victory, despite three years of continuous operations. American resolve and troop levels gradually declined, and the 1973 Paris Peace Accords formally ended U.S. involvement in Vietnam.

Despite this ultimate defeat, the policy of containment and Cold War hysteria nevertheless forged an ideological justification for American involvement in Vietnam that influenced countless numbers of young men coming of age during the Vietnam War era, including many Chicanos. Steadfast principles grounded in family, culture, patriotism, assimilation, and religion were paramount considerations within this mind-set. Moreover, the prospect of first-class citizenship reinforced a connection between these attributes and military service, as it had for earlier generations that had fought in World War II and Korea. As Raymond Buriel from Riverside, California, said, "These thoughts about freedom of religion, the domino theory, and your legitimacy here made me think, if I went into the military and served, nobody could ever question . . . our [Mexican American community] place here."[10] Tony López, also born in Riverside to conservative Catholic parents, recalled the value his father placed on certain principles during his childhood: "My dad taught me that there's three important things in life—my family, my [Catholic] faith, and my culture."[11] The need to protect these principles from perceived Communist aggression influenced his decision to volunteer for Officer Candidate School (OCS) in the U.S. Marine Corps upon his graduation from the University of San Diego in 1964. He would ultimately serve two tours in Vietnam, maintaining an unflappable sense of purpose: "I felt pretty strong that the United States needed to show its presence and try to help that country be a democratic country."[12] Across the nation in Lansing, Michigan, John Sánchez was motivated by a similar rationale:

> The domino theory was one of the reasons I volunteered for Vietnam . . . We were a family of patriots. My father was in World War II . . . then I had an uncle that was in Korea . . . I just admired the service. I grew up watching a lot of war

movies, Audie Murphy . . . John Wayne, all of that . . . When my time came, I volunteered.[13]

Sánchez's words point to another powerful medium for inculcating Cold War rationale—Hollywood films—particularly war movies. Hollywood personnel, such as the decorated World War II veteran-turned-actor Audie Murphy; popular film star John Wayne; and Vic Morrow, the lead in the weekly hit series *Combat*, were household names among young men nationwide. John Wayne's role as Sergeant Stryker in *The Sands of Iwo Jima* was a particular favorite. While these childhood experiences were immortalized by Ron Kovic's autobiography, *Born on the Fourth of July*, set in the small Long Island town of Massapequa, similar experiences during the Cold War undoubtedly affected a wide range of young men coming of age in the decade preceding the Vietnam War.[14] Within the Mexican American community, the case of Jim Acevedo, an agricultural worker from Scottsbluff, Nebraska, is suggestive. He offered the following recollection when asked about the role of the media in his decision to enlist in the Marine Corps in 1962 at the age of eighteen:

> At that time, it was Mom's apple pie and the American flag. It was the thing to do. Everybody spent a tour in the military. It was all based on nationalism. It was based on the movies that we went to as a kid, your John Wayne movies . . . You see all these things, and you just kind of felt obligated to pull a tour for your country.[15]

John Rodríguez offered equally compelling testimony in his response, also describing the influential nature of Hollywood war movies during his childhood. Moreover, there were images that he ultimately carried with him to Vietnam after he enlisted in the army in 1968:

> It's funny, I haven't told this to many people, but when I got wounded, one of the first things I said, out of just sheer, not knowing what to say . . . was, "They got me." That was John Wayne . . . I had taken [the media] to 'Nam, and I was wounded, and I said some words that reflected John Wayne. What a trip, man . . . Yeah, I've been influenced by the media.[16]

Frank Reyes, from Los Angeles, was so fascinated by the military and the popular song "Ballad of the Green Berets," that he would eventually become a Green Beret himself. Recalling the war games of his childhood and the wartime memories of male family members, he said, "Growing up, all I ever wanted to be was a soldier . . . I would go in the backyard and play army . . . I would listen intently, and [their war stories] always fascinated me."[17]

Wartime memories conveyed by World War II and Korean War veterans to younger family members also fostered a powerful sense of duty and desire for military service. George Mariscal, also from Los Angeles, offers a potent example, as he recalled his father's innumerable war stories:

> [The military] was a presence, always in my family, because all my uncles had served, and my father was a World War II vet, a Marine Corps vet, and that was very important to him. We had in our garage growing up . . . two samurai swords and a Japanese flag, a blood-splattered Japanese flag, and an old M-1 rifle . . . and he always had very exotic stories about Japan . . . So it was a big thing for him, and there were a lot of stories.[18]

This generational transfer of memories during the Cold War often produced a chain reaction within Mexican American families whereby many sons and brothers felt compelled to follow in the footsteps of relatives who had served in World War II and Korea. For example, Victor Ramírez, born and raised in Del Rio, Texas, remembers that his childhood dream was to enlist in the military, due especially to the strong influence of his older brother, a Korean War veteran: "I wanted to follow my brother . . . [He] instilled a lot of pride in me."[19] Growing up in Saginaw, Michigan, Gilbert Guevara was fascinated with the military uniforms of his three older brothers, who were in the army, Marine Corps, and air force: "When I used to see those uniforms, them shiny gold buttons, and all that stuff, I thought, that's the coolest thing I ever seen in my life . . . I need to be dressed like that."[20] Daniel Cano, a Los Angeles native, also came from a military family. In his words: "I had always heard about the Army and the military through family, parties, so for me it was . . . a natural progression."[21]

Tony Moreno, however, offered another more pragmatic perspective on military service during the Vietnam War when he stated:

> I was in the military because I got drafted and I was there strictly because I got drafted. I didn't get into the ideals . . . I just knew that once I was in the military, and I was out there in Vietnam, I was gonna do the best job I could.[22]

Despite the numerous draft notices that fellow Saginaw residents were receiving, Moreno was nevertheless shocked when he was drafted in June 1969 at the age of twenty-one while working as a junior accountant at Saginaw Steering

Gear, a subsidiary of General Motors. Recently married and with a newborn son, Moreno explored the possibility of securing an exemption through his local draft board. He offered the following on his efforts:

> I explored it, but I didn't get it. I went . . . and I told [the draft board], "Hey, I'm married and I have a son." . . . I knew there's things they could have done, but they didn't, and I knew they weren't going to do it for me . . . I pursued it as far as I could . . . Bottom line was . . . the date came, I had to go, and I went . . . I [also] think it had a lot to do with being a minority, being Hispanic. Because there was a lot of people that I knew that were white that didn't have to go . . . probably 'cause they knew people and we didn't.[23]

Moreno's commentary serves as a reminder that Cold War rhetoric and other ideological motivations were not the only factors that facilitated entry into the armed forces for service in Vietnam. As American involvement escalated, so too did the U.S. military's manpower needs, which, in turn, accelerated the draft system.[24] With no intention of mobilizing the reserves or dramatically altering the stationing of regular military units, President Johnson gambled that increased draft calls would receive the least public attention.

With 27 million baby boomers of prime draft age from 1964 to 1973, the increase in monthly draft calls affected a relatively small percentage. However, as historian Beth Bailey eloquently argues, this was also the source of potential bias within the draft system:

> Over the preceding decade, the selective service system had developed an extensive system of deferments, meant to manage the overabundance of potential draftees . . . The deferments had generated little concern while draft calls were low and the nation was at peace. But as draft calls increased, and as more and more American servicemen died on foreign soil, these deferments mattered.[25]

During the Vietnam War, these exemptions rather quickly became synonymous with class privilege—most notably student deferments, which enabled youth from more affluent families to avoid the draft while enrolled as full-time students. Additionally, potential draftees with social connections and economic clout had an added advantage in securing an exemption, especially one based on a physical or mental condition. Official documentation, which family doctors and psychiatrists could provide, were often crucial factors in convincing draft board members to approve an exemption. These institutional factors arguably placed a disproportionate burden on the working class for military service in Vietnam, and the labeling of the conflict as the "working-class war" has received considerable, though not universal, acceptance.[26]

With minimal educational and technical skills to offer once inducted into the military, the working poor were often relegated to the combat arms (infantry, artillery, engineers) due to their inability to score well enough on the Armed Forces Qualification Test (AFQT) to win entry into more technical fields.[27] This did not go unnoticed by high-level public officials who believed in the military's capacity to function as an agent of social uplift. In 1966, Secretary of Defense Robert McNamara instituted a program called Project 100,000, which authorized an annual quota of 100,000 men who had previously failed the AFQT, most of whom were from poor and single-parent homes.[28] With little or no intention of offering specialized training to these men, however, most were simply trained for combat duty as the military's manpower needs escalated. While no statistics for Spanish-surnamed individuals are available, authors Lawrence M. Baskir and William A. Strauss discovered some rather alarming data:

> From 1966 to 1968 Project 100,000 brought in 240,000 recruits, usually to the Army and Marines . . . Forty-one percent were black, and almost 50 percent came from the South . . . More than 40 percent had a reading ability at less than a sixth-grade level, and almost 15 percent read below fourth-grade . . . Half the Army and Marine contingent went to Vietnam.[29]

The consequences were tragic for these men, who suffered a casualty rate twice as high as U.S. forces overall. Sal Martínez, who transitioned from an enlisted member of the Marine Corps to a commissioned officer, observed the impact of the program firsthand:

> Project 100,000 was to put what was then referred to as category-five individuals, those who were basically illiterate, who could not pass the armed forces examination test under normal circumstances . . . into the service. Well, the majority of those people were minorities and almost all of them went into the infantry.[30]

Moreover, local draft boards all too often mirrored federal programs such as Project 100,000 in forging class distinctions within the armed forces by channeling the working poor into the military at an alarming rate. As documented by historian Christian G. Appy, "Draft boards were overwhelmingly controlled by conservative, white, prosperous men in their fifties or sixties . . . only 9 percent had blue-collar occupations . . . Only 1.3 percent were black."[31] Meant to operate as "little groups of neighbors on whom is placed the responsibility to determine who is to serve the nation in the armed forces and who is to serve in industry, agriculture, and other deferred classifications," the 4,000 draft boards nationwide were given wide latitude in the enforcement of the general guidelines established by the Selective Service and its director, General Lewis B. Hershey.[32] As director from 1947 to 1970, General Hershey viewed the Selective Service as an instrument of human-resource planning in order to channel people into a variety of occupations considered to be in the national interest. The underlying message was that gifted individuals, especially in the area of scholasticism, inherently deserved exemptions. After all, the very notion of selective service clearly implied deferments. Such an approach, however, inevitably made working-class and impoverished young men increasingly vulnerable to the draft.

What all of this meant for the Mexican American community was the inability of most working-class Chicanos to navigate this system to avoid military service if they were inclined to do so. Indeed, childhood poverty and a working-class upbringing remained an everyday reality for large elements of the community. Moreover, such an existence discouraged full-time enrollment at institutions of higher learning in order to obtain a student deferment, the result of inferior educational opportunities and the inability to afford the tuition necessary for university or vocational training. For example, at the University of Texas, during the 1966–67 academic year, 634 students were Mexican American from an overall enrollment of 22,259, for a paltry 2.6 percent.[33] The situation in California was equally grim. Within the University of California system in 1971, less than 1 percent of the total student population of 97,000 was Mexican American.[34]

Did these factors, largely created by structural inequalities, produce disproportionate representation by Mexican Americans in relation to their actual numbers in society at large? And did this inevitably heighten battlefield casualties? In other words, did race play a factor in the community's vulnerability to the draft system during the Vietnam War as indicated by Tony Moreno? For Chicano activists within the burgeoning Chicano movement, the answer was a resounding yes. Labeling themselves a nonwhite racial minority, Chicana/o activists sought to promote cultural awareness, ethnic pride, and *hermandad* (brotherhood and spiritual unity for the Mexican American community) by distancing themselves from mainstream American values.[35] Other components of the Chicano movement included the United Farm Worker movement led by Cesar Chavez, student activism at the high school and university level, and a highly vocal antiwar movement. Operating under the banner "la batalla esta aqui" ("the battle is here"), antidraft counseling was increasingly directed toward Chicano youth, and antiwar rallies, organized by the National Chicano Moratorium Committee, denounced the hypocrisy of American involvement in Vietnam, while the Chicana/o community endured a variety of social, political, and economic contradictions.

As they further emphasized, these inequalities channeled young Chicanos into the military at an alarming rate, producing disproportionate battlefield casualties in the process. One study examined casualty figures of Mexican Americans from five southwestern states (Arizona, California, Colorado, New Mexico, and Texas) and concluded that of the 6,335 deaths in Vietnam from December 1967 to March 1969, 19 percent had distinctive Spanish surnames, at a time when the 1960 census estimated the Latina/o population of that region to be 11.8 percent.[36] However, another study conducted in 1989 by geographers Brady Foust and Howard Botts offered a much smaller disproportionate representation. They examined casualty rates nationwide and concluded that Latinos comprised 6 percent of Vietnam's war dead at a time when the 1970 census estimated the Latina/o population to be 4.6 percent of the total U.S. population.[37] Comparatively, in 1970 sociologist Charles C. Moskos published a comprehensive study of the military's rank and file, and with data provided by the Department of Defense he demonstrated that black casualty rates were high in the early years of the Vietnam War in relation to their actual numbers in Southeast Asia, especially so in the army and the Marine Corps.[38] Such casualty rates steadily decreased and were slightly disproportionate by the war's midpoint in June 1968. Ultimately, this data on Chicanos and African Americans indicates that these two communities clearly endured more than their fair share of the hazards associated with military service during the Vietnam War. To conclude, however, that communities of color were specifically targeted for their race is shortsighted. Rather, the institutions most responsible for channeling young men into the military, including the draft, exploited the working poor throughout the nation, including working-class whites. For the Mexican American community, the intersection between class and race was such that the community's socioeconomic marginalization left young Chicanos with few alternatives other than military service. And thus, while the Vietnam War was the first conflict fought by integrated armed forces, the institutional apparatus of the United States engineered a military along class lines, not race. As Appy further remarked, "Though racial discrimination and racist attitudes surely persisted in the military, class was far more important than race in determining the overall social composition of American forces. Precisely when the enlisted ranks were becoming increasingly integrated by race, they were becoming ever more segregated by class."[39]

Once inducted into the military, contact with military canon and prescribed behavior was inevitable. As in World War II and Korea, this process first began with initial recruit training, a universal ordeal also known as boot camp, which aimed to destroy all vestiges of civilian identity and produce a redefined sense of self in accordance with military doctrine. Recruits were exposed to a continuous stream of crude language and behavior that continued beyond basic training and was often exacerbated by the Communist insurgency in South Vietnam, where the Viet Cong and the NVA's guerrilla tactics left American forces with relatively few sanctuaries free from enemy activity. Furthermore, a powerful sense of pride characterized completing basic training, and the acknowledgement received from family and friends. Eddie Solís, for example, was especially proud, "When I came out of boot camp, I thought bullets would bounce off me."[40] A subsequent leave period of varying length preceded final deployment, during which youthful exuberance and a call to duty masked a multitude of sensations and fears that undoubtedly affected each individual. Arriving as a unit or as individual replacements, a one-year tour of duty—thirteen months for Marine Corps personnel—began.

HUMPING HILLS AND CONFRONTING "CHARLIE"

Drafted in March 1968 at the age of nineteen while working a variety of odd jobs in Long Beach, California, George Mariscal recalled his shock and disbelief upon learning of his designation as a military policeman (MP) and guard-dog handler as he neared the completion of basic training. As he remembered, the majority of his fellow recruits were assigned as infantrymen: "I firmly believe that that happened because of the testing that they gave us, these pseudo-IQ tests. And I scored very high . . . And when the assignments came out [for all recruits] at the end of basic training, I can remember looking at the bulletin board and [seeing] straight columns of 11B [infantry] and then I'm sitting there, 95B."[41] Briefly assigned to Fort Story, Virginia, where he guarded nuclear missiles, Mariscal ultimately received orders to Vietnam after eight months in the army. He described his first reaction upon arrival: "My first memory of Vietnam is landing, and the heat."[42] With no sentry dogs to manage in Vietnam, Mariscal was assigned to patrolling the base perimeter, where encounters with enemy forces and guerrilla tactics were quite common:

> I was never on long range patrols . . . [Combat] situations would either be perimeter situations where we'd be on guard duty and [enemy] sappers would come under the wires. That happened a lot. And then rocket and mortar attacks we had a lot of . . . [Also,] there were booby traps where I was, but we [didn't] know who set 'em. Clearly, because we had Vietnamese working on the base, there's no doubt in my mind that a lot of 'em were VC. They were the people calling in the mortar and rocket attacks at night.[43]

Rising to the rank of specialist fourth class (E-4) by the completion of his tour in January 1970, Mariscal rotated home and was immediately released from active duty with an honorable discharge.

Leroy Quintana, born in Raton, New Mexico, in 1944, decided to volunteer for the draft in 1967 while enrolled as a college student at the University of New Mexico. He offered an explanation: "I wasn't doing too well in school and I thought I needed some kind of direction."[44] As a child his mother impressed upon him the value of military service, which motivated Quintana to enlist and to also volunteer for rigorous airborne training with the army. He subsequently deployed to Vietnam as a member of the famed 101st Airborne Division, where he was assigned to a five-man team that conducted long-range reconnaissance patrols (LRRP). As he described, Quintana and his fellow team members were directed to avoid combat engagements: "Recon is a little safer because your job is to stay away from action and just report what you see."[45] Nevertheless, as he detailed one harrowing incident, LRRP teams were in a constant state of vulnerability as they shadowed enemy forces: "One particular instance, it was raining . . . and I turned my face and there was a bunch of Viet Cong guys nearby. How they didn't see us, I don't know, man. Holy shit!"[46]

These reconnaissance teams also maintained a rather hectic schedule: "It [was] a situation where we were four, five, [or] six days in the field, then back to base camp for a while."[47] And it was in base camp that the drudgery of life in Vietnam often manifested itself in the form of menial and grimy tasks. He recalled, "One of the worst things in the world was that you were in Vietnam doing kitchen police [KP]. Everybody pulled KP. And everybody burned shit in barrels."[48] Such tasks also provide the context for Quintana's recollection of a Mexican national that served in his unit:

> This guy from Mexico, I don't know what the condition was. He apparently was going to become a citizen if allowed to serve in Vietnam. And that guy got chosen for everything in his squad . . . He was a very nice guy. He looked like [the actor] Ricardo Montalban. And [the VC] were hiding in the bush one day and the sergeant that he had that was always pickin' [him] for details . . . the VC came up behind him and blew [his] head off. And [the Mexican] was shattered for life. He said he didn't care about being a citizen anymore.[49]

Much to his dismay, KP and other loathsome tasks remained an everyday reality upon Quintana's return to Fort Bragg, North Carolina, in 1968. He stated: "I came back from Vietnam and pulled KP, which I thought was a shitty thing to do . . . so the army never let you kind of rest . . . [Also,] we came back from Vietnam and we had to go to the field and do field exercises."[50] As Quintana recalled his release from active duty three months later, he simply stated: "I was glad to get out."[51] He was honorably discharged as a specialist fourth class in 1969.

Bored with school in his hometown of Los Angeles and looking to follow in the footsteps of his father and uncle, both paratroopers during World War II, Daniel Cano joined the army and volunteered for airborne training in April 1966 at the age of nineteen. While grateful for the additional $50 stipend, Cano was adamant that a sense of tradition, rather than financial gain, was the primary motivation for his decision to become a paratrooper. In fact, Cano declined an initial set of orders for Germany in order to attend jump school, which virtually guaranteed a deployment to Vietnam. He arrived in October 1966 as a member of the 101st Airborne Division, where his light artillery unit supported infantry units on various missions. In his words:

> Out of the 365 days [I was there], I'd say I was in the field at least 330 days . . . Usually you set up on a mountaintop or a clearing. [We] put sandbags around us [and] they'd helicopter the guns in and then we'd support the infantry operating around us . . . Two days later or a month later, we're up and we're gone.[52]

Repeatedly probed most evenings by local VC elements—or, as he described—"usually young kids from the neighboring town," Cano was wounded by shrapnel from a grenade in December 1966, which required a week of rehabilitation at a nearby field hospital.[53] He also provided vivid commentary on one of the more powerful sources of frustration for U.S. forces—the unreliability and generally poor performance of the Army of the Republic of (South) Vietnam (ARVN). He stated, "You were always afraid to be around the ARVN because you never knew what they were gonna do . . . We didn't really trust them because they were known to not fight . . . or to be Viet Cong."[54] Upon his departure from Vietnam in October 1967, Cano was stationed at Fort Bragg, North Carolina, where he served the remainder of his three-year enlistment with the 82nd Airborne Division. He remarked: "After I got back I had a month of leave and [then] I had to go back to North Carolina for eighteen months . . . We had all kinds of [field] exercises."[55] Rising to the rank of sergeant (E5), Cano was honorably discharged in 1969.

Frank Reyes, meanwhile, took rigorous specialized training one step further by becoming a member of the U.S. Special Forces established under President Kennedy in 1960. Upon his graduation from high school in Los Angeles in 1968, Reyes enlisted into the army and successfully became an engineer and demolitions expert with the Army Rangers before joining the Green Berets.[56] He offered a more simplified description of his duties as a member of a twelve-man A-Team: "I got to blow things up, in other words, but you're [also] cross-trained with everyone else in your particular detachment."[57] Reyes also described the intense camaraderie that existed in such units, which was further reinforced for him by the itinerant nature of his childhood while raised by a single mother and extended family members:

> I never really had a family because every time I'd get comfortable in one setting, boom, I'd end up having to pack my things and move on. The only time I thought I really had a family was when I was in the service . . . Both my detachment and my teams I was with, we pretty much stayed together for quite a while, more than a year or two. We became friends [and] we became family. When somebody got hurt, it hurt [all of] us.[58]

Throughout the majority of this process, he was joined by a Mexican national, Ramiro Salinas, who enlisted in an effort to gain his citizenship. He said, "When

Ramiro first joined the army and we went through basic [training], we went through Ranger [training], [and] we went through Special Forces training . . . Ramiro did not speak a lick of English. He had just [come] over from Guanajuato, Mexico . . . He did two tours with us."[59]

Arriving in Vietnam in April 1969, Reyes would himself serve three consecutive tours with the Rangers and Green Berets, during which he participated in combat missions into Laos, Cambodia, and North Vietnam.[60] The consummate military man, he felt obligated to remain where he thought he was most needed rather than the politically divisive environment that characterized the United States. He offered the following recollection:

> Honestly, I didn't want to do stateside duty . . . At the end of the tour, you'd end up having to go back stateside anyway. And in the short time I [was] back, I really didn't like any of the things and the politics and the pettiness that was going on back here in the states . . . The first chance [I and others] did was . . . sign a [Form] 1049 . . . a request for transfer back to whatever active units that were back there [in Vietnam]. They needed experienced NCOs, so it wasn't a problem.[61]

Reyes was captured during one mission in October 1971—or, as he put it—"I got to be a guest of the North Vietnamese for eighteen months."[62] He has received little fanfare in comparison to the more celebrated cases of navy and air force pilots; nevertheless, the treatment Reyes received by his captors was every bit as brutal. He provided a brief glimpse of his ordeal and his effort to cope and survive: "I was young, I was dumb . . . There was a lot of physical beatings, a lot of mental [abuse]. And there was a lot of work."[63] Released in early 1973 following the signing of the Paris Peace Accords, Reyes and other POWs returned to the United States via West Germany, where they were debriefed and medically examined. Years later, in 1987, he was notified by the Judge Advocate General (JAG) that his role in that mission warranted the Medal of Honor. Reyes refused, however, and he explained why: "I was supposed to be awarded the Medal of Honor, but I turned it down. I don't want a medal to remember something that brought back a lot of bad memories."[64] Altogether, Reyes served nine and a half years and was honorably discharged in 1977 as a staff sergeant (E6).

Born in Texas in 1944 but raised in Corona, California, Eddie Solís was on the path of juvenile delinquency, prompting his father to present him with an ultimatum: "I wasn't going to school [and] I was ditching . . . When I started getting in trouble, my dad [said], 'You go to school or you join the service.'"[65] Nervous and exited, Solís was seventeen years old when, with his father's consent, he enlisted into the Marine Corps in 1962 for a four-year term.[66] Initially assigned to Cuba as an interpreter, he deployed to Vietnam as an advisor with a company of fellow marines for a one-year tour, from 1963 to 1964. In this capacity, he illegally entered into combat situations with ARVN troops, a precarious position that was further jeopardized by the warning provided by his superiors: "They called us advisors, but we were in the thick of it. And they told us, 'If you get caught . . . we don't know who the hell you are."[67] Of the ARVN personnel he trained, he offered the following: "They were very willing to fight [but] it was hard to trust 'em. A lot of times you [reluctantly] depended on what they said because they knew [the terrain]."[68] By contrast, he expressed a grudgingly favorable opinion of the Viet Cong he encountered: "You didn't see 'em . . . I never knew whether I got one or not, to tell you the truth . . . They were dedicated and they were well trained."[69] After returning from Vietnam, Solís got married as the manpower needs in Vietnam skyrocketed, two factors that prompted his decision to leave the Marine Corps. As he recalled, it was not without regret:

> I got married when I was in the service . . . and I got [forcibly] extended for four months . . . And then that's when [the fighting in] Vietnam really broke out and [my wife] was pregnant with twins, so I had to get out . . . [However,] I wish I would have stayed in, I wish I [had] made a career of it.[70]

After serving four years and four months, Solís was honorably discharged as a lance corporal (E3) in 1966.

Raymond Buriel enlisted into the Marine Corps in June 1967 after his graduation from high school. Because of the larger Cold War context and the looming conflict in Vietnam, for Buriel it almost seemed like a fait accompli: "Most of the guys from around here [in Riverside] that were my age, it was just a given that you were gonna go into the military whether you were drafted or you enlisted."[71] Assigned to the Third Marine Division as a rifleman, Buriel spent the majority of his deployment in I Corp, including the 1968 Battle of Khe Sanh. Situated on a remote mountaintop along with a few other hilltop outposts, the area was surrounded by two or three NVA divisions for approximately five months and was regularly bombarded. He offered a brief glimpse of the daily routine: "In Khe Sanh, we were dug in . . . for weeks. We'd get shelled and shit, [and we] quit doing patrols because we were surrounded. And so, basically, there was a lot of taking orders [and] building more trenches [and] putting up more barbed wire [and] putting up more sandbags."[72]

After being relieved and nearing the end of his tour, he also recalled the shock and unease he felt in moving further south and confronting Vietnamese villagers and the Viet Cong's guerrilla tactics on a more consistent basis. As he described, this different tactical environment further south also provoked tragic reprisals by U.S. personnel:

> All the areas where we were at [in the north], civilians had already been evacuated, and so when we were hit, we knew who was hitting us . . . It wasn't until my last three weeks in country when we went, [to] what we used to call down south, [near] Da Nang . . . And we were around villagers, and it was really there that I saw a lot of booby traps. Up north there's no booby traps . . . And you didn't know who it was, and so the only people you saw around there were villagers. And that's when some of the guys in our unit really started to go ballistic towards these villagers.[73]

Amid these combat experiences, Buriel found a bit of refuge in his capacity as a letter writer for himself and others. He reminisced: "When you're overseas, you write a lot because you look forward to getting letters back. I used to write letters and I used to write letters for other guys [who were not literate] . . . I'd read their letters [to them]; I'd write their letters [for them]."[74] This talent served him well upon his departure in January 1969 and, somewhat to his dismay, Buriel was reassigned as an office clerk while stationed at Camp Pendleton. Rising to the rank of corporal (E4), Buriel was honorably discharged the following summer.

A child prodigy, Alfredo Vea was drafted into the army in 1966 at the age of sixteen while enrolled at the University of California, Berkeley. He offered the following explanation: "When I was twelve years old, I said I was sixteen [and] I got a driver's license, a work permit, a Social Security card, [and] I got a job driving a truck. When you lived by yourself, that's what you do."[75] With the help of a lawyer, Vea postponed his departure for one year; nevertheless, he departed for basic training at the age of seventeen and trained as a radio telephone operator (RTO) at Fort Monmouth, New Jersey, where he often traveled into New York City for its cultural and intellectual environment. He stated: "I used to go into the East Village from Fort Monmouth . . . and listen to poetry and listen to music."[76] In fact, Vea was often recognized by fellow soldiers for an intellect that was indeed readily apparent: "In Vietnam, I got the nickname of 'poet' and . . . a lot of people used to come and ask me to write poems . . . [And] I remember writing [letters] to a lot of families [for them]."[77]

Vea arrived in Vietnam a week before the Tet Offensive and served primarily in I Corp with the Americal, or 23rd Infantry, Division.[78] Due to battlefield casualties in the division, he was promoted rather rapidly at the tender young age of eighteen: "I was a staff sergeant for about two weeks . . . [However,] I got into a fight with another sergeant and I went back to [sergeant] E5."[79] Vea also recalled the strong Mexican American presence within the division: "Most of the time, I was attached in Chu Lai and Da Nang [to the] Americal [Division]. It was all Mexican. In fact, we had dudes from Mexico trying to get their citizenship that didn't even speak English. One of 'em was a really good friend of mine. [He] stepped on a land mine and that was the end of him."[80] As an RTO, he was assigned on another occasion to the defense of a radio station on a remote hilltop that became the target of an entire NVA regiment of approximately three thousand men. While highlighting the futility of defending a hilltop that served as a decoy, the following vivid testimony also illustrates that the NVA was not averse to open-field engagements:

> There was one really bad three-day period . . . on that hill. That was the worst . . . It was the absolute ultimate [fear] for me, to be surrounded by North Vietnamese troops who were in the open, walking around, [and] getting ready to assault this hill. Fuck! It was just the most surreal experience I've ever had . . . They had five times more men than we had. I had never seen them that close. I had never seen them with full uniforms, black backpacks, and dark green bandoliers . . . [However,] we were a decoy. The real radio station was like thirty miles [away]. I didn't know we were a decoy; somebody told me that later.[81]

Moreover, as Vea's departure neared, he was forcibly extended for another three months to his dismay due to the critical shortage of RTOs: "I thought I was going home. That was a real grim day, boy."[82] Upon his return to the United States, Vea was honorably discharged as a sergeant (E5) after eighteen months of military service. He offered this final summation: "I didn't like any day in the U.S. Army; not one day did I enjoy. I felt like it was repressive."[83]

Across the country, John Sánchez toiled alongside his family as a seasonal laborer throughout Michigan's Saginaw Valley. As he recalled, it was a job that offered valuable lessons: "That was not the best job . . . I've ever had, but it certainly was the most important job . . . You learned the discipline of work . . . the value of work . . . the dignity of work . . . You also learned how to dream. And it taught me that I did not want to do this [for] the rest of my life."[84] A fascination with airplanes also developed, which motivated his decision in July 1966, while enrolled at two-year Lansing Community College, to volunteer for flight school in the U.S. Army at the age of twenty-one: "When I was out in the fields, I would see airplanes and the vapor trails they would leave . . . Every time I got up to stretch . . . there'd be an aircraft . . . just streaming across the sky."[85] Commissioned as a chief warrant officer (CWO), Sánchez also realized that his training as a helicopter pilot ensured a deployment overseas: "98 percent of our flight class . . . had orders to go to Vietnam . . . I knew that the price for me to learn to fly was to go to Vietnam."[86]

He arrived in August 1967, and recalled his first impression: "When I got out of the airplane . . . It's like someone had put a blanket that had been in an oven, on me. And it never went away until I left . . . It was either hot and dry or hot and wet."[87] Assigned to the 188th Assault Helicopter Company, Sánchez and his fellow pilots conducted search-and-rescue and medevac operations as well as the insertion and extraction of special combat assault groups in South Vietnam and neighboring countries. He described in his own words the harrowing nature of these missions, including one exceptionally difficult extraction:

> We were always aware of where the demarcation line was. And they cautioned us about going [across], but . . . we had to get our people out. I flew military air command (MAC) flights . . . Those [were] basically . . . secret missions, where you had a composite [group] of navy [and] Marine Corps [personnel] . . . And we were asked not to take any identification along with us. Specifically, [on] one mission, we went in and for two days, we tried to get 'em out. And there were aircraft on the sides of this mountain, American aircraft . . . [Previous attempts] had gone in and they just got beat up [and] shot down . . . So, it's my turn. We went in [and] landed on top of the [mountain]. The first thing we would load was the bodies of Americans that had already lost their lives [and left].[88]

As he further reminisced, the constant danger that confronted Sánchez was indeed extraordinary: "I went down six times . . . I was shot down twice [and four mechanically] . . . and that's by God's grace, only by God's grace [I survived]."[89] Such inherent danger and the birth of his son in November 1967 during his deployment were powerful factors in his decision to refuse a promotion that would have guaranteed an additional tour in Vietnam. He said, "I was offered a direct commission to captain, but that would have required an additional tour in Vietnam . . . Those six times going down was enough for me."[90] Upon his departure in August 1968, Sánchez spent the remainder of his time in the army as an instructor pilot at Fort Walters, Texas, and he was honorably discharged as a CW02 in February 1970 after four years of military service.

Influenced by his father's service in World War II, Charley Trujillo joined the U.S. Army in 1968 at the age of eighteen for a three-year enlistment. He also highlighted a number of additional reasons for doing so: "Patriotism, [to] be a hero like I saw in the movies . . . Loyalty to the country, [to] fight communism . . . family tradition [and] adventurism . . . [And] socioeconomic mobility. We were farmworkers . . . [If] I go to the military, I'd get the GI Bill when I [got] out, and I'd be able to go to school."[91] Rising tension at home with his father was yet another factor, who admonished Trujillo that his time in the military would not be enjoyable. As he quickly discovered, his father was right: "When I got off in Fort Ord [for basic training] . . . I said, 'man, I fucked up! What the fuck did I do! I knew right then that I wasn't gonna like it [and] my dad was right.'"[92] Assigned to a mechanized infantry unit in Germany in January 1969, Trujillo was further dismayed by the primitive and hostile environment he encountered:

> I volunteered to go to Vietnam from Germany. I couldn't take Germany. We [were] in the infantry and we were way out in the boonies, man. It was too much stress . . . We were in open bay [barracks], old army style with forty guys . . . We [were] always ready . . . to fight the Communists. They always had us ready, like dogs in a kennel. And then the [racial] situation was bad [between] the blacks and the whites . . . You had the Black Panthers [and] the Black Muslims . . . that [were] drafted from the inner cities . . . and guys from Mississippi. [It was] a whole melting pot of the working class of the United States. And then you [had] these honky guys from the South that [were] sympathetic to the Ku Klux Klan . . . Everybody carried knives![93]

Trujillo arrived in Vietnam in January 1970 as an infantryman and survived several close encounters with the NVA while on patrol. As frustrations mounted for himself and fellow soldiers, a questioning attitude began to emerge that was fueled by the tenacity and fighting spirit of the NVA. On one occasion in April or May 1970, Trujillo and his fellow soldiers were on the verge of the unthinkable after several days of fighting. He described this volatile situation:

> [After] four or five months I was there, we [were involved] in a big operation . . . the first one I had ever been in, because most of the time we [were] just out in patrols in the jungle . . . The North Vietnamese, we started scuffling with them for three days [or] four days . . . The third day we were there, we didn't want to go back in because they had kicked our butts the day before. They made us [retreat] . . . And so . . . we started going on strike, man . . . kind of like [a] semi-mutiny. We argued all night . . . In jail, you're alive . . . [Were] they gonna put us all in jail? I don't think so. [However,] in the morning, one of the guys broke the strike.[94]

In an engagement soon thereafter, Trujillo suffered massive head trauma, including the loss of an eye, and he was transferred to Japan, where he recovered from his injures. In August 1970, Trujillo was released with an honorable discharge as a sergeant (E5) after approximately two and a half years of military service.

Enamored with the Marine Corps as a child and hoping to mature before moving on to another occupation, Sal Martínez enlisted in the Marine Corps for four years after his high school graduation in 1959. As he stated, his upbringing in New York City steeled him to the rigors of basic training:

> I could not take boot camp serious[ly]. I could not believe . . . that our leaders were really serious about what they were doing. As rough and tough as they may have been in the things that they did, it always struck me as rather humorous. So, the disciplining and all that other stuff, I fell into it relatively easy . . . I figured I could take on whatever they could dish at me.[95]

Deployed to Bolivia as an embassy guard during the Cuban Missile Crisis, Martínez recalled the frenzied mob that approached the U.S. embassy in the capital city of La Paz: "The American embassy in La Paz was attacked for two straight days by the pro-Castro [forces] and the pro-Communists. There were six Marines to defend it, me being one of them. And there was about ten thousand people out there yelling [and] screaming for our blood and our heads."[96] Recently married and enticed by the $850 reenlistment bonus, Martínez continued in the Marine Corps as the war in Vietnam escalated. He ultimately deployed for the first time in 1966, and as he recalled, escalating casualties, especially among junior officers, thrust senior noncommissioned officers (NCO) into positions of greater authority: "I now started experiencing taking over greater responsibility and authority because of the number of people that were getting killed or seriously hurt over there. Those of us that were . . . staff NCOs, were occupying a lot of officer positions."[97] On one occasion, his entire platoon was decimated: "I went into combat in one situation where I was the platoon commander even though I was a staff sergeant . . . I took in fifty-six guys and only seven of us came out."[98]

Intrigued by the possibility of leaving the military, Martínez was convinced to stay when he was offered a temporary commission as an officer: "I received a combat commission out of Vietnam . . . through what they called the Temporary Commissioning Program at the time . . . But they only promised you two years as an officer."[99] Much to his delight, he was subsequently selected to retain the commission; however, a lingering doubt also accompanied Martinez's permanent transition to an officer. He explained:

> I was basically selected, I like to think, on merit . . . Twenty-two of us were picked out of twenty two hundred . . . But the most disappointing thing to me . . . was when I was selected to be one of that one percent that got selected to retain the commission. I firmly believed at the time that I was the token Puerto Rican. There were very, very few Latino officers in the Marine Corps at that time . . . in the late sixties.[100]

As an officer, he remained in the infantry and eventually returned to Vietnam for a second tour in the late sixties: "[I] was a combat commander in the field running a company of marines . . . as a second lieutenant . . . as a first lieutenant . . . [and] as a captain. I spent most of my career in the infantry, mostly by choice because I enjoyed being a grunt."[101] Martínez also offered a stark assessment of the racial divide that existed in the military during the Vietnam War era: "Race relations were atrocious. There were riots. There was great confrontation many times."[102] As he continued, one particular inspection at Camp Pendleton emphasized the difficulty in melding a racially diverse and contentious group:

> We had the inspector general come out . . . to inspect my organization . . . And they determined that twenty-seven percent of my company was made up of Latinos, 26 percent of it was made up of African Americans . . . I had as mixed a group as you ever want to see that you're trying to put together to make work as a team . . . There was constant tension and conflict.[103]

A number of different job assignments followed, and after twenty-one years of honorable service, largely in the combat arms, Martínez retired in 1980 as a major (O4).

NAVIGATING AN INTEGRATED MILITARY

The latter two testimonies illustrate the endemic nature of racial discord in the U.S. military. Unlike Mexican American veterans of World War II and Korea, however, Chicanos that served in the Vietnam War found themselves in the unique position as an intermediate group between black and white animosity in an integrated military that was often characterized by violence and rioting. One of the more dramatic incidents occurred in the summer of 1968, when over 250 black inmates in the Long Binh Stockade outside Saigon took part in a race riot, controlling the compound for over a month. As an MP assigned to the base, George Mariscal offered an eyewitness account of the mob violence: "When I was in Long Binh . . . there were race riots right on base, black on white. I remember being woken up at night and looking out and you could see gangs of guys with bats going to settle a score. So, that was totally out of control."[104] This was part of a series of serious disturbances following the assassination of Martin Luther King Jr. on April 4, 1968, an event that several narrators described as having a galvanizing effect on African American troops in Vietnam. For example, Alfredo Vea offered the following: "There was a discussion among black troops about [having] a one-day refusal . . . and there was a discussion among officers about whether or not these troops should be arrested."[105] Raymond Buriel also recalled the enraged state of African American marines: "We heard about [the assassination] about two weeks later or three weeks later. And this coincided right after . . . Khe Sanh. And I remember the blacks saying . . . 'What the fuck are we doing here? They're killing us here [in Vietnam]. They're killing us over there [in the U.S.].'"[106] Gilbert Guevara, drafted into the army in 1967, offered a similar recollection: "When it came back to us that he was killed, that's when the Negroes just turned . . . They didn't want to do shit . . . And then . . . Bobby Kennedy got killed . . . And that even made it more for them to say, 'Fuck the man. Fuck this army.'"[107]

Despite the predominant nature of the black-white racial fault line that existed in the United States, my narrators and many other Chicanos that served during the Vietnam War were invariably confronted with discriminatory behavior and racial epithets during their military service. Jesus Barragan, who served in Vietnam as a navy medic with the 1st Marine Division in 1968, offers one of the more vicious examples while stationed at the Oakland Naval Supply Center after his return:

> I had decided to grow a mustache . . . but the rule [was], only if it's on your ID [card]. Well, there was this higher noncommissioned officer, an idiot, who had been kind of bullying me and harassing me . . . And he started to make comments about the mustache, so I thought, I'd better go have my new ID taken . . . The [prints] they didn't use, they gave them to me and I threw 'em [in] the trash can [in the] dispensary . . . They found them, my fellow servicemen, and they got a picture and Xeroxed it on a piece of paper and left it on my desk. And it said, "Wanted, dead or alive, preferably dead, for Frito stealing, carnage of the English language, [and] illegal entry into the country . . . Reward, one-tenth of a penny."[108]

Such encounters were especially prevalent for service members that received training at military bases located in the South, where confrontations were numerous both on and off base. An example of the former is offered by Frank Reyes, who described one encounter at Fort Benning, Georgia: "We had just finished airborne training . . . [And] a couple of us went to the movies [on base] and that night we were confronted by about four or five white guys . . . They kept calling me 'beaner' and all kinds of things . . . But we walked away, they didn't."[109] Meanwhile, Lupe Alviar, who enlisted in the Marine Corps in April 1965, recalled the following incident at a Southern bar: "In 1969, I was in a town called Waldenboro, South Carolina . . . A bunch of us were in drill instructor school for the Marine Corps and I went out to a bar with the rest of 'em and ordered a drink, and all my buddies got served and I didn't."[110]

Once overseas, where the immediate task of confronting the enemy outweighed racist attitudes, warfare was a great equalizer. Rear areas, however, were usually splintered into a variety of cliques, with race (and, to a lesser extent, class) serving as an important factor in determining one's immediate social group. Joe Rodríguez, deployed to Vietnam as a navy medic for eleven months from 1965 to 1966, offered commentary in that regard: "My experience [was] that racism was just so pervasive that there was just no way to get around it. I can remember bases being closed. I can remember firefights between troops . . . [There was] name calling [and] certain places you just knew better than to go . . . It was like everybody had their own turf. You didn't mix."[111] Jim Acevedo offered a similar assessment:

> Everybody kind of stuck to their own little groups. [For example,] *La raza* stuck to *la raza*, the blacks stuck to [fellow] blacks [and] the whites stuck to [fellow] whites. But yet, you would intermingle sometimes, especially when you were in the heat of combat or when you were trying to accomplish something as a unit . . . [But] the cliques were definitely there.[112]

Such divisiveness usually coincided with incessant name-calling, which Eddie Solís readily acknowledged: "They called me beaner [and] wetback and this [and that]."[113] He also confessed to returning racial epithets and conceded that a racialized pecking order existed: "The [African Americans] were treated . . . worse than I was."[114] Meanwhile, for approximately four months, Lupe Alviar was subjected to a harsh display of verbal abuse by his immediate superior officer, leaving him powerless to respond:

> I was an intelligence clerk and I used to type up plans where you talk about the enemy [and] what you knew about the enemy . . . And I had an officer that must of really disliked Mexicans because . . . I could make one lousy little typo mistake and he would say, "You dumb wetback." He constantly was always making these references at me. But you can't tell an officer anything.[115]

No such power relationship existed for John Sánchez, however, who decided to take matters into his own hands when confronted with a derisive term that fellow soldiers began to employ with alarming regularity: "I didn't care for the name Speedy Gonzales. I also made it known, so eventually that went away."[116]

While the transition to an integrated military was fraught with considerable hostility, camaraderie and cohesiveness were also possible. As Frank Reyes argued, his comrades among the Special Forces were a multiracial but tight-knit group. Moreover, it was a racial setting that was further reinforced by his no-nonsense commanding officer: "We were an all-volunteer unit and . . . My detachment commander . . . [was] a very large black man . . . He did not tolerate any type of racism. He said, 'The only color I see in this outfit is OD [olive drab] green.'"[117] Another perspective is offered by Everett Álvarez as he described what he considered to be very amicable relationships with fellow naval aviators: "I just figured myself as one of the guys and conducted myself [accordingly] and I found that it was reciprocal. I never figured myself different and I was never treated differently."[118] Furthermore, Eddie Solís's commentary suggests the awareness that ability and dedication could win over discrimination: "I guess you figured that it's a place where there is prejudice, but if you do the job, you can get ahead."[119] Jesus Barragan offers a case in point as he described his immediate superior while stationed at the Oakland Naval Supply Center: "I'll never forget him, Chief King, a big Archie Bunker type . . . Bigoted as hell."[120] While assigned to the night shift, an unpopular posting with other sailors, Barragan's exemplary work ethic and attention to detail led to the following acclamation from Chief King: "I did my work and I did it well . . . Well, I won him over . . . The day I got out of the service, the Chief handed me a letter that he had written on my behalf . . . He said that it was a real loss to the navy for me to be discharged."[121]

Likewise, as in World War II and Korea, the multicultural milieu of the U.S. military did facilitate temporary and long-term interracial friendships, an aspect of military service that a clear majority of my narrators confirmed. For instance, Fred Medel, who served as an army RTO in Vietnam from early 1970 to early 1971, offered the following: "I had all [types of] friends, black, white, or brown."[122] Eddie Solís called to mind a similar development: "I had [African American] friends and I had [white] friends."[123] In addition, black-white tension within the military and society at large sometimes gave rise to a neutral ground that enabled Chicanos to avoid the full impact of racial hostility, which arguably allowed for enhanced maneuverability between the two groups. Recalling his time spent at Fort Gordon, Georgia, Leroy Quintana vividly remembers escaping the racism directed toward black comrades one particular evening while traveling with a multiracial group: "It was a Southern typical town. One night . . . and this included some white guys, too, we went across the river . . . [into] South Carolina. And they were going to serve all of us, except one or two black guys that were with us. Why they saved me from that, I don't know . . . You saw that kind of stuff very, very often."[124] Daniel Cano recalled a similar incident at Fort Bragg, North Carolina, after his return from Vietnam: "I remember going to a bar one night with some Chicanos from Texas and we had this one black friend . . . We went into the bar and they made him leave, so we all left."[125]

George Mariscal offered a comparable scenario of his time at Fort Gordon while speculating that a de facto association with whiteness was responsible: "I remember a lot of white-on-black and black-on-white problems there, but the Mexicans were kind of invisible . . . I guess I was just another white person . . . People thought I was a foreigner out in the community, that I was white but from another country."[126] Such treatment continued at Fort Story, Virginia: "There was a lot of racial stuff there . . . But again, they didn't really know what I was."[127] Ted Samora, an army volunteer in 1965, also suspected an association with whiteness for Chicanos as he underwent military intelligence training at Fort Bragg: "The Mexicans were considered white. We were allowed into bars, but the blacks weren't"[128] All in all, Frank Reyes offered a matter-of-fact summation that highlighted the intermediate status of Chicanos in the military: "You were white or you were black. There was no in between."[129]

CONCLUSION

Direct encounters with racist attitudes were a common occurrence; nevertheless, it seems that on a case-by-case basis, Chicanos were afforded the opportunity to navigate the prevailing racial fault line to their advantage due to a black-white binary that categorized them as the latter. A more sinister and prejudicial reality were the social, political, and economic contradictions in U.S. society that channeled young Chicanos and other working-class groups into the military while providing few viable alternatives. This operated in tandem with Cold War rhetoric that overshadowed such inequalities while producing a missionary idealism in the quest to combat the perceived monolithic threat posed by communism. Also at play for Chicanos were traditional notions of masculine honor often associated with Latin machismo—what George Mariscal has conceptualized as a type of warrior patriotism. As with previous generations of Mexican Americans that fought in World War II and Korea, the connection between patriotism, assimilation, and machismo motivated countless numbers of young Chicanos to enlist or accept their draft notice.

This attempt to claim full citizenship rights and fulfill a masculine rite of passage during wartime thus offers an excellent opportunity to explore how military service provided a central reference point for personal and masculine conduct that enabled Chicanos to adjust to life in the armed forces and make sense of their military service. Indeed, a military setting is an especially important arena to examine the pursuit of masculinity by Mexican American males since the U.S. military symbolized an idealized version of masculine honor. The impact on gender identity varied, however, because the connection between military service and traditional manifestations of masculinity is much more complex. Rather, a diverse range of personal, masculine, and sexual behaviors existed in this landscape of possible male identities, and it is to these varied expressions by Chicano servicemen that we now turn.

6

MAKING MASCULINITY IN THE U.S. MILITARY

Chicano Soldiering, Sexuality, and Manhood

"The military did then what it does now. It sells sexual license, it sells sexual prowess . . . to boys . . . Sexual license is very important to young men and the idea of sexual prowess being equated to violence is very important to young men. And that's what they sold."

"I had to lie on my application when they [military authorities] asked me, 'Are you a homosexual?' I could of said yes, right there and then. I could of showed up with pink panties for my physical."

AS A SOCIAL SPACE imbued with its own martial and masculine ethos, the military provides an ideal location to study the behaviors of Mexican American youth, not only because men were the dominant gender in the military from 1940 to 1975, but also because the military's emphasis on conventional, often aggressive, displays of male sex role behaviors paralleled, and often reinforced, idealized notions of the warrior associated with machismo and militarized citizenship. However, the forms of masculinity displayed by Mexican American males, both homosexual and heterosexual, were multilayered and complex and, in general, evolved from World War II to the Vietnam era with a greater willingness to challenge and openly critique the warrior ethos in the latter conflict. The result was a myriad of approaches to military service and masculine honor—a layered process that does not overlook the problematic relationship between combat veterans and machismo, nor fully dislodge the significance of hegemonic paradigms, but also did not always require conventional displays of masculinity or a direct connection to combat duty.[1] That efforts to minimize or completely avoid combat experience and other conventional masculine behaviors were sometimes unsuccessful in no way diminishes the challenge such efforts posed to idealized notions of the warrior ethos. Rather,

I argue they illustrate the contested nature of military service and the nuanced approaches to masculinity displayed by young Mexican Americans as they struggled to adjust to life in the military and return home safely. Gay men, in particular, often utilized creative methods that included emulating and embracing martial behavior in an effort to pass as heterosexual and assimilate in accordance with military canon and reconcile their sexuality with community expectations.

NEGOTIATING MACHISMO

Patriarchal norms and other conventional displays of machismo, as epitomized by the following World War II–era Mexican corrido, or ballad, were often vehicles for the transition to military life. The ballad describes a young Mexican American soldier leaving for the war who clearly espouses a traditional notion of masculinity that connects masculine honor and patriotism with bravery on the battlefield, while also expressing a profound sense of patriarchal responsibility toward his mother, who is left behind and needs to be cared for. He calls on the Virgin Mary, the ceremonial mother of all Mexicans and the embodiment of self-abnegation, to protect his "poor mother," and by doing so he affirms assigned gender roles that emphasize docility and obedience for females and agency and virility for males. Consider the following:

Soldado Razo
(Common Soldier)

I leave as a common soldier.
I'm going to join the ranks.
I will be among the Brave boys
who leave their beloved mothers
and sweethearts in tears,
crying for their departure.
I'm leaving for the war, contented.
I have my rifle and gun ready.
When all the shooting is over,
I will return as a Sergeant.
The only one thing I regret,
is leaving my poor Mother alone.

Oh brunette Virgin, please take care of her.
Watch over her, she is a wonderful person.
Please take care of her till I return.
I will depart at early morn tomorrow,
right at the break of day.
And so . . . hereforth goes another Mexican
who is willing to gamble his life.
And I say goodbye with this song . . .
Long live this Country of mine.[2]

Another example is provided by Alfredo Vea's reliance on chauvinist networks as he was cared for by other bachelors as they traveled from camp to camp harvesting crops along the West Coast in the early 1960s. He vividly remembered the ethnically mixed nature of the work force, which included Mexicans, Filipinos, African Americans, Native Americans, and working-class white Americans. This ethnic intermixture, which paralleled the cultural diversity present within the armed forces, eased his transition into the military. So, too, did the all-male environment and exaggerated displays of masculine behavior he countered: "[The migrant camps were] all male . . . which impacted how I viewed the world and later relationships with females. It also made it very easy to be in the army."[3] His familiarity with impoverished and communal living conditions, harsh work schedules, occasional knife fights, and prostitution provided a foundation for the experiences he would later encounter as a soldier.

An additional dimension of conventional machismo, and a key component of the generational focus on martial citizenship within the Mexican American community, was the emphasis placed on fulfilling idealized notions of masculine honor. For many, warfare became a necessary stepping-stone to manhood, what Joe Rodríguez described as "a way to test this macho thing and find out about war . . . 'cause that's kind of an ultimate male test."[4] As Alfredo Vea bluntly stated, "There is a rite of passage into manhood, if not adulthood, and that rite of passage is the warrior."[5] Moreover, for Raymond Buriel, joining the military also required membership in the branch of the armed forces long considered the most challenging. Thus his decision to enlist in the Marine Corps in 1966 at the age of eighteen: "If you were gonna be in the military, you wanted to be in the baddest unit . . . where nobody could question your role in the military."[6] The Marine Corps has long been considered an elite fighting force composed of battle-ready men never short on bravado and always ready to live up to its motto: "First to fight, first to die." The Marine Corps has steadily reinforced this image in its efforts to recruit new troops by asking young men (and, more recently, women) if they have the physical and mental stamina to be part of "the few, the proud, the Marines." Such masculine rhetoric and imagery, epitomized by its colorful uniform, also lured Jim Acevedo in 1960. As he recalled, "Originally, I was going to join the navy, but . . . at that time, you know, young and stupid, I liked the uniform of the Marine Corps . . . so I joined the marines."[7] Robert Castro was also swayed by the Marine Corps image in 1946: "I heard that they were a hard unit and I liked the uniform."[8] Gene Bejarano offered a similar rationale for his decision to enlist in the Marine Corps in 1950: "I just wanted to be a he-man, I guess . . . We were machos all the way and that's why I chose the marines . . . We were gung ho. We wanted to go and fight and just be . . . like John Wayne."[9]

Another challenging environment was the rigorous conditioning and expertise associated with the army's airborne training, which provided an additional $50 monthly stipend.[10] Daniel Cano explained:

> You're put through a lot of obstacle courses . . . You think you can't do it, but when you finish those obstacle courses, all of a sudden, [you are astounded by] the surprise you have. And then you jump out of airplanes and you become part of an elite group like the 101st Airborne Division. Or if you're in the Special Forces, you [finish] and you know only so many guys made it.[11]

Several other narrators, through previous commentary, also highlight the prestige derived from becoming a paratrooper. Mike González served as a paratrooper in Korea, and offered the following reason for his interest: "It [was] something exciting [and] more than just regular infantry."[12] Meanwhile, Richard Domínguez volunteered for jump school in World War II for a number of different reasons: "They did pay an extra [$50] bonus . . . that would be one [reason]. I think, also, the dress [uniform]. They were able to wear the jump boots and blouse . . . And [it was] a little prestigious thing [for me] . . . When they trained you, they said you were better than all the rest."[13] Carlos Santillán also volunteered for airborne training in World War II, which he attributed to a combination of youthful bravado and monetary gain: "I felt that it was better than being just a foot soldier, and they get more money, too."[14] It should be noted that while the stipend loomed large in some of the aforementioned reminiscences, it did not serve as the primary incentive to seek additional training and qualifications. Rather, the decision to do so was personal and masculine in nature. Extra monetary benefits were considered as nothing more than hard-earned bonuses for the hazards such training often incurred. Greater personal reward lay in the accomplishment of such physically demanding feats and in surviving the dangerous combat assignments that followed.

This pressure to uphold a tradition of masculine honor through military service could also produce a mind-set that placed little value on alternative choices when confronted with the prospect of military service. John Rodríguez put the matter succinctly as he recalled the youthful naïveté that propelled his entrance into the military for service in Vietnam:

> It's amazing how we become cattle . . . and I think it really had something to do with family, more cultural . . . I took responsibility at age eighteen, and part of that responsibility was to enter the military, and I followed those steps without question.[15]

George Mariscal furnished a corresponding perspective on the pervasiveness of established tradition as he recalled the arrival of his draft notice in March 1969: "It never occurred to me to resist, but I wasn't gung ho. But neither did I have any ability to think I should not be doing this because it was so natural in the *familia* [family] structure."[16] Ruben Moreno, when queried years later by a fellow Korean War veteran, came to a similar conclusion as he considered the cultural emphasis on expected standards of masculine behavior. Moreover, his insightful analysis makes a persuasive argument for linking communal notions of male bravado with the military's own masculine ethos:

> I attended a reunion over in Jacksonville, Florida, and I ran into one of my assistant gunners who I hadn't seen for forty-eight years. And he asked me, "What was it with you Mexicans, why were you so brave?" [I responded,] "I don't think we were any braver than anybody else" . . . And I came home [and] I start[ed] to ponder that . . . I think I got it all figured out. The Marine Corps was very much like the upbringing we [Mexicans] had as we were growing up . . . [If] you'd fall down as a kid and you start[ed] to cry, [some adults would shout], "No llores cabrón, eres hombre [Don't cry, asshole, you're a man]." You had to be a man [and] you couldn't cry. It's pretty much the same deal that the marines gave you, "You're a marine and you can take it" . . . The marines' doctrine wasn't any different than what we were getting at home. We were already brainwashed.[17]

Additionally, Tony López offered a more abstract but similar assessment of the lifelong influence of communal standards and the complementary nature of military service: "That machismo thing, I think, has a lot to do with the way that we [Chicano males] do things . . . Going with it into the military, learning it while in the military, and then, taking it with you after you leave the military."[18]

The Vietnam War, in particular, offers powerful examples of the fealty expected by an older generation and the pressure to carry on the banner of service and sacrifice in defense of la patria. Consider the following excerpt, taken from a letter written by a World War II veteran to his son, Douglas MacArthur Herrera, who was in the military but refused to be deployed to Vietnam:

> Dear Son: Your mom and I were very shocked to read your letter and you know we have never had a Herrera yet who has refused to serve his country. Your family will never live it down and your life will be ruined. You should not question your country's motives and its foreign policy, and in the overall picture someone must suffer . . . Your objections will be widely publicized here in Texas and your family will probably have to move out of Texas to get over the embarrassment and humiliation of what you are doing . . . Don't break our hearts. Please call us and tell us that you are going to do the right thing to your country and to your family.[19]

The father's profound concern that his son's refusal would forever shame the family is unmistakable. What is also clear, however, is that young Douglas, despite being named after the famous World War II general, was willing to openly challenge these cultural, masculine, and patriotic expectations and defy official military orders.

Herrera's defiance was symptomatic of a growing ambivalence in the late 1960s about U.S. objectives in Vietnam, both across the nation and within the Chicano movement. In particular, in the pursuit of first-class citizenship, Chicano activists openly criticized the unqualified patriotism expressed by an earlier generation that served in World War II and Korea. They likewise challenged prescribed codes of masculine pride and military service, as illustrated by the following excerpt of an essay by Joseph Arellano that appeared in *El Grito del Norte*, a newspaper based in New Mexico that catered to the Chicana/o community:

> MACHISMO—we all know it is a quality of manhood that runs deep in our culture. We see it all around us, in the courts and with authority figures, our men never asking for a break because it runs against our grain.

> MACHISMO is expressed in our foot-stomping music, in our lusty folk songs, now in our vengeful grito of Viva Zapata! Viva la Revolución! But perhaps it is also machismo that accounts for many of our brothers not returning from World War II, Korea—and now the war in Vietnam.[20]

A modicum of Chicano male activists did refuse induction into the military as the war progressed; nevertheless, the overwhelming obligation to serve in tandem with the community's marginalization discussed earlier were often insurmountable barriers to most Chicanos. They responded with the same sense of duty and internalized canon that inspired their elders in World War II and Korea. Mark Rocha offers one final example as he remembered the profound sense of shame he felt when he was ordered back to the United States after being diagnosed with a bad eye while deployed to Japan during the Korean War. He stated, "I had come here to serve my country and now this idiot doctor wanted to send me back . . . I didn't want to be a disappointment to my grand folks."[21]

SOLDIERING AND MASCULINITY IN THE U.S. MILITARY

While the experience of being a Chicano service member often encouraged adherence to traditional, even hegemonic, norms of masculinity, Chicanos also negotiated such ideal forms of warrior masculinity as they served in the military, and their behavior revealed a more fluid gendered process than either the U.S. military or their cultural upbringing sanctioned. One of the more powerful manifestations of such variance was the ability of individual servicemen to challenge more conventional models of behavior by negotiating the terms that dictated their entrance into the military and, thus, their subsequent careers in the armed forces. This included choosing to serve in a variety of different capacities that perhaps did not involve direct exposure to combat. Such was the case for Ted Samora, who volunteered for a three-year enlistment in the army in 1965. Doing so provided him with greater latitude in choosing his military occupational specialty (MOS), and he decided to join the intelligence community in a deliberate effort to avoid the traditional combat forces and deployment to Vietnam. While his plan failed, and he arrived in Vietnam the following year, his decision clearly demonstrates that his notion of masculine honor was not directly linked to combat duty, which he did not experience. Rather, he sought to minimize the potential for danger once inducted into the armed forces.

Motivating his decision to enlist was the childhood struggle to reconcile his homosexuality with community expectations. Growing up in Madera, California, he remained committed to hiding his homosexuality: "I knew that I was different. I knew that girls didn't interest me, but guys did. But I didn't show [my homosexuality] 'cause . . . I wanted to be masculine. I was trying to [run] away from my sexuality."[22] His reaction was due, in large part, to the overwhelming presence of the U.S. military within his immediate and extended family. His father and five uncles had served in the army during World War II, while a sixth uncle had served in the navy.[23] Samora also encountered ridicule and abusive behavior from classmates as he toiled alone with his sexual and emotional development, especially after being voted head cheerleader during his junior year in high school. Despite the obvious popularity he enjoyed, the abuse he received from Mexican American students was especially troublesome: "I enjoyed [high school] overall, but I didn't enjoy . . . the Mexican students. The Mexican students [were] the ones that called me names [like] . . . queer, *joto* [faggot], and all that."[24] As a result of these childhood ordeals, Samora resigned himself to a tour in the military. He said:

> Growing up as a kid, I knew that I had to go [in]to the military. It was kind of a macho thing . . . I had to serve 'cause my dad served. And being known in high school as a pansy guy, I thought the service would prove to them that, hey, I'm a military guy.[25]

An idealized vision of warrior masculinity clearly influenced Samora's decision to enter the military to prove his manliness. Nevertheless, by deliberately choosing an occupation with less hazardous requirements, he also demonstrated the ability to navigate the traditional military model and not succumb to it entirely.

Raúl Mosqueda also deliberately avoided the traditional combat forces while stationed on Taiwan from 1970 to 1972 as a navy dental technician, where he supported American servicemen on rest and relaxation (R&R) from Vietnam. Upon graduating from high school in La Pryor, Texas, Mosqueda moved to Saginaw, Michigan; he was drafted in 1968. Warned by his older brother to avoid service in the army, if drafted, given the increased likelihood of becoming a combat infantryman, Mosqueda decided on the U.S. Navy:

> When we [draftees] were at the induction center in Detroit . . . they started saying, "People who want to volunteer for the navy, move this way . . . You want to go air force, go that way . . . You want to stay for the army, stay right here" . . . So I chose the navy, keeping in mind what my brother had told me about the army.[26]

Conventional notions of masculine honor often associated with machismo clearly did not influence Mosqueda, and a more ambivalent attitude characterized his departure for military service. In fact, he freely admitted that he would not have entered the military voluntarily. As he stated, "Was I really gung ho about the service? No."[27] Furthermore, by volunteering for a four-year enlistment, he was able to choose his occupation, deciding on dentistry in a deliberate effort to lessen his chances of serving in Vietnam—a strategy that ultimately proved successful.

A similar strategy characterized the entrance of other narrators into the military during my chosen time period. Recall the rationale offered by John Sótelo in his decision to volunteer for the navy during World War II: "Most of the Mexican American friends [I] had wound up in the army and the infantry divisions, so I didn't want any part of that."[28] Moreover, as he continued, Sótelo's enlistment enabled him to choose the navy's motor machinist (MM) rating in order to acquire vocational training for later use: "I was gonna be drafted anyway . . . [By enlisting] I had a chance to [choose] what I wanted to do."[29] Simultaneously, Gene García clearly intended to use his enlistment in the air force in 1951 as a springboard for future success, so he avoided the traditional combat arms. He stated, "At that time, I had just started going to junior college and I saw an opportunity that, if I went into the air force . . . there was a better chance of continuing college after I got out of there . . . I just kind of had a feeling that when I joined the air force, there was more opportunity to learn, instead of carrying a rifle and pulling a trigger."[30] In 1960, Victor Ramírez also enlisted into the air force with a similar motivation: "You know that machismo thing that says, 'I want to go fight.' [Rather,] my attitude was to serve my country, but at the same time, get an education."[31] Frank Gonzales provides another worthy comparison as he explained his decision to enlist in the navy in 1949 and thus avoid a combat assignment: "The little bit that I knew about the navy was that I knew that I wasn't gonna be in a foxhole in strange terrain. I was gonna be on a ship and I was gonna . . . be able to take a shower. And I was gonna get a good meal."[32]

Interestingly, additional nuance in one's approach to military service can also be observed in individuals assigned to a traditional combat unit. Lupe Alviar, for example, so thoroughly enjoyed his initial stationing on Okinawa in 1966 as an intelligence analyst with an artillery unit that he endeavored to extend his tour there. In order to do so, however, a six-month deployment to Vietnam was required. He describes his subsequent train of thought as he confronted this requirement:

> There was a unit just leaving Okinawa to go to Vietnam, but before they went to Vietnam, they were gonna go to the Philippines . . . [for] two months . . . So, I said [to myself] . . . "If I go [to] this unit and I go to Vietnam, I'm gonna have two months knocked out of a six month tour in Vietnam."[33]

Unfortunately, his plan did not materialize after the unit was immediately rerouted to Vietnam as a special landing task force, where he witnessed considerable combat. Nevertheless, Alviar did employ some cunning strategy in an effort to limit his exposure to danger, and, ultimately, his actions were somewhat fruitful in that he served in Vietnam for six months rather than the usual thirteen months that typified a Marine Corps tour of duty.

By comparison, Everett Álvarez's experiences as a prisoner of war (POW) point to another dimension of Chicano soldiering: the development of bonds of brotherhood among those serving in the military. These homosocial bonds often encouraged much more intimate expressions of male feeling than the warrior ideal allowed, even as Chicanos also, simultaneously, lived up to the ideal in other ways. From Salinas, California, twenty-six-year-old navy lieutenant, junior grade, Álvarez was shot down the evening of August 6, 1964, in response to an attack on the USS *Maddox*. He half-jokingly stated, "When I was shot down, they [Congress] went out and passed the Gulf of Tonkin Resolution right after that . . . I started the war!"[34] Wounded and in shock, he was captured almost immediately and remained a POW until February 1973. As the years passed, a steady influx of navy and air force pilots became fellow prisoners. He was moved periodically, including stops at the infamous POW camp in Hanoi that was sarcastically referred to as the Hanoi Hilton, and Álvarez and the other pilots lived a brutish day-to-day existence, deprived of sanitation and proper nutrition and constantly subjected to physical and mental abuse by their North Vietnamese captors.[35]

The brutality of this environment often required a stoic and martial demeanor, and individuals were forced to find inner strength and personal fortitude. Principles based on family, patriotism, and religion were especially important in maintaining this mind-set. As Álvarez explained, "I prayed a lot, I talked to God a lot initially when I was by myself for the first year [and I relied on] my upbringing . . .

keeping [my] wits . . . not letting myself be duped."[36] Also at work was a military code of conduct that mandated loyalty and obedience from all POWs. For a community often considered the ideal embodiment of warrior masculinity through its courage, daring, and technical expertise of complex machinery, this code of conduct, in tandem with inhumane conditions, often played a critical role in reinforcing a more conventional masculine sense of self. However, the bonds of brotherhood established by these pilots also allowed for a more intimate sense of camaraderie that involved emotional and psychological release with fellow cellmates through dialogue and personal encouragement. According to Álvarez, "In order to survive, we opened up to each other every day . . . So every day while we were there, we had our own [therapy] session."[37] Indeed, Álvarez credits this congenial behavior with helping him to survive eight and a half years of captivity and avoid major symptoms of post-traumatic stress disorder.

The bonds of brotherhood established through warfare were also crucial for Tony Moreno as he adjusted to life in the military and overseas deployment. Drafted in 1969, Moreno was assigned to the army's 11th Armored Cavalry, which participated in the invasion of Cambodia in 1970. He recalled the military's preparation for the assault: "I was there watchin' the whole borderline get bombed by B-52s . . . the earth shaking and the red glare . . . And then about eight o'clock in the morning, all the tanks as far as you could see left [and as] far as you could see right, went on line in the jungle . . . until we got to Cambodia."[38] The tension of each day was alleviated by the camaraderie that emerged with fellow soldiers—in particular, the type that developed among Chicanos—one that emphasized cultural and ethnic kinship. As Moreno explained: "All these guys that were in my squad . . . they become like family to you. But mostly . . . Canuto Albear . . . because he was Mexican, we stuck together."[39] He described one surreal yet joyous moment he shared with Albear in a Cambodian jungle:

> My wife would send me a care package every now and then, and we got one when we were in Cambodia. I opened this box up, and my wife had sent me a can of tamales and a can of chili that had carrots in there, *vinagre* [vinegar], the onions, and the jalapeños in there. We couldn't wait to cook it . . . You dig a hole, you take your helmet off . . . [and] put your food there. C4 is that dynamite [explosive] . . . It won't blow up unless it's on fire and you smack it. You can use it to burn . . . and man, me and Canuto, we had a banquet out there. We took the tortillas that already had hair [mold] on it . . . and we took our bayonets and kinda just scraped that off . . . Man, it was like Christmas.[40]

Tony Moreno's friendship with Canuto Albear also highlights the relational dimension of masculine behavior that influenced the development of these homosocial bonds and the key role that cultural networks often played in shaping these interrelationships, while also facilitating the transition to military life. The social circle of choice for many young Chicanos was largely culturally defined, and the friendships that were forged often developed in relationship to cultural attributes they were already accustomed to. Eddie Trujillo offers a powerful example of these very bonds that united Latinos on the battlefront in Korea: "After every battle, the first thing we'd go look for was La Raza and Puerto Riquenos. Every time we used to look for each other . . . [and see] who got killed and who got hurt. And if nobody got hurt, we used to feel good."[41]

In the same manner, Daniel Cano related: "We were always moving from one army post to another army post . . . so the first friends I always made . . . were other Chicanos."[42] Eddie Trujillo similarly commented on the strong camaraderie that connected fellow Chicano marines: "Chicanos used to hang around together. We had the guitars and somebody would break out some tortillas . . . We used to have a lot of parties."[43] Fred Medel encountered similar experiences when off-duty:

> Yeah, Mexicans, we all got together . . . It was like home, you know, when you [were] around other Mexicanos . . . Everybody always had something hidden. A bottle of whiskey . . . They were sent from home a pack of tortillas . . . chorizo . . . [And] they'd put it on the table and we'd all feast and drink.[44]

George Mariscal, meanwhile, offered a broader perspective that placed cultural ties within a larger network that encompassed the working class overall. He stated, "The Chicanos hung out together . . . The Puerto Ricans hung out mainly with the blacks but sometimes with us. The working class, like Italians from New York, hung out with us. It wasn't just about race . . . class position had a lot to do with it too."[45] As he continued, however, the significance of cultural bonds remained readily apparent:

> For all the machismo, we'd all wind up being at the same Mass together on Sunday morning. A lot of us who never went to church back in the States, after a few weeks in Vietnam, we were going to Mass. So the *catholicismo* [Catholicism] kind of unified us. And then little things like getting care packages from home [such as] tortillas . . . tamales . . . And people would just share it. So, those kind of cultural signs [were present].[46]

However, such camaraderie could also challenge the assumption that all individuals of Mexican descent behaved the same and shared very similar cultural attributes. According to Raymond Buriel, "When I was in the service I really learned for the first time that all Chicanos [were] not alike."[47] The term *Chicano* was employed by individuals "mostly from California . . . 'cause the guys from Texas, they were Tejanos."[48] As George Mariscal explained further, a "varying social hierarchy," based on geography, typified these differences.[49] This was clearly evident when Chicanos from the Southwest and Midwest came into contact. Surprise and humor were some of the expressed emotions, as related by Gilbert Guevara in describing his many encounters with southwestern Chicanos:

> When I told them that I was from Michigan, they would say, "What!" . . . And I remember one of the guys saying, "They got Mexicanos in Michigan?" . . . I said, "My parents are from Mexico . . . there's people from Texas that are in Michigan." I guess they didn't realize that there were Mexicanos in the Midwest.[50]

In the case of Fred Medel, some badgering also developed: "Occasionally, you'd get somebody that heckled you because you [did not] know the [Spanish] language, you [did not] speak it well."[51] Jim Acevedo, from the small agricultural community of Scottsbluff, Nebraska, encountered a similar form of harassment, especially from Tejanos:

> My own race discriminated against me because I didn't speak good Spanish . . . The worst Hispanic to get along with, for me, was probably *raza* from Texas. We could not get along and my parents are from Texas. The Tejanos were their own different kind of Mexican . . . [On the other hand,] the Mexicans from California, those guys were cool.[52]

Another dimension of these bonds of brotherhood, and a more direct method of reinforcing prototypical male sex role behaviors in the military, were the many spaces established by locals to cater to a variety of sexual and other basic needs, such as cooking and laundry services, for off-duty servicemen. In the case of World War II, the brutal nature of close-quarter combat in the Pacific and the shifting front lines as the Allies advanced across Europe arguably curtailed the commercialization of sex on a larger basis. However, occupation duty after the completion of hostilities witnessed the proliferation of red-light districts in Germany and Japan. David Fuentes, for example, arrived in the latter in

September 1945 and remained stationed there for one year. He fondly recalled his many excursions to Tokyo, suggesting the availability of various forms of nighttime entertainment: "It was a vacation for me . . . I used to go to Tokyo . . . every day . . . We used to go dancing. We went every night. I used to go with a bunch of guys."[53] Carlos Santillán likewise encountered a similar environment in Berlin for several months until his discharge in November 1945. In particular, he described a thriving black-market economy: "We used to get passes to go to Berlin, to the Tea Garden . . . It was like a black market; you'd sell anything there."[54]

For Korean War–era veterans, Japan once again figured prominently in their recollections. A case in point is offered by Gene Bejarano, who found occupation duty there to be the "life of Riley . . . We [fellow marines] were a bunch of *borachos* [drunks] . . . Wine, women, and song."[55] Vincent Pardo Jr. discovered that "living in Japan was really an experience . . . We'd get liberty [and] we'd go into these small towns close to our camp . . . And we would go for the food, for the bars, [and] the clubs."[56] Gene García also ventured into the red-light districts of Japan, participating in excessive drinking and carousing. He said, "I would say that the majority of us . . . drank a lot . . . [Especially] with the Puerto Ricans and my Chicano buddies. We always partied."[57] So did David Carillo, on R&R from the fighting in Korea: "When they brought us back to Japan for R&R [rest and recuperation] . . . we got passes and we went to the town of Beppu . . . We drank and we danced and we enjoyed ourselves. After all, that's what you were there for, rest and recuperation."[58] Robert Villegas, on the other hand, acquired a steady girlfriend, named Kako, while stationed at Camp Gilford, adjacent to Osaka. He described one surreal exchange between them as they heatedly discussed the loss of loved ones in World War II. Recall that Villegas's older brother, Darío, was posthumously awarded the Medal of Honor:

> I met her about a month after we got there. And we stayed together all throughout [my deployment]. In fact, one day . . . we were in the room . . . talkin' and carrying on . . . The conversation came to [World War II]. She goes, "You know who killed my father?" I said, "Probably the Americans . . . the Allied forces." She said . . . you marines, [with] fire in her eyes. So, about that time, I go, "Well, you know who killed my brother? You, Japs, man. He was killed by you Japanese." She goes, "No pissed off, Bobby, no pissed off."[59]

By comparison, numerous "Boomtowns" were an especially striking feature of the Vietnam War, as depicted by sociologist Charles Moskos in his 1970 study of American enlisted men. He stated, "These Boomtowns—with their bars, laundries, tailor shops . . . massage parlors, and houses of prostitution—are a constituent part of the overseas military community."[60] In South Vietnam, these red-light districts were readily available in major urban centers and in most local towns. An example is offered by Jesus Barragan who recalled that "every village had a 'juicy Lucy,' the black-market coordinator" who provided access to alcohol and local prostitutes.[61] Meanwhile, George Mariscal clandestinely traveled with comrades to Saigon from the nearby stockade of Long Binh: "Even though it was against the rules, we used to sneak off base and catch rides to Saigon . . . and stay in hotels [and] do a lot of pot and prostitutes . . . Red-light district stuff."[62] Gilbert Guevara also remembered the accessible nature of prostitution and its medical impact on U.S. personnel: "I don't think that I knew too many guys that didn't do it. But the bad thing about it is that it wasn't the cleanest thing because a lot of guys ended up with the crabs."[63] For Alfredo Vea, however, such medical concerns in Vietnam were paramount. Rather, he engaged in commercial sex in Australia, providing commentary that also highlights the extensive sexual network that catered to American GIs throughout the Pacific Rim: "Fuck, there was guys getting' all kinds of diseases there [in Vietnam] . . . I went to Australia. They had prostitutes there and [thongs] hangin' on the wall from their last doctor's appointment."[64]

Brothel services also became mobile, and as Daniel Cano moved from one location to the next with his light artillery unit, he recalled that traveling brothels would often follow: "Sometimes you'd go into the field, and [at] our staging area when we [went] back twenty days later, there [would] be . . . a brothel set up."[65] Moreover, American servicemen's steady income and the long separation that married couples endured while husbands were deployed to Vietnam often provided ample opportunities for sexual encounters with military wives and local women other than prostitutes. On Taiwan, Raúl Mosqueda soon realized that his companionship was in high demand, and would remain so for his two-year tour in Taipei:

> Girls were a dime a dozen. They're knockin' on the [front] door, looking . . . for American GIs . . . In addition to that, there were a lot of women whose husbands were in Vietnam, and they're lookin' for . . . action. We were workin' there at the dental office cleaning teeth and assisting dentists. So, a lot of times, women would come in there and they'd get friendly, and before you know it, you'd end up going out with them . . . We had an enormous amount of access to women.[66]

For gay servicemen, the need to conceal their homosexuality required a cautious and creative approach to sexual encounters that often included deliberate efforts to pass as heterosexual.[67] For Ted Samora, this included joining fellow service members in their visits to the many brothels in Saigon. As he explained:

> I used to go to downtown Saigon, to the whore houses . . . I went with my best friend once and I went with the black guys . . . a couple of times. But I used to fake it. They couldn't understand the Vietnamese girl anyway.[68]

Back in the United States, his efforts at concealment were often hindered by evenings filled with alcohol and youthful exuberance: "Of course I kept it [homosexuality] hidden because of my [security] clearance. [But] when I got drunk, once in a while . . . some of it would come up, especially if me and a guy got drunk and we went to the barracks together."[69] Alcohol was also the reason for Jesus Barragan's one sexual encounter with a fellow sailor. As he stated:

> One time, I'm at the Enlisted Man's Club . . . [I] got good and drunk. I'm going back to my barracks [and] I run into [fellow sailor] Jim, who's also good and drunk. We go into his room. He peels off his clothes, I peel mine . . . And then the next morning, it's "Oh, shit!" And not a word was ever said.[70]

Barragan avoided further sexual encounters with military personnel by remaining sexually active only on weekends in his hometown of San Jose, away from the Oakland Naval Supply Center, where he was stationed.

With a particular focus on the Vietnam War, there nevertheless existed social networks at U.S. bases that catered to homosexual men, with an assortment of gestures and behaviors that signaled other would-be suitors. As Samora described, "There was some type of language. [A] look in the eyes, gestures . . . the way they walked . . . or by a wink . . . by looking at you and not . . . turning away . . . [However], in the military, you had to be more careful."[71] A sexual topography was also evident that imbued certain on-base locations, including shower stalls, with special significance. As Samora further explained, "I could tell in the shower how they looked at each other who was gay and who wasn't."[72] A vibrant nightlife in adjacent communities also provided off-base counterparts, as he discovered in Augusta, Georgia, while stationed at nearby Fort Story after his return from Vietnam: "There used to be gay bars in Augusta, Georgia . . . I was in military intelligence . . . and I used to go to this gay bar and there were a bunch of soldiers there."[73] Ironically, one of his many responsibilities as a member of the intelligence community was to perform background checks on military personnel for a wide variety of offenses, including homosexuality. In this capacity, Samora utilized his insight to the benefit of other gay soldiers, which included warning them that both accuser and accused would be discharged if the offense involved homosexual activity. He detailed one occasion: "One person . . . came in and he wanted to report somebody [who] fooled around with him, and I told him on the side, 'If you report this . . . you're gonna be discharged dishonorably.' He pulled back [the complaint]."[74]

These gay social networks are testament to the multiple sexual economies and sexual identities that flourished in the U.S. military. The dogmatic insistence on compulsory heterosexuality belied the fluid environment created by youthful exuberance, hazardous assignments, and the largely all-male environment of the armed forces. Moreover, the many cautious and creative methods employed by homosexual men were bolstered by the willingness of military authorities—and more importantly, fellow service members—to turn a blind eye to such activities, if dedication and commitment to the task at hand was clearly evident. Indeed, among the more powerful goals of the many homosexual soldiers, sailors, airmen, and marines was the desire to be judged on work ethic and commitment to duty, not their sexual orientation.

A concluding story—that of Jesus Barragan—highlights this dynamic. Long prior to his arrival in Vietnam as a navy hospital corpsman in 1968, Barragan felt secure in his sexual orientation. He stated: "I believe I was born this way, 'cause as far back as I can remember, I felt something [different]."[75] A loving, supportive mother stood in stark contrast to the appalling displays of masculine behavior he encountered in his adolescent years: "What I came to realize, as far as what is a man [is this] . . . My father was a gambler [and] ran around with other women . . . And [with] a lot of the fathers in the area. . . . there was a lot of alcohol, a lot of wife beating."[76] In fact, years later, Barragan recalled the following humorous incident with his mother that was simultaneously a final coming out and a reflection on her many heartaches:

> One time, my ma was asking me, "When are you gonna get married?" I said, "Ma, I like men." So, she looked at me, and in Spanish she said, "Son, that's okay, but when you get tired of men, marry a woman because you know how men are!"[77]

With the draft looming while enrolled part time at two-year San Jose City College, Barragan decided to dictate his entrance into the military by volunteering for the U.S. Naval Reserve (USNR) in August 1965 at the age of twenty. He offered the following reflection as he contemplated his choices: "I volunteered knowing I would be drafted. I had no respect for the army. I thought [they were] a bunch of losers. I thought the air force was a bunch of sissies. The marines were too rough. So, I thought, I'll join the navy."[78]

Stationed near the DMZ, Barragan accompanied marines as they patrolled the countryside, and was responsible for their care in the event of injury. As he stated: "The DMZ was walking distance. I could see the hills of North Vietnam."[79] He maintained a candid demeanor with regard to his homosexuality that openly challenged the military's enforcement of compulsory heterosexuality, and his sexuality became a topic of interest for some of the troops, leading to the following humorous encounter:

> At one point there was a river, so some of us went swimming . . . and this one white guy, I guess, he'd been dying to ask. So he said, "Hey doc, back in the world, were you a female impersonator?" . . . And I looked at him and I said, "Well, if I was and if you get hurt, you're gonna have to wait till I put on my lipstick before I patch you up." And everybody cracked up and they dropped it.[80]

While his decision to volunteer for the USNR was a deliberate effort to avoid service in Vietnam (and serves as another example of resistance to the macho ethic of military service), once overseas after being forcibly reassigned as a combat medic, Barragan performed his duties with skill and dedication. He remembered one particular incident when a U.S. tank hit an enemy mine and exploded: "I grabbed my bag because I knew all eyes were on me . . . Without any thought of my own life or safety, I ran as hard as my legs could carry me [to treat the wounded]."[81] Such commitment earned him the respect of the marines he served with, and they disregarded his sexual orientation. Barragan's experiences reveal that it was possible for Chicanos to simultaneously challenge and live up to the warrior ideal.

CONCLUSION

Clearly the perception of military service as a stepping-stone into manhood influenced many Mexican Americans coming of age from 1940 to 1975. Indeed, it seemed quite clear to many at an early age, and on a regional basis, that part of their civic and masculine responsibilities required a tour of duty in the U.S.

military. Even those willing to challenge prescribed codes of masculine behavior were often enamored, to some extent, with the military's all-male environment and the bravado it inevitably reinforced. George Mariscal's following reflection offers a case in point: "It's this weird male culture that, I think, even if we have criticisms of it, there's times when we like to hang just with men. In this [day], they call it homosocial behavior, but there is something appealing to it."[82] However, by providing a revisionist approach to the study of machismo that illustrates the contradictions in the construction of masculine identity, these stories teach us that individual Chicanos, both gay and straight, pushed boundaries and reinterpreted and crafted their own definitions of manhood, despite the existence of hegemonic ideals within the larger Mexican American community and the U.S. military.

A similar revisionist mind-set has characterized more recent examinations of the 1944 Servicemen's Readjustment Act, more commonly known as the GI Bill. While the significance of the various benefits provided by the bill cannot be overlooked, when examined from the vantage point of nonwhite men, women, and gay servicemen, the GI Bill's limitations in orchestrating social engineering as advocated by noted historian Lizabeth Cohen can be called into question. I engage this debate in the following chapter by extending coverage of the bill's effects to the Mexican American community. Moreover, as a benefits package that would be renewed in 1952 for Korean War veterans and made a permanent feature of military service in 1966, I extend coverage of the GI Bill well beyond the original version enacted in 1944, and in so doing, I clearly illustrate diminishing entitlements for discharged veterans, and thus, change over time for the worse.

7

THE GI BILL

"I went and applied for it, and I was starting to go to school . . . but under the GI Bill, they paid you not very often. Sometimes it was three, four months before you got your check . . . and a lot of fellas dropped out of school."

"For a lot of blacks and Chicanos and Latinos, it's what has made them getting training and an education affordable."

PERHAPS IT WAS INEVITABLE that the GI Bill would provoke a variety of opinions, and recent scholarship has indeed turned its attention to the many limitations, outright exclusions, and declining benefits associated with the bill's capacity to promote socioeconomic mobility for discharged veterans. In particular, the original version, signed into law in 1944, has come under intense scrutiny. For example, the localized nature of the bill's implementation forced black veterans to deal with existing discriminatory practices as an everyday reality. Moreover, the specific focus on returning soldiers, both wounded and able-bodied, rather than on a larger community that encompassed defense workers or the public at large, ensured a heterosexual norm that filtered benefits to male heads of households to the overwhelming exclusion of women. Furthermore, the Veteran's Administration (VA) view of homosexuality left veterans who had been discharged "undesirably," an ambiguous administrative term, without benefits. Lastly, these biases often operated in tandem with logistical issues common to any bureaucracy as vast as the VA to limit the effectiveness of the Serviceman's Readjustment Act.

Like members of other marginalized communities, Mexican Americans encountered various difficulties in their attempt to access the bill's entitlements. Their experiences, however, challenge conclusions that the bill was simply exclusionary. Training received under the bill, and one's status as a veteran, did facilitate a "bridging environment" to improved socioeconomic status for some veterans.[1]

Therefore, less monolithic depictions of the bill that embrace an either/or binary must be utilized. Rather, the bill's effects were more nuanced.[2] In addition, this complicated matrix of the many positive and potentially negligible outcomes associated with the 1944 GI Bill must also be extended to subsequent versions that provided benefits to veterans that served in Korea and Vietnam (and beyond). It is important to remember that the GI Bill has evolved since its original 1944 version, and in the case of the latter two conflicts, declining benefits were a tragic reality, producing a supplementary stipend in the pursuit of various educational and other training endeavors, rather than a livable wage that supported veterans and their dependents as occurred after World War II.

RETURN TO CIVILIAN LIFE

The transformative potential of the 1944 GI Bill of Rights cannot be ignored. In terms of scale and generosity, no previous legislative effort to recruit and retain military personnel, or deal with disabled veterans and the widows of those killed in action, matched the sheer amount of resources disbursed by the federal government after World War II. Moreover, the focus on providing a benefits package to the able-bodied was without precedent.[3] As recently as 1932, World War I veterans—the so-called Bonus Army—who were encamped in Washington, DC, in an effort to secure early payment of promised bonuses were forcibly removed by the U.S. Army and publicly ridiculed.[4] Nevertheless, the social insurance programs of the New Deal; the lobbying efforts of the American Legion, the main veterans' organization; and fears of a possible recession upon demobilization motivated new thinking that ultimately produced a stimulus package for individual servicemen. As described by historian Keith Olson, "the economy needed federal help; the veterans served as a convenient, traditional, and popular means to provide that assistance."[5] The result was a range of entitlements that enabled returning servicemen to access low-interest loans for homes, farms, and businesses; educational assistance at the collegiate and subcollege level; unemployment compensation for fifty-two weeks at $20 a week, also known as the 52–20 Club; and job-placement services. All returning veterans were entitled to receive these benefits if they had been released from active duty with a discharge other than dishonorable.

Of these various entitlements, particular attention has been placed on the education and training benefits that 7.8 million veterans would ultimately utilize.

By far the largest subgroup—5.6 million—chose to attend vocational or business schools or participate in on-the-job and on-the-farm training. Among the beneficiaries of these programs, John López decided to become a carpenter's apprentice in 1948 after working multiple odd jobs following his discharge in December 1945. As he described it, "The GI Bill paid for it, tools . . . whatever I needed."[6] After acquiring a journeyman classification in 1951, he remained a carpenter for the next fifty years, finding steady employment through Los Angeles–based Local 235 of the United Carpenters of America, an affiliate of the American Federation of Labor. López was unstinting in his praise of the GI Bill: "I wouldn't have what I have now if it wasn't for the help [training and benefits] from the military."[7]

David Fuentes returned to Los Angeles in November 1946 to care for his ill mother and decide on a future. His initial desire was "to go to school, I wanted to go to dentistry school, but there was a two-year waiting list."[8] Fuentes would instead utilize the tailoring skills he had learned from his father: "I did a lot of sewing . . . 'cause my father showed me when I was a little boy, and so I went to tailoring school. I went to Glover's Institute and then I was a pattern maker for women's dresses and slacks."[9] He remained in this occupation for the next forty-four years, providing him with a comfortable middle-class lifestyle. Meanwhile, Raúl Medina returned to Fresno, California, to find that his wife had deserted him and sold the house they were in the process of purchasing: "When I came home, I came home to nothing. I didn't have anything."[10] He credits the GI Bill with helping him to become a successful upholsterer: "I got the on-the-job training program . . . for upholstery, and that was always good to me because it's not a high-class, high-tech trade. You work with your hands and have a little bit of imagination. And I liked that."[11] Across the country in eastern Michigan, Guadalupe "Lupe" Ortega decided to further the haircutting skills he acquired as an army soldier and also become a homeowner after his discharge sometime in 1946. As he described: "I went to [trade] school on the GI Bill . . . Greens Barber College . . . It was only six months . . . in Detroit . . . And I got a loan to buy a house here [Saginaw, Michigan]."[12] He successfully operated Lupe's Barber Shop in Saginaw for the next twenty-five years.[13]

With the bill's generous financial provisions, the remaining 2.2 million veterans enrolled in a variety of public and private four-year universities as well as two-year junior colleges. As described by Suzanne Mettler in *Soldiers to Citizens: The G.I. Bill and the Making of the Greatest Generation*, "All tuition and fees were covered, up to a total of $500 per year—more than any university charged at that time—and veterans received monthly subsistence payments of $75 if single, $105 with one dependent, and $120 with two or more dependents."[14] For example, Jesse Ybarra enrolled at Trinity University in his hometown of San Antonio, Texas, after his discharge in December 1945; he later recalled, "At that time, they [GI Bill] would pay everything . . . schooling, books, everything you needed, they paid for."[15] He successfully acquired a bachelor's degree through the GI Bill, and a master's degree at his own expense, which he used to become a counselor at youth centers in Texas and California working with juvenile delinquents. Furthermore, the training he received as a medic in the U.S. Army also proved to be quite helpful in this occupation. He described one such episode: "A guy got shot, and I had to use a tourniquet . . . I had to apply the very thing [I learned in the army]."[16] Rolando Hinojosa also acquired a bachelor's degree after returning to the University of Texas in 1952. He offered a glowing account of the educational benefits that made this possible: "It was great! They paid for your tuition . . . We got . . . free books. We got protractors, compasses, slide rules, pencils, ink, everything."[17] He believed that many fellow veterans from his hometown of Mercedes, Texas, similarly benefitted: "That little area produced a lot of college kids because of the GI Bill, either [through service in] World War II, or in my case, the Korean War."[18] Hinojosa would continue his pursuit of higher education, ultimately acquiring a doctorate in English from the University of Illinois in 1968, whereby he entered academia, culminating in his present position at the University of Texas. Along the way, Hinojosa has become one of the more renowned figures in Chicano literature.[19]

By comparison, William Sánchez returned to the United States a changed man following his ordeal as a Japanese prisoner of war (POW) from May 1942 to September 1945: "You come back, you're totally a different person, you are never the same."[20] After three weeks of rigorous physical and mental-health examinations at Fort Lewis, Washington, he received his entire back pay in one lump sum, which enabled him to purchase a home in Los Angeles. He soon attended Woodbury College on the GI Bill, acquiring a bachelor's degree in business administration with a focus in international trade and finance. Ultimately, the bill's entitlements and his POW status, which has included a tax-exempt status on all private property, enabled Sánchez to become a successful businessman. As he stated: "I'm very fortunate . . . because of my service . . . I don't have to worry [financially]."[21]

Another veteran, Francisco Vega, was discharged at Fort Sam Houston in San Antonio, Texas, in December 1945. Recently married in May 1946, he decided to move to the Upper Midwest with his wife, a former resident of Illinois: "I was trying to get into the University of Michigan . . . But every state university was just getting a flood of veterans . . . and these states were giving preference to their residents who were born there. So I couldn't get into [the] U[niversity] of M[ichigan]."[22] In order to establish residency, Vega decided to enroll at Aquinas College, a small liberal arts academy in Grand Rapids, Michigan. For Aquinas and other similar institutions, returning veterans represented "money. I mean tuition, money for food, money for housing."[23] After two years at Aquinas, Vega transferred to the University of Michigan, and he and his wife lived in a barracks in nearby Ypsilanti that formerly housed defense workers that built bombers during World War II. He and fellow veterans bussed to the university, where Vega was immediately shocked by the huge class sizes and the difficult curriculum. As frustration and poor grades mounted, Vega decided to transfer back to Aquinas after one year; he graduated in 1950 with a bachelor's degree in Spanish and a minor in business economics. These experiences at both institutions, paid for by the GI Bill, provided Vega and his wife with a crowded yet comfortable lifestyle. He recalled: "We had money for food, for rent, and so on."[24]

Richard Domínguez returned to Los Angeles in March 1946 and became a member of the acclaimed 52–20 Club. He supplemented this income by renewing his membership in the Screen Actors Guild, an occupation he had begun prior to World War II and which allowed him to serve as an extra in a number of Hollywood films. After his discharge, this income provided a bare level of subsistence, yet he remained in no hurry to pursue a career. As he described, "I wanted to celebrate . . . and then I started school and finally got down to business. It took me a couple of years to do that."[25] Using the GI Bill's education benefits, Domínguez eventually acquired an associate's degree from East Los Angeles Junior College.[26] While on campus, he noticed advertisements seeking recruits for the Los Angeles Police Department (LAPD). Domínguez readily admits that his veteran status and his military training as a paratrooper in the 11th Airborne Division were critical factors in his acceptance into the police academy in November 1948: "Most of the fellows in the [recruit] class, well, the majority, were veterans from the armed services . . . and they [gave] you some points on the civil service examination."[27] Similarly, George Castrueta also responded to an advertisement while enrolled at East Los Angeles Junior College through the GI Bill. He applied for a job with the Los Angeles County Fire Warden and, much like Domínguez, he was glad to receive the ten additional points that his veteran status provided. However, he was not without company in this regard: "Everybody that took the exam were all veterans . . . everybody had ten points!"[28]

Such comments highlight a long-standing effort to examine the capacity of the armed forces to function as a "bridging environment" that can nurture improved socioeconomic status. In addition to GI Bill entitlements, preferential hiring practices, military training, and exposure to bureaucratic structures have also benefitted veterans as compared to their nonveteran counterparts. Furthermore, veteran status for socially marginalized groups would seemingly enhance this bridging process as a result of their less advantageous position. A 1973 study by Harley L. Browning, Sally C. Lopreato, and Dudley L. Poston Jr. showed an estimated average gross difference of $711 between veteran and nonveteran status for Mexican Americans across a variety of professional and more labor-intensive occupations. For white Americans, by contrast, the average difference was $122. As can be seen in table 1, veteran status for Mexican Americans produced a positive mean difference across the board and was especially pronounced in the least-skilled occupational groups—sales, service, and laborers—where a bridging process would most likely be expected to occur.[29] Meanwhile, aside from professionals, white veterans benefitted less from their veteran status; two categories—managers and clerical—actually suffered as a result of their military service.[30]

Another study, completed in 1979, utilizing data drawn from three 1/100 Public Use Samples of the 1970 U.S. Census, identified a $1,795 difference in mean income favoring Mexican American veterans over nonveterans of World War II. As highlighted in table 2, this is double the amount that existed between white veterans and nonveterans, which stood at $895.[31] The Korean War produced a net difference of $1,725 and the Vietnam War $587, again favoring veterans. What is telling, however, is that Mexican American veterans nevertheless earned less than both white veterans and nonveterans in terms of overall average income across three generations.

Suzanne Mettler expanded on this concept of a bridging environment to include a positive effect on the political and civic engagement of World War II veterans. As she noted, "Veterans typically found the GI Bill's benefits to be readily accessible and smoothly administered. Program implementation conveyed to them powerful messages not only about the value of one particular program but also, more broadly, about government's responsiveness to people like them."[32] Based on surveys collected from over 1,500 individuals, Mettler found a generation of veterans boosted into the ranks of the middle class and committed to public life and participatory democracy. Moreover, among black respondents

TABLE 1. Mean Differences between Veteran and Nonveteran Income in Specific Occupational Groups

OCCUPATIONAL GROUP	MEXICAN AMERICAN MEAN VETERAN INCOME	DIFFERENCES BETWEEN MEXICAN AMERICAN VETERAN, NONVETERAN INCOME	ANGLO MEAN VETERAN INCOME	DIFFERENCES BETWEEN ANGLO VETERAN, NONVETERAN INCOME
Professionals	$7,175	$207	$8,892	$453
Managers	$6,533	$175	$8,762	–$716
Clerical	$5,089	$967	$5,956	–$62
Sales	$6,001	$1,222	$7,502	$74
Craftsmen	$5,355	$131	$6,421	$6
Operatives	$4,807	$490	$5,797	$178
Service	$4,471	$1,133	$5,584	$185
Laborers	$4,891	$1,225	$5,075	$238
Total	—	$711	—	$122

SOURCE Harley L. Browning, Sally C. Lopreato, and Dudley L. Poston Jr., "Income and Veteran Status: Variations Among Mexican Americans, Blacks, and Anglos," *American Sociological Review* 33 (1973): 74–85; the information is drawn from table 3.

TABLE 2. Mean Differences in Income between Mexican American Veterans/Nonveterans and Anglo Veterans/Nonveterans

COHORT	MEXICAN AMERICAN VETERANS	MEXICAN AMERICAN NONVETERANS	ANGLO VETERANS	ANGLO NONVETERANS
World War II	$7,857	$6,062	$9,480	$8,585
Korea	$8,051	$6,326	$9,694	$8,978
Vietnam	$6,538	$5,951	$7,823	$8,315

SOURCE Melanie Martindale and Dudley L. Poston Jr., "Variations in Veteran/Nonveteran Earning Patterns Among World War II, Korea, and Vietnam War Cohorts," *Armed Forces & Society* 5 (1979): 219–43; the information is drawn from tables 2 and 3.

to her questionnaire, the bill positively influenced their civil rights activism and other challenges to the racial status quo present within the United States.

Such depictions, however, perpetuate the tendency to view World War II as a type of watershed for marginalized communities, a process immortalized as "Double V." Originally coined by African Americans to depict their struggle for a double victory over the Axis powers abroad and for civil rights at home, this concept celebrates the opportunity provided by World War II to secure first-class citizenship through dedicated military service. Yet the notion of World War II as a turning point for the Mexican American community has drawn some criticism. Historian George Sánchez argued that "there is a tendency in Chicano history to view World War II as a watershed, a period . . . when returning servicemen for the first time fought for their rights as citizens. I argue, rather, that much of the cultural identity and sense of self . . . was already shaped before the war."[33] Dennis Valdés provided a more blunt assessment in his analysis of the Mexican community residing in the Midwest: "Demographically, World War II was not a watershed in the history of the Mexican community . . . [W]orld War II did not profoundly alter the occupational profile of all Mexicans, particularly those in the Midwest, and its immediate impact on upward mobility among families, a key aspect of the American Dream, was inconsistent."[34]

These observations depict a more complicated and uneven reality, underscoring the need to reexamine the 1944 GI Bill of Rights and its impact on Mexican American veterans. For example, logistical issues and lack of awareness often coexisted with varying degrees of outright racism within the Veterans Administration and society at large to hamper the ability of many veterans to utilize the full range of benefits offered or led them to shun the program altogether. African American veterans of World War II were especially vulnerable, and in April 1947 "the VA found only 5 percent of all black veterans enrolled in courses and programs under the education benefit."[35] Thus, the notion of World War II and the GI Bill as marking a watershed for African Americans is also suspect. Rather, the Deep South entered into a new era of social and political flux at war's end, revealing a racial landscape "evolving beyond the certainties of an older era toward a different and undefined future—moving out of the past, but not wholly escaping it, either."[36]

Rampant discrimination in the form of redlining could also make it difficult to purchase a home through the bill's low-interest loan program. George Castrueta, for example, detailed his effort to buy a home in Whittier, California, a predominantly white suburban enclave in Los Angeles County: "In around

1952, there were still some areas . . . where they frowned on selling you [Mexican Americans] a home . . . the salesperson was a young guy and it wasn't up to him, he had been given the word . . . I wasn't gonna press it . . . there [were] a lot of other areas."[37] The following year Richard Domínguez also acquired a home in Whittier, despite having his initial housing application denied due to exclusionary practices. The reaction from his neighbors was less than friendly, a hostility apparently exacerbated by the growing size of his family, which ultimately included five sons and three daughters: "Sometime in 1958 or so . . . I got a letter in the mail . . . and it said . . . 'Why don't you go back to Mexico where you belong. All you do is know how to have children. We don't want you around here.' "[38] Further inland, in Riverside, California, Mike García encountered an equally harsh environment: "I tried to get a house in town when I first got out of the service, but they flatly told me 'we don't sell to Mexicans, to niggers, or to Orientals.' "[39]

Aside from bigotry, navigating the massive bureaucracy associated with the GI Bill and the VA in order to receive benefits or deal with problems also explains underutilization by some veterans. In the case of Alfred Aguirre, the reasons included complete ignorance of what the law entailed: "I didn't understand all the benefits we had. I learned later on, but at the time I didn't know. Nobody told me about it."[40] Late payment on a monthly basis could also produce a general indifference toward the bill, as described by John Sótelo in this chapter's epigraph: "Sometimes it was three, four months before you got your check . . . and a lot of fellas dropped out of school."[41] Meanwhile, Nick Salazar was immediately frustrated with the sheer size of the veteran student population, a reality that also prevented David Fuentes from pursuing dentistry: "I was gonna go to school . . . I went to UCLA to start with, but in those days . . . there's thousands of veterans. It was all the way around the block, the line, four deep . . . to hell with it. I came home, I went to trade school."[42] He enrolled at Trade Technical Institute in Los Angeles and eventually became a printer.

Frustration over the training received also left some veterans disillusioned if such training did not produce immediate results. Newly married and in need of employment after receiving his discharge in September 1946, Mike García decided to pursue certification in watchmaking and repair. As he explained, the results were less than satisfactory: "That was nothing but a small course, and then I tried to get a job, and they wouldn't hire an apprentice . . . then later on I got involved into construction but I went to school on my own. I put in three years of apprenticeship."[43] Martin Morales was also disappointed with the training he received in cabinetmaking. However, the monthly subsistence of $75 provided financial incentive to remain in the course for approximately six months. As he stated, "If you went to school on the GI Bill of Rights, they would pay you [a monthly subsistence]. I didn't learn anything, [however]. I went . . . for the money . . . I was just killing time."[44] Finally, many veterans were simply unable to take advantage of the GI Bill due to family and other household responsibilities. As Arnulfo "Arnif" Nerio recalled, "I should of [used the bill], but I had . . . my kids . . . and I had to keep on working at . . . General Motors [in Saginaw, Michigan]."[45] Moreover, a middle-class or lower-middle-class lifestyle was indeed possible without federal assistance, as was the case for Salvador Marez. After his discharge from the navy in January 1946, Marez found steady foundry work throughout the Upper Midwest until his retirement in Grand Rapids, Michigan, in 1986. On the nonuse of his entitlements, he simply stated: "'Cause I didn't need to . . . I was able to do everything that I wanted to do [without my GI Bill benefits]."[46]

All in all, while participation was not widespread, nor did veterans utilize the full range of benefits provided, these diverse experiences challenge conclusions that the 1944 GI Bill of Rights was simply faulty and exclusionary. After all, training received under the bill, and one's status as a veteran, did facilitate a degree of social mobility for some while also promoting activism in the pursuit of social equality. This "bridging environment" played a key role in fostering professional careers and a variety of trade skills acquired through vocational training. Furthermore, this complicated reality associated with the original 1944 bill sets the stage for a similar examination of GI Bill entitlements encountered by Korean and Vietnam War veterans. In the case of the former, lawmakers, veterans' organizations, and a majority of the public favored a continuation of benefits for able-bodied servicemen upon their release from active duty. Yet cost concerns—in particular, various abuses encountered in the administration of the first bill—dampened congressional activity on the matter. The outbreak of hostilities on the Korean Peninsula at the height of the Cold War, however, provided the needed pressure for a new benefits package.

KOREA AND THE COLD WAR

Cold War tension with the Soviet Union and a stimulus package meant to help both the economy and returning veterans were important factors in the creation of a second GI Bill. Moreover, as Melinda L. Pash expressed in her recent study, *In the Shadow of the Greatest Generation: The Americans Who Fought the Korean War*, "81 percent of those who served overseas felt entitled to the same educational opportunities afforded earlier veterans, and another 78 percent believed the government should offer their generation low-cost home loans."[47] Signed into law on July 14, 1952, Public Law 500, also known as the Veterans' Readjustment Assistance Act, provided many of the same entitlements that World War II veterans received, such as educational benefits, loan guarantees, assistance in securing employment, and unemployment compensation. Those that served after June 27, 1950, whether service was performed in the Korean combat zone or in any other military location, and who separated from the military with ninety days of active service and with a discharge other than dishonorable were eligible to receive these benefits.

Notable modifications included a maximum of thirty-six months of benefits, in contrast to the original bill's four years. Also, the 1952 act did not include payment to colleges and training institutions for tuition, books, and fees. Rather, "the government directly paid this new wave of GI students monthly stipends, making them responsible for covering both tuition and living expenses. Those returning to school full time received between $110 and $160 a month depending upon the number of their dependents."[48] While these and other modifications were meant to curb corruption and waste, they also made it more difficult for many returning veterans to access their educational benefits. For example, individual payments hampered many veterans in their ability to pay tuition and other registration costs prior to the commencement of the academic year as required by most universities and training institutions. Most importantly, however, stipends did not keep pace with inflation and other living expenses, requiring most veterans to supplement their stipend with full- or part-time employment, a reality that also forced many to reduce their academic or training workload and become part-time students. This was indeed a common experience shared by many Korean War veterans and is a testament to the inability of the 1952 act to provide a living wage in contrast to the earlier bill.

Testimony is provided by Michigan resident John López, who served in the U.S. Air Force from 1948 to 1952 and subsequently enrolled at DeVry Institute in Chicago to study electronics for one year: "They [GI Bill] paid for your books and stuff like that, but you didn't have enough money left over to pay your rent . . . It paid quite a bit, [but] I'm not saying it paid [for] everything."[49]

Vincent Pardo provided similar commentary on his experience at the same DeVry Institute following a three-year tour (1952–55) in the U.S. Marine Corps:

> We [students] were getting only money once a month to pay for the classes. But they [VA] would not pay for sustaining yourself or [for] your [rent] where you were living. We would work five days a week [for] four hours in the morning in the places where they wanted to hire students . . . And then we'd go to school from four o'clock in the afternoon till eight o'clock at night. And then we were also working extra, like Saturday or Sunday . . . And that's what paid for my upkeep."[50]

William J. Fisher, meanwhile, resumed his pursuit of a bachelor's degree at the University of Arizona after being demobilized from his status as a naval reservist in September 1951. However, family and other household responsibilities required an income much greater than the monthly stipend provided by the 1952 GI Bill. He described his circumstances:

> At one time, I was working for the [U.S.] Post Office, going to school [part time], [I was] in the [USMC] reserves, and working at a liquor store at night . . . My wife wasn't working and I had two kids. By being in the reserves, it was just . . . extra money. And then going to school was also extra money [from the GI Bill].[51]

After fourteen years as a part-time student attending evening and summer classes, he received a bachelor's degree in elementary education in 1962.[52]

Ruben Moreno also pursued a more gradual approach to his apprenticeship training as he struggled to support his family: "I took an apprenticeship as a cabinetmaker . . . After four years of going to school at night and working at it, I was able to get my master's [certification]."[53] Eddie Trujillo took a similar approach: "I started going to school at night [in a] machine shop . . . I used it [GI Bill benefits] all."[54] His veteran status also facilitated needed instruction in basic literacy skills. As he stated, "[Nearby administrators] had a school for Korean War veterans in L.A. [where] I was learning to read and write [and] arithmetic and all that."[55] Robert Villegas utilized his education benefit to acquire certification as a hairstylist in order to supplement his primary income as a factory worker. He recalled, "I went to . . . a cosmetology class . . . A friend of mine had a beauty shop . . . [and] this looked very [promising]."[56] He received additional help in his effort to purchase a home: "My [home] loan, I got it through the GI Bill. That was very convenient. I didn't have to give a down payment [and] the interest rate was fairly low."[57]

Other challenges associated with the 1952 act included frustration over training received that left many veterans feeling embittered in a manner similar to some World War II beneficiaries. For example, Ray Gomez decided to become a barber following a four-year tour in the U.S. Army from 1948 to 1952: "I went to American Barber College in Los Angeles and I graduated from there, but I could never make any money cutting hair . . . There's no money in that profession . . . So I winded up as a machinist [for] forty years."[58] Furthermore, such frustration was often exacerbated by rampant discrimination that often nullified the training received by individual veterans or simply halted the training program altogether. José Domínguez encountered the latter upon his return to Las Cruces, New Mexico, following a four-year stint in the army from 1948 to 1952. As he described, the local white power structure was intent on maintaining the racial status quo, which included disrupting classes with a large Mexican American presence: "I did [go] to [a] . . . school for mechanic [training] under the GI Bill, but it didn't last long. [As a result], everybody disappeared from the school and before you [knew] it, it was all over."[59]

Gene García also confronted racial hostility. However, through sheer perseverance he ultimately acquired a rewarding career. He detailed his ordeal:

> I wanted to become a mechanic, I think, for the simple reason that my dad was a mechanic . . . so I went to . . . trade school in Los Angeles [to become an] automotive diesel mechanic . . . I finished trade school [and received] my diploma . . . [However], in those days they wouldn't hire Chicanos in the garages . . . and I looked and I looked . . . So continuing [the use of] my GI Bill, I went to body and fender school in Los Angeles.[60]

After a promising start, García was laid off, forcing him to turn yet again to his GI Bill entitlements. He continued: "I went back to college, and this time I went . . . for general academic [training] . . . [And] I got my [associates of arts] degree [at Riverside Community College]."[61] While on campus he encountered an old friend that provided a recommendation for employment in the missile-defense industry, a career that ultimately spanned thirty-two years. He described his rapid advancement: "I was able to build all these valves and all this hardware that went on the missiles without any problem . . . I started out as

TABLE 3. Comparison of Training Participation Rates for the Three GI Bills

PROGRAM	NUMBER ELIGIBLE	NUMBER OF TRAINEES	PERCENTAGE OF TRAINEES
World War II (1944–56)	15,614,000	7,800,000	49.9
Korean Conflict (1952–65)	5,708,000	2,391,000	41.8
Vietnam Era (1966–June 20, 1972)	6,303,000	2,400,000	40.9*
Total	27,625,000	12,591,000	41.6

SOURCE U.S. Veterans Administration Information Service pamphlet, *G.I. Bill of Rights, 25th Anniversary, 1944–1969* (Washington, DC: Veterans Administration Main Office, 1969), 6–10.
*Eligibility under the Veterans Readjustment Benefits Act of 1966 continued for another eight years after separation from service.

an assembler, from there I went to a test technician, and then . . . to a development technician."[62]

Overall, despite these challenges, the administration of the 1952 act occurred with fewer problems in comparison to the earlier bill, and many abuses were corrected. Nevertheless, as table 3 illustrates, approximately 2.4 million veterans, or about 42 percent, availed themselves of their educational, training, and other benefits, while half of those eligible after World War II did so.[63] In particular, the less generous provisions of the 1952 GI Bill stands as the most striking difference between the two acts that inherently made the pursuit of an education and other forms of training a more challenging endeavor for returning veterans, one that required supplementary forms of income and a more gradual pursuit of educational goals and other forms of certification. The financial disparity between the two bills would also establish a precedent for subsequent legislation that would ultimately leave returning veterans from yet another U.S. conflict with even fewer benefits from which to draw.

THE VIETNAM WAR

With the termination of eligibility for the Korean War GI Bill in 1955, the idea for permanent financial assistance as a form of veteran readjustment increasingly gained public and congressional support. However, fears of an expanding federal government and financial considerations played a key role in establishing an opposition that delayed action on a permanent benefits program. An increased tempo of American involvement in Vietnam in the mid-1960s was needed to obtain results. Signed into law on March 3, 1966, Public Law 89–358, also known as the Veterans' Readjustment Benefits Act, retroactively provided a comprehensive benefits package to all peacetime and combat veterans that had served 180 days since January 31, 1955. Furthermore, no termination date existed for this latest GI Bill legislation, as was the case with the previous two enactments. Thus it established the GI Bill as a permanent feature of military service in the United States.

In addition to support for education and vocational training, the Vietnam-era GI Bill provided home loans, medical care, preference in civil service positions, and free counseling. The most prominent modification from the first two bills, however, was that eligible veterans were to receive one month of benefits for each month of active service—up to a maximum of thirty-six months—while the first two bills provided 1.5 months of assistance. This meant that a service member had to serve three years to be entitled to the equivalent of four academic years. Moreover, like its predecessor, the actual assistance took the form of a direct grant to the returning veteran with the following rates: single veterans enrolled full time received a $100 allowance; with one dependent, $125; and with two or more dependents, $150.[64] Regrettably, these initial rates were noticeably lower than those provided to Korean War veterans, and consistent sentiment for a general increase led to a series of modifications between 1967 and 1972 that more than doubled monthly stipends.[65] More importantly, the prevailing perspective associated with this latest version was its supplemental nature rather than a subsistence wage meant to support veterans and their dependents. As J. Peter Matilda concluded in his 1978 study, "At its peak in 1949, monthly G.I. Bill benefits were 53.9 percent of monthly wages in manufacturing . . . At its peak in 1975, Vietnam era enrollees received only 34.3 percent of average monthly wages in manufacturing."[66] Indeed, the following experiences conveyed by Mexican American veterans of the Vietnam War clearly demonstrate that transition in GI Bill benefits.

George Mariscal returned from Vietnam in 1970 and, as he stated, "I came back and went right back to the city college I had flunked out of [prior to being drafted]. And there were a lot of vets there."[67] Expediting his return was the military's "early out" option, which enabled service members who had served a tour in Vietnam to complete their contractual obligation early, by several months, if evidence was provided that such a request would enable the individual to attend a college or vocational training. As he described: "At that time, they had what was called an 'early out' [option] . . . If you could prove [that] you were going to get into a college program . . . they'd let you out [a few] months early."[68] Mariscal's frugal endeavors upon his return to Long Beach City College, which continued at California State University, Long Beach, after his transfer, capture the supplementary nature of the Vietnam-era GI Bill:

> I used the whole thing. It was [approximately] $250 a month . . . I came back to city college, which was cheap. In those days, it was like $10 to register, [so] I was saving a lot of that . . . [Also], the first year or so, I lived at home. But then, in those days . . . an apartment [was] $95 a month. It was doable. Plus . . . I was going home and eating a lot.[69]

A variety of odd jobs throughout his academic training, culminating in a doctorate in Spanish literature from the University of California, Irvine, provided additional income.[70]

Several other narrators would also acquire advanced degrees, and their GI Bill stipends provided support in the early stages of their academic training. Among them was Joe Rodríguez, who also utilized the military's early out option and returned to San Diego from Vietnam in 1966. He offered the following: "I was able to get out and go to school. In fact, you could get out early if you went to college."[71] He offered a more glowing appraisal of the GI Bill and other military benefits: "[It was] good value . . . I was able to finish my BA [at San Diego State] . . . [And I] was able to go to school just on VA benefits and live comfortably."[72] Moreover, as he described, his training as a navy hospital corpsman also facilitated his endeavors:

> How I put myself through school was to . . . work as a nurse [at] Scripps Memorial Hospital. I used to work up on the fifth floor in orthopedics while I was going to grad school after my [GI Bill] benefits ran out.[73]

Meanwhile, Raymond Buriel first enrolled at Riverside Community College, where he utilized his monthly stipend after completing his tour in the Marine Corps: "I went through junior college with that . . . I milked that thing . . . It was very beneficial."[74] He also recounted the impression he made on his employers at the Claremont Colleges after acquiring both a bachelor's and a doctorate at the University of California, Riverside:

> It was a two-year [appointment] . . . I figured . . . this will pay for the bills for two years while I get some publications . . . [Campus administration ultimately] said, "This is what we had always been wanting for Chicano Studies. Why don't you stay and we'll make you a tenure-track professor in Chicano Studies, the first one."[75]

Another veteran, Leroy Quintana, left the army in 1969 and enrolled at the University of New Mexico, where he ultimately acquired a bachelor's degree. As he recalled, his monthly stipend was quite helpful: "It helped [and I am] glad I got it . . . I got married . . . a year after I came back. So that really helped in terms of finances . . . 'cause it allowed me to be free to go to school . . . I did a lot of odd jobs, but not as many as I otherwise [would have had to]."[76] Daniel Cano offered a more pragmatic appraisal of the GI Bill after he returned to Los Angeles following his discharge from the army in 1967: "It supplemented [my pursuit of a bachelor's] . . . but I had to still work."[77] His need for employment increased following his marriage and the birth of a child in 1971, which ultimately delayed the completion of his bachelor's coursework until 1978:

> I started . . . at Santa Monica Community College [in 1969] and then I went to Cal State Domínguez Hills . . . In 1973, I got really serious about college, but then, by that time, I couldn't go to school full time because I had to work full time. So I went to school at night. That's why it took so long.[78]

Alfredo Vea, however, decided to delay the use of his GI Bill benefits after he left the army in 1969 until he enrolled at law school at the University of California, Berkeley. As he stated, his work ethic provided the necessary income to support himself and pay for his undergraduate degree: "I waited [because] I didn't know what I wanted to do. Plus, I always worked. I was a contractor when I was getting my BA . . . [I went] through nine years of [academic training] without owning a dime. I worked at night. I was just used to working."[79]

Across the country, Raúl Mosqueda completed his four-year tour in the navy (1968–72) and returned to Saginaw, Michigan, where he found himself recruited by a number of universities offering financial assistance for underprivileged students who had been part of the migrant labor work force. Through funds provided by United Migrants for Opportunity Inc. (UMOI), he decided to attend the University of Michigan in the fall of 1972. As he described, however, a surplus of funds did have its drawbacks:

> I think it made things too easy for me because [I] had this special program that was paying [my] tuition, room, and board. And then, on top of that, I had my GI Bill. What happened with me . . . I started to drink a little bit . . . and so . . . I got off track."[80]

After acquiring a bachelor's in general studies in 1980, he enrolled in dental school at Indiana University from 1981 to 1985, where he found his prior training as a dental technician quite helpful. In fact, Mosqueda offers the clearest example of a service member whose job in the military laterally transferred to the civilian sector with excellent results. He offered the following reminiscence:

> That gave me the edge . . . [I had] some problems with the academic part, but all of the practical part . . . doing the extractions [and] doing the denture work . . . all of that I could whiz right through it . . . Having the experience of [being] a dental tech gave me . . . confidence.[81]

Gilbert Guevara also returned to Saginaw, Michigan, after a two-year tour in the army from 1967 to 1969, and he found his veteran status helpful in returning to his job at Saginaw Steering Gear. He recalled that "I still had a job there. They said to me, 'Because you were drafted, your job will be here when you come back.'"[82] Rather than return, he instead decided to enroll at Saginaw Valley State University. Unfortunately, family and community responsibilities prevented his completion of a bachelor's degree: "I was married [and] then I got involved in the community, and one thing led to another, so that I just gradually was [attending fewer classes] . . . [However, the GI Bill] paid for the classes that I took."[83]

In addition to these various educational endeavors after being discharged from active service, career officers in the armed forces are provided with the opportunity to pursue a master's degree at the military's expense while also acquiring GI Bill benefits for later use. As an officer in the Marine Corps for twenty-two years, Tony López utilized both options to his advantage. He explained:

> I got a master's in management . . . and then I got a [second] master's in education . . . The master's in management was from Pepperdine [while in the service] and the master's in education was from [California State University,] San

> Bernardino . . . as soon as I got out of the service. I was able to do it through the [GI Bill] benefits that I accrued from my military career.[84]

Similarly, Everett Álvarez retired from the navy in 1980 after a twenty-year career, during which he earned an MS in operational research and systems development from the navy's postgraduate school in Monterey, California. While stationed in Washington, DC, he also decided to utilize his GI Bill benefits to attend law school as he neared retirement:

> I started going to school at night, 'cause I knew I wanted to learn more. So I would work all day and go to school at night, five nights a week, to law school . . . [at] George Washington University . . . When I retired, I clerked in a law firm . . . [But] after three or four months I decided that was not for me. [It was] too boring.[85]

Álvarez subsequently decided to join President Ronald Reagan's administration, and a series of government posts followed:

> I had other choices. One of them was to come into the Reagan administration . . . as a political appointee . . . I was the number two at the Peace Corps for a year and a half. And then I moved over to the Veterans Administration. I was the number two at the VA for the next four years.[86]

These latter two stories highlight the enhanced opportunities afforded to officers in the U.S. military. Unfortunately, precious few Mexican Americans obtained a commission from World War II through Vietnam, leaving the overwhelming majority enlisted men unable to access these additional perks and other advantages.

CONCLUSION

The reminiscences provided by these Mexican American veterans offer examples of various achievements in a variety of different occupations and other professional endeavors. However, in the case of Korea and Vietnam, the supplementary nature of their monthly stipends is also readily apparent. Moreover, quantitative data has illustrated that in the aftermath of the Vietnam War,

Hispanic veterans had less formal education vis-à-vis non-Hispanic veterans. In particular, the VA's *Chart Book on Black and Hispanic Veterans* listed 843,700 male Hispanic veterans in the United States in 1980. Of this figure, approximately 10 percent had completed four or more years of college whereas approximately 20 percent of the 26.5 million, or 5.2 million, non-Hispanic male veterans had done so.[87] Thus, despite opportunities for socioeconomic advancement commonly associated with the GI Bill, the data indicate that a bridging process did occur for many Mexican American veterans that served between 1940 and 1975, just not as many as one might assume. A variety of factors offer an explanation, including personal indifference, uneven implementation, social and educational discrimination, and the declining value of monthly stipends that left Korean and Vietnam War veterans with fewer benefits from which to draw. Additionally, many returning veterans confronted more personal battles with the physical and emotional scars acquired while in uniform. And in the ongoing debate over the GI Bill's ultimate impact, the psychiatric and medical services provided by the Veterans Administration to wounded GIs as part of the original bill's appropriations have been largely overlooked in favor of the direct benefit programs. Nevertheless, the VA, as a health-care system, would play no less a central role in the postwar lives of many veterans than the more celebrated forms of direct assistance.

8

THE VETERANS ADMINISTRATION

"We got one foot in the grave, they're [VA] gonna throw us a goddamm bone, and that's what it amounts to. I feel that as far as the Veterans Administration [is concerned] . . . we were treated just plain goddamm rotten."

"You . . . hear and see on TV and [in] the newspaper[s] that the government takes care of its soldiers . . . and it's just a bunch of bull."

THE EFFECTIVENESS OF THE GI BILL, and military service overall, in promoting socioeconomic mobility for Mexican American and other veterans must take into consideration the physical and mental scars acquired while in service. For example, alcoholism and post-traumatic stress disorder are among the maladies that many veterans have endured well beyond their tours of duty, which the following reminiscences furnished by my narrators clearly attest to. Consequently, the psychiatric and medical services provided by the Veterans Administration (VA) have remained one of the more important facets of military service that many veterans have utilized for the remainder of their lives. Differing opinions over proper compensation, however, in addition to poor services, discriminatory practices, and other inconsistencies often generated scathing criticism or an indifferent attitude to the VA's services by Mexican American veterans. In fact, the VA has remained an object of intense scrutiny by veterans and civilians alike, including those more patriotically inclined.

THE VA HEALTH-CARE SYSTEM

The sheer number of World War II veterans, some 16 million, including 670,846 Americans who suffered nonfatal wounds due to both combat and noncombat-related accidents, required an immediate attempt to modernize, expand, and improve health-care services available to veterans.[1] Several different agencies had operated previous to 1930, when President Herbert Hoover centralized veteran services under the reorganized Veterans Administration. So began a concerted effort to build new facilities throughout the nation and, "in 1947 alone, the VA expended $153 billion in the construction of hospitals . . . By 1950, the VA administered 136 hospitals, which had a total of 577,715 admissions that fiscal year."[2] Public Law 293 passed in January 1946 and linked VA hospitals with medical schools, staffing the former with eager and innovative residents, while the establishment of "hometown care" the following year enabled veterans to obtain medical services from a local physician contracted by the VA rather than an actual VA facility, which could involve long distances for many. This hospital system would also service Korean War veterans, in which of the 1.8 million personnel who served, 36,940 were killed in action and 92,134 suffered nonfatal wounds.[3] In the case of Vietnam, the U.S. military commitment involved 2.7 million troops and produced approximately 58,000 casualties by March 1973, when the last combatants left Vietnam. Another 270,000 were wounded.[4]

In an effort to provide compensation for all service-related injuries, the VA also began offering medical pensions after World War II, utilizing a rating system from zero to one hundred that was based "on the degree to which a disease or injury caused an 'impairment of earning capacity' to the veteran in civilian life . . . Pensions were based on economic concerns, and not necessarily on the severity of the injury."[5] The total cost of these medical disability pensions was unprecedented, averaging $74 million a month in 1950. Documentation was critical when filing a claim, which a review board ultimately approved or denied after conducting a medical examination. If approved, the disability rating was simultaneously determined; it was periodically reviewed and possibly removed at a future date. This process easily generated conflicting opinions over the severity of a veteran's injury and the extent to which the U.S. military should be held accountable, frequently producing angry veterans who somehow felt mistreated, even cheated, by the VA when their claims were denied.

As with the more celebrated forms of direct assistance provided by the GI Bill, many veterans did not fully avail themselves of the medical and counseling services provided by the VA. In particular, Angelita García-Cabrera discovered that Mexican American, Puerto Rican, and other Hispanic veterans displayed a disturbing indifference to such services. Her conclusions, drawn from a questionnaire distributed to Hispanic veterans ages nineteen through ninety-five at ten VA hospitals in the United States and Puerto Rico, focused on the following four concerns: "(1) culture-related behavior; (2) language-related barriers; (3) geographical isolation; (4) lack of knowledge about the VA services."[6] As these problem areas illustrate, organizational ineptness and cultural insensitivity, including the lack of bilingual staff, were some of the more prominent barriers to increased utilization. An apathetic attitude toward "the system" in general and the VA in particular could be reinforced by the caste-like nature of treatment, which was based on seniority, that often worked to the detriment of many low- and intermediate-rank Mexican American veterans. Having retired as a major in the Marine Corps, Sal Martínez described the biased working environment of the VA: "It's a caste system that works very, very well, in the sense that if you're an officer you are obviously gonna have easier, faster treatment."[7] While stressing its centrality in maintaining discipline, Tony López also agreed with the notion of a caste system in the treatment afforded to officers when he stated: "The military life . . . gave me more than what I had before . . . particularly into the officer status . . . you kind of get put in a different situation where things are available for you very readily . . . not only material things, but certain privileges, benefits, those types of things."[8]

Moreover, cultural factors played a role, including the stigma often attached to mental illness and the tendency to suffer in silence or use nontraditional folk medicine. As Alfredo Vea succinctly stated, "Mexicans don't go to doctors."[9] Frank Reyes offered similar commentary: "I was raised to believe that you take care of your own [self] . . . I did have my pride. I didn't want to ask for help."[10] Meanwhile, Jim Acevedo relied on a self-described "tough-guy" attitude: "You get this [attitude] where you don't wanna ask or you don't want no help. You think you can do it [on your own], but you could use the help but you don't do [so]."[11] Rosina M. Becerra and Milton Greenblatt confirmed these attitudes and findings while examining a wide variety of social and cultural factors particular to the Hispanic veteran population from three eras in an effort to explain such underutilization. The issue of discrimination received particular attention and, as highlighted in table 4, they asserted that Vietnam veterans were much more decisive than their counterparts in World War II and Korea in reporting discriminatory practices.[12] At first glance, table 4 portrays a sample of World War II Hispanic veterans who overwhelmingly characterized the VA as respectful toward the veteran and his family, and as providing services on a par with those received by the entire veteran population. One noteworthy observation, however, was the less satisfactory approval rating offered in connection to the

TABLE 4. Attitudes Toward Discrimination* (Hispanics Only) (Percentage Responding "Agree" and "Strongly Agree").

QUESTIONS POSED	WORLD WAR II (N = 188)	KOREAN WAR (N = 141)	VIETNAM WAR (N = 235)	TOTAL SAMPLE (N = 564)
VA doctors do not treat Hispanics with respect.	13.3	18.4	20.4	17.6
VA staff respects feelings of the family of the Hispanic veteran.	86.7	73.0	60.4	72.3
VA does not provide the Hispanic veteran with respect.	17.6	21.3	28.5	23.0
VA staff treats Hispanic veterans with respect.	87.2	73.0	66.0	74.8
VA has bilingual personnel to help Hispanic veterans.	52.7	38.3	40.0	43.8
VA doctors treat Hispanic veterans the same as all veterans.	93.6	80.1	77.4	83.5
VA doctors are not considerate of the Hispanic veteran's family.	11.2	24.1	23.0	19.3
VA doctors give same care to Hispanic veterans as they do to all veterans.	96.8	87.9	77.4	86.5

SOURCE Rosina M. Becerra and Milton M. Greenblatt, *Hispanics Seek Health Care: A Study of 1,088 Veterans of Three War Eras* (Lanham, MD: University Press of America, 1983), 90–91; also cited in Lea Ybarra, *Vietnam Veteranos: Chicanos Recall the War* (Austin: University of Texas Press, 2004), 9.

*These percentages include only those who were familiar with VA services and benefits.

availability of bilingual personnel. The overall positive appraisal by these veterans prompted Becerra and Greenblatt to offer a possible reason:

> Vietnam veterans had a significantly stronger sense of being discriminated against than their older peers . . . The older veteran was more likely to accept discriminatory treatment because by doing so he had learned to survive as a minority person in a majority culture. He was more likely to say things were fine at the V.A. because the organization treated him similarly to how he had been treated by other institutions in the past.[13]

While open to discussion, this explanation merits consideration, given the contemporary practices that maintained a racial dividing line within the United States. Ultimately, as a health-care system, the Veterans Administration proved to be a complex and sometimes frustrating experience for Mexican American veterans as military service left them with an assortment of physical injuries and psychiatric problems.

RECEIVING CARE BACK HOME

Carlos Santillán was wounded during the Battle of the Bulge by a piece of shrapnel embedded deep within his calf. Rather than choose immediate treatment, Santillán opted to return to his unit, given the urgent need for manpower to stop the German advance. The shrapnel was never removed, and he received a 10 percent disability rating. Jesse Ybarra suffered extensive injury to five vertebrae when his patrol was ambushed and his vehicle overturned during fighting in the Ruhr Pocket in the spring of 1945; terrible pain eventually necessitated back surgery at a VA hospital in Long Beach, California, in 1965, and in tandem with a diagnosis of post-traumatic stress disorder (PTSD), he was provided with a disability rating of 100 percent. Nick Salazar spent six months recovering in military hospitals from injuries also suffered in the Ruhr Pocket; his injuries required VA treatment for some time thereafter, earning him a disability rating of 45 percent. Arnif Nerio, too, suffered an assortment of injuries, including burst eardrums, from artillery fire on New Guinea in 1944. Sometime in the 1950s he decided to file a grievance with the VA due to constant ringing in his ears. As he recalled, some persistence was involved: "I had to fight for it. It took me about a year before I could get it . . . They were [initially] giving me ten percent . . . I fought it and they put me in a hearing [room] . . . They came to that conclusion. It was 60 percent."[14]

Vincent Pardo Jr. arrived in Korea with his Marine Corps unit just prior to the July 1953 cease-fire. While his unit did not deploy in support of combat operations, conditions still proved to be hazardous when he suffered a broken eardrum that subsequently became infected after his vehicle accidently rolled down an embankment. Constant swelling and occasional hearing loss continued for some time after his discharge in 1954, and Pardo repeatedly sought treatment at the VA hospital in Saginaw, Michigan. He described his mounting frustration with what he considered to be exceptionally poor treatment:

> They [VA] would give medicine. They would look at it . . . [and] send me [home]. There was times where [I] would go to the hospital and . . . sit there, two or three hours waiting for attention. Then, all of a sudden, they [would] come out and say, "Well, the doctor didn't show up. You [are] gonna have to come back next week." And then again, next week [same experience], and again, next week. And it seemed like all they could give [me] was pills. And that went on for quite a while to the point where I decided that I didn't want to go to the [VA] hospital [anymore] . . . I didn't put in for compensation because I got discouraged.[15]

By comparison, George Castaneda experienced extensive combat in Korea and was wounded multiple times. Upon his discharge in 1952, he underwent a physical exam at the VA hospital in Detroit, which led to a 10 percent disability rating. He regretfully remembered the lost opportunity to receive more:

> They gave me a whole bunch of X-rays . . . and then they said, "Well, how much money do you think . . . you should get?" And that's where I messed up because I told 'em . . . maybe about 10 percent. I should of asked for more . . . [A]nd they start[ed] sending me a check every month . . . A little check. Not much.[16]

Ruben Moreno was discharged in 1952 with a 10 percent disability rating due to a separated shoulder. However, his repeated attempts to receive further treatment for PTSD and symptoms related to frostbite suffered during the Battle of Chosin Reservoir, including loss of sensation, blackened toenails, and body rashes, were ignored by the VA hospital in Tucson, Arizona. He recalled his frustration: "I haven't really been helped by the VA hospital here. I even got into an [argument] with a doctor. I had always tried [receiving treatment] a long time back. [I said], 'Well, the heck with 'em. I don't need 'em. I'll pay for my doctoring.'"[17] After joining the Chosin Few sometime in the 1980s—an organization for army and Marine Corps survivors of the Battle of Chosin Reservoir that conducted intense political lobbying on their behalf—he received a 70 percent disability rating, which was ultimately upgraded to 100 percent in 2000. He offered a final sarcastic remark on his ordeal: "I'm glad they didn't wait till I died before okaying it."[18]

As a navy hospital corpsman assigned to the 1st Marine Division, Jesus Barragan was part of Operation Pegasus—a push to lift the Battle of Khe Sanh, a marine outpost near the demilitarized zone (DMZ) separating North and South Vietnam. As he traveled on a transport jeep on Easter Sunday 1968, it overturned and left Barragan with torn ligaments in his left knee. As he convalesced at the Oakland Naval Hospital, Barragan realized the fortuitous circumstances he derived from his injury. He said: "That injury, no doubt . . . saved my life because I ran into this guy that was in [my] unit . . . and he told me, 'Remember so and so? Killed.' He said they were hit bad going into Khe Sanh about three days after I was medevac'd."[19] He continued his convalescence at the Oakland Naval Supply Center, where he was ultimately discharged in December 1969 with a 30 percent disability rating. As he stated, "It's . . . $376.00 for life . . . [And] they give you a little more every so often."[20] Moreover, he underwent total knee-replacement surgery in March 2009, paid for by the VA, and he offered high praise for the services he received:

> The VA has a policy that anytime a veteran is in the hospital for their service-connected condition . . . thirty days or more, you go to 100 percent temporary disability . . . I was in the hospital [for] thirty-seven days. [It consisted of] excellent food, excellent care, excellent physical therapy, and then outpatient [treatment]. So, for thirteen months, I got approximately $2,700 from the VA . . . a month.[21]

By contrast, John Rodríguez prematurely left the VA hospital system despite not being fully recovered from the extensive physical injuries he suffered from mortar fire along the Cambodian border in May 1969. He remarked, "I did experience a number of things that told me that I . . . was a burden."[22] Along with a diagnosis of PTSD, Rodríguez would ultimately attain a rating of 100 percent. So too, did Charley Trujillo after suffering massive head trauma, including the loss of an eye, as well as PTSD. He offered the following commentary on his experiences with the VA: "There's a lot of bureaucracy that you have to put up with . . . [However,] I've gotten good medical service, I must admit. But you have to hassle with 'em. You have to persevere . . . A lot of guys aren't willing to do that."[23]

Furthermore, many veterans returned with diseases common to the battlefields of the Pacific and Southeast Asia, such as malaria and jungle rot. In the case of World War II, for example, John Sótelo suffered from malaria well beyond his discharge from the navy, and Darío Villegas experienced persistent episodes of jaundice for approximately two years after his tour of duty. On the other hand, Mike García received a 10 percent disability rating for jungle rot, but a subsequent review by the VA terminated this benefit. Raúl Medina also suffered jungle rot, and he spent four or five months in military hospitals in Leyte and Honolulu. His combination of ailments, including a PTSD diagnosis, eventually resulted in a 100 percent disability classification in 2002, a full fifty-seven years after World War II ended. As he described in the epigraph, he offered a scathing indictment of the VA: "We got one foot in the grave, they're [the VA] gonna throw us a goddamm bone, and that's what it amounts to. I feel that as far as the Veterans Administration [is concerned] . . . we were treated just plain goddamm rotten."[24] Moreover, during the Vietnam War, other notable health problems developed as the result of exposure to Agent Orange. Approximately 20 million gallons of herbicides were used from 1962 to 1971 in an effort to remove unwanted foliage that provided cover for enemy forces.[25] Eddie Solís's diabetes, poor eyesight, and poor liver and kidney function were linked to Agent Orange, which, in tandem with PTSD, produced a rating of 100 percent. Meanwhile, Tony Moreno vividly recalled his exposure to Agent Orange while on patrol: "We stirred up this powder and right away [we] had to put on our [gas] masks . . . It just burned and burned . . . our skin and eyes."[26] Despite having no medical symptoms, such exposure, along with a minor shrapnel wound, provided him with a rating of 10 percent.

As some of these stories illustrate, psychiatric problems were also numerous and not unexpected. A generation of Vietnam War veterans would provide the context that ultimately established a clinical diagnosis for veterans suffering from combat-related trauma—PTSD. However, these symptoms—which include recurring nightmares, flashbacks, anxiety, and emotional paralysis, referred to as combat fatigue during World War II—have remained one of the more tragic consequences of military service in any period. For example, Raúl Medina can be instantly reminded of his combat experiences in the Philippines: "You see something and it creates a reflex, it takes you back."[27] He has relied extensively on "rap sessions," where a group of individuals gather to openly discuss their experiences. Jesse Ybarra offered a similar appraisal for this therapeutic approach: "Mostly the counseling has helped . . . Guys sit and talk out [their] experiences. They [rap sessions] had Korean and Vietnam veterans as [well]."[28]

The many horrors endured by William Sánchez as a Japanese prisoner of war (POW) during World War II remain ever present. Together with British POWs, he and other Americans made quite a stir upon arriving in Tokyo in November 1942. Employed as a stevedore, his daily diet consisted of one bowl of rice and soup. Such labor, however, did have its benefits, despite the inherent danger involved: "We used to be able to steal stuff, like sugar, salmon . . . because we unloaded a lot of stuff for the Japanese army. Of course, if you got caught you took a horrific beating, but it was worth it."[29] In November 1944, the first B-29s began arriving over Japan, and in March 1945 he witnessed the terrible toll caused by the firebombing of Tokyo: "There was children, there was women, there was young kids floating down the canal. It was devastating . . . But we knew the war was coming to an end."[30] After Japan's formal surrender on September 2, 1945, Sánchez and other POWs encountered U.S. occupation forces in Yokohama: "They took us to a warehouse; they deloused us, and gave us a uniform. God, it felt good to have clean underwear, clean everything . . . and then we were put on a hospital ship."[31] During our conversation, he also revealed: "I can . . . be asleep, and I'll wake up in the middle of the night thinking I'm in prison camp, sweating and everything."[32] Amazingly, he initially received a disability rating of 70 percent for his ordeals as a POW and was at last upgraded to 100 percent in 2000. His longevity was unusual, given the high mortality rate for prisoners of the Japanese, in comparison to American POWs' experience in Europe. Historian Mark D. Van Ells discovered that "in the six years following the war, ex-POWs from the Pacific . . . were three times more likely to die of cardiovascular diseases, four times more likely to die of digestive disorders, and nine times more likely to die of tuberculosis than normal."[33]

Similarly, Guadalupe "Lupe" Ortega has endured a lifetime of PTSD after participating in a 375-mile forced march from northern Burma through southern China that sabotaged Japanese supply lines. The thousand men that began the march in early 1945 under General Joseph Stillwell's command repeatedly engaged Japanese forces and suffered from a variety of diseases, such as malaria, dysentery, and jungle rot. Of the latter disease, he remembered that "pieces of meat fall off of you."[34] Those too sick or wounded to continue the march, including men that suffered mental breakdowns, were left behind. As he recalled, such action essentially meant leaving these men to their demise: "[We] laid 'em by the side and hoped somebody would pick them up."[35] Ultimately, only four hundred men survived the five-month ordeal. Afterwards, a cursory medical evaluation discovered no physical ailments; however, soon after his return to his hometown of Saginaw, Michigan, Ortega suffered a nervous breakdown. He tearfully said: "When I got home, I was hospitalized for three months . . . They sent me to Ann Arbor [Michigan], the psychiatric ward."[36] Indeed, nightmares and flashbacks remain a constant feature of Ortega's life. Fortunately, the VA has provided quality service, including an immediate 100 percent disability rating: "I've been satisfied . . . Believe me, they go out of their way to treat me [well]."[37]

Alfred Aguirre also suffers from PTSD; his symptoms include headaches, body aches, and nightmares that first manifested themselves during the latter stages of his participation in the invasion of Okinawa in April 1945. He was hospitalized by the military for two months, yet the VA denied his claim, and he pursued no further action. Francisco Vega, by comparison, recalled one particular incident soon after being discharged from the army in late 1945: "I remember waking up in bed and yelling . . . And I was perspiring . . . Right then and there . . . I said, I gotta get [a] hold of this."[38] He credits his deep Catholic faith, including evening prayers, with helping him to thwart PTSD symptoms and avoid VA health-care services altogether. Meanwhile, Darío Villegas developed a dependence on alcohol and cigarettes in an effort to cope with his symptoms and deal with the discrimination at his job site: "I didn't get promoted like I should [have] and I knew the job real good."[39] He would ultimately confront one particularly difficult individual by displaying his honorable discharge listing his battlefield exploits, and it had an immediate positive effect. However, his failure to utilize the counseling services provided by the VA stemmed in large part from the cursory medical examination he received as he demobilized. As he recounted, the officer in charge stated: "'Anybody who's got complaints about their health, get in that line over there.' So I got in the line . . . [Do] you know what he [the doctor] told me . . . 'You oughta be grateful you're back, 'cause a lot of men never made it back. Next!'"[40]

As with World War II veterans, mental and emotional distress typified military service during the Korean War and, once again, the VA's health-care services elicited a variety of responses. Gene Bejarano testified that "there's nights when I wake up and I'm just totally soaked in sweat."[41] His PTSD has remained a lifelong problem, and his claim with the VA produced only a 10 percent rating, leaving him angry and frustrated. As he described in the epigraph: "You . . .

hear and see on TV and . . . the newspaper[s] that the government takes care of its soldiers . . . and it's just a bunch of bull."[42] Similarly, Ruben Moreno's nightmares were equally profound: "I kicked the wife out of bed one time with the nightmares I was having."[43] Coincidentally, Rolando Hinojosa found his attention span suffering during his first semester at school following his discharge: "I had a bad time in that spring semester when I came back. I would be very interested in some things . . . but at other times, I would be in Korea, or I would be in Japan."[44] Mike González was rated 30 percent for symptoms that include flashbacks and panic attacks; nevertheless, he lauded the services provided by the VA and he seemed confident that a higher rating was forthcoming. He stated, "It's been very helpful. They've been really [great]."[45] However, Robert Castro, a Marine Corps veteran of Korea and Vietnam, placed little value on claims involving PTSD: "I think, sometimes, this is imaginary . . . for whatever reason."[46] Castro would receive a 45 percent disability rating for an assortment of physical injuries, but he steadfastly denied having PTSD and has never sought treatment.

Other Mexican American veterans of the Korean War have also not pursued treatment, or else did so after a considerable amount of time had passed, and complete ignorance of VA services is to blame, a point highlighted earlier by Angelita García-Cabrera. For example, José Domínguez ultimately filed a claim with the VA in 1997; in 2002 he subsequently received a 100 percent rating for PTSD. Eddie Trujillo also admitted to a lengthy wait. He explained why: "You know, for forty-eight years, I did not know. . . . that I could get help. [My] friend from Oklahoma . . . he was the one that told me about [the VA services] . . . not the government."[47] Trujillo filed a claim in 2000 despite having been discharged from the army in 1952; in 2002 he received a 100 percent rating for PTSD. Meanwhile, Ray Gomez has never received treatment despite lifelong symptoms that stem from his combat experiences and the mass graves he encountered as allied forces pressed northward into North Korea. He offered the following: "In Pyongyang, when we got there, I [saw] thousands of people, dead, in there . . . It still bothers me off and on . . . when I see a combat movie . . . Sometimes, I have to turn [the television] off."[48] When asked to offer an explanation for his nonutilization of VA services, he simply stated: "I don't know what to do."[49]

For Vietnam War veterans, personal narratives of the trauma associated with PTSD also emerge rather forcefully. In fact, according to the National Vietnam Veterans Readjustment Study conducted in 1988, Hispanic Vietnam veterans were found to be suffering from PTSD at an astounding rate of 27 percent, while black and white veterans suffered at a rate of 19 and 14 percent, respectively.[50] Alfredo Vea offers a powerful case study as he described his personal battle with PTSD:

> I just didn't know how terrorized I'd been. It took years for me to stop being terrorized . . . I had nightmares for years . . . I didn't think I believed in PTSD for myself. I thought, I'm a fucking lawyer, I make a lot of money, I write books . . . But I have trouble being emotionally honest. I have trouble with women because I'm a male tribal member, and in Vietnam, it was a male tribe. I was just perfect for that. Now, it's taken a lot of work for me to be emotionally honest and learn how to communicate with people.[51]

John Rodríguez's aggressiveness, which stemmed in large part from the poor treatment he received by the VA while recovering from his injuries, produced constant confrontations with law enforcement. He recalled, "I've probably seen every jailhouse in this area, from San Jose all the way down to Palo Alto [California] . . . I was . . . combating authority, which was now the police."[52] Incongruously, Eddie Solís feels a strong sense of remorse for not having returned to Vietnam after his deployment as an advisor to the South Vietnamese Army from 1963 to 1964. As he described, "We came back . . . and half of the guys that came back with me, they went back, and I feel kind of guilty."[53] Moreover, greeting the returned remains of fallen marines while playing "Taps" also left him emotionally scarred, resulting in a 100 percent rating for PTSD. Chappo López also received a 100 percent rating for an assortment of physical injuries and PTSD stemming from his two tours in Vietnam as a Marine Corps rifleman. He offered the following praise for the VA when asked to describe the quality of care: "Very helpful . . . I got my own personal doctor looking after me. I also [have] a psychiatrist . . . They take care of me."[54] Similarly, Frank Reyes's decision to utilize the VA's counseling services just prior to this interview provided long overdue therapy and a 100 percent rating: "It's taken me a long time to come to terms with what happened in Southeast Asia. I'm doing it now and I'm doing real good, for the first time in a long time."[55] However, Raymond Buriel, despite combat experiences that include having a "guy . . . in your arms and the last thing you hear him say is 'mama,'" claims no mental irregularities.[56] He firmly believes that his strong Catholic faith and the spiritual services provided by his grandmother, a quasi-*curandera*, or folk healer, upon his return from Vietnam helped ameliorate any harmful consequences. As he recalled:

> When I came back . . . my grandmother . . . told me very sternly, "Vienes manana, porque te voy a curar el susto . . . Tu haz pasado por mucho. Te puede afectar" (Come tomorrow, because I'm going to calm your emotional state. You have experienced much. It may negatively affect you) . . . More out of respect than anything, I went through the whole thing.[57]

As a radio telephone operator (RTO), Fred Medel was responsible for the quick transmission of various directives and other messages—a job that provided a significant degree of stress that was exacerbated by the knowledge that enemy forces eagerly targeted RTOs due to their crucial role in maintaining lines of communication. His frequent assignment to one remote mountaintop and its radio station was especially nerve-racking:

> I hated that goddamm mountain. But I was one of the best . . . Up there you had to talk to three people and take down sorties . . . air strikes . . . coordinates for artillery to fire . . . it was very stressful. And you coped the best you could. And I coped by drinking Southern Comfort and smokin' dope [marijuana].[58]

Other combat experiences, including the loss of a dear friend, further scarred Medel, and he began experiencing multiples symptoms of PTSD soon after his discharge from the army in 1972. He described his emotional state and the tragic consequences on his wife: "[My wife] put up with my shit for years. I'd [wake] up and be in the corner of the bedroom tryin' to call artillery or I'd [wake] up with my hands around her throat."[59] He continued: "Mentally, after I came back here [Saginaw, Michigan], I was broken . . . I drank, smoked [marijuana], didn't care about my wife or my kid . . . I was a bum . . . But finally, I [calmed] down and buckled down to work . . . But I still had issues."[60] The disability rating ultimately provided by the VA in 2009 included 50 percent for PTSD, 20 percent for ulcers, and 10 percent for a lingering ringing in his ears, for a total of 80 percent.

The dependence on alcohol and narcotics highlighted by Medel provides additional context for understanding some of the many physical and emotional scars that often endure long after one's tour of duty and the tactics employed in an effort to cope. Moreover, exposure to drugs and alcohol often began while in uniform and was especially prominent during the Vietnam War. Indeed, a pervasive drug culture increasingly characterized daily existence in Vietnam as the conflict progressed into a war of attrition. While some journalists and scholars have equated drug use with growing dissent among U.S. troops, I argue that drugs were most valued for their ability to provide euphoric escape from the anxieties associated with combat. In particular, drug use heightened considerably after the Tet Offensive in 1968 as the logic underlying American objectives and the policy of containment increasingly proved hollow. Marijuana and alcohol became the drugs of choice; yet heroin and other narcotics were also used. As authors Lawrence M. Baskir and William A Strauss discovered:

> Between 1966 and 1967 . . . the number of soldiers under criminal investigation for marijuana use climbed from fewer than one hundred to more than thirteen hundred . . . By 1969–70, military police in Vietnam were making more than eleven thousand drug arrests per year, 90 percent involving marijuana . . . Yet despite this crackdown, the proportion of pot-smoking soldiers in Vietnam rose from 29 percent in 1967 to almost 60 percent in 1971. More than half were heavy smokers.[61]

Comparatively, no prevalent drug culture typified military service during the Second World War, which the veterans present within this study corroborate. Several narrators, however, claimed to have witnessed the use of narcotics by troops during the Korean War era, perhaps a precursor to the drug culture that would typify the U.S. military during the Vietnam War. In particular, occupation duty in Japan proved to be a particular hot spot. For example, Eddie Trujillo admitted the following: "Friends used to give it to me . . . here and there . . . opium."[62] Robert Villegas also encountered drugs while stationed in Japan at Camp Gilford: "I [saw] a little bit of *mota* [marijuana]."[63] And Ray Gómez witnessed some casual use of marijuana and other drugs: "I saw some [use], yes, by my comrades."[64]

In Vietnam, Daniel Cano immersed himself into this drug and alcohol underworld during his tour of duty: "[There was a] lot of drugs [and a] lot of alcohol. They gave us the alcohol, we bought the drugs ourselves."[65] For Fred Medel, the availability of marijuana and other, more lethal, narcotics was astounding: "Anything you want[ed]. Anything from opium . . . to hash, to coke . . . to weed . . . anything you could imagine, you could get there."[66] Chappo López further described this escalating use of narcotics in Vietnam: "In the first tour that I went, '65–'66 . . . [narcotics] wasn't that noticeable . . . Then, when I went back in 1968, in my second tour, it was pretty well in the open. Some touched it, some didn't. Somebody like me . . . would just drink, which I did. I preferred to drink."[67] George Mariscal offered similar commentary: "Near the end of my tour, it was at the point where it was shifting to the hard stuff, late '69. [For example], a lot of speed. Guys who I walked on patrol with were shooting up all the time . . . I smoked a lot of pot both on duty and off."[68] Alfredo Vea also confronted a prevalent drug culture in his tour. However, he strictly confined his participation to his off-duty hours. He explained, "We had a lot of pot [and] Thai sticks and we had opium. But [I] never [used them] in the field. I was too scared not to be able to concentrate."[69] Meanwhile, as a stevedore and truck driver stationed at a supply depot, Gilbert Guevara and his comrades were provided with no other alternatives for recreation during off-duty hours. Therefore, they "drank a lot of beer [and] there was a lot of smoking [marijuana] going on."[70]

Raymond Buriel marveled at the ability of fellow marines to obtain drugs despite repeated deployments to isolated areas near the DMZ that separated North and South Vietnam. As he described, "There were a lot of drugs . . . I still don't know how those guys got it . . . [We were] way out in the middle of nowhere . . . [However], I didn't do drugs. I can tell you honestly."[71] Joe Rodríguez wondered why more service members did not refrain from the use of narcotics given the guerrilla tactics that endangered military personnel on a daily basis: "It always amazed me . . . Why would you want to walk around stoned? People are shootin' at you."[72] For John Rodríguez, the application of morphine was a medical necessity after being severely wounded by a mortar attack; it also proved quite addictive. As he explained, "When I got wounded and they hit morphine on me, it was heaven . . . it was something I had never felt in my life. When I came home, they had turned me on to a whole new different world of alcohol [and] drugs . . . everything that was there that could destroy me."[73] Ted Samora offered similar commentary on the lasting consequences of drug and alcohol abuse that first began in the military: "I think I became a drug addict and an alcoholic in Vietnam, 'cause when I got out I continued drinking [and] I continued taking drugs."[74]

The rising prevalence of narcotics during the Vietnam War was superseded only by the abuse of alcohol, which was cheap and made readily available by the military in all three conflicts studied here. World War II veteran Jesse Ybarra offered the following: "I used to drink and smoke a lot, 'cause they would give us cigarettes . . . with the K rations . . . Beer was available to us [also], so I drank a lot."[75] This is reinforced by Richard Domínguez, who recalled nights of revelry with fellow comrades during off-duty hours: "We put on some good ones sometimes . . . We'd really get *pedo* [drunk]."[76] The rough-and-tumble life that typified Martin Morales's adolescence and adulthood was exacerbated by the hard-nosed work environment that characterized his squadron in the Army Air Corps, where alcohol consumption occurred on a frequent basis. He said: "Everybody that was in that squadron was a hell-raiser. They [would] fight you in a minute."[77] He continued: "I always drank. I drank because I liked it."[78] Mike García, however, claimed a tenuous connection between alcoholism and his military experiences. As he simply stated, "I don't know."[79] Rather, he believes the camaraderie he developed with fellow construction workers and his ownership of a bar precipitated his alcoholism. Salvador Marez also admitted to abusing alcohol, and in a manner similar to Mike García, downplayed any connection to his time in the navy from 1943 to 1946. And yet, excessive drinking characterized his life for some time after his discharge, and it was especially pronounced on weekends: "It [drinking] used to be routine every Friday."[80]

Exposure to alcohol was especially prevalent during off duty hours, and once more Japan figured prominently in these reminiscences as discussed earlier in my examination of the homosocial bonding that characterized trips to red-light districts. For instance, Gene Bejarano described his time in Japan to be the "life of Riley . . . We [fellow marines] were a bunch of *borachos* [drunks] . . . Wine, women, and song."[81] Vincent Pardo Jr. also commented that "living in Japan was really an experience . . . We'd get liberty [and] we'd go into these small towns close to our camp . . . And we would go for the food, for the bars, [and] the clubs."[82] As a sailor assigned to the USS *Bonhomme Richard*, an aircraft carrier that launched air strikes on enemy targets while stationed off the coast of Korea, Frank Gonzales fondly remembered the ship's return to various ports in Japan that included Sasebo, Yokosuka, and Yokohama. As he stated: "I liked Japan . . . I enjoyed myself going there . . . We'd go there for so many days . . . then we'd go back out to our task force."[83] By comparison, Robert Villegas offered a more lively reminiscence of his time in Japan: "It was great! We drank . . . not [too] excessively overboard."[84] Gene García also engaged in excessive drinking with other Latino service members: "I would say that the majority of us . . . drank a lot . . . [Especially] with the Puerto Ricans and my Chicano buddies. We always partied."[85]

Rolando Hinojosa, on the other hand, quickly discovered that the fluid nature of the front lines in Korea allowed him to enjoy the alcohol rations provided to combat units, which consisted of one case of beer or one bottle of whiskey a week. He usually chose the former: "I used to drink a lot [of beer] . . . Hell, I wanted to relax."[86] According to Hinojosa, however, such drinking did not carry over into civilian life. Rather, he found comfort largely through his many literary accomplishments. His first publication dealing specifically with the Korean War, titled *Korean Love Songs*, first appeared in 1978. His second, *Useless Servants*, published in 1993, was a deliberate effort to exorcise a few remaining demons. He said, "I think it was like a catharsis. Finally, 'alright, I'm done with this.'"[87] Mike González, however, drank excessively in order to cope with PTSD: "I'd come home at night . . . I was with the bottle. That's why my first wife left me."[88] Mark Rocha offered a matter-of-fact appraisal of the military's role in promoting his alcohol consumption, which continued with coworkers after being discharged from the navy: "I never drank or smoked until I went into the service . . . I would go to the EM [Enlisted Men's] Club."[89]

In the case of the Vietnam War, alcohol also figured prominently, including the practice of assigning alcohol rations to troops on combat assignments, as Hinojosa described. As Tony Moreno recalled, the Cambodian jungle provided a surreal backdrop while his unit participated in the invasion of Cambodia in the spring of 1970: "Choppers used to bring it out to us in the field, cases and cases of beer . . . and ice."[90] Joe Rodríguez offered a more blunt assessment of the military's drinking culture: "Everybody used alcohol . . . There was a lot of booze, a lot of people drunk."[91] Robert Castro witnessed the tragic consequences of alcohol abuse on enlisted personnel while assigned as a prison warden during the Vietnam War era: "I saw what liquor did to people [and] how it would affect them . . . saying and doing things that they would later regret."[92] For Tony López, meanwhile, the stress associated with the responsibilities of leading a rifle company as a Marine Corps officer increasingly prompted his alcohol consumption: "I used to drink a lot over there, and when I came back I had a hard time getting out of that."[93] Marine Corps major Sal Martínez also noted: "The big problem in the military . . . was alcohol. The military was part of the macho syndrome . . . The club systems . . . in the military were set up to be very inexpensive."[94] Victor Ramírez offered similar commentary while crediting the military for his excessive drinking, which continued after his discharge: "I drank pretty heavy when I got out of the service [and the military] had something to do with it . . . When we were stationed in Iceland, there was nothing to do but go to the beer garden and drink."[95] Added Charley Trujillo: "I started drinking when I was seventeen, eighteen [years of age], but not like I did after [being discharged]."[96] He fully blamed the military's drinking culture and his PTSD for his abuse of alcohol. And for Eddie Solís, exposure to drugs and alcohol in the military would produce tragic consequences on his family life: "I lost one marriage over it . . . heavy drinking [and] drugs."[97]

In a manner similar to Rolando Hinojosa and his effort to cope with his wartime experiences in Korea, several narrators have become successful writers, and their prose has been heavily influenced by their participation in the Vietnam War. For example, the war sits squarely at the center of Charley Trujillo's volume of oral history interviews, *Soldados: Chicanos in Viet Nam*, and his novel, *Dogs of Illusion*, both published by Trujillo's Chusma House Publishing Company, located in San Jose, California.[98] Other examples include Alfredo Vea's *Gods Go Begging*, Daniel Cano's *Shifting Loyalties*, Joe Rodríguez's *Oddsplayer*, and Leroy Quintana's *Interrogations*. As illustrated by Daniel Cano, writing has proven to be a cathartic endeavor for each author. He offered the following: "Every time I went back to the stories [in *Shifting Loyalties*], I went right back to Vietnam. So it was a very difficult book to write."[99] Alfredo Vea offered a similar perspective that described his lifelong efforts to come to terms with his experiences in Vietnam. As he stated, "For me, the answer was writing [which] is what I still do. And I still have a long way to go."[100] Indeed, the effort to reconcile with combat and other traumatic experiences has remained a lifelong endeavor, and these literary accomplishments represent a more constructive effort to do so as opposed to the more harmful efforts that have tormented many veterans.

CONCLUSION

The recollections provided in this chapter clearly indicate the significance of the VA's psychiatric and medical services for discharged veterans across three generations while also demonstrating diverse appraisals of these services, which included indifference and anger in addition to more complimentary assessments. Furthermore, these well-documented physical and psychological consequences of military service also illustrate the connection between health care and social activism, as returning veterans, most notably those that served in World War II and Korea, returned to civilian life with a profound sense of entitlement and began to tackle the social, economic, and racial inconsistencies that plagued American society. As described by historian Lorena Oropeza, "ethnic activists frequently mentioned the battlefield exploits of Mexican American soldiers as irrefutable proof that the ethnic group was deserving of first-class citizenship."[101] The various complications associated with the VA's health-care services, in tandem with second-class citizenship, played a key role in that process, resulting in a sincere ideological transformation within many veterans. For Mexican American veterans of the Vietnam War, however, this change in consciousness was much more diverse and complex, including sentiments that challenged the patriotism of an earlier generation.

9

TRANSFORMED IDENTITIES AND POLITICAL MOBILIZATION

"I think in the Latino/Chicano culture . . . to serve your country, to be in the military, is huge . . . It's a validation that you really belong here. Plus, it was a chance to get some training. It was an opportunity in life that you might not otherwise get if you didn't go."

"It [Vietnam War] helped me see the contradictions in United States policy toward other countries. I question everything now because of the Vietnam War."

THE MILITARY'S CAPACITY to foster a politicized consciousness among the clear majority of Mexican American men that served between 1940 and 1975 must be seen as the most prominent legacy of their service. I highlight that process by first analyzing the post–World War II generation, which struggled to overcome institutionalized discrimination by linking first-class citizenship with their military performance. The patriotic, integrationist, and anti-Communist policies of organizations such as the American GI Forum, and its founder, Dr. Hector Perez García, will merit special attention, as well as their handling of the Felix Longoria incident and the GI Bill's uneven implementation in southern Texas. On the other hand, the Vietnam War offered an altogether different platform for returning veterans and thus provides clear evidence of an evolution in Mexican American identity. For many Chicano servicemen, their experiences with poverty and social and educational discrimination, in tandem with the growing futility of American strategic aims in Southeast Asia, fostered an increased willingness to openly challenge the community's marginalization and the venerable tradition of military service as the path to civil rights. Rather, powerful emotions that encompassed anger and disillusionment, and even anti-U.S. sentiments, characterized the postwar consciousness of these veterans.

FIGHTING THE PEACE AT HOME

In response to the many difficulties associated with the GI Bill's implementation in southern Texas, a meeting of Mexican American veterans took place in Corpus Christi on March 26, 1948, with Dr. Hector Perez García acting as temporary chair. As described in the minutes of this first meeting, the purpose "was to demand the rights of veterans consisting of Draft Boards, Bonus, Hospitalization, [and] immediate action on checks."[1] Concerned with the lack of Mexican American representation on local draft boards, Dr. García also continued his aggressive campaign to expand and improve the hospital facilities available to veterans in southern Texas. The denial of services had become commonplace, and four hardship cases involving sick veterans drew particular attention, including the following two:

> Benito Padilla of 748 Cheyenne St. One day Mr. Padilla brought his sick wife to the doctor and begged him to take care of her until his check arrived. He had not received a check since six months ago, and he had his wife and child to support. The Red Cross has been helping him out . . . He has been to the Veterans Administration fourteen times and yet nothing has been done.

> Jesus Ramos of 905 Duncan St. One day Mr. Ramos came to see the doctor because of his painful stomach. The doctor's diagnosis was possible appendicitis. The doctor sent him to the Veteran Administration with [form] P-10, and from there he was sent to the base [Corpus Christi] hospital, where the doctor again, just felt his stomach and told him to come back. He came to see his doctor again and was sent to the VA and from there to the hospital, and at the hospital they told him he had to get a letter from San Antonio. In the meantime, Ramos is suffering from pain.[2]

The issue of delayed checks was another hot topic. Such delays impeded the ability of many veterans to pursue training and other educational endeavors. John Huey, a local city and county service officer who pledged his continued support in expediting the process, underscored the problem by announcing that three hundred veterans had finally received payment in January, despite their having enrolled in various training programs the previous September. He offered a list of veterans, including the length of delay:

> Rafael Alvarado, one child, check delayed six months.
> Santos Barron, check delayed three months.

Eddie Barrera, check delayed two months.
Rafael Cavazos, check delayed five months.
Crispin Espinosa, check delayed five months.
Amados Garcia, check delayed five months.
Fidel Marroquin, one child, check delayed five months.
Martin Martinez, check delayed five months.
Conrado Mayorga, one child, check delayed six months.
Benito Padilla, one child, check delayed six months.
Edinco Perales, check delayed six months.
Juan Rosales, check delayed five months.
Frank Schwing, check delayed five months.[3]

Securing veterans rights and entitlements became vital to Dr. García. As a licensed surgeon and member of the Army Medical Corps, he had served with distinction in the European theater and risen to the rank of major. After returning to his hometown of Corpus Christi and setting up practice in 1946, he welcomed the financial opportunity to handle the large caseload of veterans needing treatment when the local director of the VA approached him. In this capacity, Dr. García saw firsthand the physical and mental maladies that continued to plague veterans long after their military service. He realized the tremendous difficulties that Chicano veterans encountered when dealing with the VA's bureaucratic red tape. When coupled with the rampant discrimination that continued to exist in southern Texas, Mexican American veterans—and indeed much of the Mexican American community—suffered from a combination of poor health, lower socioeconomic standing, and social and educational discrimination. Dr. García carried these concerns with him to that first meeting, from which emerged the American GI Forum as an advocacy group for veterans' rights. He became the forum's first president, a position he would occupy many times in the future.[4] Other meetings followed in 1948 (see figures 2 and 3), and this newly established veterans' organization continued to grow in size and reputation, enabling it to respond to a blatant act of discrimination in early January 1949 that propelled Dr. García and the GI Forum to the forefront of civil rights activism on behalf of the entire Mexican American community.

In November 1948, Beatrice Longoria was notified by the army that the remains of her husband, Private Felix Longoria, would be arriving in San Francisco the following January. He had entered the army in November 1944 and served as an infantryman in the reconquest of Luzon (an island in the Philippines), where he was killed in action on June 16, 1945, when his patrol was ambushed by Japanese snipers (see fig. 4). His widow needed to find a burial site; she ultimately settled on his hometown of Three Rivers, Texas, about a two-hour drive northwest of Corpus Christi. Excerpts from a notarized statement detail the series of events that unfolded in her efforts to reinter her husband in Three Rivers:

> On January 7, 1949, I went to Three Rivers, Texas, my former hometown, to make arrangements for my husband's . . . funeral. I went to the Rice Funeral Home [the] only funeral home in Three Rivers . . . owned by Mr. T.W. Kennedy to have the funeral arrangements made. He agreed to handle the arrangements, but when I told him I wanted his body kept at the chapel, he said, "Well, Mrs. Longoria, I have lots of Latin friends but I can't let his body rest at this chapel because the whites won't like it." I returned to Corpus Christi to consult with my family about the incident. One of my sisters immediately got in contact with the "American GI Forum" . . . and I authorized Dr. García to try to get the use of the chapel for my husband's services . . . Dr. García then called Mr. Kennedy and was told by Mr. Kennedy that "they had never let the Latin Americans use the chapel and were not starting now, even if he was a soldier killed in action."[5]

In response to this outrage, Dr. García wired telegrams to state and federal officials. He also organized a meeting with members of the American GI Forum at Lamar Elementary School in Corpus Christi on January 11, 1949. The community responded, producing a meeting charged with anticipation. A decorated American soldier who had made the ultimate sacrifice was returning home, yet his Mexican ancestry denied him the dignified burial he deserved. Something had to be done. All the meeting's participants had been treated as second-class citizens in one way or another, and now the opportunity to take action presented itself. At the meeting, Dr. García read the following telegram from Texas senator Lyndon Baines Johnson:

> I deeply regret to learn that the prejudice of some individuals extends even beyond this life. I have no authority over civilian funeral homes. Nor does the federal government. However, I have today made arrangements to have Felix Longoria buried with full military honors in Arlington National Cemetery here at Washington . . . Or, if his family prefers to have his body interred nearer his home, he can be reburied at Fort Sam Houston National Military Cemetery at San Antonio. There will be no cost.[6]

FIGURE 2. Caption reads: "Attention Veterans! Gathering of Veterans, Thursday, December 30, 1948." (Source: Hector P. Garcia Papers, Special Collections and Archives, Mary and Jeff Bell Library, Texas A&M University–Corpus Christi.)

FIGURE 3. One of the first gatherings of the American GI Forum; date unknown. (Source: Hector P. Garcia Papers, Special Collections and Archives, Mary and Jeff Bell Library, Texas A&M University–Corpus Christi.)

Thus, with Beatrice Longoria's approval, Dr. García presented the audience with three options: burial in Arlington, San Antonio, or Three Rivers. The majority voted to accept Senator Johnson's offer.

In the days and weeks that followed, the civic leaders of Three Rivers and the state of Texas began a concerted effort to change Mrs. Longoria's mind and spare Texas negative publicity in the process.[7] Guadalupe Longoria, Felix's father, was pressured to sign a falsified affidavit stating that "Felix's wife would not speak to me because I objected to the association she was having with another man . . . He [Felix] is my boy, and I want his body brought back to his home in Three Rivers . . . I do not know this García from Corpus Christi and [I] do not want any trouble from him."[8] Through its own seemingly unbiased investigation, the American Legion's local chapter found "not . . . the least trace of any act of Un-American activities or racial discrimination practiced in this matter."[9]

FIGURE 4. Private Felix Longoria; date unknown. (Source: Hector P. Garcia Papers, Special Collections and Archives, Mary and Jeff Bell Library, Texas A&M University–Corpus Christi.)

And the Texas Good Neighbor Commission attempted to remind Dr. García "that the reputation of Texas will be at stake in history's recording of our handling of this very delicate matter."[10] Furthermore, the committee assigned by the Texas House of Representatives to investigate the matter released its final report on April 7, 1949. After compiling 372 pages of affidavits, interviews, and other documentation, the report concluded with this simple statement: "This committee . . . concludes that there was no discrimination on the part of the undertaker of Three Rivers, Texas, relative to the proposed burial of the body of the deceased Felix Longoria."[11] Four of the five committee members signed the report, but Representative Frank C. Oltorf filed a dissenting minority report, ending with a straightforward assessment of the incident: "I cannot look into the heart of Mr. Kennedy to ascertain his true intent, but can only accept his oral words, which appear to me discriminatory."[12]

Meanwhile, the American GI Forum began a collection to raise the $1,500 necessary to cover the airline expense to Washington, DC. Donations poured in from across the United States and from individual members of the Mexican and Mexican American communities of central and southern Texas. The latter contributed what they could, in amounts that taxed their meager resources, yet the opportunity to participate in this civil rights victory was overwhelming. In attendance at the funeral on February 16, 1949, were Beatrice Longoria; her daughter, Adelita; Felix's mother; and five siblings. The return of his remains and the controversy surrounding his burial undoubtedly generated considerable heartache for his family. Yet his body finally lay at rest, with the full honors he so richly deserved (see fig. 5).

This victory for civil rights bolstered a broad spectrum of social activism that emerged after World War II in an effort to combat segregation and other discriminatory practices.[13] It displayed a galvanized consciousness and sense of entitlement that utilized the community's exploits and dedicated service as irrefutable proof that the Mexican American community deserved first-class citizenship. Mexican American veterans, in particular, recognized the many inconsistencies that remained in American society, despite their having championed democratic principles in the struggle against fascism. This included repeated encounters with overt acts of racism, often while in uniform. For example, Medal of Honor recipient Macario García detailed one such episode in an affidavit to civil rights activist and League of United Latin American Citizens (LULAC) leader Alonso S. Perales, who would gather a collection of similar affidavits and publish *Are We Good Neighbors?* in 1948, which detailed a clear pattern of discrimination against

FIGURE 5. Family members present at the burial of Felix Longoria, February 16, 1949. (Source: AP Photo/LBJ Presidential Library.)

Mexican Americans in Texas after World War II. García's following testimony describes the series of events that led to his arrest:

> My name is Macario García. I am 26 years of age . . . I served in the United States Army two years, ten months, and twenty-eight days, eleven months and six days of which I served overseas. On August 23, 1945, President Harry S. Truman bestowed upon me the Congressional Medal of Honor . . . On October 10, 1945, about 11:15 p.m., I went into the Oasis Café . . . and I sat at the counter and ordered a cup of coffee. One of the waitresses . . . then said to me: "I cannot serve you" . . . because Mexicans were not served at the place . . . Then her husband, came to me and [said] . . . "She told you why, so there is the door" . . . I stood up. There was a sugar bowl on the counter and what he had told me made me so angry that I pushed the sugar bowl off the counter . . . I was wearing the uniform of the United States Army at the time.[14]

Tragically, discriminatory encounters remained an everyday reality despite dedicated military service in yet another conflict that followed soon thereafter—the Korean War. A case in point is offered by Frank Ornelas, who recalled a humiliating incident in 1951 as he traveled home to Saginaw, Michigan, while on leave following the completion of basic training at Fort Bliss, Texas:

> Coming back [to Michigan] after basic training, they gave me ten days to lay en route, so I could report to Camp Edwards [Massachusetts]. We stopped in Oklahoma on the bus coming home, and I had my military uniform on . . . There was two or three of us, maybe more, military guys, but I was the only Mexican. And I went through the [front] door and [the owner] said, "No. You don't come [through] here. If you want to eat, go to the back door and there's a window there. Knock there and tell 'em what you want." I [said], "You know what, I'm not going in anyway to your place."[15]

In response to such treatment, civic engagement proved the inevitable result for many of these veterans. Indeed, problems of inclusion vis-à-vis military benefits and, more broadly, the American Dream pushed veterans and nonveterans alike to continue the pursuit of social equality, a process already begun prior to World War II. After the war, linking citizenship to military service provided a new course of action in that struggle, which would continue through the Korean conflict and the Cold War. Political theorist and feminist Cynthia Enloe drove home this point in her examination of plural societies and the ethnic soldiers who are often called upon to defend them:

> When such groups discover upon demobilization that their political power is no greater than it was before conscription, they may be disillusioned . . . Their mistake was to believe that they were taking part in a nation-state process, that their maps and those of the authorities conscripting them were identical. One consequence of conscripts forming mental maps that are out of line with elite maps can be a postwar politicization of ethnic groups led by their respective veterans' organization.[16]

However, as the Korean War raged and the United States' relationships with foreign nations came under increased scrutiny, a simultaneous fear of potential Communist infiltration into the United States became manifest, reaching its climax in the early 1950s. Symbolized by the massive witch hunts led by the House Committee on Un-American Activities (HUAC) and Senator Joseph

McCarthy, domestic hysteria swept the nation and organizations such as the American GI Forum remained hard pressed to continually prove their loyalty and counter the charge that political activism in the pursuit of racial equality was Communist inspired.[17]

Caught in the crossfire over potential Communist infiltration were undocumented migrants from Mexico that provided critically needed labor in various southwestern industries, most notably commercial agriculture. The yearlong, multiagency effort in 1954, designated Operation Wetback, conducted a series of raids designed to apprehend and deport undocumented individuals. Furthermore, as historian Mae M. Ngai eloquently argues, race played a factor in this endeavor through the creation of a Cold War "Brown Scare" that depicted not only Mexicans but also Mexican Americans as foreigners. She underscored this characterization:

> "Foreignness" was a racialized concept that adhered to all Mexicans, including those born in the United States, and carried the opprobrium of illegitimacy and inferiority. American citizenship, whether by native birth or by naturalization, accrued few benefits.[18]

Unfortunately, many of those targeted by Operation Wetback were bracero guest workers who legally entered the United States as part of the Mexican contract-labor program first established during World War II as an effort to satisfy labor shortages in the agricultural and railroad industries. This managed migration was immensely popular with agricultural interests in the United States, enabling the program to, under a series of bilateral agreements, survive from its inception in 1942 until 1964.[19]

These concerns over immigration and citizenship prompted Dr. García to steer the GI Forum to embrace the concept of whiteness in an effort to win the privileges associated with that racial classification. The community's de jure status as white enabled such an approach, which LULAC had embraced since its inception in 1929. In the following excerpt, historian Neil Foley describes the rationale underlying this effort to overcome the de facto reality of being treated as a nonwhite "other":

> Mexican Americans were accorded the racial status of white people; socially, politically, and economically, however, they were treated as nonwhites. With the rise of the so-called Mexican American generation of the 1930's, '40s, and '50s, Mexican

> Americans began insisting on their status as whites in order to overcome the worst features of Jim Crow segregation.[20]

An excerpt from a letter by Dr. García to the GI Forum's rank-and-file membership in September 1948 offers a potent example of this strategy:

> You must avoid or stop having draft registration cards filled out with "Latin American" on the card instead of "white." Be sure and protest at the draft board if there is any evidence that Latin Americans are being classified as "Latin Americans" or "Mexican" instead of "white." We are all to be classified as "white." Explain to all these veterans that the Anglos are not to be referred to as "los blancos" [the whites]. Such phrases are certainly not correct and should not be used, as we are all "white."[21]

This "possessive investment in whiteness," as coined by historian George Lipsitz, facilitated the effort to dissociate from undocumented Mexican migrants and bracero guest workers, as evidenced in an October 1949 letter from Dr. García to Senator Lyndon B. Johnson:

> We also feel that imported labor is being brought in to lower the wages per hour scale which, as it is now, is too low and is the direct cause of the migratory character of our people who go as far as Michigan [and] Colorado . . . in search of better wages . . . The first obligation of our government is to its citizens and I believe it is not too hard to see now that the whole importation of labor and the legalizing of wetbacks has only one object, "Cheap Labor" . . . You, as our Senator, know that the standard of living of 1,200,000 Americans of Mexican origins is low enough in the state, so why lower it more by importing labor and lowering the minimum standard wage?[22]

The scrutiny of the Bracero Program was consistent with Dr. García's desire, as well as other members of the GI Forum's leadership, to highlight the patriotism of Mexican Americans. Linking citizenship to military service, anti-communism, and an anti-immigrant and anti-guest-worker platform as well as a firm embrace of whiteness was a crucial linchpin in that strategy.

Other newly established associations, such as the Community Service Organization (CSO), that included a strong veteran presence, supplemented organized action by the American GI Forum in the immediate postwar environment.

The CSO contained a youthful coterie "made up predominantly of Mexican Americans—many of them veterans and their wives—and focused on various community issues, especially voter registration and getting Mexicans to become politically involved."[23] Established in Los Angeles in 1948, following the unsuccessful run by Edward R. Roybal for the Los Angeles City Council the previous year, the CSO had more than five thousand members by 1950. Such organizational activity was further supplemented by ordinary Mexican American veterans across the United States, including the narrators present within this study, who confronted discrimination and socioeconomic inequality in their respective occupational and residential environments.

Alfred Aguirre embarked on a political career in his hometown of Placentia, California, south of Los Angeles. The birth of his first son in 1946 provided Aguirre with the motivation to ensure that segregated schooling would not play a role in limiting the future possibilities of Mexican American children. On the advice of a local priest, Aguirre and several companions visited a Los Angeles attorney, C. W. Marshall, who was noted for his willingness to provide assistance in cases involving desegregation. Marshall provided legal counsel on several occasions free of charge, purportedly offering the following encouragement to push forward: "You're American citizens, you're members of the white race, you're veterans . . . and they're [school board] gonna back off."[24] Emboldened by such counsel, Aguirre and his fellow organizers confronted Placentia's all-white school board in 1949:

> We organized a group of about fifty people . . . and we bluffed the city. We told 'em we had three attorneys waiting for us and we are gonna drag you into the courts, and we're gonna beat you . . . And they're all ranchers [stating], "Well, we meant well . . . you're good at picking oranges . . . at picking up strawberries . . . We tried to help you because . . . you Mexicans are different, you can't keep up with the studies, you can't speak English . . . the white kids are too far advanced."[25]

Following the successful desegregation of Placentia public schools, Aguirre realized that further success in the city's political process required registered voters and a close affiliation with the Democratic Party, so he became a registrar of voters for approximately four years, starting in 1950. He was aided in the first year by his good friend, Bobby Moreno, a Marine Corps veteran of Iwo Jima. As Aguirre described, Placentia's Mexican American community developed its own political power base, shifting the balance of power in the city: "I registered over three hundred Chicanos in Placentia . . . For about ten to fifteen years, anybody that wanted to run under our name, we [Mexican American voters] could get them in."[26] He would himself be elected to the city council and serve from 1958 to 1962, as well as various other commissions for some time thereafter. His political activism also included becoming a California representative for LULAC and campaigning for Senator John F. Kennedy's 1960 presidential campaign. Through his involvement in the Viva Kennedy clubs, Aguirre would meet the presidential hopeful at the St. Francis Hotel in San Francisco.[27]

John Sótelo's political activism began immediately after his discharge from the U.S. Navy in May 1946. Despite having fought for the same democratic principles and shared the same misery and toil associated with military service, white members of an American Legion outpost in Riverside, California, felt compelled to maintain an exclusionary policy toward Chicano veterans:

> When we [Mexican American veterans] were ready to join the American Legion here in Riverside, we probably had 150 to 200 veterans that wanted to be a part of it, and, at that time they told us . . . that we had different cultures so why don't we form an American Legion [outpost] of [our] own.[28]

This racial dividing line characterized the social and political practices of the entire city, and Sótelo was compelled to respond the following year after a Mexican American family turned to him for help. His stature as an activist and a political candidate was apparently on the rise:

> A young [Mexican American] boy was not admitted to . . . school . . . so I told the mother, "You take him back to school" . . . And they sent him home [again] . . . and I went up to the superintendent of schools [Ira C. Landis], and I told him that I was going to go to the newspaper[s], and I was gonna get some money to hire a lawyer and we were gonna sue the school. So, he admitted the boy. They personally came in a car and picked the boy up after the third day.[29]

These actions by Sótelo and Aguirre, and the respective families involved, paralleled similar efforts by other Mexican American families to combat segregated schooling. In 1945, in the small community of Westminster, California, Gonzalo and Felicitas Méndez filed a lawsuit to ensure integrated schooling and better opportunities for their children. The original verdict in *Méndez et al. v. Westminster School District of Orange County*, upheld on appeal by the Ninth Circuit

Court in 1947, effectively ended de facto segregation for Mexican American schoolchildren in California. Moreover, citing *Méndez*, Governor Earl Warren signed into law the Anderson Act that same year, which banned all forms of segregation in public education throughout the state and served as a powerful precedent for *Brown v. Board of Education* in 1954.[30] Nevertheless, social and educational discrimination remained an everyday reality for Mexican Americans and members of other marginalized communities despite these victories.

Sótelo also became active in the American GI Forum, joining one of the first chapters in California around 1950. He frequently participated in the forum's state and national conventions, where he often interacted with Dr. García. His additional involvement with the Mexican American Political Association (MAPA), LULAC, and the Democratic Party made him a familiar face in regional and national politics.[31] Yet his primary concern lay with his hometown, where he struggled throughout the 1950s to establish a greater level of political representation for Riverside's Mexican American and African American populations. As he described, he faced an uphill battle:

> We used to have elections at large in the city of Riverside, and we [Mexican Americans] never had representation . . . We found out that all the city officials . . . the mayor and council members were all from within a four block area [of] downtown Riverside . . . We fought to change the charter . . . That was the first I ever heard of gerrymandering.[32]

Around 1960 new voting districts based on a ward system replaced the previous at-large electoral process. Seven new wards were established, and Sótelo ran a successful campaign for Ward 2 at the behest of a group of supporters who arrived en masse at his home. He remained a council member from 1961 to 1972. By the time he left office, at least one Mexican American or African American had a place on twenty-eight of the twenty-nine boards and commissions maintained by the city.

George Castrueta, by comparison, was the first Mexican American in Los Angeles County Fire Warden's Forestry Division when his career as a forestry fireman began in 1949. Despite the lack of diversity, the strong veteran presence created a sense of camaraderie with fellow firefighters. And yet, individual encounters with prejudice did occur. He described one of the more notable incidents and his combative reaction: "Some guy called me, 'How you doing Cisco?' And that was demeaning to me. But I cornered him . . . and I told him, 'You know, you don't call me that . . . My name is George. The only reason . . . I'm not gonna go walk all over you, and you know I can, is because I know your brother.' His brother was in the service with me."[33] Following his retirement in 1966, Castrueta became a vocational counselor for various high schools in Whittier and Pico Rivera, east of downtown Los Angeles. He recalled his contribution to the Chicano movement as it exploded around him in the late sixties: "My contribution was simply this . . . I made a point to spend some extra time with my . . . kids [and] delivered what I had to say. I stressed education, things of that nature."[34] His commitment to Chicano youth continued in another capacity with his simultaneous employment in the Educational Poverty Program in East Los Angeles, which he described:

> That was quite ingratiating . . . to train young kids into some kind of vocation . . . so they could provide for themselves . . . I worked with another gentleman and we were really quite conscientious about that job. It was possibly one of the happiest employments I've ever had . . . Our enrollees were principally poor kids . . . Some of 'em were gang members.[35]

Castrueta continued in this capacity to promote education and job training for the next twenty-six years until his retirement in 1993.

Across the country in Grand Rapids, Michigan, where Francisco Vega permanently settled in 1951 or 1952 as sales manager for a local cemetery, he discovered that discriminatory clauses banning nonwhites were standard practice. He explained, "They all had what they called a Caucasian clause. They would not take, not only blacks, but Indian[s] or Mexicans . . . The racism was very strong."[36] With increased sales, Vega acquired his own cemetery in 1959 and he banned any form of discrimination, a practice he continued until his retirement in 1993. However, such altruism was not well received:

> When I opened up Resurrection [Cemetery], I did not put the Caucasian clause in. I wouldn't do it. And that was the first cemetery in the history of the state of Michigan . . . And that was resented by the other cemetery owners . . . and by funeral homes . . . I had people who'd park [a] school bus, knowing that I had a funeral coming in, across the entrance.[37]

He was also an instrumental figure in bringing Texas-based civic organizations, such as LULAC and the American GI Forum, to Grand Rapids: "I started the [first] LULAC chapter here. I started the [first] GI Forum chapter here . . . to bring the information of what these organizations offered."[38] Despite the more conservative demeanor of these organizations, Vega's activism was varied and widespread. He said, "I went to [all types of] marches . . . In Washington, DC, I carried the Virgen de Guadalupe banner."[39] His efforts also brought him into contact with Cesar Chavez for the first time in the mid-sixties. It began a relationship that spanned several decades: "I knew him well . . . I [drove] him in from Lansing twice. The last time was 1993 when he died . . . It impressed me [what] a tremendous confidence this guy had."[40]

Martin Morales also developed a relationship with Cesar Chavez during the latter's multiple trips to Michigan. He did so as part of a larger agenda to promote civil rights and integration for public agencies in Grand Rapids, where Morales settled in 1968. A man of few words, he simply stated, "I pushed for them to put Latinos on their payroll."[41] He also ran for mayor twice, providing the following brief rationale for doing so: "To create the awareness that my people could do it."[42] His efforts were largely funded by his ownership of the Little Mexico Café from 1968 to 1995, a local popular eatery that attracted notable dignitaries and which served as his base of operations.[43] As he lamented, however, poor financial management was his ultimate downfall: "I gave a lot of money away. People needed homes [and] cars."[44] Meanwhile, in Saginaw, Frank Ornelas became quite active in local union and Democratic Party politics. An unsuccessful run for city council in 1969 nevertheless provided him with significant exposure, which enabled him to secure a position on the executive board of Local 668 of the United Auto Workers. He said, "By that time, I had already run for city council . . . Everybody knew me, even the Anglos."[45] In the 1970s, he was appointed to the city's planning commission and to the state labor board under Governor William Milliken. As he recalled, the seventies were a particular heyday for Latino political involvement: "Within the Latino community [in Saginaw], we had a bunch of us that . . . were very much politically [involved] . . . And we used to bring people to teach us, to train us. We used to have retreats to go train . . . for two, three days."[46] And, similar to Vega and Morales, he also befriended and supported Cesar Chavez: "I met him [a] bunch of times, in Detroit . . . and then [in] Saginaw . . . I was with him in Lansing when he went there . . . I was one of the leaders for his marches. We marched from Bay City to Saginaw and then . . . we marched from Saginaw all the way to Lansing."[47]

In Arizona, meanwhile, after acquiring a doctorate in curriculum instruction and bilingual education in 1969, William J. Fisher began a nineteen-year career as a high school principal in Tucson where Mexican Americans comprised a majority of the student population at the four schools he supervised. He offered the following commentary on his many efforts to overcome equipment, textbook, and other shortages he encountered:

> I was [a] principal at four different schools . . . In fact, two of 'em were about 90 percent Latinos . . . They lacked a lot of things at the two Latino schools, but my military training, I guess, came in handy. I was a "procurer." I was able to do extra things on my own that I did for the school[s].[48]

In addition, his work with bilingual students received national recognition in 1978 when his school became a finalist for an award from the National Association for Bilingual Education. Fisher also recalled the emergence of the Chicano movement and his willingness to provide moral, but not active, support due to concern over his job security: "I was in sympathy with it, I identified with it, but to actually get out and boycott or demonstrate, no."[49] He ultimately retired from his career in education in 1988. In the meantime, Ruben Moreno endeavored to record the oral histories of the Mexican American community in Tucson, including the large Mexican American contingent of E Company that was mobilized for service in Korea. He laughingly described the chain of events that led to his role as a "volunteer":

> We formed a club . . . here [in Tucson] that was known as the "Descedientes del Presidio" [Descendents of the Presidio]. The main reason behind it is that the historical society here in Tucson has got a bunch of early history, but mostly Anglo . . . We figured that Hispanics needed to be recognized too. The idea was to interview old folks around town and get their histories . . . And then I said, "Well, you know, it'd be a good idea if somebody would do an oral history on E Company" . . . Next thing I know, they brought me a cassette recorder and instructions and [they] said, "Go to it." I couldn't back out but the more I did it . . . the more I liked it. I figured I was doing something worth doing.[50]

Moreno has continued his association with the Arizona Historical Society in Tucson, where he has produced several pamphlets of oral histories

All in all, these efforts, large and small, that emerged after World War II and that continued through the Korean War and thereafter are indicative of the galvanized consciousness expressed by Mexican American veterans, and the community overall, in the pursuit of social and political equality. Underlying such efforts was a rather simple formula that emphasized military service, cultural notions of civic and masculine responsibility, and sincere veneration of the American Dream. All that was missing was the community's ability to engage in America's promises in an uninhibited manner, which their military record should remedy. At no point did the sociopolitical establishment of the United States or its foreign policy objectives come under scathing review. The Vietnam War, however, would offer a more complicated and critical assessment of U.S. foreign policy and the meaning of American citizenship.

A NATION DIVIDED

In November 1977, the New York City–based Center for Policy Research was commissioned by the House Committee on Veterans Affairs and the Veterans Administration to examine the adjustment patterns of Vietnam veterans in their return to civilian life using a broad survey of topics—this culminated in the publication of *Legacies of Vietnam: Comparative Adjustment of Veterans and Their Peers* in March 1981.[51] Responses to the following question by the 1,400 participants, "Looking back over your life, how would you say the Vietnam War affected your life?" offers a glimpse of the war's capacity to engineer an enhanced politicized consciousness, especially in the area of personal disillusionment. As listed in table 5, varying numbers of Vietnam veterans, military veterans that did not serve overseas, and civilians emphasized an expanded awareness of political issues and institutional corruption. Also, the first group that served in Vietnam clearly indicated a more sincere understanding of the sobering realities and consequences of warfare. And finally, the category indicating an increased appreciation for the United States generated an overwhelmingly poor response from all three groups, further highlighting the divisive nature of the Vietnam War for veterans and nonveterans alike.

Moreover, the temporal obligation employed by the U.S. military for service in Vietnam, centered on a one-year tour of duty (thirteen months for Marine Corps personnel), produced an armed forces committed to individual survival rather than a uniform experience shared by all personnel, as in the Second World War, when troops served for the duration of the conflict. Thus, for American servicemen stationed in Vietnam, this individual approach increasingly fostered a political questioning of American policies as little or no progress toward

TABLE 5. Effect of War on Perceptions by Veteran Status

	VIETNAM VETERAN	VIETNAM-ERA VETERAN	NONVETERAN	TOTAL
Broadened Political Horizons	21.4	39.0	45.2	40.7
Awareness of Political/Institutional Corruption	26.8	35.0	31.8	31.5
Enhanced Understanding of War/Violence	14.0	8.7	12.1	11.9
Increased Appreciation for U.S.	3.3	—	0.6	0.9
Decreased Appreciation for U.S.	18.9	10.2	8.2	10.1
Broadened Knowledge of Other People/Cultures	15.6	7.1	2.2	4.9
	100% (n = 85)	100% (n = 79)	100% (n = 199)	100% (n = 363)
Response Rate	28.7%	24.0%	36.2%	32.6%

Source Egendorf et al., *Legacies of Vietnam*, 412.

stated objectives was accomplished. In effect, the U.S. military's rotational policies and the United States' strategic aims encouraged a wide variety of dissent among U.S. servicemen while deployed to Vietnam. Alfredo Vea, for instance, remembered that open displays of political questioning and discussions of radical militancy, such as the Black Panther Party, were frequent topics of conversation: "I don't think there was that much resistance to that kind of talking, at least among the basic troops . . . We talked about politics all the time."[52]

In addition, the growing popularity of cultural nationalism provided a tremendous source of racial pride in the latter stages of the Vietnam War, prompting open displays of racial solidarity that defied prescribed grooming standards and other military regulations. Among black servicemen, such efforts included nonregulation-style Afro haircuts and a rather elaborate arsenal of slang terminology. George Mariscal offers vivid testimony in this regard as he compared the behaviors employed by African Americans and Chicanos:

> The most visible memory for me is African American resistance, both at the level of style and, just, behavior. It was much more theatrical . . . in terms of giant, huge anti-regulation Afros . . . the DAP, they used to call it, the handshake and the whole routine that went around it. That was heavy . . . [Meanwhile], the only visible sign of . . . Chicano identity [was that] everyone would write on their helmet liner where they were from. So . . . you'd see, "Viva La Raza," "Tejano," whatever."[53]

Latinos also resorted to speaking Spanish in an effort to communicate discreetly with each other, which provided a more mild form of open resistance in an English-dominated environment. Sal Martínez witnessed this process unfold among the Chicano troops he commanded: "[The term] 'La Raza' . . . was being used as a kind of a rallying cry . . . [And] they were speaking Spanish a lot more than they were speaking English, which was also a cause of division."[54]

Upon their return to the United States, this soul-searching process often coalesced in the tumultuous environment that encompassed the antiwar movement and various other social crusades typical of the 1960s, including the Chicano movement. The resulting change in consciousness for many veterans encompassed varying degrees of anger, disillusionment, and critiques of U.S. foreign policy and domestic inequality that paralleled the outrage of student activists. Indeed, the cultural nationalism expressed by the Chicano student movement often equated the latter two by espousing a worldview that linked their struggle for social and political equality at home with anticolonialist struggles for independence across the globe, including the Vietnamese. In the same manner that these student activists drew strength and inspiration from the mythical kingdom of Aztlán, they recognized shared circumstances in the plight of the Vietnamese farmworker as they both struggled to survive while confronting overwhelming odds. Historian Lorena Oropeza offered the following comparison:

> From a radical perspective, Chicanos and the Vietnamese were both members of the Third World in that both were a non-white people suffering from the exploitative nature of U.S. imperialism and capitalism. From this perspective, moreover, the Chicano claim to the land was an anti-colonial struggle similar to the one that the Vietnamese were waging.[55]

The rural upbringing of many Chicano servicemen reinforced this identification with the Vietnamese, including Alfredo Vea, who described his conflicted emotional state during his many confrontations with Vietnamese villagers while cognizant of the Chicano community's marginalization and his own experiences as a migrant farm worker:

> It was sort of a nebulous thing wanting to see war [and] at the same time having all this history [of inequality] in my head and all of a sudden realizing that I was the colonist . . . I was the one asking and telling these people, "Tell me where they [the enemy] are or I'll kill you" . . . And I knew they were hiding shit from us. And I knew that was the right thing for them to be doing. And I also knew that I was on the wrong side.[56]

As a result of these many experiences, Vea expressed a scathing indictment of the United States upon his return from Vietnam: "I despised the United States of America. I still in many ways do."[57] In fact, he immediately left for France, where he lived for eighteen months before returning to enroll at the University of California, Berkeley, as an undergraduate and, subsequently, as a law student. Throughout, he became an active demonstrator and ultimately worked as legal counsel for the United Farm Workers (UFW) led by Cesar Chavez. As he recalled, however, some of his experiences with the UFW proved disappointing:

> It was . . . an eye-opener to go work there and find out how many people there were just hangers-on . . . who were using their association with Cesar Chavez

> to . . . get notoriety. It wasn't what I thought it was going to be. Like an idiot, I thought this was going to be Camelot and everybody was gonna be pulling their weight. There was so much infighting, it was unbelievable. That leaves you feeling a little ill at ease about movements.[58]

John Rodríguez also harbors powerful anti-U.S. sentiments, going so far as to symbolically renounce his American citizenship:

> When I almost died in Nam, I made quite clear that two things had to be questioned a bit, and that was this society, this country, and the religion that I was into, which was Catholic[ism]. I found myself denouncing both . . . I understood that I was there for no other reason than to be eliminated. I was just a number. I was corralled, I was led, to be slaughtered . . . My coming back from Nam gave me a real clear picture as to where I stood in this society.[59]

His outrage stemmed in part from the following Western Union telegram his mother received on May 19, 1969, a few days after Rodríguez received life-threatening injuries, which included a punctured lung, nerve damage, and the removal of his spleen and a portion of his small intestine:

> The Secretary of the Army has asked me to inform you that your son, Specialist John G. Rodríguez was slightly wounded in action in Vietnam on 16 May 1969 by fragments while at base camp when the area came under a mortar attack by a hostile force. He received wounds to the abdomen, the left ankle, left tibia, left thigh, the back, the buttocks, and the left elbow, with a fracture of the left tibia. He was treated and hospitalized in Vietnam. Address mail to him or the hospital mail section APO San Francisco 96381 since he is not, repeat not, seriously wounded. No further reports will be furnished.[60]

As he continued, he participated in antiwar demonstrations upon his return: "As soon as I got out of Nam, I was going to protests . . . as a veteran and as a Chicano."[61] This formative experience, however, did offer one tangible, albeit abstract, benefit. He explained: "The only thing that has benefitted me was the experience of going through something that told me the 'truth.' And no one was telling me the truth. I had to learn the truth by that experience."[62]

Joe Rodríguez readily acknowledged his antiwar stance upon his discharge from the military, and he offered the following explanation, which included the death of his brother, a second lieutenant in the 101st Airborne Division: "It let me see a side of me that I hope I never see again. It made me afraid of people . . . I guess in a certain way, it made me cynical about patriotism . . . and I lost my brother. He was a good guy."[63] Furthermore, when asked his willingness to repeat his experience in Vietnam, he stated:

> Would I do it again? Fuck, I'd go to jail . . . I'd be straightforward [and] be the conscientious objector. I'd do my time . . . It wasn't worth it, what I saw. It was a waste. It wasn't strategic, there was no strategy . . . a lot of it was bullshit . . . When I got out I was anti-war, marched, and the whole thing. I became [an] active [demonstrator] . . . in San Diego.[64]

George Mariscal, by comparison, offered a similar response to the same question:

> A lot of Chicano vets that I know, if pushed . . . they'll say, "I would do it again." Now, I won't say that. My answer to that is, I would not do it again. In other words, if I were drafted, knowing what I know now, I'd be so down deep in [the Mexican state of] Oaxaca that you'd have trouble finding me.[65]

In a manner similar to John Rodríguez, he also credits his military service in Vietnam as the source of his political awakening: "The only . . . advantage I find, and it's kind of abstract . . . is being politicized, which basically, is a counter product of what they were trying to do . . . What really did change for me was my political awareness. And that's only grown since then."[66] He became an avid demonstrator in the Chicano movement, where he encountered tremendous rage and frustration. He recalled one especially powerful sign, held by a mother that had lost her only son in Vietnam: "The anger was so great. I remember a protest sign at a demonstration that said, 'A mi me dieron diez mil y una medalla por mi único hijo' [They gave me ten thousand dollars and a medal for my only son]."[67] In addition, Leroy Quintana likewise stated his unwillingness to repeat his experience: "I was very much more politicized and aware of the situation [and] the futility of being there . . . Had I been smarter . . . it would have been nice to go to Canada [and] hide there."[68] What's more, he described his transformed consciousness as "the biggest advantage of all" stemming from his time in the military.[69]

Coincidentally, Charley Trujillo also refers to his political transformation as the most prominent outcome of his military service. Indeed, upon his return in

1970, he was ready to take a violent stand against the United States: "I wanted to start fighting here. It crossed my mind more than once. Remember, [it] was 1970 [during the] Chicano Moratorium. I got home in August 1970 . . . My political identity as a Chicano solidified in Vietnam so I was ready to fight these guys, the gringos."[70] Used throughout the twentieth century to refer to lower-class Mexican Americans and juvenile delinquents, the term *Chicano* came to symbolize a bold sense of self-assertion and cultural pride during the Chicano movement. As Trujillo explained, this new political consciousness first developed in Vietnam as he contemplated the tenacity and sense of purpose he observed in the enemy:

> I saw these Vietnamese guys fighting, when we were fighting real close . . . I started wondering about that. I said these guys are fighting real hard to the death [and] they're Communists . . . We used to try and figure that out, "Why are these guys fighting so hard?" . . . We were basically fighting for survival, whereas they had a political cause . . . I started thinking . . . "Why am I fighting in this army?" This is the same army that took the land away from our people . . . They still got us fucked up at home . . . What am I doing fighting these *vatos* [people]? I kinda even look like 'em. Some of the white soldiers would tell me . . . "Hey, watch out. You look like a gook from behind."[71]

For Daniel Cano, however, a similar questioning attitude took some time to develop after he returned home in October 1967. Nevertheless, the final withdrawal of the United States from Saigon in 1975 cemented a more cynical mind-set that has also called into question his involvement in Vietnam. He said:

> And that's the most frustrating thing. That's why it's kind of a double-edge sword [for me], the dichotomy. When you asked if I regret going over there or getting out of it [in hindsight] and I said I wouldn't have given it up. But at the same time, I wouldn't have been over there had I not been lied to in the first place. So, in some ways, do I wish the Vietnam War had never happened? And I would have to say yes, because the guys that died over there shouldn't have died.[72]

He summed up his new demeanor: "I question everything now because of the Vietnam War."[73]

It is also important to remember that such political questioning and changed consciousness manifested itself differently in each veteran. For Raymond Buriel, involvement in antiwar activities was unacceptable, and he explained why: "I have to admit that I could understand what they [demonstrators] were doing, but I couldn't get into it because it would be sort of throwing into doubt everything I had done for the last thirteen months."[74] Rather, Buriel became a tutor to student radicals: "All of these guys [activists] that were out there raising Cain were failing, and I would tutor them so that they could stay in school. And I figured this is my way of making my contribution to the movement."[75] Jesus Barragan offered a comparable rationale that took into account the value placed on military service by large elements of the Chicano community. He said, "I never came [out] against the war because I understood . . . I wish I had not gone over there, but I'm proud of having served in the military."[76] On the other hand, as he continued his education after being discharged in August 1969, he became active in the Communist Party, which he indicated was influential in motivating his political activism: "It's like I was able to peel away how I had been trained to think and had the courage to look at it from a different point of view."[77]

In 1975, Barragan was one of the founding members of the Gay Latino/Latina Alliance (GALA) in San Francisco, which endeavored to create political space and promote an agenda friendly to gay Latinas/os, including working with the city's affirmative action compliance office.[78] Such efforts drew the attention of the famed Harvey Milk, the nation's first openly gay elected official. When he successfully ran for a position on San Francisco's Board of Supervisors in 1977, Barragan recalled that Milk received GALA's endorsement, albeit with some apprehension: "When he was running for supervisor, he came to us [GALA] to endorse him, and we [did] . . . But it haunts me to this day. He said something [about Latinos] and one of our members called him on it . . . and Harvey said, 'Well, you guys are gonna have to teach me [how] to be a good racist.'"[79] Barragan simultaneously worked as a therapist with the city's veteran center, where he encountered incredible stories related by gay servicemen. He described:

> From 1981 through 1990, I worked at the veteran's center . . . for PTSD [cases] . . . I started as a counselor and then [as a] therapist. And I was shocked to have these vets come in, identify themselves as gay, and tell me that "my lover died in my arms over there." I almost fell out of my chair.[80]

After being passed over for the center's directorship, he then moved to Child Protective Services and soon began addressing the department's rather poor services to Latino families: "When I got there, I was appalled at the lack of services and sensitivity for Latino/Chicano Spanish-speaking families. So I kept my mouth shut for six months and once I became permanent, I picked up the Mexican banner and led the charge."[81] All in all, until his retirement in 1999, Barragan maintained a prolific and admirable activist career that served a variety of different constituencies.

In Michigan, Gilbert Guevara could never bring himself to openly critique or demonstrate against the Vietnam War upon his return in 1968. While deployed overseas, however, he did realize that a career in political activism was in his future:

> I thought, "I'm going back home and somehow I'm gonna get involved in something" . . . I didn't know what yet. I didn't know what the [Chicano] movement was, because all we saw . . . was all the protesting . . . So when I went back . . . that's when I started to see that there was some movement [activities] in Michigan . . . The lack of recognition of Hispanics in terms of their accomplishments [and] their contributions, that's what got me involved. [However,] I didn't get critical of Vietnam.[82]

With funds provided by the Great Society's Model Cities Program and Housing and Urban Development, Guevara initially worked for Saginaw's poverty program as its Spanish-speaking coordinator. He also joined the Brown Berets, one of the more militant organizations to emerge during the Chicano movement. He offered the following: "My job as a Brown Beret was to get into [city] boards and commissions and figure what they were doing and see if they were serving . . . Chicanos and our community."[83] Guevara next worked for Saginaw's Catholic Archdiocese from 1980 until his retirement in 2005 as coordinator of immigration work, community affairs, and youth ministry. And along with his wife, his many responsibilities also provided religious guidance to the area's migrant farmworkers through what they called "Tailgate Ministry." He recalled: "I had a truck and I used to carry tables and chairs . . . My wife would lay this kind of [cloth] and she'd put a candle and a little crucifix and the Bible, and we would preach to the kids."[84] Moreover, he rendered crucial immigration services, which he described: "A lot of them were undocumented, so my job was to do all the paperwork, submit it to Detroit, take them to Detroit . . . and then get them work authorization, and then eventually . . . their permanent residency."[85]

For Guevara, such religious activism clearly moved beyond spiritual matters and acquired a distinctly political dimension as had his earlier work. They are testament to his dedicated pursuit of social justice and first-class citizenship for migrant workers and the Mexican American community.

Nevertheless, public activism stemming from various forms of alienation and disillusionment did not emerge as the sole consequence of military service in Vietnam. An equally profound ideological transformation reinforced a sense of patriotism, insisting that the men who fought the war were not allowed to win due to larger political factors in the United States. This "we should have won" perspective espoused by Chappo López has been part of an effort to describe American defeat as political, rather than military. Adding to this frustration was the reality that well into the 1980s the war remained an unspoken topic, finding little avenue for public discussion other than a handful of Hollywood films—some of which attempted to rewrite history by promoting a winning portrayal of American involvement through the superheroic feats of characters such as Rambo, a disgruntled veteran who finds personal redemption by returning to Vietnam to save Americans listed as missing in action. According to historian Christian Appy, this "way of thinking often leads veterans to rage against the various people and groups they believe were responsible for sending them to fight an unwinnable war, for not finding a way to win, or for the deep divisions at home that widened as the war continued."[86] Chappo López, for instance, offers a powerful example when he stated: "The things we could have done [but] they wouldn't let us do. 'Cause over there our hands were tied in a lot of situations . . . My anger is with the politics and the people back here."[87] John Sánchez offered a similar reminiscence: "We did not lose. We were held back. The rules of engagement, in essence, [we] performed . . . with one hand tied behind our back. We were never given the opportunity to fully do what we were capable of doing."[88] And Tony López also believes that American military might was held back: "I regret that we didn't do what we should have done, gone all the way to Hanoi."[89]

Additionally, the anti-troop sentiments often expressed by antiwar demonstrators fostered hostility toward peace groups, including Eddie Solís, who offered the following: "I can get excited in no time at all, especially when I was younger and I was ready to fight if anybody said anything wrong . . . I stayed away from them."[90] Victor Ramírez further lamented the lack of any welcoming process as enjoyed by World War II veterans: "You came back, there was no confetti or anything thrown over your head. You came home by yourself."[91] Frank Reyes described a similar form of frustration: "We were not ever given proper respect . . . I got spit on. I got called all kind of names."[92] Furthermore, for some, the Chicano movement also came under scathing review, including Everett Álvarez, who returned from his captivity to find the country and the Mexican American community in turmoil. He explained:

> When I came back there was this big Chicano movement. When I grew up, Chicano was a familiar term. It became very political. I didn't understand what the heck they were trying to do, especially the students . . . When I came back in the seventies, it was very politicized and militant. And I said, "Wait a minute." I fought for something which is counter to what these people are doing.[93]

Tony López, meanwhile, was more direct in his condemnation of the movement: "I personally categorize them [militants] more as an anti-American group."[94]

And yet, lingering frustration such as this, as well as principles highlighting patriotism, teamwork, and a fraternal brotherhood did not deter López from becoming a high school guidance counselor in Moreno, California, where he works with the large Latino student population and their parents to promote education and the English language. He said:

> The academic [program] is referred to as the English Limited Development Program [for] those kids that have English as their second language. So, in [my] school, we've got probably about a thousand kids. I specialize mainly [in] working with their parents [and] kind of empowering their parents to give them the resources . . . [and stressing] the benefits of education, those types of things.[95]

John Sánchez, by comparison, began a job as a wage claims supervisor for the state of Michigan while he apprenticed at night for State Farm Insurance. As he recalled, despite the many challenges he confronted in the performance of his duties, he persevered in order to safeguard the livelihood of agricultural laborers, a job he performed himself as a child:

> I was their token Hispanic. I would go . . . to the west side of the state making sure that the growers were paying their [migrant workers] . . . the right amount of wages per hour. And I needed to see [their] books. And they would call me a

> Communist . . . I was Hispanic also . . . I feared that almost more than being in Vietnam . . . That took a certain amount of skill, dedication, and courage to face those growers in their homes.[96]

These latter two stories demonstrate that more conventional and patriotically inclined methods of working for the betterment of the Mexican American community continued through the Vietnam War and were not specific to the generations that fought in World War II and Korea. Indeed, the former methods largely typified the thirty-five-year time period under investigation, while the more critical mind-set that emerged during the Vietnam War served as a more unique, though no less significant, consequence of military service that impacted the postwar consciousness of Chicano veterans.

CONCLUSION

Returning once again to Cynthia Enloe, she offers another powerful assessment of ethnic soldiers in plural societies: "The military is part—often the most crucial part—of a political order. The absence or over-representation of any ethnic group in the military . . . should tell us something about that political order and how groups with widely different political resources cope with that order."[97] In the case of the Mexican American community, large numbers emphasized military service as the proper avenue to full citizenship rights through a sincere demonstration of civic and masculine responsibility, as did other marginalized communities. This was especially the case in the aftermath of World War II, when returning Mexican American veterans were emboldened by their wartime service and struggles ensued in education, political representation, and economic advancement, to name a few. Moreover, this communal sense of obligation continued through the Korean and Cold War in response to the new threat posed by the Soviet Union and the Eastern Bloc. It also provided significant motivation to once again answer the call in the defense of South Vietnam; but the divisive nature of American involvement diversified the political awakening that many veterans experienced, and prototypical sentiments that encompassed pride and patriotism coexisted with angrier and more critical assessments of U.S. foreign policy and domestic inequality. What is ultimately clear, however, is that Mexican American veterans that served from World War II through the Vietnam War demanded the full privileges of American citizenship for themselves and their community, and they used their military service as a springboard for individual and collective action to achieve that goal. Finally, as the Latina/o community continued to grow at an exceptional rate beyond 1975, did a similar emphasis on military service emerge? And if so, what politicized ramifications awaited these new recruits?

EPILOGUE

BY MAPPING THE CULTURAL CONTEXT that influenced large elements of the Mexican American community from 1940 to 1975, this analysis illustrates how military service provided a central reference point in the attempt to understand citizenship and lay claim to national belonging. Additionally, as a social space imbued with its own masculine ethos, as well as the entitlements derived from a tour of duty, the U.S. military offers an ideal location to study the gendered behaviors and socioeconomic aspirations of these young men. As Gina M. Perez has persuasively argued in a more recent examination of Latina/o military service, "The U.S. military is an especially important institution to examine regarding . . . moments of inclusion and exclusion, not only because it symbolizes a vision of citizenship that rests on sacrifice, honor, and patriotism, but also because it is an invaluable vehicle for economic mobility for many working-class families."[1] Within my sample of narrators, the GI Bill was especially helpful in funding the costs associated with the pursuit of undergraduate and advanced degrees for some, producing a middle- and upper-middle-class lifestyle as lawyers, writers, and university professors. A larger number acquired a variety of different trade skills as carpenters, welders, and machinists. These latter occupations usually provided steady employment and financial security, which union membership reinforced.

For many others, however, the GI Bill and their military service did promote a bridging process to improved socioeconomic status, although not always in a straightforward manner. Uneven implementation of the program's direct forms of assistance and declining benefits across three generations were also compounded by the more personal battles with physical and emotional scars acquired while in uniform. In the case of the latter, the health-care practices of the Veterans Administration stimulated a variety of appraisals from veterans in all three conflicts, most notably frustration and anger. Still others were provided with few transferable skills and were unwilling or unable to access their various benefits, and thus experienced minimal gains upon reentering the civilian labor force. All in all, it is necessary to remember that no uniform experience characterized Mexican American military service from World War II through the Vietnam War. And whether veterans are critical of their time spent in the military or proud and eager to provide a celebratory and patriotic assessment, the clear evolution of Mexican American identity that is central to my analysis facilitated greater levels of political activism in communities across the Southwest and the Great Lakes region. For instance, voter-registration drives, student outreach and integration efforts, immigration services, and deliberate attempts to exercise political clout in local jurisdictions were but a few of the endeavors to combat discrimination and other forms of inequality by the interviewees. And while these efforts illustrate the drive for inclusion into the American mainstream, they simultaneously convey a clear celebration of their Mexican heritage. Equally important, moreover, is the fact that Mexican American servicemen negotiated cultural expectations and the martial values of the U.S. military on an individual basis, allowing for a wide range of ideological, masculine, and ethnic identities to flourish both during and after their military service, despite the existence of hegemonic ideals within the armed forces and the larger Mexican American community.

But what of the Mexican American and Latina/o presence in the U.S. military since 1975? To answer that question, a comparative approach with the African American community is warranted since participation by the two communities has differed substantially since March 1973, when the nation's first peacetime draft, instituted by the Selective Training and Service Act of September 1940, came to an end in favor of a market-driven all-volunteer force (AVF). This transition was accompanied by initial fears that the overall capabilities of the armed forces would suffer if, as expected, minority groups increasingly turned to the U.S. military as a source of employment. As described by historian Beth Bailey, "debates about quality and the AVF were also driven by the fallout of the social change movements of the 1960s . . . In the 1970s, every discussion of 'quality' and the army was shadowed by assumptions about race."[2] In fact, the perception of the U.S. military as providing a social welfare role intensified as the African American presence developed at an exceptional rate. In 1972, African Americans comprised 11.1 percent of all active-duty military personnel, an amount that jumped dramatically to 20.8 percent by 1990—a figure considerably higher than their 12.1 percent representation in the census conducted that same year.[3] This overrepresentation continued through the 1990s, and by 2001, African American enlisted personnel were 22.45 percent of the armed forces despite composing only 12.73 percent of the civilian workforce in the 18–44 age group.[4] More recently, by 2013, the African American enlisted presence had decreased to 18.9 percent, a figure that was nevertheless somewhat higher than the community's percentage of the civilian workforce, ages 18–44, which stood at 13.5 percent.[5] Ultimately, for African Americans, the long-held perception of the U.S. military as an agent of social and economic uplift has indeed continued into the present day.

In sharp contrast, the Latina/o presence has increased more slowly, but steadily, since the transition to an AVF. In 1972, the Latina/o proportion of all active-duty personnel was 3.6 percent, which increased slightly to 4.6 percent in 1990.[6] This slower growth pattern seemed especially striking given the rapid increase of the Latina/o population in the 1980s, a decade immortalized as the "Decade of the Hispanic," producing a community that constituted approximately 9 percent of the U.S. population in the 1990 census.[7] The following decade witnessed considerable growth, however, and by 2001, Latinos constituted 9.49 percent of all enlisted personnel while accounting for 13.35 percent of the eligible civilian workforce, ages 18–44.[8] Representation was highest in the enlisted communities of the marines and navy, with 13.8 and 10.28 percent, respectively. Interestingly, in that same year, Latinas constituted 9.35 percent of all enlisted females in the armed forces.[9] On the whole, Latina/o representation continued to steadily climb so that by 2013, they made up 13.2 percent of all enlisted personnel and 14.4 percent of enlisted females while constituting 20 percent of the labor force, ages 18–44.[10] Within individual branches, percentages were again highest in the marines and navy's enlisted communities, with 18.4 and 16.8 percent, respectively.[11]

More recent efforts to recruit within the growing Latina/o community have emphasized the familial nature of the U.S. military as well as the educational benefits and job security derived from a tour of duty. Since the more recent involvement of U.S. forces in Afghanistan in 2001 and Iraq in 2003 as part of the post–9/11 War on Terror, difficulties did emerge in meeting annual recruitment goals, and material incentives such as the GI Bill have attempted to compensate in order to attract young men and women. Such benefits are inevitably appealing to minority groups and working-class Americans, as they were for many of the sixty-four narrators I interviewed for this book. Furthermore, a July 2002 executive order by President George W. Bush made noncitizen members of the armed forces eligible for expedited U.S. citizenship—a more recent facet of military service that garnered considerable attention following the publicized deaths of noncitizen Latinos, dubbed "Green-Card GIs," during the invasion of Iraq. A case in point is Marine Lance Corporal José Antonio Gutierrez, an undocumented indigenous migrant from Guatemala who was posthumously awarded citizenship after being killed in action on March 21, 2003.[12] Such legislation will undoubtedly augment representation in the U.S. military as the Latina/o community, which currently constitutes one-sixth of the U.S. population, continues to grow into the twenty-first century. For many social critics and advocates of immigration reform, however, the cost for this kind of inclusion is much too high. Nevertheless, the lure of citizenship in tandem with material benefits will continue to serve as motivation to enlist, a process that has been reinforced by Spanish-language recruitment ads, as the military has begun to zero in on the Latina/o community with greater earnest. Additionally, the possibilities of public life and participatory democracy will also unfold. But whether or not this current generation of Mexican American and Latino servicemen and women undergoes a personal and political transformation experienced by their predecessors that served in World War II, Korea, and Vietnam remains to be seen. Yet, service in the U.S. military certainly holds open that possibility.

As for myself, I owe a large measure of gratitude to the U.S. Navy. The professionalism I encountered during four years of active-duty service and the expanded worldview I received, especially in the area of cultural and racial diversity, provided a solid foundation for future growth and success. It furthered my transformation into a mature adult with career goals and provided the motivation and confidence to achieve them as I embarked on a career in academia. My participation in the United States Naval Reserve all these years has only enhanced these positive consequences while providing continued access to material benefits (GI Bill, health care, pay, and entitlements) that have promoted socioeconomic mobility. Indeed, my status as a naval officer and a university professor are the twin pillars of my adult professional life. This is not to say, however, that my time in the navy has not been nuanced and free of difficulty.

More robust notions of masculinity, a regimented and limited freethinking environment, and occasional episodes of racial hostility have been some of the more negative aspects that I have encountered in my naval career. And yet, I've been able to navigate these ordeals without letting them affect me in overly adverse ways. In fact, these adverse qualities have repeatedly challenged me to explore what it means to be a man, an intellectual, and a Chicano. I've also been fortunate that my enlisted occupation as an operations specialist and my commission as a human resources officer steered me away from combat environments and the tragedy and trauma associated with those assignments. Were I a combat veteran, perhaps my reminiscence would be laden with more angst and frustration in a manner similar to some of the narrators I interviewed. Ultimately, it is the totality of my experiences in the navy, both positive and negative, that has informed my political and masculine sense of self as a loyal and proud American that takes pride in his Mexican ancestry and who has simultaneously learned the value of confident yet compassionate masculinity. And for that, I am eternally grateful.

APPENDIX A

INTERVIEW QUESTIONS

1. Where are you from and where did you grow up?
2. How old were you when you entered the military, and in what branch did you serve?
3. How many years did you serve? (For officers: What school did you graduate from?)
4. What was the highest rank you were able to attain?
5. Were you drafted or did you volunteer?
6. If you volunteered, why? And why did you pick the branch of service that you did?
7. Before entering the service did you think of the military as a source of employment and a way to improve your life? (For officers: Why join the military after finishing college? Did it help pay for some, or all, of your college expenses?)
8. What were your feelings about entering the service? Were you afraid, proud, angry, etc.?
9. What was the pay like? Did it meet your needs?
10. Did you send any money home to your family? Did you save any?
11. What were the food and living conditions like?
12. Was there adequate health care?
13. Were there any educational or other training opportunities available? If so, did you make use of them?

14. Did being in the military help you to speak and understand English better if you were not already fluent prior to joining?
15. How difficult was it to attain rank? (For officers: Were there many other Hispanic officers during your time in the military? Were opportunities for all officers equitable, despite one's ethnicity? Or were minority officers mainly found in certain types of roles/duties?)
16. What were race relations like while you were in the military?
17. Did you experience any type of discrimination?
18. Did you have any friends who were not Mexican American? (For officers: Did any enlisted men, white or nonwhite, disrespect your authority because of your ethnicity?)
19. Were Mexican Americans or other minorities overly represented in certain jobs, such as the infantry?
20. In combat, did too many Mexican Americans or other minorities have certain types of duty that were hazardous?
21. Did many Mexican Americans volunteer for these hazardous types of duty? Did you? If so, why?
22. What were your feelings when you left the service?
23. Did you think your self-esteem suffered or benefitted?
24. Did military service increase your pride in being Mexican American?
25. Did military service increase your job opportunities when you became a civilian again?
26. Did any of the training you received in the military prove to be beneficial later on?
27. Did you receive and use the GI Bill? If so, how effective was it in paying for school and living expenses?
28. If you didn't receive the GI Bill, or just didn't use it, why not?
29. Did military service expose you to drugs and/or alcohol?
30. If you developed a substance abuse problem, was it a result of your time in the military?
31. Did you (do you) suffer from nightmares and flashbacks from your combat or other military experiences?
32. Has the VA helped you overcome these and any other problems you acquired as a result of being in the military? In other words, have the health care services provided by the VA been adequate?
33. Overall, what advantages did you derive from military service? What disadvantages? (For officers: Were you satisfied with your retirement package?)

APPENDIX B

NARRATORS

WORLD WAR II

NAME	BIRTHDATE	BIRTHPLACE	BRANCH OF SERVICE
Aguirre, Alfred	July 22, 1920	Placentia, CA	U.S. Army Air Corps
Bablot, Alfred	April 7, 1925	Jerome, AZ	U.S. Army
Castrueta, George	February 24, 1925	Los Angeles, CA	U.S. Naval Armed Guard
Domínguez, Richard*	June 27, 1924	Los Angeles, CA	U.S. Army
Fuentes, David	December 4, 1925	Los Angeles, CA	U.S. Army
García, Mike	May 8, 1925	Los Angeles, CA	U.S. Army
López, John	August 11, 1923	Mexico; Raised in Los Angeles	U.S. Army Air Corps
Marez, Salvador	December 9, 1925	Corona, MI	U.S. Navy
Medina, Joe B.	August 24, 1924	Granada, CO	U.S. Army
Medina, Raúl	January 15, 1925	El Paso, TX	U.S. Army
Morales, Martin	November 11, 1928	Rio Grande City, TX	U.S. Army Air Corps
Nerio, Arnulfo "Arnif"	September 29, 1922	San Antonio, TX	U.S. Army
Ortega, Guadalupe "Lupe"	March 19, 1921	Ashington, TX	U.S. Army
Salazar, Nick "Nicho"	October 9, 1923	Long Beach, CA	U.S. Army
Sánchez, William	July 19, 1918	El Paso, TX	U.S. Army
Santillán, Carlos	August 4, 1923	Tampico, Mexico	U.S. Army
Sótelo, John	January 19, 1925	Riverside, CA	U.S. Navy
Vega, Francisco	February 28, 1922	San Antonio, TX	U.S. Army Air Corps
Villegas, Darío	June 2, 1925	Riverside, CA	U.S. Army
Ybarra, Jesse	September 18, 1916	San Antonio, TX	U.S. Army

* Also served in Korea

DRAFTED/ ENLISTED	RANK UPON DISCHARGE	PRIMARY OCCUPATION(S)
Drafted	Corporal, E-4	General Contractor; City Council Member
Drafted	Corporal, E-4	Postal Service
Drafted	Petty Officer, Third Class, E-4	Firefighter
Drafted	Sergeant, E-5	Police Officer
Drafted	Private First Class, E-3	Tailor and Pattern Maker
Drafted	Private First Class, E-3	Carpenter
Drafted	Private First Class, E-3	Carpenter
Enlisted	Petty Officer, First Class, E-6	Foundry Work
Drafted	First Lieutenant, O-2	Lawyer
Drafted	Private First Class, E-3	Upholsterer
Enlisted	Unknown	City Service; Entrepreneur
Drafted	Private First Class, E-3	General Motors
Drafted	Corporal, E-4	Barber; Electrician
Enlisted	Private First Class, E-3	Lithographer
Enlisted	Sergeant, E-5	Trade & Finance
Drafted	Private First Class, E-3	Machinist
Enlisted	Petty Officer, Second Class, E-5	Auto Mechanic; City Council Member
Enlisted	Staff Sergeant, E-6	Sales/Entrepreneur
Drafted	Private First Class, E-3	Civil Service
Drafted	Private First Class, E-3	Counselor

KOREAN WAR ERA

NAME	BIRTHDATE	BIRTHPLACE	BRANCH OF SERVICE
Bejarano, Gene	July 10, 1931	La Union, NM	U.S. Marine Corps
Carillo, David	April 13, 1930	Riverside, CA	U.S. Army
Castaneda, George	July 27, 1927	Dallas, TX	U.S. Army
Castro, Robert L.*	April 6, 1925	Miami, AZ	U.S. Marine Corps
Domínguez, José	January 21, 1930	Las Cruces, NM	U.S. Army
Domínguez, Richard	June 27, 1924	Los Angeles, CA	National Guard (CA)
Fisher, William James	September 16, 1927	Wilmar, CA	U.S. Navy/U.S. Marine Corps Reserve
Garciá, Gene	April 16, 1932	San Diego, CA	U.S. Air Force
Gómez, Ray	September 9, 1931	Anthony, NM	U.S. Army
Gonzales, Frank	October 7, 1930	Saginaw, MI	U.S. Navy
González, Mike	September 29, 1929	Los Angeles, CA	U.S. Army
Hinojosa, Rolando	January 21, 1929	Mercedes, TX	U.S. Army
López, John	December 24, 1929	Tuscola County, MI	U.S. Air Force
Lovio, Eddie	October 14, 1932	Tucson, AZ	U.S. Marine Corps Reserve
Moreno, Ruben	December 25, 1927	Tucson, AZ	U.S. Navy/U.S. Marine Corps Reserve
Ornelas, Frank	February 21, 1931	Henrietta, OK	U.S. Army
Pardo, Vincent, Jr.	March 22, 1931	Saginaw, MI	U.S. Marine Corps
Rocha, Mark	October 7, 1932	Indio, CA	U.S. Navy
Trujillo, Eddie	May 16, 1931	Silver City, NM	U.S. Army
Villegas, Robert	July 20, 1935	Riverside, CA	U.S. Marine Corps

* Also served in Vietnam

DRAFTED/ ENLISTED	RANK UPON DISCHARGE	PRIMARY OCCUPATION(S)
Enlisted	Corporal, E-4	Silk Screen Industry
Enlisted	Sergeant First Class, E-7	General Contractor
Enlisted	Sergeant, E-5	General Motors
Drafted/Mobilized	Master Gunnery Sergeant, E-9	U.S. Marine Corps
Enlisted	Corporal, E-4	Mechanic
Mobilized	First Sergeant, E-8	Police Officer
Enlisted/Mobilized	First Sergeant, E-8	High School Principal
Enlisted	Staff Sergeant, E-5	Machinist
Enlisted	Corporal, E-4	Machinist
Enlisted	Petty Officer Third Class, E-4	Sales/Management
Enlisted	Staff Sergeant, E-6	Welder/Manufacturing
Enlisted/Recalled to Active Duty	Sergeant, E-5	University Professor; Writer
Enlisted	Staff Sergeant, E-5	General Motors
Mobilized	Sergeant, E-5	Firefighter
Enlisted/Mobilized	Sergeant, E-5	Carpenter
Drafted	Staff Sergeant, E-6	General Motors; Emergency Services
Drafted	Corporal, E-4	General Motors
Enlisted	Petty Officer Third Class, E-4	Machinist
Enlisted	Corporal, E-4	Machinist
Enlisted	Private, E-1	Factory Work

VIETNAM

NAME	BIRTHDATE	BIRTHPLACE	BRANCH OF SERVICE
Acevedo, Jim	1943	Scottsbluff, NE	U.S. Marine Corps
Álvarez, Everett	December 23, 1937	Salinas, CA	U.S. Navy
Alviar, Guadalupe "Lupe"	February 16, 1947	Muskegon, MI	U.S. Marine Corps
Barragan, Jesus	October 15, 1944	Glendale, AZ	U.S. Naval Reserve
Buriel, Raymond	December 27, 1948	Riverside, CA	U.S. Marine Corps
Cano, Daniel	August 1, 1947	Los Angeles, CA	U.S. Army
Castro, Robert L.	April 6, 1925	Miami, AZ	U.S. Marine Corps
Guevara, Gilbert	September 25, 1942	Saginaw, MI	U.S. Army
López, "Chappo"	1947	San Diego, CA	U.S. Marine Corps
López, Tony	1942	Riverside, CA	U.S. Marine Corps
Mariscal, George	1949	Los Angeles, CA	U.S. Army
Martínez, Salvador "Sal"	1941	Puerto Rico; Raised in New York City	U.S. Marine Corps
Medel, Fred	October 23, 1951	Saginaw, MI	U.S. Army
Moreno, Tony	October 24, 1948	Saginaw, MI	U.S. Army
Mosqueda, Raúl	September 22, 1948	Benton Township, OH	U.S. Navy
Quintana, Leroy	June 10, 1944	Raton, NM	U.S. Army
Ramírez, Victor	July 28, 1941	Del Rio, TX	U.S. Air Force
Reyes, Frank	February 1952	Los Angeles, CA	U.S. Army
Rodríguez, Joe	November 4, 1943	Oahu, HI	U.S. Naval Reserve
Rodríguez, John	1950	San Jose, CA	U.S. Army
Salcedo, Jesse	1948	Hollister, CA	U.S. Army
Samora, Ted	October 1, 1943	Madera, CA	U.S. Army
Sánchez, John	March 28, 1945	Alma, MI	U.S. Army
Solís, Eddie	1944	Weslaco, TX	U.S. Marine Corps
Trujillo, Charley	November 6, 1949	Hanford, CA	U.S. Army
Vea, Alfredo	June 28, 1950	Phoenix, AZ	U.S. Army

DRAFTED/ ENLISTED	RANK UPON DISCHARGE	PRIMARY OCCUPATION(S)
Enlisted	Staff Sergeant, E-6	Firefighter
Enlisted	Commander, O-5	U.S. Navy/Public Service/Consulting Firm
Enlisted	Staff Sergeant, E-6	Disabled; Veterans Outreach
Mobilized	Petty Officer, Third Class, E-4	Therapist; Civil Servant
Enlisted	Corporal, E-4	University Professor
Enlisted	Sergeant, E-5	University Professor; Writer
Enlisted	Master Gunnery Sergeant	U.S. Marine Corps
Drafted	Unknown	City Employment; Catholic Archdiocese
Enlisted	Gunnery Sergeant, E-7	U.S. Marine Corps Reserve; Postal Service
Enlisted	Lieutenant Colonel, O-5	U.S. Marine Corps; High School Guidance Counselor
Drafted	Specialist, E-4	University Professor
Enlisted	Major, O-4	U.S. Marine Corps; Job Training
Enlisted	Specialist, E-4	Construction; General Maintenance
Drafted	Specialist, E-4	General Motors
Drafted	Petty Officer, Third Class, E-4	Dentist
Enlisted	Specialist, E-4	University Professor; Writer
Enlisted	Staff Sergeant, E-5	Materials and Inventory Control
Enlisted	Staff Sergeant, E-6	Sheriff's Deputy; Truck Driver
Mobilized	Petty Officer, Third Class, E-4	University Professor; Writer
Enlisted	Specialist, E-4	Electronics; Photography
Drafted	Sergeant, E-5	General Contractor
Enlisted	Sergeant, E-5	Computer Technician
Enlisted	Chief Warrant Officer 2, CWO2	Insurance
Enlisted	Lance Corporal, E-3	Construction; Refrigeration
Enlisted	Sergeant, E-5	University Lecturer; Writer
Drafted	Sergeant, E-5	Defense Lawyer; Writer

NOTES

INTRODUCTION

1. I received a BA in history from the University of California, San Diego, and a PhD in history from the University of California, Irvine. An initial appointment as a visiting assistant professor in the Department of American Cultures at Loyola Marymount University in Los Angeles was followed by a tenure-track position in the Department of History at Grand Valley State University in Grand Rapids, Michigan. I currently teach in the Department of History at the University of Arkansas.
2. Markers of identification for communities of Hispanic descent have become commonplace. I employ *Mexican American* to describe individuals of Mexican ancestry having U.S. citizenship through birth or naturalization. More specifically, *Tejana/o* refers to Texas residents with Mexican ancestry. The term *Chicano* references the era of the Chicano Movement and the Vietnam War, roughly 1965–75. Lastly, I utilize the terms *Latino* and *Hispanic* as all-encompassing forms of identification. Meanwhile, for the sake of simplicity, I employ the phrase *white* to signify the dominant segment of the American mainstream whose members have historically benefitted from social and racial privileges, largely through their European ancestry.
3. On the idea of a social contract I am influenced by Cecilia Elizabeth O'Leary, *To Die For: The Paradox of American Patriotism* (Princeton, NJ: Princeton

University Press, 1999) and Claire R. Snyder, *Citizen-Soldiers and Manly Warriors: Military Service and Gender in the Civic Republican Tradition* (Lanham, MD: Rowan and Littlefield, 1999).

4. Lucy E. Salyer, "Baptism by Fire: Race, Military Service, and U.S. Citizenship Policy, 1918–1935," *Journal of American History* 91, no. 3 (2004): 851.
5. As part of the Immigration Act of 1917, an Asiatic zone was established that barred immigration from Asia while severely limiting the flow of legal migration through the creation of a quota system. For additional information see Mae M. Ngai, *Impossible Subjects: Illegal Aliens and the Making of Modern America* (Princeton, NJ: Princeton University Press, 2005). It was not until 1935, with the passage of the Nye-Lea bill, that Asian veterans were finally granted citizenship.
6. Following the Treaty of Guadalupe Hidalgo, which ended the Mexican American War (1846–48), citizenship was granted to former Mexican nationals who remained north of the U.S.-Mexico border. This would begin a political association with de jure whiteness that was reinforced by the black-white racial binary that labeled Mexican Americans as part of the country's white population. The 1980 census provided the option to self-identify as "Spanish/Hispanic origin descent."
7. Although beyond the scope of my analysis, this connection between military service and citizenship can also be extended to World War I. See Emilio Zamora, *The World War I Diary of José De La Luz Sáenz* (College Station: Texas A&M University Press, 2014); José A. Ramírez, *To the Line of Fire: Mexican Texans and World War I* (College Station: Texas A&M University Press, 2009); Alexander Mendoza, "Tejanos at War: A History of Mexican Texans in American Wars," in *Texans and War: New Interpretations of the State's Military History*, ed. Alexander Mendoza and Charles D. Grear (College Station: Texas A&M University Press, 2012). See also Adriane Lentz-Smith, *Freedom Struggles: African Americans and World War I* (Cambridge, MA: Harvard University Press, 2009) and Nancy Gentile Ford, *Americans All! Foreign-born Soldiers in World War I* (College Station: Texas A&M University Press, 2008).
8. A sampling of such works include Aaron Belkin, *Bring Me Men: Military Masculinity and the Benign Façade of American Empire, 1989–2001* (New York: Oxford University Press, 2012); Michael Hughes, *Forging Napoleon's Grand Armée: Motivation, Military Culture, and Masculinity in the French Army, 1800–1808* (New York: New York University Press, 2012); Dagmar Herzog, ed.,

Brutality and Desire: War and Sexuality in Europe's Twentieth Century (New York: Palgrave Macmillan, 2011); Joshua S. Goldstein, *War and Gender: How Gender Shapes the War System and Vice Versa* (Cambridge: Cambridge University Press, 2003); Cynthia Enloe, *Bananas, Beaches, and Bases: Making Feminist Sense of International Politics* (Berkeley: University of California Press, 2000).

9. The play was first performed on April 3, 1971, one of many performances by Teatro Campesino (Peasant Theater), founded by Valdez in 1965 to support the grape strike being conducted by the United Farm Workers led by Cesar Chavez. Operating from flatbed trucks, union halls, and agricultural fields, the troupe performed *actos*, or short skits, that dramatized the plight of migrant farm workers and the Chicano community. The Vietnam War was increasingly targeted for criticism, and in "Soldado Razo," life is a tale told by Death, who appears in the robes of a Franciscan friar. Ultimately, this is an old-fashioned morality play involving a mother and father, their twenty-year-old son Johnny, Johnny's fiancée, and his little brother, as Johnny goes off to die in Vietnam. A Mexican corrido, or ballad, by the same name also first appeared during World War II and has been performed by a variety of noted Mexican musicians, including Jorge Negrete, Pedro Infante, and more recently, by Ramón Ayala. A detailed analysis of the ballad's lyrics appears in chapter 6.
10. Examples include David D. Gilmore, *Manhood in the Making: Cultural Concepts of Masculinity* (New Haven, CT: Yale University Press, 1991) and Oscar Lewis, *The Children of Sánchez: Autobiography of a Mexican Family* (New York: Random House, 1961).
11. Octavio Paz, *The Labyrinth of Solitude and Other Writings*, trans. Yara Milos, Lysander Kemp, and Rachel Philips (New York: Grove/Atlantic, 1994). Defensive masculinity is also central to the work of Marvin Goldwert, *Machismo and Conquest: The Case of Mexico* (Lanham, MD: University Press of America, 1983). Another psychoanalytic profile of the Mexican national character with a particular focus on the aggressive posturing of the *pelado*, or lower-class male, can be found in Samuel Ramos, *Profile of Man and Culture in Mexico*, trans. Peter G. Earle (Austin: University of Texas Press, 1972).
12. Scholarship that examines the linkages between state power, Mexican citizenship, machismo, and cultural productions include Sergio de la Mora, *Cinemachismo: Masculinities and Sexuality in Mexican Film* (Austin: University of Texas Press, 2006) and Robert McKee Irwin, *Mexican Masculinities* (Minneapolis: University of Minnesota Press, 2003). By comparison, monolithic depictions of the Mexican/American male (and female) have an established

precedence in U.S. Hollywood films. See Mary C. Beltrán, *Latina/o Stars in U.S. Eyes: The Making and Meanings of Film and TV Stardom* (Champaign: University of Illinois Press, 2009); Clara Rodríguez, *Heroes, Lovers, and Others: The Story of Latinos in Hollywood* (New York: Oxford University Press, 2008); Charles Ramírez Berg, *Latino Images in Film: Stereotypes, Subversion, and Resistance* (Austin: University of Texas Press, 2002).

13. See Richard Rodríguez, *Hunger of Memory: The Education of Richard Rodríguez* (New York: Random House, 1983); Ernesto Galarza, *Barrio Boy* (Notre Dame, IN: University of Notre Dame Press, 1971); José Antonio Villareal, *Pocho* (New York: Knopf, 1970); Américo Paredes, *"With His Pistol in His Hand": A Border Ballad and Its Hero* (Austin: University of Texas Press, 1958).
14. Examples include Lionel Cantú Jr., *The Sexuality of Migration: Border Crossings and Mexican Immigrant Men*, ed. Nancy A. Naples and Salvador Vidal-Ortiz (New York: New York University Press, 2009); Gloria González-López, *Erotic Journeys: Mexican Immigrants and Their Sex Lives* (Berkeley: University of California Press, 2005); Matthew C. Gutman, ed., *Changing Men and Masculinities in Latin America* (Durham, NC: Duke University Press, 2003); Alfredo Mirandé, *Hombres y Machos: Masculinity and Latino Culture* (Boulder, CO: Westview Press, 1997); Matthew C. Gutman, *The Meanings of Macho: Being a Man in Mexico City* (Berkeley: University of California Press, 1996). Studies of male gender in Europe and the United States include George L. Mosse, *The Image of Man: The Creation of Modern Masculinity* (New York: Oxford University Press, 1996); Michael Kimmel, *Manhood in America: A Cultural History* (New York: Oxford University Press, 1996); Gail Bederman, *Manliness and Civilization: A Cultural History of Gender and Race in the United States, 1880–1917* (Chicago: University of Chicago Press, 1996); George Chauncey, *Gay New York: Gender, Urban Culture, and the Making of the Gay Male World, 1890–1940* (New York: Basic Books, 1995); Harry Brod and Michael Kaufman, ed., *Theorizing Masculinities* (Thousand Oaks, CA: Sage, 1994).
15. R. W. Connell, *Masculinities* (Berkeley: University of California Press, 1995), 76.
16. Frank J. Barrett, "The Organizational Construction of Hegemonic Masculinity: The Case of the U.S. Navy," in *The Masculinities Reader*, ed. Stephen M. Whitehead and Frank J. Barrett (Malden, MA: Blackwell, 2001), 342.
17. A partial listing of accounts that analyze the bill's exclusions based on race and gender include Kathleen J. Frydl, *The GI Bill* (New York: Cambridge University Press, 2009); Lizabeth Cohen, *A Consumer's Republic: The Politics of*

Mass Consumption in Postwar America (New York: Knopf, 2003); and David H. Onkst, "'First a Negro . . . Incidentally a Veteran': Black World War Two Veterans and the G.I. Bill of Rights in the Deep South, 1944–1948," *Journal of Social History* 31 (1998): 517–44. For accounts of homosexual exclusion, see Allan Bérubé, *Coming Out Under Fire: The History of Gay Men and Women in World War II* (New York: Free Press, 2000) and Margot Canaday, "Building a Straight State: Sexuality and Social Citizenship Under the 1944 G.I. Bill," *Journal of American History* 90 (2003): 935–57.

18. Some of the more prominent examples include Rosina M. Becerra and Milton Greenblatt, *Hispanics Seek Health Care: A Study of 1,088 Veterans of Three War Eras* (Lanham, MD: University Press of America, 1983); Arthur Egendorf et al., *Legacies of Vietnam: Comparative Adjustment of Veterans and Their Peers* (Washington, DC: Government Printing Office, 1981); Angelita García-Cabrera, "The Hispanic Veteran of the Armed Services and in the Veterans Administration" (PhD diss., Brandeis University, 1978); Walter E. Penk et al., "Ethnicity: Post-Traumatic Stress Disorder (PTSD) Differences Among Black, White, and Hispanic Veterans Who Differ in Degrees of Exposure to Combat in Vietnam," *Journal of Clinical Psychology* 45 (1989): 729–35; J. I. Escobar et al, "Post Traumatic Stress Disorder in Hispanic Vietnam Veterans: Clinical Phenomenology and Sociocultural Characteristics," *Journal of Nervous and Mental Disease* 171 (1983): 585–96; Richard Strayer and Lewis Ellenhorn, "Vietnam Veterans: A Study Exploring Adjustment Patterns and Attitudes," *Journal of Social Sciences* 31 (1975): 81–93.

19. See Michelle Hall Kells, *Hector P. Garcia: Everyday Rhetoric and Mexican American Civil Rights* (Carbondale: Southern Illinois University Press, 2006); Lorena Oropeza, *Raza Si! Guerra No! Chicano Protest and Patriotism During the Viet Nam War Era* (Berkeley: University of California Press, 2005); Patrick J. Carroll, *Felix Longoria's Wake: Bereavement, Racism, and the Rise of Mexican American Activism* (Austin: University of Texas Press, 2003); Ignacio García, *Hector P. Garcia: In Relentless Pursuit of Justice* (Houston: Arte Publico Press, 2003). A broader, detailed history of the American GI Forum can be found in Henry A. J. Ramos, *The American GI Forum: In Pursuit of the Dream, 1948–1983* (Houston: Arte Publico Press, 1998).

20. Maggie Rivas-Rodríguez, ed., *Mexican Americans & World War II* (Austin: University of Texas Press, 2005); Maggie Rivas-Rodríguez and Emilio Zamora, eds., *Beyond the Latino World War II Hero: The Social and Political Legacy of a Generation* (Austin: University of Texas Press, 2009); Maggie Rivas-Rodríguez

and B. V. Olguín, *Latina/os And World War II: Mobility, Agency, and Ideology* (Austin: University of Texas Press, 2014).

21. In 2010, the project's name was changed to the Voces (Voices) Oral History Project, reflecting its expansion into the Korean and Vietnam Wars.
22. Spurred to action, Professor Rivas-Rodríguez and other activists established the "Defend the Honor" campaign, calling on Burns to shoot extra footage and incorporate it into the final edition. The subsequent public relations scramble, which included abrasive commentary by Burns and PBS officials, produced a compromise that called for the inclusion of two Chicano veterans and one Native American. Rather than seamlessly reedit the actual documentary, however, the three interviews were awkwardly appended to the end of three of the seven episodes. The result was the transformation of the Chicano contribution to the war effort into an addendum, attached but not fully integrated into the body politic and the memorialization of the Second World War.
23. Everett Álvarez Jr. and Anthony S. Pitch, *Chained Eagle* (New York: Dell, 1989) and Roy Benavidez and Oscar Griffen, *The Three Wars of Roy Benavidez* (San Antonio, TX: Corona, 1986).
24. Department of Defense, *Hispanics in America's Defense* (Washington, DC: Office of the Deputy Assistant Secretary of Defense for Military Manpower and Personnel Policy, 1988). Altogether, the Hispanic community has earned thirty-seven such medals, the highest total of any minority group in U.S. military history. Two Medals of Honor were awarded in the Civil War, one for service during the Boxer Rebellion, one for service in World War I, twelve during World War II, eight for the Korean War, and thirteen for the Vietnam War. While admittedly not an accurate indicator, by using birthplace, the awardees assumed to be of Mexican ancestry include the one recipient for service in World War I, eleven recipients for service in World War II, six for service in the Korean War, and eight for service in the Vietnam War, for a total of twenty-seven. However, it is my contention that the discriminatory policies encountered by the African American community prevented this community from receiving its fair share of our nation's most esteemed award for valor on the battlefield.
25. Scholarly monographs include Oropeza, *Raza Si! Guerra No!* (2005) and George Mariscal, *Aztlán and Viet Nam: Chicano and Chicana Experiences of the War* (Berkeley: University of California Press, 1999). A sampling of fictional works are Alfredo Vea, *Gods Go Begging* (New York: Plume, 1999); Daniel Cano, *Shifting Loyalties* (Houston: Arte Publico Press, 1995); Charley Trujillo,

Dogs from Illusion (San José: Chusma House Publications, 1994); Joe Rodríguez, *The Oddsplayer* (Houston: Arte Publico Press, 1988). Another autobiography of note is Juan Ramírez, *A Patriot After All: The Story of a Chicano Vietnam Vet* (Albuquerque: University of New Mexico Press, 1999).

26. The two notable examples involving the Mexican American community are Lea Ybarra, *Vietnam Veteranos: Chicanos Recall the War* (Austin: University of Texas Press, 2004) and Charley Trujillo, *Soldados: Chicanos in Viet Nam* (San José, CA: Chusma House Publications, 1990). For similar efforts dealing with other marginalized communities, see Toshio Welchel, *From Pearl Harbor to Saigon: Japanese American Soldiers and the Vietnam War* (New York: Verso, 1999); Tom Holm, *Strong Hearts, Wounded Souls: The Native American Veterans of the Vietnam War* (Austin: University of Texas Press, 1996); Wallace Terry, *Bloods: An Oral History of the Vietnam War by Black Veterans* (New York: Ballantine, 1984).

27. See Rolando Hinojosa-Smith, *The Useless Servants* (Houston: Arte Publico Press, 1993) and Rolando Hinojosa-Smith, *Korean Love Songs from Klail City Death Trip* (Berkeley: Editorial Justa Publications, 1978). Hinojosa-Smith is currently a professor emeritus in the Department of English at the University of Texas.

28. The Southwestern collection is subdivided into three samples consisting of fifteen World War II veterans, fourteen from the Korean War, and nineteen that served during the Vietnam War. The interviews were largely conducted in four counties within Southern California—Los Angeles, Orange, Riverside, and San Diego. Smaller sets of interviews were also collected in the California cities of San Francisco and San José and in Tucson, Arizona. An additional interview was conducted in Mesa, Arizona. The Michigan sample consists of five World War II veterans, five from the Korean War, and six that served during the Vietnam War. Twelve interviews were conducted in Saginaw, three in Grand Rapids, and one in Muskegon. Lastly, naval aviator Everett Álvarez, who was interviewed in McLean, Virginia, was born and raised in Salinas, located in California's San Joaquin Valley. However, his adult life was largely spent living elsewhere.

29. A limited but growing body of scholarship has documented the contours of the Mexican American labor experience and selected aspects of daily life in the Midwest, with a particular focus on industrial labor within metropolitan centers—namely Chicago, Detroit, and St. Paul. See Michael Innis-Jiménez, *Steel Barrio: The Great Mexican Migration to South Chicago, 1915–1940* (New

York: New York University Press, 2013); Lilia Fernández, *Brown in the Windy City: Mexican and Puerto Ricans in Postwar Chicago* (Chicago: University of Chicago Press, 2012); Marc Simon Rodríguez, *The Tejano Diaspora: Mexican Americanism and Ethnic Politics in Texas and Wisconsin* (Chapel Hill: University of North Carolina Press, 2011); Gabriela F. Arredondo, *Mexican Chicago: Race, Identity, and Nation, 1916–1939* (Champaign: University of Illinois Press, 2008); Dionicio N. Valdés, *Barrios Nortenos: St. Paul and Midwestern Mexican Communities in the Twentieth Century* (Austin: University of Texas Press, 2000); Zaragosa Vargas, *Proletarians of the North: A History of Mexican Industrial Workers in Detroit and the Midwest, 1917–1933* (Berkeley: University of California Press, 1999).

30. There are officially sixty-three Mexican American veterans in this study. One individual, Sal Martínez, is a Vietnam veteran of Puerto Rican descent. Our interview had concluded before I ascertained his ethnic background. Nevertheless, his commentary is quite compelling and thought-provoking, so I have decided to include him in my research sample. Furthermore, he will allow for an admittedly brief, but informative, comparison with another Latino community.
31. Sal Martínez arrived from Puerto Rico as a nine-month-old infant with his parents during World War II.
32. Two veterans were participants of two conflicts. Richard Domínguez served in World War II and Korea. He was drafted for service in the former and mobilized from his status as an army reservist for service in the latter. Robert Castro was a drilling reservist in the United States Marine Corps Reserve and was mobilized for service in Korea. He subsequently transitioned into the active duty Marine Corps where he ultimately deployed for combat service in Vietnam. Meanwhile, Rolando Hinojosa-Smith initially served in the army from August 1946 until December 1947 but was recalled to active duty in November 1949 and was assigned to Japan as part of the occupation forces. He subsequently deployed to Korea following the North Korean invasion of the south in June 1950. This latter reactivation is due to the temporal obligation that defines the labor contract between enlisted personnel and the U.S. government, which is eight years in length. Upon completion of one's initial tour of duty, the remaining time is spent in a nonmobilized status, serving as a pool of available manpower liable for reactivation.
33. A chief warrant officer is considered a technical leader and specialist and is an officer in a military organization who is designated by a warrant as distin-

guished from a commissioned officer who is designated an officer by a commission. Within my sample, John Sánchez served as an army helicopter pilot in Vietnam rising to the rank of CW02, based on a ranking system that ranges from CW01 to CW05.

34. A list of the questions can be found in the appendix.
35. Donald A. Ritchie, *Doing Oral History: A Practical Guide* (New York: Oxford University Press, 2003), 29.
36. Ronald J. Grele, "Oral History as Evidence," in *Handbook of Oral History*, ed. Thomas L. Charlton, Lois E. Myers, and Rebecca Sharpless (Lanham, MD: Alta Mira Press, 2006), 87–88.
37. Michael H. Frisch, *A Shared Authority: Essays on the Craft and Meaning of Oral and Public History* (Albany: State University of New York Press, 1990).
38. One heralded community in the Midwest that contributed nearly eighty young men for service in World War II and Korea, including eight combat deaths, was the Mexican American community in Silvis, Illinois. Second Street, where most of the young men lived, would later be renamed Hero Street in their honor. Their exploits are chronicled in Marc Wilson, *Hero Street, USA. The Story of Little Mexico's Fallen Soldiers* (Norman: University of Oklahoma Press, 2009).

CHAPTER 1

1. George Sánchez, *Becoming Mexican American: Ethnicity, Culture, and Identity in Chicano Los Angeles, 1900–1945* (New York: Oxford University Press, 1995), 20.
2. A sampling of monographs that examine the many facets of the Mexican Revolution include Frank McLynn, *Villa and Zapata: A History of the Mexican Revolution* (New York: Basic Books, 2002); Friedrich Katz, *The Life and Times of Pancho Villa* (Palo Alto, CA: Stanford University Press, 1998); John M. Hart, *Revolutionary Mexico: The Coming and Process of the Mexican Revolution* (Berkeley: University of California Press, 1987); Alan Knight, *The Mexican Revolution, Volume 1: Porfirians, Liberals, and Peasants* (Lincoln: University of Nebraska Press, 1986); Alan Knight, *The Mexican Revolution, Volume 2: Counter-revolution and Reconstruction* (Lincoln: University of Nebraska Press, 1990).
3. Cited in Devra Weber, *Dark Sweat, White Gold: California Farm Workers, Cotton, and the New Deal* (Berkeley: University of California Press, 1994), 40–41. Additional scholarship that highlights this first wave of northward migration

includes Kelly Lytle Hernández, *Migra! A History of the U.S. Border Patrol* (Berkeley: University of California Press, 2010); José Alamillo, *Making Lemonade out of Lemons: Mexican American Labor and Leisure in a California Town, 1880–1960* (Champaign: University of Illinois Press, 2006); Gilbert G. González, *Culture of Empire: American Writers, Mexico, and Mexican Immigrants, 1880–1930* (Austin: University of Texas Press, 2004); Matt García, *A World of Its Own: Race, Labor, and Citrus in the Making of Greater Los Angeles, 1900–1970* (Chapel Hill: University of North Carolina Press, 2001); David G. Gutierrez, *Walls and Mirrors: Mexican Americans, Mexican Immigrants, and the Politics of Ethnicity* (Berkeley: University of California Press, 1995); Ricardo Romo, *East Los Angeles: History of a Barrio* (Austin: University of Texas Press, 1983).

4. Sánchez, *Becoming Mexican American*, 51. See also Roger Daniels, *Guarding the Golden Door: American Immigration Policy and Immigrants Since 1882* (New York: MacMillan, 2005); Mae M. Ngai, *Impossible Subjects: Illegal Aliens and the Making of Modern America* (Princeton, NJ: Princeton University Press, 2004); Erika Lee, *At America's Gates: Chinese Immigration During the Exclusion Era, 1882–1943* (Chapel Hill: University of North Carolina Press, 2004).
5. Jesse Ybarra, interview by Steven Rosales, January 14, 2003, Riverside, California, audio tape (in author's possession).
6. Ibid.
7. Ibid.
8. Alfred Bablot, interview by Steven Rosales, April 24, 2003, Los Angeles, California, audio tape (in author's possession).
9. John Sótelo, interview by Steven Rosales, February 4, 2003, Riverside, California, audio tape (in author's possession).
10. Raúl Medina, interview by Steven Rosales, February 18, 2003, Riverside, California, audio tape (in author's possession).
11. Ibid.
12. Carlos Santillán, interview by Steven Rosales, March 14, 2003, Norwalk, California, audio tape (in author's possession).
13. Further compounding the situation for those of Mexican ancestry was the focus placed on those deemed to be a burden on the American taxpayer, producing a repatriation drive intent on reducing the Mexican population living in the United States. Checkpoints and other coercive methods were utilized by local authorities, yet the most prominent method was simply to deny access to relief programs made available by President Franklin Delano Roosevelt's

New Deal and other social services. Against this backdrop, approximately 500,000 individuals were deported or left voluntarily, often taking their U.S.-born children with them. Within my collection, only one individual endured this ordeal. His experience is discussed in chapter 2.

14. Joe B. Medina, interview by Steven Rosales, January 21, 2003, Los Angeles, California, audio tape (in author's possession).
15. Ibid.
16. Maria E. Montoya, "The Roots of Economic and Ethnic Division in Northern New Mexico: The Case of the Civilian Conservation Corps," *Western Historical Quarterly* 26, no. 1 (1995): 18. For additional information on the Civilian Conservation Corps and its connection to environmentalism, see Neil M. Maher, *Nature's New Deal: The Civilian Conservation Corps and the Roots of the American Environmental Movement* (New York: Oxford University Press, 2009).
17. Ybarra, interview.
18. Alfred Aguirre, interview by Steven Rosales, April 22, 2003, Placentia, California, audio tape (in author's possession).
19. Ruben Moreno, interview by Steven Rosales, August 9, 2002, Tucson, Arizona, audio tape (in author's possession).
20. Ibid.
21. David Carillo, interview by Steven Rosales, January 23, 2003, Riverside, California, audio tape (in author's possession).
22. Ibid.
23. Ray Gómez, interview by Steven Rosales, August 10, 2003, Mesa, Arizona, audio tape (in author's possession).
24. José Domínguez, interview by Steven Rosales, January 28, 2003, Moreno Valley, California, audio tape (in author's possession). Ray Gómez and José Domínguez have remained lifelong friends.
25. Ibid.
26. Eddie Trujillo, interview by Steven Rosales, April 19, 2003, Victorville, California, audio tape (in author's possession).
27. Ibid.
28. Alfredo Vea, interview by Steven Rosales, December 14, 2002, Oakland, California, audio tape (in author's possession).
29. Victor Ramírez, interview by Steven Rosales, March 6, 2003, Riverside, California, audio tape (in author's possession).
30. Ibid.

31. Joe Rodríguez, interview by Steven Rosales, December 23, 1997, San Diego, California, audio tape (in author's possession).
32. Jesus Barragan, interview by Steven Rosales, August 17, 2011, San Francisco, California, audio tape (in author's possession).
33. Ibid.
34. Everett Álvarez, interview by Steven Rosales, July 29, 2003, McLean, Virginia, audio tape (in author's possession).
35. Jesse Salcedo, interview by Steven Rosales, December 28, 1999, San Francisco, California, audio tape (in author's possession).
36. Gene García, interview by Steven Rosales, March 2, 2003, Riverside, California, audio tape (in author's possession).
37. Medina, interview.
38. Gómez, interview.
39. Moreno, interview.
40. Eddie Lovio, interview by Steven Rosales, August 10, 2003, Tucson, Arizona, audio tape (in author's possession).
41. Barragan, interview.
42. Robert L. Castro, interview by Steven Rosales, August 9, 2003, Tucson, Arizona, audio tape (in author's possession).
43. Ibid.
44. Ibid.
45. Ibid.
46. Ibid.
47. Sótelo, interview.
48. Postwar civil rights efforts by returning veterans is more fully covered in chapter 9. Founded in 1929 in Corpus Christi, Texas, LULAC emerged as the most prominent Mexican American civil rights organization. With an emphasis on legal, political, and educational initiatives, American citizenship was also required for membership in an effort to differentiate between Mexican Americans and more recent arrivals from Mexico. A more thorough examination of the organization can be found in Craig A. Kaplowitz, *LULAC: Mexican Americans and National Policy* (College Station: Texas A&M University Press, 2005); David Gutiérrez, *Walls and Mirrors*, 1995); Benjamin Marquez, *LULAC: The Evolution of a Mexican American Political Organization* (Austin: University of Texas Press, 1993).
49. María Eva Flores, "What a Difference a War Makes!" in *Mexican Americans & World War II*, ed. Maggie Rivas-Rodríguez (Austin: University of Texas Press,

2005), 193. The swimming pool and bath house were ultimately desegregated in 1948.

50. A partial inventory of scholarship that examines the segregation of Mexican American schoolchildren includes Richard R. Valencia, *Chicano Students and the Courts: The Mexican American Legal Struggle for Educational Equality* (New York: New York University Press, 2008); Gilbert González, *Chicano Education in the Era of Segregation* (Philadelphia: Balch Institute Press, 1990); Guadalupe San Miguel Jr., *"Let All of Them Take Heed": Mexican Americans and the Campaign for Educational Equality in Texas, 1910–1981* (College Station: Texas A&M University Press, 1987); Thomas P. Carter, *Mexican Americans in School: A History of Educational Neglect* (New York: College Entrance Examination Board, 1970).
51. Mike García, interview by Steven Rosales, March 4, 2003, Riverside, California, audio tape (in author's possession).
52. He was ultimately forced to leave high school after his father's death in order to help his family financially through employment.
53. Aguirre, interview.
54. Moreno, interview.
55. García, interview.
56. Ramírez, interview.
57. Charley Trujillo, interview by Steven Rosales, December 27, 1999, San José, California, audio tape (in author's possession).
58. Eddie Solís, interview by Steven Rosales, February 17, 2003, Riverside, California, audio tape (in author's possession).
59. His brother would eventually acquire a doctorate in botany from the University of California, Los Angeles.
60. The daily academic and religious regimen proved to be too much for Buriel, and he transferred to an integrated public high school, which he described as racially harmonious.
61. Tony López, interview by Steven Rosales, January 18, 2003, Riverside, California, audio tape (in author's possession).
62. Bablot, interview.
63. Sótelo, interview.
64. Barragan, interview.
65. Salcedo, interview.
66. Vicki L. Ruiz, *From Out of the Shadows: Mexican Women in Twentieth-Century America* (New York: Oxford University Press, 1998), 50.

67. Edward J. Escobar, *Race, Police, and the Making of a Political Identity: Mexican Americans and the Los Angeles Police Department, 1900–1945* (Berkeley: University of California Press, 1999), 166. Additional in-depth analysis of the zoot suit is provided by Luis Álvarez, *The Power of the Zoot: Youth Culture and Resistance During World War II* (Berkeley: University of California Press, 2008).
68. Eduardo O. Pagan, *Murder at the Sleepy Lagoon: Zoot Suits, Race, and Riot in Wartime L.A.* (Chapel Hill: University of North Carolina Press, 2003), 129.
69. Medina, interview.
70. John López, interview by Steven Rosales, March 9, 2003, Riverside, California, audio tape (in author's possession).
71. Ramírez, interview.
72. Carillo, interview.
73. John Rodríguez, interview by Steven Rosales, December 28, 1999, San José, California, audio tape (in author's possession).
74. Ibid.
75. Ibid. It is important to note that other factors also played a role, including the dire socioeconomic circumstances he encountered as a youngster and the cultural, masculine, and patriotic responsibilities he perceived.
76. Sal Martínez, interview by Steven Rosales, December 22, 1997, Oceanside, California, audio tape (in author's possession).
77. Ibid.
78. Josh Sides, *L.A. City Limits: African American Los Angeles from the Great Depression to the Present* (Berkeley: University of California Press, 2003), 44.
79. Douglas Flamming, *Bound for Freedom: Black Los Angeles in Jim Crow America* (Berkeley: University of California Press, 2005), 100.
80. Sánchez, *Becoming Mexican American*, 76.
81. George Castrueta, interview by Steven Rosales, May 1, 2003, Whittier, California, audio tape (in author's possession).
82. Ibid.
83. Ibid.
84. Richard Domínguez, interview by Steven Rosales, March 26, 2003, Whittier, California, audio tape (in author's possession).
85. Ibid.
86. José Domínguez would develop into a well-known actor often typecast into stereotypical character roles while starring in films such as *Red River* with John Wayne and *Viva Villa!* with Wallace Berry.
87. Ibid.

88. David Fuentes, interview by Steven Rosales, April 24, 2003, Los Angeles, California, audio tape (in author's possession).
89. This skill would serve Gabaldon well after his enlistment in the Marine Corps. In 1944, on the enemy-held island of Saipan, he would be credited with the capture of over fifteen hundred Japanese soldiers. His exploits were commemorated in the 1960 film *Hell to Eternity*.
90. Fuentes, interview.
91. Nick Salazar, interview by Steven Rosales, March 29, 2003, Commerce, California, audio tape (in author's possession).
92. Ibid.
93. Much like the Rose Gregory Houtchen Settlement, a Methodist community center in El Paso, Texas, documented by Vicki L. Ruiz in *From Out of the Shadows*, various medical services and other social and educational endeavors were the primary tactics utilized by Protestant evangelists to simultaneously Americanize and proselytize.
94. Ibid.
95. Moreno, interview. Later in his adulthood, he would convert back to Catholicism at the insistence of his soon-to-be wife.
96. Trujillo, interview.
97. Ramírez, interview.

CHAPTER 2

1. Dennis Valdés, *Al Norte: Agricultural Workers in the Great Lakes Region, 1917–1970* (Austin: University of Texas Press, 1991), 3. Also see Kathleen Mapes, *Sweet Tyranny: Migrant Labor, Industrial Agriculture, and Imperial Politics* (Champaign: University of Illinois Press, 2009).
2. Edson's field notes are part of the Paul S. Taylor Collection, Bancroft Library, University of California, Berkeley (Hereafter cited as PTC).
3. George T. Edson, "Mexicans in the North Central States," 1927, file folder 13.38, PTC.
4. Valdés, *Al Norte*, 15.
5. "Menominee River Sugar Co.," 1926–27, file folder 12.3, PTC. English translation provided by the author.
6. "Michigan Sugar Company," October 22, 1926, file folder 13.42, PTC. English translation provided by the author.

7. Maria S. Montano, "My Experience in the United States," 1928 [estimated], file folder 11.69, PTC.
8. George T. Edson, "Mexicans in Saginaw," October 22, 1926, file folder 13.31, PTC.
9. Javier Tobar, July 30, 1928, file folder 11.69, PTC.
10. John López, interview by Steven Rosales, May 22, 2010, Saginaw, Michigan, audio tape (in author's possession).
11. George Castaneda, interview by Steven Rosales, June 14, 2010, Saginaw, Michigan, audio tape (in author's possession).
12. Ibid.
13. Ibid.
14. Frank Ornelas, interview by Steven Rosales, May 28, 2010, Saginaw, Michigan, audio tape (in author's possession).
15. Ibid.
16. Arnulfo Nerio, interview by Steven Rosales, May 29, 2010, Bay City, Michigan, audio tape (in author's possession).
17. Ibid.
18. Ibid.
19. Salvador Marez, interview by Steven Rosales, June 2, 2010, Grand Rapids, Michigan, audio tape (in author's possession). Marez moved to Michigan in 1952 and ultimately settled in Grand Rapids.
20. Martin Morales, interview by Steven Rosales, October 5, 2009, Grand Rapids, Michigan, audio tape (in author's possession). Morales settled in Grand Rapids in 1969.
21. Ibid.
22. A sampling of monographs that examine the repatriation efforts of the Great Depression include Kelly Lytle Hernandez, *Migra! A History of the U.S. Border Patrol* (Berkeley: University of California Press, 2010); Dennis Valdés, *Barrios Nortenos: St. Paul and Midwestern Mexican Communities in the Twentieth Century* (Austin: University of Texas Press, 2000); Francisco E. Balderrama and Raymond Rodríguez, *Decade of Betrayal: Mexican Repatriation in the 1930s* (Albuquerque: University of New Mexico Press, 1995); Camille Guerin-Gonzales, *Mexican Workers and American Dreams: Immigration, Repatriation, and California Farm Labor, 1900–1939* (New Brunswick, NJ: Rutgers University Press, 1994).
23. Vincent Pardo Jr., interview by Steven Rosales, May 23, 2010, Saginaw, Michigan, audio tape (in author's possession).

24. Marez, interview.
25. "470 Mexicans Leaving Today," *Saginaw Daily News*, November 22, 1932.
26. "Mexican Population Here Believed Reduced by 300," *Saginaw Daily News*, September 3, 1931.
27. The figures for 1930 are from the U.S. Census using "Mexican" as a general descriptor. The source for 1940 is U.S. Census, "Figure 31: Mexicans in Michigan Cities, 1940–1950."
28. "Sugar Beet Farm Hands Arrive Here," *Saginaw News*, May 15, 1938.
29. Pardo, interview.
30. Gilbert Guevara, interview by Steven Rosales, June 14, 2010, Saginaw, Michigan, audio tape (in author's possession).
31. John Sánchez, interview by Steven Rosales, November 15, 2009, Saginaw, Michigan, audio tape (in author's possession).
32. Ibid.
33. Raúl Mosqueda, interview by Steven Rosales, June 13, 2010, Saginaw, Michigan, audio tape (in author's possession). Mosqueda moved to Saginaw in 1968.
34. Guadalupe Alviar, interview by Steven Rosales, April 30, 2010, Muskegon, Michigan, audio tape (in author's possession).
35. Fred Medel, interview by Steven Rosales, April 18, 2010, Saginaw, Michigan, audio tape (in author's possession).
36. Sánchez, interview.
37. Ornelas, interview.
38. Guadalupe Ortega, interview by Steven Rosales, May 29, 2010, Saginaw, Michigan, audio tape (in author's possession).
39. Frank Gonzales, interview by Steven Rosales, May 22, 2010, Saginaw, Michigan, audio tape (in author's possession).
40. Tony Moreno, interview by Steven Rosales, November 15, 2009, Saginaw, Michigan, audio tape (in author's possession).
41. Castaneda, interview.
42. Edson, "Mexicans in Saginaw."
43. George T. Edson, "Mexicans in Detroit," October 15, 1926, file folder 13.31, PTC.
44. Zaragosa Vargas, *Proletarians of the North: A History of Mexican American Industrial Workers in Detroit and the Midwest, 1917–1933* (Berkeley: University of California Press, 1993), 94. Additional scholarship on the auto industry includes Douglas Brinkley, *Wheels for the Road: Henry Ford, His Company, and a Century of Progress* (New York: Penguin, 2004); Steven Watts, *The People's*

Tycoon: Henry Ford and the American Century (New York: Knopf, 2006); David Farber, *Sloan Rules: Alfred P. Sloan and the Triumph of General Motors* (Chicago: University of Chicago Press, 2002); Joyce S. Peterson, *American Automobile Workers, 1900–1933* (Albany: State University of New York Press, 1987); Stephen Meyer, *The Five Dollar Day: Labor Management and Social Control in the Ford Motor Company, 1908–1921* (Albany: State University of New York Press, 1981).

45. Vargas, *Proletarians of the North*, 51.
46. Guevara, interview.
47. Nerio, interview.
48. Castaneda, interview.
49. Ornelas, interview.
50. Castaneda, interview.
51. Ortega, interview.
52. Edson, "Mexicans in Saginaw."
53. Gonzales, interview.
54. Pardo, interview.
55. Guevara, interview.
56. Ibid.
57. Moreno, interview.
58. López, interview.
59. Ornelas, interview.
60. Pardo, interview.
61. Marez, interview.
62. Edson, "Mexicans in Saginaw."
63. Gonzales, interview.
64. Moreno, interview.
65. Guevara, interview.
66. "Negroes, Mexicans Cause of Protest," *Saginaw News Courier*, July 13, 1926.
67. Pardo, interview.
68. Medel, interview.
69. Pardo, interview.
70. Edson, "Mexicans in Saginaw."
71. Guevara, interview.
72. López, interview.
73. Guevara, interview.
74. López, interview.

75. Gonzales, interview.
76. Pardo, interview.
77. See Elena Ruiz Sanchez, *Remembrances of Guadalupe* (Saginaw, Michigan, 2005).
78. López, interview.
79. Sánchez, *Remembrances of Guadalupe*, 79.
80. "Mexican Mission Five Years Old," *Saginaw Daily News*, December 1, 1934.
81. Sánchez, interview.

CHAPTER 3

1. Ernie Pyle, *Brave Men* (Lincoln: University of Nebraska Press, 2001), 66–68. Only Bill Mauldin, the cartoonist responsible for the characters Willy and Joe, approached Pyle's acclaim.
2. Department of Defense, *Hispanics in America's Defense* (Washington, DC: Office of the Deputy Assistant Secretary of Defense for Military Manpower and Personnel Policy, 1988), 27. Exact numbers are imprecise because, with the exception of 53,000 Puerto Ricans, data on Mexican Americans and other Latinos were not maintained by the Department of Defense.
3. William Sánchez, interview by Steven Rosales, April 29, 2003, Monterey Park, California, audio tape (in author's possession).
4. Ibid.
5. Richard Domínguez, interview by Steven Rosales, March 26, 2003, Whittier, California, audio tape (in author's possession).
6. Francisco Vegas, interview by Steven Rosales, September 15, 2009, Grand Rapids, Michigan, audio tape (in author's possession).
7. Nick "Nicho" Salazar, interview by Steven Rosales, March 29, 2003, Los Angeles, California, audio tape (in author's possession).
8. For more on the rise and fall of Nazi Germany and the war in Europe, see Antony Beever, *D-Day: The Battle for Normandy* (New York: Penguin, 2009); John Keegan, *The Second World War* (New York: Penguin, 2005); Richard Overy, *Russia's War: A History of the Soviet Effort, 1941–1945* (New York: Penguin, 1998); Richard Overy, *Why the Allies Won* (New York: W. W. Norton, 1997); William L. Shirer, *The Rise and Fall of the Third Reich* (New York: Simon & Schuster, 1990).
9. The rise and fall of the Japanese Empire and the war in the Pacific is documented in Ian W. Toll, *The Conquering Tide: War in the Pacific Islands,*

1942–1944 (New York: W. W. Norton, 2015); Michael J. Lyons, *World War II: A Short History* (New York: Pearson, 2009); Ian W. Toll, *Pacific Crucible: War at Sea in the Pacific, 1941–1942* (New York: W. W. Norton, 2011); Iris Chang, *The Rape of Nanking* (New York: Penguin, 1997); John W. Dower, *War Without Mercy: Race and Power in the Pacific War* (New York: Pantheon, 1987); Saburo Ienaga, *The Pacific War, 1931–1945* (New York: Pantheon, 1968).

10. Also established was the Citizens' Military Training Camps (CMTC) that offered monthlong training over four consecutive summers from 1921 to 1940 with the goal of establishing a diverse pool of men that could serve as commissioned officers in a time of national emergency. Funds for the CMTC were discontinued in 1940, thus ending the program. For more information, see Donald M. Kington, *Forgotten Summers: The Story of the Citizens' Military Training Camps, 1921–1940* (San Francisco: Two Decades, 1995).
11. Victor Vogel, *Soldiers of the Old Army* (College Station: Texas A&M University Press, 1990), ix–xi.
12. Additional coverage of U.S. foreign policy prior to World War II and U.S. military preparedness can be found in Stephen E. Ambrose and Douglas G. Brinkley, *Rise to Globalism: American Foreign Policy Since 1938* (New York: Penguin, 1997) and Arnold A. Offner, *America and the Origins of World War II, 1933–1941* (Boston: Houghton Mifflin, 1971).
13. Approximately two weeks after the Japanese attack on the Philippines, elements of the 200th would be reconstituted as the 515th Coast Artillery Regiment.
14. Dorothy Cave, *Beyond Courage: One Regiment Against Japan, 1941–1945* (Santa Fe: Sunstone Press, 2006), 45.
15. Sánchez, interview.
16. Ibid.
17. Ibid.
18. For additional information, see Michael Norman and Elizabeth M. Norman, *Tears in the Darkness: The Story of the Bataan Death March and Its Aftermath* (New York: MacMillan, 2010); Cave, *Beyond Courage*. 2006.
19. Sánchez, interview.
20. His ordeal in Japan is recounted with greater detail in chapter 8.
21. Sánchez, interview.
22. Overy, *Why the Allies Won*, 6. A comparison between Japanese Bushido and Mexican machismo can be made since both placed a profound emphasis on martial manhood and honor. For more on Bushido, see Oleg Benesch, *Invent-*

ing the Way of the Samurai: Nationalism, Internationalism, and Bushido in Modern Japan (New York: Oxford University Press, 2016).

23. Dower, *War Without Mercy*, 34. The Japanese American community also suffered from racial antipathy, including xenophobic legislation that culminated in presidential Executive Order 9066, which provided for the removal of Japanese immigrants and their U.S.-born children to one of ten internment camps situated in isolated areas of the American West and Arkansas. For more information, including the military exploits of second-generation Nisei men in units such as the famed 442nd Regimental Combat Team, see Ronald Takaki, *Double Victory: A Multicultural History of America in World War II* (Boston: Back Bay Books, 2000); Valerie J. Matsumoto, *Farming the Home Place: A Japanese American Community in California, 1919–1982* (Ithaca, NY: Cornell University Press, 1993); Gary Okihiro, *Cane Fires: The Anti-Japanese Movement in Hawaii, 1865–1945* (Philadelphia: Temple University Press, 1992).
24. Raúl Medina, interview by Steven Rosales, February 18, 2003, Riverside, California, audio tape (in author's possession).
25. Ibid.
26. Ibid.
27. Ismael Villegas was posthumously awarded the Medal of Honor for his gallant charge against a number of Japanese foxholes on March 20, 1945, while serving on the island of Luzon. His brother, Darío, became active in the communal effort to establish a memorial in honor of Ismael. Such activism has produced a park, statue, mural painting, and a middle school named in his honor.
28. Villegas departed for basic training in April 1944 after receiving his draft notice the previous June, soon after his eighteenth birthday. However, an X-ray revealed a pulmonary condition, which delayed his departure for ten months.
29. Darío Villegas, interview by Steven Rosales, February 27, 2003, Riverside, California, audio tape (in author's possession).
30. Ibid.
31. Domínguez, interview. Two older brothers also entered the U.S. Marine Corps in 1942. Eugene was killed on the island of Saipan in 1944, while complications from injuries suffered on Iwo Jima led to Joe Jr.'s untimely death in 1956.
32. Ibid.
33. Ibid.
34. Ibid.

35. Alfred Aguirre, interview by Steven Rosales, April 22, 2003, Placentia, California, audio tape (in author's possession).
36. Ibid.
37. Ibid.
38. Ibid.
39. Ibid.
40. John Sótelo, interview by Steven Rosales, February 4, 2003, Riverside, California, audio tape (in author's possession).
41. Ibid.
42. Ibid.
43. An unnamed perceived physical defect provided García with a 4F disqualified rating that was subsequently overturned.
44. Mike García, interview by Steven Rosales, March 4, 2003, Riverside, California, audio tape (in author's possession).
45. Ibid.
46. Ibid.
47. Ibid.
48. George Castrueta, interview by Steven Rosales, May 1, 2003, Whittier, California, audio tape (in author's possession).
49. The LAPD's dragnet netted over six hundred Mexican American "suspects," most notably the members of the local 38th Street gang. Twenty-two were ultimately indicted and the anti-Mexican bias of the presiding judge and the prosecuting attorney was clearly evident throughout the trial. Seventeen were found guilty of various charges and given various sentences ranging from life imprisonment to one year in the county jail. For more information on the trial, the successful effort to free the boys, and the Zoot Suit Riots, see Luis Álvarez, *The Power of the Zoot: Youth Culture and Resistance During World War II* (Berkeley: University of California Press, 2009); Eduardo O. Pagán, *Murder at the Sleepy Lagoon: Zoot Suits, Race, and Riot in Wartime L.A.* (Chapel Hill: University of North Carolina Press, 2003); Edward J. Escobar, *Race, Police, and the Making of a Political Identity: Mexican Americans and the Los Angeles Police Department, 1900–1945* (Berkeley: University of California Press, 1999); Mauricio Mazón, *The Zoot Suit Riots: The Psychology of Symbolic Annihilation* (Austin: University of Texas Press, 1984).
50. For off-duty sailors, the shortest route from the training center to downtown Los Angeles lay through Chavez Ravine, where they were often confronted by local youth.

51. The rioting officially began on June 3 and lasted through June 9. By declaring Los Angeles off limits to all military personnel, the rampage was brought to an end by military authorities.
52. Castrueta, interview.
53. Ibid.
54. His tour included stops in the Pacific islands of Guadalcanal and New Caledonia, the city of Freemantle in western Australia, Ceylon, Calcutta, South Africa, Nigeria, the Ivory Coast, and Liberia before sailing across the Atlantic Ocean to New York City. A subsequent train ride across the United States to Los Angeles completed the tour.
55. Arnulfo Nerio, interview by Steven Rosales, May 29, 2010, Bay City, Michigan, audio tape (in author's possession).
56. Ibid.
57. Ibid.
58. Ibid.
59. Ibid.
60. Ibid.
61. Ibid.
62. Ibid.
63. Ibid.
64. Joe B. Medina, interview by Steven Rosales, January 21, 2003, Los Angeles, California, audio tape (in author's possession).
65. Ibid.
66. Ibid.
67. Ibid.
68. Its all-Tejano personnel remains a bit of a mystery since Mexican Americans were not formally segregated into their own units. One possibility is the simple fact that as a National Guard unit based out of the city of El Paso, Company E reflected the city's large Mexican American population base. However, the existence of an El Paso-based, all-white Company H offers credible evidence that segregationist policies could indeed exist against Mexican American servicemen.
69. Raúl Morín, *Among the Valiant: Mexican Americans in World War II and Korea* (Los Angeles: Borden, 1966), 59. It should be noted that as the company suffered casualties, the consistent arrival of new replacement soldiers from all across the United States would have diminished the unit's initial Tejano composition.

70. Of the four thousand men that participated in the assault, less than half did not return. Controversy surrounding this ill-fated attack resulted in a congressional hearing by the Committee of Military Affairs in early 1946 that proved inconclusive. An aspect of this controversy involved Company E's commanding officer at the time of the attack, Lieutenant Gabriel Navarrete, who became a bit of a cause célèbre for his efforts to stop the attack. After leading a small reconnaissance team across the river that ascertained the strength of enemy forces, he informed his battalion commander, promising to return and forcibly confront him if the attack continued. True to his word, General Walton Walker defused the situation by transferring Lieutenant Navarrete to another unit. For more information on the Rapido crossing and the 36th Infantry Division, see Dave Gutíerrez, *Patriots from the Barrio* (Bloomington: Xlibris, 2014); Duane Schultz, *Crossing the Rapido: A Tragedy of World War II* (Yardley, PA: Westholme, 2010); Lee Carraway Smith, *A River Swift and Deadly: The 36th "Texas" Infantry Division at the Rapido River* (Austin: Eakin Press, 1989); Robert Wagner, *The Texas Army: A History of the 36th Division in the Italian Campaign* (Austin, TX: Western Publications, 1972).
71. Francisco Vega, interview by Steven Rosales, September 15, 2009, Grand Rapids, Michigan, audio tape (in author's possession).
72. Ibid.
73. Ibid.
74. Ibid.
75. Jesse Ybarra, interview by Steven Rosales, January 14, 2003, Riverside, California, audio tape (in author's possession).
76. Ibid.
77. Ibid.
78. Ibid.
79. Ibid.
80. Carlos Santillán, interview by Steven Rosales, March 14, 2003, Norwalk, California, audio tape (in author's possession).
81. Ibid.
82. Ibid.
83. Ibid.
84. Ibid.
85. Ibid.
86. Ybarra, interview.
87. Villegas, interview.

88. Medina, interview.
89. Maggie Rivas-Rodríguez, ed., *Mexican Americans & World War II* (Austin: University of Texas Press, 2005), xviii.
90. Mae M. Ngai, *Impossible Subjects: Illegal Aliens and the Making of Modern America* (Princeton, NJ: Princeton University Press, 2004), 4.
91. Lorena Oropeza, *Raza Si! Guerra No!: Chicano Protest and Patriotism During the Viet Nam War Era* (Berkeley: University of California Press, 2005), 35.

CHAPTER 4

1. Max Hastings, *The Korean War* (New York: Touchstone, 1987), 58.
2. A more thorough analysis of the Cold War and U.S. foreign policy is conducted in chapter 5, where I examine the United States' role in the Vietnam War.
3. Rolando Hinojosa, interview by Steven Rosales, March 26, 2005, Austin, Texas, audio tape (in author's possession). Born to a naturalized Mexican father and an English-born mother, Hinojosa did not employ the hyphenated surname of "Hinojosa-Smith" while in the military, which he would ultimately utilize later in life.
4. Ibid.
5. Ibid.
6. Following the North Korean invasion, a unanimous UN Security Council resolution condemned the attack and pledged immediate assistance to the South Korean government. Operating under UN authority, the subsequent effort over the next three years was classified as a "police action," a term coined by a reporter at a White House press conference and agreed to by President Harry Truman.
7. Hastings, *The Korean War*, 194–95. President Truman replaced General Douglas MacArthur, the initial supreme allied commander, with General Matthew B. Ridgway in December 1950. An armistice declaring a cease-fire was signed on July 27, 1953, and the initial boundaries of North and South Korea remained intact. To this day, no formal end to hostilities has been negotiated, and the two countries remain divided by a demilitarized zone.
8. Ruben Moreno, interview by Steven Rosales, August 9, 2003, Tucson, Arizona, audio tape (in author's possession).
9. Ibid.

10. Ibid.
11. Altogether, 258 officers and enlisted men were mobilized in order to bring the 1st Marine Division, based at Camp Pendleton, California, to full strength. Upon arrival, the personnel of Company E were utilized as a replacement pool and parceled out to other individual units within the division. Approximately 80 percent of the company was of Mexican ancestry.
12. Moreno, interview. Ultimately, twelve of the unit's personnel would be killed in action.
13. Ibid.
14. Ibid.
15. Ibid.
16. David Carillo, interview by Steven Rosales, January 23, 2003, Riverside, California, audio tape (in author's possession).
17. Ibid.
18. Ibid.
19. Ibid.
20. Gene García, interview by Steven Rosales, March 2, 2003, Riverside, California, audio tape (in author's possession).
21. Ibid.
22. Ibid.
23. Frank Gonzales, interview by Steven Rosales, May 22, 2010, Saginaw, Michigan, audio tape (in author's possession).
24. Ibid.
25. Ibid.
26. Ibid.
27. Mike González, interview by Steven Rosales, February 13, 2003, Los Angeles, California, audio tape (in author's possession).
28. Ibid.
29. Ibid.
30. Ibid.
31. George Castaneda, interview by Steven Rosales, June 14, 2010, Saginaw, Michigan, audio tape (in author's possession). I did not ascertain whether Castaneda and González were acquaintances in the 187th Regimental Combat Team.
32. Ibid.
33. Ibid.
34. Ibid.

35. Ibid.
36. William James Fisher, interview by Steven Rosales, August 10, 2003, Tucson, Arizona, audio tape (in author's possession). Fisher was born to a Mexican mother from the state of Sonora and an Irish-American father.
37. Ibid.
38. Ibid.
39. Ibid.
40. Placed on alert for the Cuban Missile Crisis in 1962, Fisher recalled that no indication of possible mobilization occurred during the Vietnam War.
41. Robert L. Castro, interview by Steven Rosales, August 9, 2003, Tucson, Arizona, audio tape (in author's possession).
42. Ibid.
43. Ibid.
44. A master gunnery sergeant is considered an expert in a particular military occupational specialty and is equal to the more popularized rank of sergeant major (E9). Castro would also serve two tours of duty in Vietnam. Some of his experiences following his permanent return to active duty in 1952 are recounted in chapter 8.
45. Hinojosa, interview.
46. Ibid.
47. Rolando Hinojosa, *Korean Love Songs: From Klail City Death Trip* (Berkeley: Editorial Justa, 1978).
48. Hinojosa, interview.
49. Ibid.
50. Frank Ornelas, interview by Steven Rosales, May 28, 2010, Saginaw, Michigan, audio tape (in author's possession).
51. Ibid.
52. Ibid.
53. Ibid.
54. Ibid.
55. Robert Villegas, interview by Steven Rosales, March 7, 2003, Riverside, California, audio tape (in author's possession).
56. Ibid.
57. Ibid.
58. Ibid.
59. Ibid.
60. Ibid.

61. Ibid.
62. Eddie Lovio, interview by Steven Rosales, August 10, 2003, Tucson, Arizona, audio tape (in author's possession).
63. Ibid.
64. Ibid.
65. Ibid.
66. Ibid.
67. Ibid.
68. Upon his return to Tucson he remained affiliated with Company E, serving six years altogether in the USMCR. Lovio subsequently transferred to the U.S. Army Reserve, where he served for another four years.
69. Lovio, interview.
70. Lorena Oropeza, *Raza Si! Guerra No! Chicano Protest and Patriotism During the Viet Nam War Era* (Berkeley: University of California Press, 2005), 40.
71. The subsequent war in Vietnam would become the first conflict fought by a fully integrated U.S. military.
72. Eddie Trujillo, interview by Steven Rosales, April 19, 2003, Victorville, California, audio tape (in author's possession).
73. González, interview.
74. Ibid.
75. Carillo, interview.
76. Ornelas, interview.
77. Vincent Pardo Jr., interview by Steven Rosales, May 23, 2010, Saginaw, Michigan, audio tape (in author's possession).
78. Ibid.
79. Mark Rocha, interview by Steven Rosales, February 6, 2003, Riverside, California, audio tape (in author's possession).
80. Castro, interview.
81. Moreno, interview.
82. Ibid.
83. Fisher, interview.
84. A captain's mast is nonjudicial punishment imposed by a unit's commanding officer—it involves committing a minor violation. It is not an admission of guilt; it simply means that the accused individual does not elect a judicial process. Meanwhile, a summary court martial provides a simplified trial for the handling of charges involving minor incidents of misconduct.
85. Fisher, interview.

86. García, interview.
87. Carillo, interview.
88. Trujillo, interview.
89. González, interview.
90. José Domínguez, interview by Steven Rosales, January 28, 2003, Moreno Valley, California, audio tape (in author's possession).
91. Castro, interview.
92. Lovio, interview.
93. Hinojosa, interview.
94. Castaneda, interview.
95. García, interview.
96. Carillo, interview.
97. Ray Gómez, interview by Steven Rosales, August 10, 2003, Mesa, Arizona, audio tape (in author's possession).
98. Gonzales, interview.
99. Pardo Jr., interview.
100. Moreno, interview.
101. Castro, interview.
102. Oropeza, *Raza Si! Guerra No!*, 46.

CHAPTER 5

1. Paul Rosenfeld and Amy L. Culbertson, "Hispanics in the Military," in *Hispanics in the Workplace*, ed. Stephen B. Knouse, Paul Rosenfeld, and Amy L. Culbertson (Thousand Oaks, CA: Sage, 1992), 213.
2. Stephen E. Ambrose and Douglas G. Brinkley, *Rise to Globalism: American Foreign Policy Since 1938* (New York: Penguin, 1997), 82. Other authoritative monographs on the Cold War and Vietnam include Mitchell K. Hall, *The Vietnam War* (New York: Longman, 2008); John L. Gaddis, *The United States and the Origins of the Cold War* (New York: Columbia University Press, 2000); Stanley Karnow, *Vietnam: A History* (New York: Penguin, 1997); Guenter Lewy, *America in Vietnam* (New York: Oxford University Press, 1980).
3. In 1883, Vietnam became a French protectorate and, along with Laos and Cambodia, formed French Indochina.
4. Karnow, *Vietnam*, 148.
5. Philip Caputo, *A Rumor of War* (New York: Henry Holt, 1977), xiv.

6. Ambrose and Brinkley, *Rise to Globalism*, 173.
7. A detailed analysis of the events in the Gulf of Tonkin, and the growing presence of American advisors and other military and logistical aid to South Vietnam can be found in Robert S. McNamara, *In Retrospect: The Tragedy and Lessons of Vietnam* (New York: Knopf, 1995); Karnow, *Vietnam*, 1997.
8. For an excellent discussion of the tactics and overall strategy employed by the U.S. military to secure victory in Vietnam, see Christian G. Appy, *Working-Class War: American Combat Soldiers and Vietnam* (Chapel Hill: University of North Carolina Press, 1993); Karnow, *Vietnam*, 1997.
9. The geography of the hilly northern highlands, less populated but covered in dense jungle foliage, differed from the more heavily populated lowlands of central and southern Vietnam, the latter also containing the Mekong Delta, a labyrinth of sinuous waterways that extended south from Cambodia.
10. Raymond Buriel, interview by Steven Rosales, December 30, 2002, Riverside, California, audio tape (in author's possession).
11. Tony López, interview by Steven Rosales, January 18, 2003, Riverside, California, audio tape (in author's possession).
12. Ibid.
13. John Sánchez, interview by Steven Rosales, November 15, 2009, Saginaw, Michigan, audio tape (in author's possession).
14. See Ron Kovic, *Born on the Fourth of July* (New York: Pocket Books, 1976).
15. Jim Acevedo, interview by Steven Rosales, December 23, 1997, San Diego, California, audio tape (in author's possession).
16. John Rodríguez, interview by Steven Rosales, December 28, 1999, San José, California, audio tape (in author's possession).
17. Frank Reyes, interview by Steven Rosales, April 17, 2003, Los Angeles, California, audio tape (in author's possession).
18. George Mariscal, interview by Steven Rosales, December 11, 1997, San Diego, California, audio tape (in author's possession).
19. Victor Ramírez, interview by Steven Rosales, March 6, 2003, Riverside, California, audio tape (in author's possession).
20. Gilbert Guevara, interview by Steven Rosales, June 14, 2010, Saginaw, Michigan, audio tape (in author's possession).
21. Daniel Cano, interview by Steven Rosales, November 26, 2002, Los Angeles, California, audio tape (in author's possession).
22. Tony Moreno, interview by Steven Rosales, November 15, 2009, Saginaw, Michigan, audio tape (in author's possession).

23. Ibid.
24. Except for the time period from March 1947 through mid-1948, the draft would remain in effect until the transition to an all volunteer military in March 1973.
25. Beth Bailey, *America's Army: Making the All-Volunteer Force* (Cambridge: Belknap Press, 2009), 13. Additional analysis of the draft system during the Vietnam War era and the controversy over class, race, and recruitment can be found in Appy, *Working-Class War*, 1993; George Q. Flynn, *Lewis B. Hershey: Mr. Selective Service* (Chapel Hill: University of North Carolina Press, 1985); James W. Davis Jr. and Kenneth M. Dolbeare, *Little Groups of Neighbors: The Selective Service System* (Westport, CT: Greenwood, 1981); Lawrence M. Baskir and Wiliam A. Strauss, *Chance and Circumstance: The Draft, the War, and the Vietnam Generation* (New York: Random House, 1978).
26. Draft reforms in 1969 did establish a lottery in an effort to produce a more equitable class representation of inductees; nevertheless, educational deferments continued until 1971, when troop withdrawals had minimized the need for increased draft quotas.
27. The test placed recruits into one of five groups ranked from one (the highest) to five (the lowest). Recruits that scored in the upper three categories were accepted, while those classified as category five were disqualified from military service. It was within category four that standards were altered in response to the increased need for manpower. As a matter of fact, prior to the Vietnam War, category-four individuals were routinely rejected due to mental inadequacy.
28. McNamara drew on the recommendations provided by Assistant Secretary of Labor Daniel P. Moynihan. In 1964, Moynihan chaired a task-force study, *One Third of a Nation*, which called on the military to lower its entrance requirements and thus provide the working poor with an opportunity to receive training, benefits, and improved self-esteem.
29. Baskir and Strauss, *Chance and Circumstance*, 129.
30. Martínez, interview.
31. Appy, *Working-Class War*, 35.
32. Davis Jr. and Dolbeare, *Little Groups of Neighbors*, 57.
33. Thomas P. Carter, *Mexican Americans in School: A History of Educational Neglect* (New York: College Entrance Examination Board, 1970), 30.
34. Ralph Guzman, "Mexican American Casualties in Vietnam," *La Raza* (1969): 13.
35. A thorough analysis of the Chicano movement is beyond the scope of this manuscript. For additional reading, see Mario T. García and Sal Castro, *Blowout!*

Sal Castro and the Chicano Struggle for Educational Justice (Chapel Hill: University of North Carolina Press, 2011); David Montejano, *Quixote's Soldiers: A Local History of the Chicano Movement, 1966–1981* (Austin: University of Texas Press, 2010); Carlos Muñoz Jr., *Youth, Identity, Power: The Chicano Movement* (New York: Verso, 2007); George Mariscal, *Brown-Eyed Children of the Sun: Lessons from the Chicano Movement, 1965–1975* (Albuquerque: University of New Mexico Press, 2005); Lorena Oropeza, *Raza Si! Guerra No! Chicano Protest and Patriotism During the Vietnam War Era* (Berkeley: University of California Press, 2005); Ernesto Chávez, *Mi Raza Primero! Nationalism, Identity, and Insurgency in the Chicano Movement in Los Angeles, 1966–1978* (Berkeley: University of California Press, 2002).

36. Guzman, "Mexican American Casualties in Vietnam," 12–16. In 1969, Octavio I. Romano V, a senior fellow at the Center for Advanced Mexican-American Social Research at the University of California, Berkeley, published a list of casualties with Spanish surnames from the United States and Puerto Rico. His list totaled 2,035 casualties from December 1967 to May 1969. See Octavio I. Romano, "Spanish Surname War Dead Vietnam," *El Grito* (1969): 6–31.
37. Foust and Botts as cited in Oropeza, *Raza Si! Guerra No!*, 216, 251.
38. See Charles C. Moskos Jr., *The American Enlisted Man* (New York: Russell Sage Foundation, 1970), 218. For more on the African American experience in Vietnam, see James E. Westheider, *The African American Experience in Vietnam: Brothers in Arms* (Lanham, MD: Rowman and Littlefield, 2007); Wallace Terry, *Bloods: An Oral History of the Vietnam War by Black Veterans* (New York: Ballantine Books, 1984); Martin Binkin et al., *Blacks and the Military* (Washington, DC: Brookings Institute, 1982); Arthur Egendorf et al., *Legacies of Vietnam: Comparative Adjustment of Veterans and Their Peers* (Washington, DC: Government Printing Office, 1981).
39. Appy, *Working-Class War*, 22.
40. Eddie Solís, interview by Steven Rosales, February 17, 2003, Riverside, California, audio tape (in author's possession).
41. Mariscal, interview.
42. Ibid.
43. Ibid.
44. Leroy V. Quintana, interview by Steven Rosales, February 11, 1998, San Diego, California, audio tape (in author's possession).
45. Ibid.
46. Ibid.

47. Ibid.
48. Ibid. More formally known as "mess duty," KP is relegated to junior enlisted personnel that are assigned to the kitchen staff on a rotational basis. Excluding cooking, responsibilities can include food preparation, dish washing, wiping tables, and serving food.
49. Ibid.
50. Ibid.
51. Ibid.
52. Cano, interview.
53. Ibid. Immediately following his departure in October 1967, Cano's unit was attacked by an NVA regiment that evening, leaving several comrades dead and wounded. Despite his fortuitous timing, this major assault has provided Cano with a lingering sense of remorse.
54. Ibid.
55. Ibid.
56. With physical fitness and training standards above and beyond that imposed on regular army personnel, Green Berets conducted clandestine operations in hostile territory and trained indigenous populations to fend off Communist infiltration. Such counterinsurgency tactics were highly suitable for the type of guerrilla warfare that typified the Vietnam War.
57. Reyes, interview.
58. Ibid.
59. Ibid.
60. The details of these missions remain classified.
61. Reyes, interview.
62. Ibid.
63. Ibid.
64. Ibid.
65. Solís, interview.
66. Solís celebrated his eighteenth birthday in basic training and would ultimately acquire his certificate in General Educational Development (GED) during his enlistment.
67. Solís, interview.
68. Ibid.
69. Ibid.
70. Ibid.
71. Buriel, interview.

72. Ibid.
73. Ibid.
74. Ibid.
75. Alfredo Vea, interview by Steven Rosales, December 14, 2002, Oakland, California, audio tape (in author's possession). He attended another unnamed institution prior to his enrollment at UC Berkeley (UCB), an interruption that voided his student exemption despite being enrolled at UCB as a full-time student.
76. Ibid.
77. Ibid.
78. Established on the island of New Caledonia in 1942, the division remained in operation in the U.S. Army through the Vietnam War and was ultimately deactivated following its withdrawal in November 1971.
79. Vea, interview.
80. Ibid.
81. Ibid.
82. Ibid.
83. Ibid.
84. Sánchez, interview.
85. Ibid.
86. Ibid.
87. Ibid.
88. Ibid.
89. Ibid.
90. Ibid.
91. Charley Trujillo, interview by Steven Rosales, December 27, 1999, San José, California, audio tape (in author's possession).
92. Ibid.
93. Ibid.
94. Ibid. Trujillo provided no indication of legal consequences for himself or any of the other men involved.
95. Sal Martínez, interview by Steven Rosales, December 22, 1997, Oceanside, California, audio tape (in author's possession).
96. Ibid. Despite orders to resist to the last man, the protestors never penetrated the grounds of the embassy.
97. Ibid.
98. Ibid.

99. Ibid.
100. Ibid.
101. Ibid.
102. Ibid.
103. Ibid.
104. Mariscal, interview.
105. Vea, interview.
106. Buriel, interview.
107. Guevara, interview.
108. Jesus Barragan, interview by Steven Rosales, August 17, 2011, San Francisco, California, audio tape (in author's possession).
109. Reyes, interview.
110. Guadalupe Alviar, interview by Steven Rosales, April 30, 2010, Muskegon, Michigan, audio tape (in author's possession).
111. Joe Rodríguez, interview by Steven Rosales, December 23, 1997, San Diego, California, audio tape (in author's possession).
112. Acevedo, interview.
113. Solís, interview.
114. Ibid.
115. Alviar, interview.
116. Sánchez, interview.
117. Reyes, interview.
118. Everett Álvarez, interview by Steven Rosales, July 29, 2003, McLean, Virginia, audio tape (in author's possession).
119. Solís, interview.
120. Barragan, interview.
121. Ibid.
122. Fred Medel, interview by Steven Rosales, April 18, 2010, Saginaw, Michigan, audio tape (in author's possession).
123. Solís, interview.
124. Quintana, interview.
125. Cano, interview.
126. Mariscal, interview.
127. Ibid.
128. Ted Samora, interview by Steven Rosales, January 4, 2010, San Francisco, California, audio tape (in author's possession).
129. Reyes, interview.

CHAPTER 6

1. I am influenced by the work of sociologist Raewyn (R. W.) Connell and her focus on the contested nature of masculine identity, despite the existence of hegemonic forms of masculinity in many cultures. See R. W. Connell, *Masculinities* (Berkeley: University of California Press, 1995).
2. Quoted in Raúl Morin, *Among the Valiant: Mexican Americans in World War II and Korea* (Alhambra, CA: Borden, 1966), 91.
3. Alfredo Vea, interview by Steven Rosales, December 14, 2002, Oakland, California, audio tape (in author's possession).
4. Joe Rodríguez, interview by Steven Rosales, December 23, 1997, San Diego, California, audio tape (in author's possession).
5. Vea, interview.
6. Raymond Buriel, interview by Steven Rosales, December 30, 2002, Riverside, California, audio tape (in author's possession).
7. Jim Acevedo, interview by Steven Rosales, December 23, 1997, San Diego, California, audio tape (in author's possession).
8. Robert L. Castro, interview by Steven Rosales, August 9, 2002, Tucson, Arizona, audio tape (in author's possession).
9. Gene Bejarano, interview by Steven Rosales, February 16, 2003, Chino Hills, California, audio tape (in author's possession).
10. To my knowledge, the stipend remained fixed at $50 throughout my chosen time period.
11. Daniel Cano, interview by Steven Rosales, November 26, 2002, Los Angeles, California, audio tape (in author's possession).
12. Mike González, interview by Steven Rosales, February 13, 2003, Los Angeles, California, audio tape (in author's possession).
13. Richard Domínguez, interview by Steven Rosales, March 26, 2003, Whittier, California, audio tape (in author's possession).
14. Carlos Santillán, interview by Steven Rosales, March 14, 2003, Norwalk, California, audio tape (in author's possession).
15. John Rodríguez, interview by Steven Rosales, December 28, 1999, San José, California, audio tape (in author's possession).
16. George Mariscal, interview by Steven Rosales, December 11, 1997, San Diego, California, audio tape (in author's possession).
17. Ruben Moreno, interview by Steven Rosales, August 9, 2003, Tucson, Arizona, audio tape (in author's possession).

18. Tony López, interview by Steven Rosales, January 18, 2003, Riverside, California, audio tape (in author's possession).
19. Quoted in George Mariscal, *Aztlán and Viet Nam: Chicano and Chicana Experiences of the War* (Berkeley: University of California Press, 1999), 29. The letter is dated October 25, 1967.
20. Ibid., 204–5. The essay is dated June 5, 1971. Founded by Elizabeth "Betita" Martínez in New Mexico, this bilingual newspaper (1968–73) sought to organize and inform the Chicana/o populace about various local and international issues important to the community. Of particular concern was the recovery of lost land rights in the aftermath of the Mexican-American War (1846–48).
21. Mark Rocha, interview by Steven Rosales, February 6, 2003, Riverside, California, audio tape (in author's possession). After several medical examinations, Rocha returned to Japan, where he was stationed for a total of twenty-eight months.
22. Ted Samora, interview by Steven Rosales, January 4, 2010, San Francisco, California, audio tape (in author's possession). A separate interview of Samora can also be found in the Library of Congress Veterans History Project, collection number AFC/2001/001/5877.
23. Three older brothers also preceded Samora into the military.
24. Samora, interview.
25. Ibid.
26. Raúl Mosqueda, interview by Steven Rosales, June 13, 2010, Saginaw, Michigan, audio tape (in author's possession).
27. Ibid.
28. John Sótelo, interview by Steven Rosales, February 4, 2003, Riverside, California, audio tape (in author's possession).
29. Ibid.
30. Gene García, interview by Steven Rosales, March 2, 2003, Riverside, California, audio tape (in author's possession).
31. Victor Ramírez, interview by Steven Rosales, March 6, 2003, Riverside, California, audio tape (in author's possession).
32. Frank Gonzales, interview by Steven Rosales, May 22, 2010, Saginaw, Michigan, audio tape (in author's possession).
33. Lupe Alviar, interview by Steven Rosales, April 30, 2010, Muskegon, Michigan, audio tape (in author's possession).
34. Everett Álvarez, interview by Steven Rosales, July 29, 2003, McLean, Virginia, audio tape (in author's possession).

35. Such torture was occasionally supervised or conducted by Soviet Bloc personnel, including a sadistic Cuban, dubbed Fidel, who took particular interest in Álvarez due to his Mexican ancestry. The pursuit of forced confessions attesting to war crimes was the primary objective. His ordeal is recounted in Everett Álvarez Jr. and Anthony S. Pitch, *Chained Eagle* (New York: Dell, 1989).
36. Álvarez, interview.
37. Ibid.
38. Tony Moreno, interview by Steven Rosales, November 15, 2009, Saginaw, Michigan, audio tape (in author's possession).
39. Ibid.
40. Ibid.
41. Eddie Trujillo, interview by Steven Rosales, April 19, 2003, Victorville, California, audio tape (in author's possession). The moniker La Raza is an all-encompassing form of identification for individuals of Mexican ancestry that was especially utilized during the era of the Chicano movement and thereafter.
42. Cano, interview.
43. Eddie Solís, interview by Steven Rosales, February 17, 2003, Riverside, California, audio tape (in author's possession).
44. Fred Medel, interview by Steven Rosales, April 18, 2010, Saginaw, Michigan, audio tape (in author's possession).
45. Mariscal, interview.
46. Ibid.
47. Buriel, interview.
48. Ibid.
49. Mariscal, interview.
50. Gilbert Guevara, interview by Steven Rosales, June 14, 2010, Saginaw, Michigan, audio tape (in author's possession).
51. Medel, interview.
52. Acevedo, interview.
53. David Fuentes, interview by Steven Rosales, April 24, 2003, Los Angeles, California, audio tape (in author's possession).
54. Santillán, interview.
55. Bejarano, interview.
56. Vincent Pardo Jr., interview by Steven Rosales, May 23, 2010, Saginaw, Michigan, audio tape (in author's possession).

57. García, interview.
58. David Carillo, interview by Steven Rosales, January 23, 2003, Riverside, California, audio tape (in author's possession).
59. Robert Villegas, interview by Steven Rosales, March 7, 2003, Riverside, California, audio tape (in author's possession).
60. Charles C. Moskos, *The American Enlisted Man* (New York: Russell Sage Foundation, 1970), 85.
61. Jesus Barragan, interview by Steven Rosales, August 17, 2011, San Francisco, California, audio tape (in author's possession).
62. Mariscal, interview.
63. Guevara, interview.
64. Vea, interview.
65. Cano, interview.
66. Mosqueda, interview.
67. A fruitful comparison with gay British veterans and their efforts to project heterosexuality during World War II can be made. See Emma Vickers, "'The Good Fellow': Negotiation, Remembrance, and Recollection—Homosexuality in the British Armed Forces, 1939–1945," in *Brutality and Desire: War and Sexuality in Europe's Twentieth Century*, ed. Dagmar Herzog, (New York: Palgrave Macmillan, 2011).
68. Samora, interview.
69. Ibid.
70. Barragan, interview.
71. Samora, interview.
72. Ibid.
73. Ibid.
74. Ibid.
75. Barragan, interview.
76. Ibid.
77. Ibid.
78. Ibid. His enlistment contract required an initial two-year affiliation with the naval reserve, which was to be followed by two years in the regular navy and a final two years in the reserves. However, largely due to an injury, he ultimately performed thirty-eight months of active duty and was released on a medical (and honorable) discharge in December 1969.
79. Ibid.
80. Ibid.

81. Ibid.
82. Mariscal, interview.

CHAPTER 7

1. A partial listing of scholarship that generally supports a more positive depiction of the 1944 GI Bill and its transformative potential include Glen C. Altschuler and Stuart M. Blumin, *The GI Bill: A New Deal for Veterans* (New York: Oxford University Press, 2009); Suzanne Mettler, *Soldiers to Citizens: The G.I. Bill and the Making of the Greatest Generation* (New York: Oxford University Press, 2009); Michael J. Bennet, *When Dreams Come True: The GI Bill and the Making of Modern America* (Washington, DC: Potomac Books, 1999); Harold M. Hyman, *American Singularity: The 1787 Northwest Ordinance, the 1862 Homestead and Morrill Acts, and the 1944 GI Bill* (Athens: University of Georgia Press, 1986); Keith W. Olson, *The G.I. Bill, the Veterans, and the Colleges* (Lexington: University Press of Kentucky, 1974); David R. B. Ross, *Preparing for Ulysses: Politics and Veterans During World War II* (New York: Columbia University Press, 1969).
2. An exception is Kathleen Frydl, *The GI Bill* (New York: Cambridge University Press, 2009). While this book illustrates the tragic role that racial politics played in limiting the bill's overall effectiveness for African Americans, its nuanced and carefully balanced assessment also highlights the resilient determination by African American veterans to maximize the opportunities made available to them by the GI Bill and their military service.
3. Recent scholarship on the evolution of assistance provided to veterans prior to World War II include Frydl, *The GI Bill*, and Altschuler and Blumin, *The GI Bill*.
4. Additional information on the Bonus marchers can be found in Stephen Ortiz, *Beyond the Bonus March and GI Bill: How Veteran Politics Shaped the New Deal Era* (New York: New York University Press, 2009).
5. Olson, *The G.I. Bill, the Veterans, and the Colleges*, 24.
6. John López, interview by Steven Rosales, March 9, 2003, Riverside, California, audio tape (in author's possession).
7. Ibid.
8. David Fuentes, interview by Steven Rosales, April 24, 2003, Los Angeles, California, audio tape (in author's possession).

9. Ibid.
10. Raúl Medina, interview by Steven Rosales, February 18, 2003, Riverside, California, audio tape (in author's possession).
11. Ibid.
12. Guadalupe Ortega, interview by Steven Rosales, May 29, 2010, Saginaw, Michigan, audio tape (in author's possession).
13. Ortega also began taking electrician classes at night school at his own expense, and eventually earned his master contractor's license. He again started his own business, Ortega Electrical Contracting Inc., which he operated for approximately forty years until his retirement.
14. Mettler, *Soldiers to Citizens*, 7.
15. Jesse Ybarra, interview by Steven Rosales, January 14, 2003, Riverside, California, audio tape (in author's possession).
16. Ibid.
17. Rolando Hinojosa, interview by Steven Rosales, March 26, 2005, Austin, Texas, audio tape (in author's possession).
18. Ibid. As described in chapter 4, Hinojosa initially served in the U.S. Army from August 1946 until December 1947 but was recalled to active duty in November 1949, ultimately acquiring extensive combat experience during the Korean War. Due to his initial seventeen-month tour of duty, however, he was entitled to receive twenty-four months of benefits under the Servicemen's Readjustment Act of 1944 in addition to an unspecified amount from the Korean War version.
19. His first job as an assistant professor at Trinity University in San Antonio, Texas, was followed by other academic appointments, and in 1981, he joined the Department of English at the University of Texas. He is currently a professor emeritus.
20. William Sánchez, interview by Steven Rosales, April 29, 2003, Los Angeles, California, audio tape (in author's possession).
21. Ibid.
22. Francisco Vega, interview by Steven Rosales, September 15, 2009, Grand Rapids, Michigan, audio tape (in author's possession).
23. Ibid.
24. Ibid.
25. Richard Domínguez, interview by Steven Rosales, March 26, 2003, Whittier, California, audio tape (in author's possession).
26. He subsequently attended California State University, Los Angeles, and

completed a third year of college coursework using the GI Bill. However, family and work obligations left him several classes shy of acquiring a bachelor's degree.

27. Domínguez, interview.
28. George Castrueta, interview by Steven Rosales, May 1, 2003, Whittier, California, audio tape (in author's possession).
29. Harley L. Browning, Sally C. Lopreato, and Dudley L. Poston Jr., "Income and Veteran Status: Variations Among Mexican Americans, Blacks, and Anglos," *American Sociological Review* 38 (1973): 74–85. Data are derived from the U.S. Census Bureau, "One in a Hundred: A Public Use of Basic Records from the 1960 Census" (April 1971). Also, the sample was restricted to veterans who served in World War II and after.
30. Roughly one half of the men in the 1/100 Public Use Sample were included in this analysis. In an effort to produce more meaningful veteran/nonveteran comparisons, restrictions were utilized based on the following criteria: (1) males drawn from five southwestern states—Arizona, California, Colorado, New Mexico, and Texas; (2) males between the ages of twenty-five and fifty; (3) exclusion of males with farm occupations; (4) males with less than five years of formal schooling; and (5) part-time employment.
31. Melanie Martindale and Dudley L. Poston Jr., "Variations in Veteran/Nonveteran Earnings Among World War II, Korea, and Vietnam War Cohorts," *Armed Forces & Society* 5 (1979): 219–43. Additional research that supports the concept of a bridging process includes John D. Kasarda and Wayne J. Villemez, "Veteran Status and Socioeconomic Attainment," *Armed Forces & Society* 2 (1976): 407–20, and Roger D. Little and J. Eric Fredlund, "Veteran Status, Earnings, and Race," *Armed Forces & Society* 5 (1979): 244–59. These latter two studies employed a "white/nonwhite" subdivision. Nevertheless, both found a positive correlation between income and veteran status, which was especially pronounced for their nonwhite cohorts.
32. Mettler, *Soldiers to Citizens*, 59.
33. George J. Sánchez, *Becoming Mexican American: Ethnicity, Culture, and Identity in Chicano Los Angeles, 1900–1945* (New York: Oxford University Press, 1993), 256.
34. Dennis Valdés, "The Mexican American Dream and World War II: A View from the Midwest," in *Mexican Americans & World War II*, ed. Maggie Rivas-Rodríguez (Austin: University of Texas Press, 2005), 136–37. Dennis Valdés's

use of the term *Mexican* incorporates both Mexican nationals and U.S. citizens of Mexican descent.

35. David H. Onkst, "'First a Negro . . . Incidentally a Veteran': Black World War Two Veterans and the G.I. Bill of Rights in the Deep South, 1944–1948," *Journal of Social History* 31 (1998): 530.
36. Jennifer E. Brooks, *Defining the Peace: World War II Veterans, Race, and the Remaking of Southern Political Tradition* (Chapel Hill: University of North Carolina Press, 2004), 11.
37. Castrueta, interview.
38. Domínguez, interview.
39. Mike García, interview by Steven Rosales, March 4, 2003, Riverside, California, audio tape (in author's possession).
40. Alfred Aguirre, interview by Steven Rosales, April 22, 2003, Placentia, California, audio tape (in author's possession).
41. John Sótelo, interview by Steven Rosales, February 4, 2003, Riverside, California, audio tape (in author's possession).
42. Nick Salazar, interview by Steven Rosales, March 29, 2003, Los Angeles, California, audio tape (in author's possession).
43. García, interview. Like John López, he also became a member of United Carpenters of America.
44. Martin Morales, interview by Steven Rosales, October 5, 2009, Grand Rapids, Michigan, audio tape (in author's possession).
45. Arnulfo Nerio, interview by Steven Rosales, May 29, 2010, Bay City, Michigan, audio tape (in author's possession).
46. Salvador Marez, interview by Steven Rosales, June 2, 2010, Grand Rapids, Michigan, audio tape (in author's possession).
47. Melinda L. Pash, *In the Shadow of the Greatest Generation: The Americans Who Fought the Korean War* (New York: New York University Press, 2012), 209–10.
48. Ibid., 211.
49. John López, interview by Steven Rosales, May 22, 2010, Saginaw, Michigan, audio tape (in author's possession).
50. Vincent Pardo Jr., interview by Steven Rosales, May 23, 2010, Saginaw, Michigan, audio tape (in author's possession).
51. William J. Fisher, interview by Steven Rosales, August 10, 2003, Tucson, Arizona, audio tape (in author's possession).
52. Fisher also acquired a master's degree in education from the University of

Arizona in 1966 and a doctorate in curriculum instruction and bilingual education from the University of New Mexico in 1976. He subsequently served as a principal at four schools in Tucson for nineteen years.

53. Ruben Moreno, interview by Steven Rosales, August 9, 2003, Tucson, Arizona, audio tape (in author's possession).
54. Eddie Trujillo, interview by Steven Rosales, April 19, 2003, Victorville, California, audio tape (in author's possession).
55. Ibid.
56. Robert Villegas, interview by Steven Rosales, March 7, 2003, Riverside, California, audio tape (in author's possession).
57. Ibid.
58. Ray Gómez, interview by Steven Rosales, August 10, 2003, Mesa, Arizona, audio tape (in author's possession).
59. José Domínguez, interview by Steven Rosales, January 28, 2003, Moreno Valley, California, audio tape (in author's possession).
60. Gene García, interview by Steven Rosales, March 2, 2003, Riverside, California, audio tape (in author's possession).
61. Ibid.
62. Ibid.
63. U.S. Veterans Administration Information Service pamphlet, *G.I. Bill of Rights, 25th Anniversary, 1944–1969* (Washington, DC: Veterans Administration Main Office, 1969), 6–10.
64. Additional information on the Vietnam-era GI Bill can be found in Sar A. Levitan and Joyce K. Zickler, *Swords into Plowshares: Our GI Bill* (Salt Lake City: Olympus, 1973).
65. Ibid., 51.
66. J. Peter Mattila, "G.I. Bill Benefits and Enrollments: How Did Vietnam Veterans Fare?" *Social Science Quarterly* 59 (1978): 535–45.
67. George Mariscal, interview by Steven Rosales, December 11, 1997, San Diego, California, audio tape (in author's possession).
68. Ibid.
69. Ibid.
70. He is currently a professor of literature at the University of California, San Diego.
71. Joe Rodríguez, interview by Steven Rosales, December 23, 1997, San Diego, California, audio tape (in author's possession).
72. Ibid.

73. Ibid. He would acquire a doctorate in literature from the University of California, San Diego, and at the time of this interview was a professor of Chicano and Chicana Studies at San Diego State University.
74. Raymond Buriel, interview by Steven Rosales, December 30, 2002, Riverside, California, audio tape (in author's possession). He would acquire an associate of arts in behavioral sciences from Riverside Community College in 1971 and a bachelor's in psychology in 1973 from the University of California, Riverside, where he also attained a doctorate in psychology in 1977. He is currently a professor of psychology and Chicano Studies at Pomona College.
75. Ibid.
76. Leroy Quintana, interview by Steven Rosales, February 11, 1998, San Diego, California, audio tape (in author's possession). He would also acquire a master's degree from New Mexico State University, and at the time of this interview he was employed as a professor at two-year San Diego Mesa College.
77. Daniel Cano, interview by Steven Rosales, November 26, 2002, Los Angeles, California, audio tape (in author's possession). He is currently a professor of English at two-year Santa Monica College in Los Angeles.
78. Ibid.
79. Alfredo Vea, interview by Steven Rosales, December 14, 2002, Oakland, California, audio tape (in author's possession).
80. Raúl Mosqueda, interview by Steven Rosales, June 13, 2010, Saginaw, Michigan, audio tape (in author's possession).
81. Ibid.
82. Gilbert Guevara, interview by Steven Rosales, June 14, 2010, Saginaw, Michigan, audio tape (in author's possession).
83. Ibid. Prior to being drafted, he acquired an associate of arts degree from two-year Delta College.
84. Tony López, interview by Steven Rosales, January 18, 2003, Riverside, California, audio tape (in author's possession). His career spanned 1965–87.
85. Everett Álvarez, interview by Steven Rosales, July 29, 2003, McLean, Virginia, audio tape (in author's possession).
86. Ibid. Álvarez left government service in 1986 and started his own consulting firm, which he continued to manage at the time of this interview.
87. Stephen J. Dienstfrey and Robert H. Feitz, *Chart Book on Black and Hispanic Veterans: Data from the 1980 Census of Population and Housing* (Washington, DC: Office of Information Management and Statistics, Statistical Policy and Research Service, Research Division, 1985).

CHAPTER 8

1. Mark D. Van Ells, *To Hear Only Thunder Again: America's World War II Veterans Come Home* (Lanham, MD: Lexington, 2001), 96.
2. Ibid., 122.
3. Melinda L. Pash, *In the Shadow of the Greatest Generation: The Americans Who Fought the Korean War* (New York: New York University Press, 2012), 92.
4. Lawrence M. Baskir and William A. Strauss, *Chance and Circumstance: The Draft, the War, and the Vietnam Generation* (New York: Knopf, 1978), 2–4.
5. Van Ells, *To Hear Only Thunder Again*, 118.
6. Angelita García-Cabrera, "The Hispanic Veteran of the Armed Services and in the Veterans Administration" (PhD diss., Brandeis University, 1978), 83.
7. Sal Martínez, interview by Steven Rosales, December 22, 1997, Oceanside, California, audio tape (in author's possession).
8. Tony López, interview by Steven Rosales, January 18, 2003, Riverside, California, audio tape (in author's possession).
9. Alfredo Vea, interview by Steven Rosales, December 14, 2002, Oakland, California, audio tape (in author's possession).
10. Frank Reyes, interview by Steven Rosales, April 17, 2003, Los Angeles, California, audio tape (in author's possession).
11. Jim Acevedo, interview by Steven Rosales, December 23, 1997, San Diego, California, audio tape (in author's possession).
12. Rosina M. Becerra and Milton Greenblatt, *Hispanics Seek Health Care: A Study of 1,088 Veterans of Three War Eras* (Lanham, MD: University Press of America, 1983), 9.
13. Ibid., 90–91.
14. Arnulfo "Arnif" Nerio, interview by Steven Rosales, May 29, 2010, Saginaw, Michigan, audio tape (in author's possession).
15. Vincent Pardo Jr., interview by Steven Rosales, May 23, 2010, Saginaw, Michigan, audio tape (in author's possession).
16. George Castaneda, interview by Steven Rosales, June 14, 2010, Saginaw, Michigan, audio tape (in author's possession).
17. Ruben Moreno, interview by Steven Rosales, August 9, 2003, Tucson, Arizona, audio tape (in author's possession).
18. Ibid.

19. Jesus Barragan, interview by Steven Rosales, August 17, 2011, San Francisco, California, audio tape (in author's possession).
20. Ibid.
21. Ibid.
22. John Rodríguez, interview by Steven Rosales, December 28, 1999, San José, California, audio tape (in author's possession).
23. Charley Trujillo, interview by Steven Rosales, December 27, 1999, San José, California, audio tape (in author's possession).
24. Raúl Medina, interview by Steven Rosales, February 18, 2003, Riverside, California, audio tape (in author's possession).
25. A class-action lawsuit filed in 1982 against the companies that produced Agent Orange led to a settlement in 1984. At that time, 15,000 veterans were involved, but approximately 250,000 ultimately filed claims. Under the terms of the settlement, the chemical companies agreed to provide $180 million in compensation while not having to accept blame for any injuries that occurred as a result of exposure to Agent Orange.
26. Tony Moreno, interview by Steven Rosales, November 15, 2009, Saginaw, Michigan, audio tape (in author's possession).
27. Medina, interview.
28. Jesse Ybarra, interview by Steven Rosales, January 14, 2003, Riverside, California, audio tape (in author's possession).
29. William Sánchez, interview by Steven Rosales, April 29, 2003, Los Angeles, California, audio tape (in author's possession).
30. Ibid.
31. Ibid.
32. Ibid.
33. Van Ells, *To Hear Only Thunder Again*, 107.
34. Guadalupe "Lupe" Ortega, interview by Steven Rosales, May 29, 2010, Saginaw, Michigan, audio tape (in author's possession).
35. Ibid.
36. Ibid.
37. Ibid.
38. Francisco Vega, interview by Steven Rosales, September 15, 2009, Grand Rapids, Michigan, audio tape (in author's possession).
39. Darío Villegas, interview by Steven Rosales, February 27, 2003, Riverside, California, audio tape (in author's possession).

40. Ibid.
41. Gene Bejarano, interview by Steven Rosales, February 16, 2003, Riverside, California, audio tape (in author's possession).
42. Ibid.
43. Moreno, interview.
44. Rolando Hinojosa, interview by Steven Rosales, March 26, 2005, Austin, Texas, audio tape (in author's possession).
45. Mike González, interview by Steven Rosales, February 13, 2003, Los Angeles, California, audio tape (in author's possession).
46. Robert L. Castro, interview by Steven Rosales, August 9, 2003, Tucson, Arizona, audio tape (in author's possession).
47. Eddie Trujillo, interview by Steven Rosales, April 19, 2003, Victorville, California, audio tape (in author's possession).
48. Ray Gómez, interview by Steven Rosales, August 10, 2003, Mesa, Arizona, audio tape (in author's possession).
49. Ibid.
50. United States House Committee on Veterans Affairs, *Hispanic Veterans: Contributions to the Nation and Community, Receipt of Federal Veterans Benefits, and Related Issues* (Washington, DC: Government Printing Office, 1994), 115.
51. Vea, interview.
52. Rodríguez, interview.
53. Eddie Solís, interview by Steven Rosales, February 17, 2003, Riverside, California, audio tape (in author's possession).
54. Chappo López, interview by Steven Rosales, December 22, 1997, San Diego, California, audio tape (in author's possession).
55. Ibid.
56. Raymond Buriel, interview by Steven Rosales, December 30, 2002, Riverside, California, audio tape (in author's possession).
57. Ibid.
58. Fred Medel, interview by Steven Rosales, April 18, 2010, Saginaw, Michigan, audio tape (in author's possession).
59. Ibid.
60. Ibid.
61. Baskir and Strauss, *Chance and Circumstance*, 134.
62. Trujillo, interview.
63. Robert Villegas, interview by Steven Rosales, March 7, 2003, Riverside, California, audio tape (in author's possession).

64. Gómez, interview.
65. Daniel Cano, interview by Steven Rosales, November 26, 2002, Los Angeles, California, audio tape (in author's possession).
66. Medel, interview.
67. López, interview.
68. George Mariscal, interview by Steven Rosales, December 11, 1997, San Diego, California, audio tape (in author's possession).
69. Vea, interview.
70. Gilbert Guevara, interview by Steven Rosales, June 14, 2010, Saginaw, Michigan, audio tape (in author's possession).
71. Buriel, interview.
72. Joe Rodríguez, interview by Steven Rosales, December 23, 1997, San Diego, California, audio tape (in author's possession).
73. Rodríguez, interview.
74. Ted Samora, interview by Steven Rosales, January 4, 2010, San Francisco, California, audio tape (in author's possession).
75. Jesse Ybarra, interview by Steven Rosales, January 14, 2003, Riverside, California, audio tape (in author's possession).
76. Richard Domínguez, interview by Steven Rosales, March 26, 2003, Whittier, California, audio tape (in author's possession).
77. Martin Morales, interview by Steven Rosales, October 5, 2009, Grand Rapids, Michigan, audio tape (in author's possession).
78. Ibid.
79. Mike García, interview by Steven Rosales, March 4, 2003, Riverside, California, audio tape (in author's possession).
80. Salvador Marez, interview by Steven Rosales, June 2, 2010, Grand Rapids, Michigan, audio tape (in author's possession).
81. Bejarano, interview.
82. Pardo, interview.
83. Frank Gonzales, interview by Steven Rosales, May 22, 2010, Saginaw, Michigan, audio tape (in author's possession).
84. Villegas, interview.
85. Gene García, interview by Steven Rosales, March 2, 2003, Riverside, California, audio tape (in author's possession).
86. Hinojosa, interview.
87. Ibid.
88. González, interview.

89. Mark Rocha, interview by Steven Rosales, February 6, 2003, Riverside, California, audio tape (in author's possession).
90. Moreno, interview.
91. Rodríguez, interview.
92. Castro, interview.
93. López, interview.
94. Martínez, interview.
95. Victor Ramírez, interview by Steven Rosales, March 6, 2003, Riverside, California, audio tape (in author's possession).
96. Trujillo, interview.
97. Solís, interview.
98. Trujillo acquired a bachelor's degree from the University of California, Berkeley, and a master's degree from San Jose State University with support provided by his GI Bill and disability benefits. He subsequently worked as an adjunct lecturer for twelve years.
99. Cano, interview.
100. Vea, interview.
101. Lorena Oropeza, *Raza Si! Guerra No! Chicano Protest and Patriotism During the Viet Nam War Era* (Berkeley: University of California Press, 2005), 13.

CHAPTER 9

1. Minutes, American GI Forum, March 26, 1948, semi-processed area, Hector Perez García Collection, Jeff and Mary Bell Library, Texas A&M University, Corpus Christi. Hereafter noted as HPGC, TAMUCC.
2. Ibid.
3. Ibid.
4. Membership in the American GI Forum remained open to all veterans with honorable discharges as well as interested nonveterans. It would nevertheless remain an organization primarily composed of Mexican Americans.
5. Notarized statement, Beatrice Longoria, January 8, 1949 (estimated), file folder 130.1, HPGC, TAMUCC.
6. Telegram, Lyndon B. Johnson to Hector P. Garcia, January 10, 1949 (estimated), file folder 130.4, HPGC, TAMUCC.
7. For an examination of the media coverage that accompanied the incident, see Maggie Rivas-Rodríguez, "Framing Racism: Newspaper Coverage of the

Three Rivers Incident," in *Mexican Americans & World War II*, ed. Maggie Rivas-Rodríguez (Austin: University of Texas Press, 2005).

8. File Folder 130.34, HPGC, TAMUCC.
9. File Folder 130.1, HPGC, TAMUCC.
10. Ibid. The Good Neighbor Commission (GNC) was established in 1943 to handle charges of discrimination against the Mexican American community in Texas as well as to foster binational cooperation with Mexico following the latter's decision in 1942 to ban bracero guest workers to the state, citing discriminatory practices in Texas.
11. File Folder 130.39, HPGC, TAMUCC.
12. File Folder 130.1, HPGC, TAMUCC.
13. Scholarship that establishes a decisive link between the Longoria incident and the greater social activism that followed includes Michelle Hall Kells, *Hector P. Garcia: Everyday Rhetoric and Mexican American Civil Rights* (Carbondale: Southern Illinois University Press, 2006); Patrick Carroll, *Felix Longoria's Wake: Bereavement, Racism, and the Rise of Mexican American Activism* (Austin: University of Texas Press, 2003); Rivas-Rodríguez, ed., *Mexican Americans and World War II*, 2005.
14. Alonso S. Perales, *Are We Good Neighbors?* (San Antonio, TX: Artes Grafícas, 1948), 156–57. Further discussion of the publication can be found in Lorena Oropeza, *Raza Sí! Guerra No! Chicano Protest and Patriotism During the Viet Nam War Era* (Berkeley: University of California Press, 2005).
15. Frank Ornelas, interview by Steven Rosales, May 28, 2010, Saginaw, Michigan, audio tape (in author's possession).
16. Cynthia Enloe, *Ethnic Soldiers: State Security in Divided Societies* (Athens: University of Georgia Press, 1980), 54.
17. A sampling of scholarship that examines the domestic Red Scare following World War II includes Victor Navasky, *Naming Names* (New York: Hill and Wang, 2003); Ellen Schrecker, *The Age of McCarthyism: A Brief History with Documents* (Boston: Bedford/St. Martin's, 2002); Thomas Borstelmann, *The Cold War and the Color Line: American Race Relations in the Global Arena* (Cambridge, MA: Harvard University Press, 2001); Ellen Schrecker, *Many Are the Crimes: McCarthyism in America* (Princeton, NJ: Princeton University Press, 1999).
18. Mae M. Ngai, *Impossible Subjects: Illegal Aliens and the Making of Modern America* (Princeton, NJ: Princeton University Press, 2004), 132.
19. Overall, 4.6 million contracts were issued during the program's lifetime, with

the vast majority, 72 percent, executed between 1955 and 1964. For additional information on the Bracero Program, see Natalia Molina, *How Race Is Made in America: Immigration, Citizenship, and the Historical Power of Racial Scripts* (Berkeley: University of California Press, 2014); Ana Elizabeth Rosas, *Abrazando el Espíritu: Bracero Families Confront the U.S.-Mexico Border* (Berkeley: University of California Press, 2014); Deborah Cohen, *Braceros: Migrant Citizens and Transnational Subjects in the Postwar United States and Mexico* (Chapel Hill: University of North Carolina Press, 2011); David G. Gutierrez, *Walls and Mirrors: Mexican Americans, Mexican Immigrants, and the Politics of Ethnicity* (Berkeley: University of California Press, 1995).

20. Neil Foley, "Becoming Hispanic: Mexican Americans and the Faustian Pact with Whiteness," in *Reflexiones: New Directions in Mexican American Studies*, ed. Neil Foley (Austin: University of Texas Press, 1998), 53. Also see Carlos Kevin Blanton, *George I. Sánchez: The Long Fight for Mexican American Integration* (New Haven, CT: Yale University Press, 2013); Craig A. Kaplowitz, *LULAC: Mexican Americans and National Policy* (College Station: Texas A&M University Press, 2005); Neil Foley, *The White Scourge: Mexicans, Blacks, and Poor Whites in Texas Cotton Culture* (Berkeley: University of California Press, 1999); Gutierrez, *Walls and Mirrors*, 1995; Thomas A. Guglielmo, "Fighting for Caucasian Rights: Mexicans, Mexican Americans, and the Transnational Struggle for Civil Rights in World War II Texas," *Journal of American History* 92 (March 2006): 1212–37.

21. File Folder 5, semi-processed area, HPGC, TAMUCC.

22. File Folder 147.6, HPGC, TAMUCC. The phrase is borrowed from George Lipsitz, *The Possessive Investment in Whiteness: How White People Profit from Identity Politics* (Philadelphia: Temple University Press, 2006).

23. Mario T. García, *Memories of Chicano History: The Life and Narrative of Bert Corona* (Berkeley: University of California Press, 1995), 163. For additional information on the CSO, see Shana Bernstein, "Interracial Activism in the Los Angeles Community Service Organization: Linking the World War II and Civil Rights Eras," *Pacific Historical Review* 80 (2011): 231–67; Katherine Underwood, "Pioneering Minority Representation: Edward Roybal and the Los Angeles City Council, 1949–1962," *Pacific Historical Review* 66 (1997): 399–425; Margaret Rose, "Gender and Civic Activism in Mexican American Barrios in California: The Community Service Organization, 1947–1962," in *Not June Cleaver: Women and Gender in Postwar America, 1945–1960*, ed. Joanne Meyerowitz (Philadelphia: Temple University Press, 1994).

24. Alfred Aguirre, interview by Steven Rosales, April 22, 2003, Placentia, California, audio tape (in author's possession).
25. Ibid.
26. Ibid.
27. Through public campaigning and voter registration drives, these clubs, encompassing chapters in thirty states across the United States, provided key support for the 1960 Kennedy-Johnson ticket. For a more thorough discussion, see Zaragosa Vargas, *Crucible of Struggle: A History of Mexican Americans from the Colonial Period to the Present Era* (New York: Oxford University Press, 2010); Julie L. Pycior, *LBJ and Mexican Americans: The Paradox of Power* (Austin: University of Texas Press, 1997); and García, *Memories of Chicano History*, 1995.
28. John Sótelo, interview by Steven Rosales, February 4, 2003, Riverside, California, audio tape (in author's possession).
29. Ibid.
30. A partial inventory of scholarship on *Mendéz et al. v. Westminster School District of Orange County*, and the larger process of desegregation for the Mexican American community, includes Philippa Strum, *Mendéz v. Westminster: School Desegregation and Mexican American Rights* (Lawrence: University Press of Kansas, 2010); Gilbert González, *Chicano Education in the Era of Segregation* (Philadelphia: Balch Institute Press, 1990); Thomas P. Carter, *Mexican Americans in School: A History of Educational Neglect* (New York: College Entrance Examination Board, 1970); Vicki L. Ruiz, "Tapestries of Resistance: Episodes of School Segregation and Desegregation in the Western United States," in *From the Grassroots to the Supreme Court: Brown v. Board of Education and American Democracy*, ed. Peter F. Lau (Durham, NC: Duke University Press, 2004).
31. Founded in Fresno, California, in 1960, MAPA endeavored to engage a broad coalition of workers in electoral politics. Founding member and labor activist Bert Corona provided additional information in García, *Memories of Chicano History*, 1995.
32. Sótelo, interview.
33. George Castrueta, interview by Steven Rosales, May 1, 2003, Whittier, California, audio tape (in author's possession).
34. Ibid.
35. Ibid.
36. Francisco Vega, interview by Steven Rosales, September 22, 2009, Grand Rapids, Michigan, audio tape (in author's possession).

37. Ibid.
38. Ibid.
39. Ibid.
40. Ibid.
41. Martin Morales, interview by Steven Rosales, October 5, 2009, Grand Rapids, Michigan, audio tape (in author's possession).
42. Ibid.
43. This includes presidents Richard Nixon, Gerald R. Ford, and Ronald Reagan, as well as Vice President Al Gore and multiple governors of Michigan.
44. Ibid.
45. Frank Ornelas, interview by Steven Rosales, May 28, 2010, Saginaw, Michigan, audio tape (in author's possession).
46. Ibid.
47. Ibid.
48. William J. Fisher, interview by Steven Rosales, August 10, 2003, Tucson, Arizona, audio tape (in author's possession).
49. Ibid.
50. Ruben Moreno, interview by Steven Rosales, August 9, 2003, Tucson, Arizona, audio tape (in author's possession). Moreno had collected thirty-two narrations at the time of this interview, and more were forthcoming.
51. Arthur Egendorf et al., *Legacies of Vietnam: Comparative Adjustment of Veterans and Their Peers* (Washington, DC: Government Printing Office, 1981), 412.
52. Alfredo Vea, interview by Steven Rosales, December 14, 2002, Oakland, California, audio tape (in author's possession).
53. George Mariscal, interview by Steven Rosales, December 11, 1997, San Diego, California, audio tape (in author's possession).
54. Sal Martínez, interview by Steven Rosales, December 22, 1997, Oceanside, California, audio tape (in author's possession).
55. Oropeza, *Raza Si! Guerra No!*, 95. Geographically, Aztlan referred to the territories ceded to the United States by Mexico following the Mexican-American War (1846–48); more importantly, however, it symbolized the social, political, and economic contradictions that confronted the Chicano community. Its utilization was part of a larger effort to deploy a type of rhetoric and imagery that promoted cultural nationalism by drawing strength and inspiration from a heroic Aztec past, the glorification of Mexico, the ancestral homeland of the Chicana/o community, and the celebration of their indigenous roots and,

thus, their nonwhite racial status. Additional objectives included an end to the Vietnam War; educational reform, in particular the creation of Chicano Studies programs in high schools and universities; and community issues such as police brutality, discriminatory hiring and renting practices, and teaching the characteristics of *La Causa* (The Cause) to young students. For more on the student movement and the Chicano movement overall, see Mario T. García and Sal Castro, *Blowout!: Sal Castro and the Chicano Struggle for Educational Justice* (Chapel Hill: University of North Carolina Press, 2011); David Montejano, *Quixote's Soldiers: A Local History of the Chicano Movement, 1966–1981* (Austin: University of Texas Press, 2010); Carlos Muñoz Jr., *Youth, Identity, Power: The Chicano Movement* (New York: Verso, 2007); George Mariscal, *Brown-Eyed Children of the Sun: Lessons from the Chicano Movement, 1965–1975* (Albuquerque: University of New Mexico Press, 2005); Ernesto Chávez, *Mi Raza Primero!: Nationalism, Identity, and Insurgency in the Chicano Movement in Los Angeles, 1966–1978* (Berkeley: University of California Press, 2002).

56. Vea, interview.
57. Ibid.
58. Ibid.
59. John Rodríguez, interview by Steven Rosales, December 28, 1999, San José, California, audio tape (in author's possession).
60. Copy of Western Union telegram, in author's possession.
61. Rodríguez, interview.
62. Ibid.
63. Joe Rodríguez, interview by Steven Rosales, December 23, 1997, San Diego, California, audio tape (in author's possession).
64. Ibid.
65. Mariscal, interview.
66. Ibid.
67. Ibid.
68. Leroy Quintana, interview by Steven Rosales, February 11, 1998, San Diego, California, audio tape (in author's possession).
69. Ibid.
70. Charley Trujillo, interview by Steven Rosales, December 27, 1999, San José, California, audio tape (in author's possession).
71. Ibid.

72. Daniel Cano, interview by Steven Rosales, November 26, 2002, Los Angeles, California, audio tape (in author's possession).
73. Ibid.
74. Raymond Buriel, interview by Steven Rosales, December 30, 2002, Riverside, California, audio tape (in author's possession).
75. Ibid.
76. Jesus Barragan, interview by Steven Rosales, August 17, 2011, San Francisco, California, audio tape (in author's possession).
77. Ibid. He reenrolled at San José City College in February 1970 and subsequently transferred to San José State University in 1973, where he earned a bachelor's degree in psychology in 1975, with a minor in Mexican American Studies. He then earned a Marriage, Family, and Child Counseling (MFCC) license from San Francisco State University.
78. GALA functioned from 1975 to 1983, when it disbanded in order to promote HIV/AIDS activism. For more on the organization, see Horacio N. Rocque Ramírez, "'That's My Place!': Negotiating Gender, Racial, and Sexual Politics in San Francisco's Gay Latino Alliance, 1975–1983," *Journal of the History of Sexuality* 12, no. 2 (2003): 224–58.
79. Barragan, interview.
80. Ibid.
81. Ibid.
82. Gilbert Guevara, interview by Steven Rosales, June 14, 2010, Saginaw, Michigan, audio tape (in author's possession).
83. Ibid. Formed in Los Angeles in 1967, the organization's agenda included police harassment, inadequate public schools, health care, and job training, and an active stance against the Vietnam War. Gilbert Guevara, however, claimed no knowledge of the group's more militant activities.
84. Ibid.
85. Ibid.
86. Christian G. Appy, *Working-Class War: American Combat Soldiers & Vietnam* (Chapel Hill: University of North Carolina Press, 1993), 9.
87. Chappo López, interview by Steven Rosales, December 22, 1997, San Diego, California, audio tape (in author's possession).
88. John Sánchez, interview by Steven Rosales, November 15, 2009, Saginaw, Michigan, audio tape (in author's possession).
89. Tony López, interview by Steven Rosales, January 18, 2003, Riverside, California, audio tape (in author's possession).

90. Eddie Solís, interview by Steven Rosales, February 17, 2003, Riverside, California, audio tape (in author's possession).
91. Victor Ramírez, interview by Steven Rosales, March 6, 2003, Riverside, California, audio tape (in author's possession).
92. Frank Reyes, interview by Steven Rosales, April 17, 2003, Los Angeles, California, audio tape (in author's possession).
93. Everett Álvarez, interview by Steven Rosales, July 29, 2003, McLean, Virginia, audio tape (in author's possession). Such turmoil also existed closer to home for Álvarez when he discovered upon his return that his sister, Delia, had become an ardent antiwar activist and participant of the Chicano movement. Years later, deep bonds of affection would help to reunite the two despite their political differences.
94. López, interview.
95. Ibid.
96. Sánchez, interview.
97. Enloe, *Ethnic Soldiers*, 209.

EPILOGUE

1. Gina M. Pérez, "Hispanic Values, Military Values: Gender, Culture, and the Militarization of Latina/o Youth," in *Beyond El Barrio: Everyday Life in Latina/o America*, ed. Gina M Pérez, Frank A. Guridy, and Adrian Burgos Jr. (New York: New York University Press, 2010), 169.
2. Beth Bailey, *America's Army: Making the All-Volunteer Force* (Cambridge, MA: Harvard University Press, 2009), 89.
3. Paul Rosenfeld and Amy L. Culbertson, "Hispanics in the Military," in *Hispanics in the Workplace*, ed. Stephen B. Knouse, Paul Rosenfeld, and Amy L. Culbertson (Thousand Oaks, CA: Sage, 1992), 214–15.
4. Office of the Under Secretary of Defense, Personnel and Readiness. *Population Representation in the Military Services: Fiscal Year 2001 Summary Report*, 2003, http://www.cna.org/research/pop-rep.
5. Office of the Under Secretary of Defense, Personnel and Readiness. *Population Representation in the Military Services: Fiscal Year 2013 Summary Report*, 2014, http://www.cna.org/research/pop-rep.
6. Rosenfeld and Culbertson, "Hispanics in the Military," 215.
7. Ibid.

8. Office of the Under Secretary of Defense, Personnel and Readiness. *Population Representation in the Military Services: Fiscal Year 2001 Summary Report*, 2003, http://www.cna.org/research/pop-rep.
9. Ibid.
10. Office of the Under Secretary of Defense, Personnel and Readiness. *Population Representation in the Military Services: Fiscal Year 2013 Summary Report*, 2014, http://www.cns.org/research/pop-rep.
11. Ibid.
12. For more information, see *The Short Life of José Antonio Gutierrez*. DVD. Directed by Heidi Specogna. 2006; Montreal: Atopia Distribution Inc., 2006.

BIBLIOGRAPHY

MANUSCRIPT COLLECTIONS

Hector Perez García Collection, Special Collections Archive. Jeff and Mary Bell Library, Texas A&M University, Corpus Christi. Corpus Christi, Texas.

Hoyt Library, Local History and Genealogy Collection. Public Libraries of Saginaw. Saginaw, Michigan.

League of United Latin American Citizens (LULAC) Archives. Benson Latin American Collection, University of Texas, Austin.

Marine Corps Historical Center. Washington Navy Yard, Washington, DC.

Paul S. Taylor Collection. Bancroft Library, University of California, Berkeley. Berkeley, California.

Texas Military Forces Museum. Camp Mabry, Austin, Texas.

U.S. Army Center of Military History. Fort McNair, Washington, DC.

BOOKS

Allsup, Carl. *The American G.I. Forum: Origins and Evolution*. Austin: Center for Mexican American Studies, 1982.

Altschuler, Glen C., and Stuart M. Blumin. *The GI Bill: A New Deal for Veterans*. New York: Oxford University Press, 2009.

Álvarez, Everett. *Chained Eagle*. New York: Dell, 1989.

Álvarez, Luis. *The Power of the Zoot: Youth Culture and Resistance During World War II*. Berkeley: University of California Press, 2008.

Ambrose, Stephen E., and Douglas G. Brinkley. *Rise to Globalism: American Foreign Policy Since 1938*. New York: Penguin, 1997.

Anderson, Karen. *Wartime Women: Sex Roles, Family Relations, and the Status of Women During World War II*. Westport, CT: Greenwood Press, 1981.

Appy, Christian. *Working-Class War: American Combat Soldiers and Vietnam*. Chapel Hill: University of North Carolina Press, 1993.

Arredondo, Gabriela F. *Mexican Chicago: Race, Identity, and Nation, 1916–1939*. Champaign: University of Illinois Press, 2008.

Bailey, Beth. *America's Army: Making the All-Volunteer Force*. Cambridge, MA: Harvard University Press, 2009.

Balderrama, Francisco E., and Raymond Rodríguez. *Decade of Betrayal: Mexican Repatriation in the 1930s*. Albuquerque: University of New Mexico Press, 1995.

Baskir, Lawrence M., and William A. Strauss. *Chance and Circumstance: The Draft, the War, and the Vietnam Generation*. New York: Alfred A. Knopf, 1978.

Basso, Matthew, Laura McGill, and Dee Garceau, eds. *Across the Great Divide: Cultures of Manhood in the American West*. New York: Routledge, 2001.

Becerra, Rosina M., and Milton Greenblatt. *Hispanics Seek Health Care: A Study of 1,088 Veterans of Three War Eras*. Lanham, MD: University Press of America, 1983.

Bederman, Gail. *Manliness and Civilization: A Cultural History of Gender and Race in the United States, 1880–1917*. Chicago: University of Chicago Press, 1995.

Belkin, Aaron. *Bring Me Men: Military Masculinity and the Benign Façade of American Empire, 1989–2001*. New York: Oxford University Press, 2012.

Beltrán, Mary C. *Latina/o Stars in U.S. Eyes: The Making and Meanings of Film and TV Stardom*. Champaign: University of Illinois Press, 2009.

Benavidez, Roy, and Oscar Griffin. *The Three Wars of Roy Benavidez*. San Antonio: Corona, 1986.

Benesch, Oleg. *Inventing the Way of the Samurai: Nationalism, Internationalism, and Bushido in Modern Japan*. New York: Oxford University Press, 2016.

Bennet, Michael J. *When Dreams Come True: The GI Bill and the Making of Modern America*. Washington, DC: Potomac Books, 1999.

Berg, Charles Ramírez. *Latino Images in Film: Stereotypes, Subversion, and Resistance*. Austin: University of Texas Press, 2002.

Berube, Allan. *Coming Out Under Fire: A History of Gay Men and Women in World War Two*. New York: Free Press, 1990.

Binkin, Martin, et al. *Blacks and the Military*. Washington, DC: Brookings Institution, 1982.

Blanton, Carlos Kevin. *George I. Sánchez: The Long Fight for Mexican American Integration*. New Haven, CT: Yale University Press, 2015.

Blum, John Morton. *V Was for Victory: Politics and American Culture During World War II*. New York: Harcourt Brace and Company, 1976.

Borstelmann, Thomas. *The Cold War and the Color Line: American Race Relations in the Global Arena*. Cambridge, MA: Harvard University Press, 2001.

Brod, Harry, and Michael Kaufman, eds. *Theorizing Masculinities*. Thousand Oaks, CA: Sage, 1994.

Brooks, Jennifer E. *Defining the Peace: World War II Veterans, Race, and the Remaking of Southern Political Tradition*. Chapel Hill: University of North Carolina Press, 2004.

Canaday, Margot. *The Straight State: Sexuality and Citizenship in Twentieth-Century America*. Princeton, NJ: Princeton University Press, 2009.

Cano, Daniel. *Shifting Loyalties*. Houston: Arte Publico Press, 1995.

Cantú, Lionel, Jr. *The Sexuality of Migration: Border Crossings and Mexican Immigrant Men*, ed. Nancy A. Naples and Salvador Vidal-Ortiz. New York: New York University Press, 2009.

Caputo, Philip. *A Rumor of War*. New York: Henry Holt, 1977.

Carroll, Patrick J. *Felix Longoria's Wake: Bereavement, Racism, and the Rise of Mexican American Activism*. Austin: University of Texas Press, 2003.

Carter, Thomas P. *Mexican Americans in School: A History of Educational Neglect*. New York: College Entrance Examination Board, 1970.

Cave, Dorothy. *Beyond Courage: One Regiment Against Japan, 1941–1945*. Las Cruces, NM: Yucca Tree Press, 1992.

Charlton, Thomas L., Lois E. Myers, and Rebecca Sharpless, eds. *Handbook of Oral History*. Lanham, MD: AltaMira Press, 2006.

Chauncey, George. *Gay New York: Gender, Urban Culture, and the Making of the Gay Male World, 1890–1940*. New York: Basic Books, 1995.

Chávez, Ernesto. *Mi Raza Primero! Nationalism, Identity, and Insurgency in the Chicano Movement in Los Angeles, 1966–1978*. Berkeley: University of California Press, 2002.

Cohen, Deborah. *Braceros: Migrant Citizens and Transnational Subjects in the Postwar United States and Mexico*. Chapel Hill: University of North Carolina Press, 2011.

Cohen, Lizabeth. *A Consumer's Republic: The Politics of Mass Consumption in Postwar America*. New York: Knopf, 2003.

Connell, R. W. *Masculinities*. Berkeley: University of California Press, 1995.

Cortright, David. *Soldiers in Revolt: GI Resistance During the Vietnam War*. Chicago: Haymarket Books, 2005.

Culbertson, Amy L., Stephen B. Knouse, and Paul Rosenfeld, eds. *Hispanics in the Workplace*. Thousand Oaks, CA: Sage, 1992.

Daniel, Clete. *Chicano Workers and the Politics of Fairness: The FEPC in the Southwest, 1941–1945*. Austin: University of Texas Press, 1991.

Davis, James W., Jr., and Kenneth M. Dolbeare. *Little Groups of Neighbors: The Selective Service System*. Chicago: Markham, 1968.

Department of Defense. *Hispanics in America's Defense*. Washington, DC: Office of the Deputy Assistant Secretary of Defense for Military Manpower and Personnel Policy, 1988.

———. *Population Representation in the Military Services, Fiscal Year 2001*. Washington, DC: Office of the Under Secretary of Defense, Personnel and Readiness, 2003.

Dienstfrey, Stephen J., and Robert H. Feitz. *Chart Book on Black and Hispanic Veterans: Data from the 1980 Census of Population and Housing*. Washington, DC: Office of Information Management and Statistics, Statistical Policy and Research Service, Research Division, 1985.

Dower, John W. *War Without Mercy: Race and Power in the Pacific War*. New York: Pantheon, 1986.

Dudink, Stefan, Karen Hagemann, and John Tosh, eds. *Masculinities in Politics and War: Gendering Modern History*. Manchester, UK: Manchester University Press, 2004.

Egendorf, Arthur, et al. *Legacies of Vietnam: Comparative Adjustment of Veterans and Their Peers*. Washington, DC: Government Printing Office, 1981.

Enloe, Cynthia. *Ethnic Soldiers: State Security in Divided Societies*. Athens: University of Georgia Press, 1980.

———. *Bananas, Beaches, and Bases: Making Feminist Sense of International Politics*. Berkeley: University of California Press, 1990.

Escobar, Edward J. *Race, Police, and the Making of a Political Identity: Mexican Americans and the Los Angeles Police Department, 1900–1945*. Berkeley: University of California Press, 1999.

Escobedo, Elizabeth R. *From Coveralls to Zoot Suits: The Lives of Mexican American Women on the World War II Home Front*. Chapel Hill: University of North Carolina Press, 2013.

Estes, Steve. *Ask and Tell: Gay and Lesbian Veterans Speak Out*. Chapel Hill: University of North Carolina Press, 2007.

Fernández, Lilia. *Brown in the Windy City: Mexican and Puerto Ricans in Postwar Chicago*. Chicago: University of Chicago Press, 2012.

Flamming, Douglas. *Bound for Freedom: Black Los Angeles in Jim Crow America.* Berkeley: University of California Press, 2005.

Flynn, George Q. *Lewis B. Hershey, Mr. Selective Service.* Chapel Hill: University of North Carolina Press, 1985.

Foley, Michael S. *Confronting the War Machine: Draft Resistance During the Vietnam War.* Chapel Hill: University of North Carolina Press, 2003.

Foley, Neil, ed. *Reflexiones: New Directions in Mexican American Studies.* Austin, TX: Center for Mexican American Studies, 1997.

———. *The White Scourge: Mexicans, Blacks, and Poor Whites in Texas Cotton Culture.* Berkeley: University of California Press, 1999.

Ford, Nancy Gentile. *Americans All! Foreign-Born Soldiers in World War I.* College Station: Texas A&M University Press, 2008.

Frisch, Michael H. *A Shared Authority: Essays on the Craft and Meaning of Oral and Public History.* Albany: State University of New York Press, 1990.

Frydl, Kathleen J. *The GI Bill.* New York: Cambridge University Press, 2009.

Gaddis, John L. *The United States and the Origins of the Cold War.* New York: Columbia University Press, 2000.

García, Ignacio. *Hector P. Garcia: In Relentless Pursuit of Justice.* Houston: Arte Publico Press, 2003.

García, Mario T. *Mexican Americans: Leadership, Ideology, and Identity, 1930–1960.* New Haven, CT: Yale University Press, 1989.

———. *Memories of Chicano History: The Life and Narrative of Bert Corona.* Berkeley: University of California Press, 1994.

García, Mario T., and Sal Castro. *Blowout! Sal Castro and the Chicano Struggle for Educational Justice.* Chapel Hill: University of North Carolina Press, 2011.

García, Matt. *A World of Its Own: Race, Labor, and Citrus in the Making of Greater Los Angeles, 1900–1970.* Chapel Hill: University of North Carolina, 2001.

———. *From the Jaws of Victory: The Triumph and Tragedy of Cesar Chavez and the Farm Worker Movement.* Berkeley: University of California Press, 2012.

Gilmore, David D. *Manhood in the Making: Cultural Concepts of Masculinity.* New Haven, CT: Yale University Press, 1991.

Gluck, Sherna Berger. *Rosie the Riveter: Women, the War, and Social Change.* New York: Plume, 1987.

Goedde, Petra. *GIs and Germans: Culture, Gender, and Foreign Relations, 1945–1949.* New Haven, CT: Yale University Press, 2003.

Goldstein, Joshua S. *War and Gender: How Gender Shapes the War System and Vice Versa.* New York: Cambridge University Press, 2003.

Gonzales, Manuel G. *Mexicanos: A History of Mexicans in the United States*. Bloomington: Indiana University Press, 1999.

González, Gilbert G. *Chicano Education in the Era of Segregation*. Philadelphia: Balch Institute Press, 1990.

———. *Mexican Consuls and Labor Organizing: Imperial Politics in the American Southwest*. Austin: University of Texas Press, 1999.

González-López, Gloria. *Erotic Journeys: Mexican Immigrants and Their Sex Lives*. Berkeley: University of California Press, 2005.

Guerin-Gonzáles, Camille. *Mexican Workers and American Dreams: Immigration, Repatriation, and California Farm Labor, 1900–1939*. New Brunswick, NJ: Rutgers University Press, 1996.

Gutíerrez, Dave. *Patriots from the Barrio*. Bloomington, IN: Xlibris, 2014.

Gutíerrez, David. *Walls and Mirrors: Mexican Americans, Mexican Immigrants, and the Politics of Ethnicity*. Berkeley: University of California Press, 1995.

———, ed. *Between Two Worlds: Mexican Immigrants in the United States*. Wilmington, DE: Scholarly Resources, 1996.

Gutman, Matthew C. *The Meanings of Macho: Being a Man in Mexico City*. Berkeley: University of California Press, 1996.

———. *Changing Men and Masculinities in Latin America*. Durham, NC: Duke University Press, 2003.

Hall, Mitchell K. *The Vietnam War*. New York: Longman, 2008.

Hastings, Max. *The Korean War*. New York: Touchstone, 1987.

Hernández, Kelly Lytle. *Migra! A History of the U.S. Border Patrol*. Berkeley: University of California Press, 2010.

Herrera-Sobek, Maria. *The Mexican Corrido: A Feminist Analysis*. Bloomington: Indiana University Press, 1990.

———. *Northward Bound: The Mexican Immigrant Experience in Ballad and Song*. Bloomington: Indiana University Press, 1993.

Herzog, Dagmar, ed. *Brutality and Desire: War and Sexuality in Europe's Twentieth Century*. New York: Palgrave Macmillan, 2011.

Hinojosa, Rolando. *Korean Love Songs: From Klail City Death Trip*. Berkeley: Editorial Justa, 1978.

———. *The Useless Servants*. Houston: Arte Publico Press, 1993.

Holm, Tom. *Strong Hearts, Wounded Souls: The Native American Veterans of the Vietnam War*. Austin: University of Texas Press, 1996.

Howard, John. *Men Like That: A Southern Queer History*. Chicago: University of Chicago Press, 1999.

Huebner, Andrew J. *The Warrior Image: Soldiers in American Culture from the Second World War to the Vietnam Era*. Chapel Hill: University of North Carolina Press, 2008.

Hyman, Harold M. *American Singularity: The 1787 Northwest Ordinance, the 1862 Homestead and Morrill Acts, and the 1944 GI Bill*. Athens: University of Georgia Press, 1986.

Innis-Jiménez, Michael. *Steel Barrio: The Great Mexican Migration to South Chicago, 1915–1940*. New York: New York University Press, 2013.

Irwin, Robert McKee. *Mexican Masculinities*. Minneapolis: University of Minnesota Press, 2003.

Isaacs, Arnold R. *Vietnam Shadows: The War, Its Ghosts, and Its Legacy*. Baltimore: Johns Hopkins University Press, 1997.

Kaplowitz, Craig A. *LULAC, Mexican Americans, and National Policy*. College Station: Texas A&M University Press, 2005.

Karnow, Stanley. *Vietnam: A History*. New York: Penguin, 1983.

Kells, Michelle Hall. *Hector P. Garcia: Everyday Rhetoric and Mexican American Civil Rights*. Carbondale: Southern Illinois University Press, 2006.

Kimmel, Michael. *Manhood in America: A Cultural History*. New York: Oxford University Press, 2012.

Kington, Donald M. *Forgotten Summers: The Story of the Citizens' Military Training Camps, 1921–1940*. San Francisco: Two Decades Publishing, 1995.

Kovic, Ron. *Born on the Fourth of July*. New York: Pocket Books, 1976.

Lau, Peter F., ed. *From the Grassroots to the Supreme Court: Brown vs. Board of Education and American Democracy*. Durham, NC: Duke University Press, 2004.

Levitan, Sar A., and Joyce K. Zickler. *Swords into Plowshares: Our GI Bill*. Salt Lake City, UT: Olympus Publishing Company, 1973.

Lewis, Oscar. *The Children of Sánchez: Autobiography of a Mexican Family*. New York: Random House, 1961.

Lewy, Guenter. *America in Vietnam*. New York: Oxford University Press, 1980.

Lipsitz, George. *Rainbow at Midnight: Labor and Culture in the 1940s*. Champaign: University of Illinois Press, 1994.

———. *The Possessive Investment In Whiteness: How White People Profit From Identity Politics*. Philadelphia: Temple University Press, 1998.

Longley, Kyle. *Grunts: The American Combat Soldier in Vietnam*. Armonk, NY: M. E. Sharpe, 2008.

Lyons, Michael J. *World War II: A Short History*. Englewood Cliffs, NJ: Prentice Hall, 1989.

Mapes, Kathleen. *Sweet Tyranny: Migrant Labor, Industrial Agriculture, and Imperial Politics*. Champaign: University of Illinois Press, 2009.

Mariscal, George. *Aztlan and Viet Nam: Chicano and Chicana Experiences of the War*. Berkeley: University of California Press, 1999.

———. *Brown-Eyed Children of the Sun: Lessons from the Chicano Movement, 1965–1975*. Albuquerque: University of New Mexico Press, 2005.

Márquez, Benjamin. *LULAC: The Evolution of a Mexican American Political Organization*. Austin: University of Texas Press, 1993.

Matsumoto, Valerie J. *Farming the Home Place: A Japanese American Community in California, 1919–1982*. Ithaca, NY: Cornell University Press, 1993.

Mazón, Mauricio. *The Zoot-Suit Riots: The Psychology of Symbolic Annihilation*. Austin University of Texas Press, 1984.

McNamara, Robert S. *In Retrospect: The Tragedy and Lessons of Vietnam*. New York: Vintage Books, 1995.

McWilliams, Carey. *Factories in the Field: The Story of Migratory Farm Labor in California*. Boston: Little, Brown and Company, 1935.

———. *North from Mexico: The Spanish-Speaking People of the United States*. New York: Praeger, 1948.

Mendoza, Alexander, and Charles David Grear, eds. *Texans and War: New Interpretations of the State's Military History*. College Station: Texas A&M University Press, 2012.

Mettler, Suzanne. *Soldiers to Citizens: The G.I. Bill and the Making of the Greatest Generation*. New York: Oxford University Press, 2005.

Meyer, Leisa D. *Creating GI Jane: Sexuality and Power in the Women's Army Corps During World War II*. New York: Columbia University Press, 1996.

Meyerowitz, Joanne, ed. *Not June Cleaver: Women and Gender in Postwar America, 1945–1960*. Philadelphia: Temple University Press, 1994.

Mirande, Alfredo. *Hombres y Machos: Masculinity and Latino Culture*. Boulder, CO: Westview Press, 1997.

Molina, Natalia. *How Race Is Made in America: Immigration, Citizenship, and the Historical Power of Racial Scripts*. Berkeley: University of California Press, 2014.

Montejano, David. *Anglos and Mexicans in the Making of Texas, 1836–1986*. Austin: University of Texas Press, 1987.

———. *Quixote's Soldiers: A Local History of the Chicano Movement, 1966–1981*. Austin: University of Texas Press, 2010.

Mora, Sergio de la. *Cinemachismo: Masculinities and Sexuality in Mexican Film*. Austin: University of Texas Press, 2006.

Morehouse, Maggie M. *Fighting in the Jim Crow Army: Black Men and Women Remember World War II*. Lanham, MD: Rowman and Littlefield, 2000.

Morín, Raúl. *Among the Valiant: Mexican Americans in WW II and Korea*. Los Angeles: Borden, 1966.

Moskos, Charles C. *The American Enlisted Man*. New York: Russell Sage Foundation, 1970.

Mosse, George L. *The Image of Man: The Creation of Modern Masculinity*. New York: Oxford University Press, 1996.

Muñoz, Carlos, Jr. *Youth, Identity, Power: The Chicano Movement*. New York: Verso, 1989.

Navasky, Victor S. *Naming Names*. New York: Penguin, 1981.

Ngai, Mae M. *Impossible Subjects: Illegal Aliens and the Making of Modern America*. Princeton, NJ: Princeton University Press, 2004.

Office of the Under Secretary of Defense, Personnel and Readiness. *Population Representation in the Military Services: Fiscal Year 2001 Summary Report*. 2003.

———. *Population Representation in the Military Services: Fiscal Year 2013 Summary Report*. 2014.

Offner, Arnold A. *Another Such Victory: President Truman and the Cold War, 1945–1953*. Stanford, CA: Stanford University Press, 2002.

Okihiro, Gary. *Cane Fires: The Anti-Japanese Movement in Hawaii, 1865–1945*. Philadelphia: Temple University Press, 1992.

O'Leary, Cecilia Elizabeth. *To Die For: The Paradox of American Patriotism*. Princeton, NJ: Princeton University Press, 1999.

Olson, Keith W. *The G.I. Bill, the Veterans, and the Colleges*. Lexington: University Press of Kentucky, 1974.

Oropeza, Lorena. *Raza Si! Guerra No! Chicano Protest and Patriotism During the Viet Nam War Era*. Berkeley: University of California Press, 2005.

Ortiz, Stephen. *Beyond the Bonus March and GI Bill: How Veteran Politics Shaped the New Deal Era*. New York: New York University Press, 2009.

Overy, Richard. *Why the Allies Won*. New York: W. W. Norton, 1995.

Pagán, Edguardo Obregon. *Murder at the Sleepy Lagoon: Zoot Suits, Race, and Riot in Wartime L.A.* Chapel Hill: University of North Carolina Press, 2003.

Paredes, Américo. *"With His Pistol in His Hand": A Border Ballad and Its Hero*. Austin: University of Texas Press, 1958.

Pash, Melinda L. *In the Shadow of the Greatest Generation: The Americans Who Fought the Korean War*. New York: New York University Press, 2012.

Paz, Octavio. *The Labyrinth of Solitude*. Translated by Lysander Kemp, Yara Milos, and Rachel Phillips Belash. New York: Grove, 1985.

Perales, Alonso S. *Are We Good Neighbors?* San Antonio, TX: Artes Graficas, 1948.

Perales, Monica. *Smeltertown: Making and Remembering a Southwest Border Community*. Chapel Hill: University of North Carolina Press, 2010.

Pérez, Gina M., Frank A. Guridy, and Adrian Burgos Jr., eds. *Beyond El Barrio: Everyday Life in Latina/o America*. New York: New York University Press, 2010.

Pycior, Julie Leininger. *LBJ and Mexican Americans: The Paradox of Power*. Austin: University of Texas Press, 1997.

Pyle, Ernie. *Brave Men*. New York: Henry Holt, 1944.

Ramírez, Catherine S. *The Woman in the Zoot Suit: Gender, Nationalism, and the Cultural Politics of Memory*. Durham, NC: Duke University Press, 2009.

Ramírez, José A. *To the Line of Fire: Mexican Texans and World War I*. College Station: Texas A&M University Press, 2009.

Ramírez, Juan. *A Patriot After All: The Story of a Chicano Vietnam Vet*. Albuquerque: University of New Mexico Press, 1999.

Ramos, Henry A. J. *The American GI Forum: In Pursuit of the Dream, 1948–1983*. Houston: Arte Publico Press, 1998.

Ritchie, Donald A. *Doing Oral History*. New York: Twayne, 1995.

Rivas-Rodríguez, Maggie, ed. *Mexican Americans and World War II*. Austin: University of Texas Press, 2005.

Rivas-Rodríguez, Maggie, and B. V. Olguín, eds. *Latina/os and World War II: Mobility, Agency, and Ideology*. Austin: University of Texas Press, 2014.

Rivas-Rodríguez, Maggie, and Emilio Zamora, eds. *Beyond the Latino World War II Hero: The Social and Political Legacy of a Generation*. Austin: University of Texas Press, 2009.

Rodriguez, Clara, ed. *Latin Looks: Images of Latinas and Latinos in the U.S. Media*. Boulder, CO: Westview Press, 1997.

———. *Heroes, Lovers, and Others: The Story of Latinos in Hollywood*. New York: Oxford University Press, 2008.

Rodríguez, Joe. *The Oddsplayer*. Houston: Arte Publico Press, 1988.

Rodríguez, Marc Simon. *The Tejano Diaspora: Mexican Americanism and Ethnic Politics in Texas and Wisconsin*. Chapel Hill: University of North Carolina Press, 2011.

Rodríguez, Richard. *Hunger of Memory: The Education of Richard Rodríguez*. New York: Random House, 1983.

Rosas, Ana Elizabeth. *Abrazando el Espíritu: Bracero Families Confront the U.S.-Mexico Border*. Berkeley: University of California Press, 2014.

Ruiz, Vicki L. *From Out of the Shadows: Mexican Women in Twentieth-Century America*. New York: Oxford University Press, 1998.

Sánchez, George. *Becoming Mexican American: Ethnicity, Culture, and Identity in Chicano Los Angeles, 1900–1945*. New York: Oxford University Press, 1993.

San Miguel, Guadalupe, Jr. *"Let All of Them Take Heed": Mexican Americans and the Campaign for Educational Equality in Texas, 1910–1981*. College Station: Texas A&M University Press, 1987.

Schrecker, Ellen. *Many Are the Crimes: McCarthyism in America*. Princeton, NJ: Princeton University Press, 1999.

———. *The Age of McCarthyism: A Brief History with Documents*. Boston: Bedford/St. Martin's, 2002.

Schultz, Duane. *Crossing the Rapido: A Tragedy of World War II*. Yardley, PA: Westholme, 2010.

Sides, Josh. *L.A. City Limits: African American Los Angeles from the Great Depression to the Present*. Berkeley: University of California Press, 2003.

Snyder, Claire R. *Citizen-Soldiers and Manly Warriors: Military Service and Gender in the Civic Republican Tradition*. Lanham, MD: Rowman and Littlefield, 1999.

Strum, Philippa. *Mendez v. Westminster: School Desegregation and Mexican-American Rights*. Lawrence: University Press of Kansas, 2010.

Stueck, William, ed. *The Korean War in World History*. Lexington: University Press of Kentucky, 2004.

Takaki, Ronald. *Double Victory: A Multicultural History of America in World War II*. New York: Back Bay, 2001.

Terry, Wallace. *Bloods: An Oral History of the Vietnam War by Black Veterans*. New York: Ballantine, 1984.

Toll, Ian W. *Pacific Crucible: War at Sea in the Pacific, 1941–1942*. New York: W. W. Norton, 2012.

———. *The Conquering Tide: War in the Pacific Islands, 1942–1944*. New York: W. W. Norton, 2015.

Trujillo, Charley. *Soldados: Chicanos in Viet Nam*. San José, CA: Chusma House, 1990.

U.S. Congress. House Committee on Veterans Affairs. *Hispanic Veterans: Contributions to the Nation and Community, Receipt of Federal Veterans Benefits, and Related Issues*. Washington, DC: Government Printing Office, 1994.

Valdés, Dionicio N. *Al Norte: Agricultural Workers in the Great Lakes Region, 1917–1970*. Austin: University of Texas Press, 1991.

———. *Barrios Nortenos: St. Paul and Midwestern Mexican Communities in the Twentieth Century*. Austin: University of Texas Press, 2000.

Van Ells, Mark D. *To Hear Only Thunder Again: America's World War II Veterans Come Home*. Lanham, MD: Lexington Books, 2001.

Vargas, Zaragosa. *Crucible of Struggle: A History of Mexican Americans from Colonial times to the Present Era*. New York: Oxford University Press, 2011.

———, ed. *Major Problems in Mexican American History*. Boston: Houghton Mifflin, 1999.

———. *Proletarians of the North: A History of Mexican Industrial Workers in Detroit and the Midwest, 1917–1933*. Berkeley: University of California Press, 1999.

Vea, Alfredo. *Gods Go Begging*. New York: Plume, 1999.

Villareal, José Antonio. *Pocho*. New York: Knopf, 1970.

Vogel, Victor. *Soldiers of the Old Army*. College Station: Texas A&M University Press, 1990.

Weber, Devra. *Dark Sweat, White Gold: California Farm Workers, Cotton, and the New Deal*. Berkeley: University of California Press, 1994.

Welchel, Toshio. *From Pearl Harbor to Saigon: Japanese American Soldiers and the Vietnam War*. New York: Verso, 1999.

Westheider, James E. *The African American Experience in Vietnam: Brothers in Arms*. Lanham, MD: Rowman and Littlefield, 2007.

Whitehead, Stephen M., and Frank J. Barrett, eds. *The Masculinities Reader*. Malden, MA: Polity, 2001.

Williams, Norma. *The Mexican American Family: Tradition and Change*. Walnut Creek, CA: AltaMira, 1990.

Wilson, Marc. *Hero Street, USA: The Story of Little Mexico's Fallen Soldiers*. Norman: University of Oklahoma Press, 2009.

Ybarra, Lea. *Vietnam Veteranos: Chicanos Recall the War*. Austin: University of Texas Press, 2004.

Zamora, Emilio. *The World War I Diary of José De La Luz Sáenz*. College Station: Texas A&M University Press, 2014.

ARTICLES

Becerra, Rosina M., and Milton Greenblatt. "The Mental Health-Seeking Behavior of Hispanic Veterans." *Comprehensive Psychiatry* 22, no. 1 (1981): 124–33.

———. "The Needs of Hispanic Vietnam Veterans." *Psychiatric Epidemiology and Prevention: The Possibilities*, Prevention Publication Series, UCLA Psychiatric Institute 273 (1986).

Bernstein, Shana. "Interracial Activism in the Los Angeles Community Service Organization: Linking the World War II and Civil Rights Eras." *Pacific Historical Review* 80 (2011): 231–67.

Browning, Harley L., et al., "Income and Veteran Status: Variations Among Mexican-Americans, Blacks, and Anglos." *American Sociological Review* 38 (1973): 74–85.

Bryant, Richard R., et al. "The Effect of Military Service on the Subsequent Civilian Wage of the Post-Vietnam Veteran." *Quarterly Review of Economics and Finance* 33, no. 1 (1993): 15–31.

Canaday, Margot. "Building a Straight State: Sexuality and Social Citizenship Under the 1944 G.I. Bill." *Journal of American History* 90 (2003): 935–57.

Donaldson, Mike. "What is Hegemonic Masculinity?" *Theory and Society* 22 (1993): 643–57.

Escobar, Edward J. "Bloody Christmas and the Irony of Police Professionalism: The Los Angeles Police Department, Mexican Americans, and Police Reform in the 1950s." *Pacific Historical Review* 72, no. 2 (2003): 171–99.

Escobar, Javier I., et al. "Post-Traumatic Stress Disorder in Hispanic Vietnam Veterans: Clinical Phenomenology and Sociocultural Characteristics." *Journal of Nervous and Mental Disease* 171, no. 10 (1983): 585–96.

Escobar, Javier I., et al. "Symptoms of Schizophrenia in Hispanic and Anglo Veterans." *Culture, Medicine, and Psychiatry* 10 (1986): 259–76.

Guglielmo, Thomas A. "Fighting for Caucasian Rights: Mexicans, Mexican Americans, and the Transnational Struggle for Civil Rights in World War II Texas." *Journal of American History* 92 (March 2006): 1212–37.

Gutíerrez, Ramon. "Community, Patriarchy, and Individualism: The Politics of Chicano History and the Dream of Equality." *American Quarterly* 45, no. 1 (1993): 44–71.

Guzman, Ralph. "Mexican American Casualties in Vietnam." *La Raza* 1 (1969): 12–14.

Kasarda, John D., and Wayne J. Villemez. "Veteran Status and Socioeconomic Attainment." *Armed Forces and Society* 2 (1976): 407–20.

Little, Roger D., and J. Eric Fredland. "Veteran Status, Earnings, and Race." *Armed Forces and Society* 5, no. 2 (1979): 244–59.

Martindale, Melanie, and Dudley L. Poston Jr. "Variations in Veteran/Nonveteran Earnings Among World War II, Korea, and Vietnam War Cohorts." *Armed Forces and Society* 5 (1979): 219–43.

Mattila, J. Peter. "G.I. Bill Benefits and Enrollments: How Did Vietnam Veterans Fare?" *Social Science Quarterly* 59 (1978): 535–45.

Montoya, Maria E. "The Roots of Economic and Ethnic Divisions in Northern New Mexico: The Case of the Civilian Conservation Corps." *Western Historical Quarterly* 26, no. 1 (1995): 14–34.

Onkst, David H. "'First a Negro . . . Incidentally a Veteran': Black World War Two Veterans and the G.I. Bill of Rights in the Deep South, 1944–1948." *Journal of Social History* 31 (1998): 517–44

Ornelas, Charles, and Michael González. "The Chicano and the War: An Opinion Survey in Santa Barbara." *Aztlan* 2 (1971): 23–35.

Penk, Walter E., et al. "Ethnicity: Post-Traumatic Stress Disorder (PTSD) Differences Among Black, White, and Hispanic Veterans Who Differ in Degrees of Exposure to Combat in Vietnam." *Journal of Clinical Psychology* 45, no. 5 (1989): 729–35.

Pilisuk, Marc. "The Legacy of the Vietnam Veteran." *Journal of Social Issues* 31, no. 4 (1975): 3–12.

Rocque Ramírez, Horacio N. "'That's My Place!': Negotiating Gender, Racial, and Sexual Politics in San Francisco's Gay Latino Alliance, 1975–1983." *Journal of the History of Sexuality* 12, no. 2 (2003): 224–58.

Rodela, Eduardo S., et al. "The Stressor-Strain Framework: Understanding Cross-Cultural Issues and the Hispanic Vietnam Veteran." *Journal of Multicultural Social Work* 3, no. 2 (1994): 67–85.

Romano-V, Octavio I. "Spanish Surnamed War Dead, Vietnam." *El Grito* 3, no. 1 (1969): 6–31.

Salyer, Lucy E. "Baptism by Fire: Race, Military Service, and U.S. Citizenship Policy, 1918–1935." *Journal of American History* 91, no. 3 (2004): 85.

Schwartz, Saul. "The Relative Earnings of Vietnam and Korean-Era Veterans." *Industrial and Labor Relations Review* 39, no. 4 (1986): 564–71.

Strayer, Richard, and Lewis Ellenhorn. "Vietnam Veterans: A Study Exploring Adjustment Patterns and Attitudes." *Journal of Social Sciences* 31, no. 4 (1975): 81–93.

Underwood, Katherine. "Pioneering Minority Representation: Edward Roybal and the Los Angeles City Council, 1949–1962." *Pacific Historical Review* 66 (1997): 399–425.

Velasquez, Roberto J., and Wendell J. Callahan. "MMPI Comparisons of Hispanic And White-American Veterans Seeking Treatment For Alcoholism." *Psychological Reports* 67 (1990): 95–98.

Vera, Ron. "Observations on the Chicano Relationship to Military Service in Los Angeles County." *Aztlan—Chicano Journal of the Social Sciences and the Arts* 1, no. 2 (1970): 27–37.

Ybarra, Lea. "Perceptions of Race and Class Among Chicano Vietnam Veterans." *Vietnam Generation* 1 (1989): 70–81.

Ybarra, Lea, and Nina Genera. *La Batalla Esta Aqui (The Battle Is Here): Chicanos and the War*. El Cerrito, CA: Chicano Draft Help, 1972.

DISSERTATIONS, THESES, AND UNPUBLISHED PAPERS

Cárdenas, Jaime O., Jr. "Cousins of Caliban: Nation, Masculinity, and Latino Men in California, 1945 to the mid-1960s." PhD diss., University of California, Los Angeles, 2000.

García-Cabrera, Angelita. "The Hispanic Veteran of the Armed Services and in the Veterans Administration." PhD diss., Brandeis University, 1978.

Sevilla, Exequiel R., Jr. "The Latino Soldier." PhD diss., Northwestern University, 1979.

NEWSPAPERS

Saginaw Daily News

Saginaw News

Saginaw News Courier

INTERVIEWS

Acevedo, Jim. Interviewed by the author, December 23, 1997, tape recording,

Aguirre, Alfred. Interviewed by the author, April 22, 2003, tape recording.

Álvarez, Everett. Interviewed by the author, July 29, 2003, tape recording.

Alviar, Guadalupe "Lupe." Interviewed by the author, April 30, 2010, tape recording.

Bablot, Alfred. Interviewed by the author, April 24, 2003, tape recording.

Barragan, Jesus. Interviewed by the author, August 17, 2011, tape recording.

Bejarano, Gene. Interviewed by the author, February 16, 2003, tape recording.

Buriel, Raymond. Interviewed by the author, December 30, 2002, tape recording.

Cano, Daniel. Interviewed by the author, November 26, 2002, tape recording.

Carillo, David. Interviewed by the author, January 24, 2003, tape recording.

Castaneda, George. Interviewed by the author, June 14, 2010, tape recording.

Castro, Robert. Interviewed by the author, August 9, 2003, tape recording.

Castrueta, George. Interviewed by the author, May 1, 2003, tape recording.
Domínguez, José. Interviewed by the author, January 28, 2003, tape recording.
Domínguez, Richard J. Interviewed by the author, March 26, 2003, tape recording.
Fisher, William James. Interviewed by the author, August 10, 2003, tape recording.
Fuentes, David. Interviewed by the author, April 24, 2003, tape recording.
García, Gene. Interviewed by the author, March 2, 2003, tape recording.
García, Mike. Interviewed by the author, March 4, 2003, tape recording.
Gómez, Ray. Interviewed by the author, August 10, 2003, tape recording.
Gonzales, Frank. Interviewed by the author, May 22, 2010, tape recording.
González, Mike. Interviewed by the author, February 13, 2003, tape recording.
Guevara, Gilbert. Interviewed by the author, June 14, 2010, tape recording.
Hinojosa-Smith, Rolando. Interviewed by the author, March 26, 2005, tape recording.
López, "Chappo." Interviewed by the author, December 22, 1997, tape recording.
López, John. Interviewed by the author, March 9, 2003, tape recording.
López, John. Interviewed by the author, May 22, 2010, tape recording.
López, Tony. Interviewed by the author, January 18, 2003, tape recording.
Lovio, Eddie. Interviewed by the author, August 10, 2003, tape recording.
Marez, Salvador. Interviewed by the author, June 2, 2010, tape recording.
Mariscal, George. Interviewed by the author, December 11, 1997, tape recording.
Medel, Fred. Interviewed by the author, April 18, 2010, tape recording.
Medina, Joe B. Interviewed by the author, January 21, 2003, tape recording.
Medina, Raúl. Interviewed by the author, February 18, 2003, tape recording.
Morales, Martin. Interviewed by the author, October 5, 2009, tape recording.
Moreno, Ruben. Interviewed by the author, August 9, 2003, tape recording.
Moreno, Tony. Interviewed by the author, November 15, 2009, tape recording.
Mosqueda, Raúl. Interviewed by the author, June 13, 2010, tape recording.
Nerio, Arnulfo "Arnif." Interviewed by the author, May 29, 2010, tape recording.
Ornelas, Frank. Interviewed by the author, May 28, 2010, tape recording.
Ortega, Guadalupe "Lupe." Interviewed by the author, May 29, 2010, tape recording.
Pardo, Vincent, Jr. Interviewed by the author, May 23, 2010, tape recording.
Quintana, Leroy. Interviewed by the author, February 11, 1998, tape recording.
Ramírez, Victor. Interviewed by the author, March 6, 2003, tape recording.
Reyes, Frank. Interviewed by the author, April 17, 2003, tape recording.
Rocha, Mark. Interviewed by the author, February 6, 2003, tape recording.
Rodríguez, Joe. Interviewed by the author, December 23, 1997, tape recording.
Rodríguez, John. Interviewed by the author, December 28, 1999, tape recording.

Salazar, Nick "Nicho." Interviewed by the author, March 29, 2003, tape recording.
Salcedo, J. D. Interviewed by the author, December 28, 1999, tape recording.
Samora, Ted. Interviewed by the author, January 4, 2010, tape recording.
Sánchez, John. Interviewed by the author, November 15, 2009, tape recording.
Sánchez, William. Interviewed by the author, April 29, 2003, tape recording.
Santillán, Carlos. Interviewed by the author, March 14, 2003, tape recording.
Solís, Eddie. Interviewed by the author, February 17, 2003, tape recording.
Sótelo, John. Interviewed by the author, February 4, 2003, tape recording.
Trujillo, Charley. Interviewed by the author, December 27, 1999, tape recording.
Trujillo, Eddie. Interviewed by the author, April 19, 2003, tape recording.
Vea, Alfredo. Interviewed by the author, December 14, 2002, tape recording.
Vega, Francisco. Interviewed by the author, September 15 and 22, 2009, tape recording.
Villegas, Darío. Interviewed by the author, February 27, 2003, tape recording.
Villegas, Robert. Interviewed by the author, March 17, 2003, tape recording.
Ybarra, Jesse. Interviewed by the author, January 14, 2003, tape recording.

INDEX

ABOUT THE AUTHOR

Steven Rosales received his PhD in history from the University of California, Irvine, in 2007. He is currently an assistant professor in the History Department at the University of Arkansas, where he is also affiliated faculty in Latin American and Latina/o Studies and Gender Studies. Articles by Rosales have been published in *Oral History Review*, *Pacific Historical Review*, *Michigan Historical Review*, *The Routledge Handbook of the History of Race and the American Military*, and in *Latinas in the United States: A Historical Encyclopedia* (ed. Vicki L. Ruiz and Virginia Sánchez Korrol [Bloomington: Indiana University Press, 2006]).